THE EGYPTIANS

THE EGYPTIANS

EDITED BY

Sergio Donadoni

TRANSLATED BY

Robert Bianchi

Anna Lisa Crone

Charles Lambert

AND

Thomas Ritter

THE UNIVERSITY OF CHICAGO PRESS

CHICAGO AND LONDON

SERGIO DONADONI is professor emeritus at the University of
Rome. He is the author of *La Religione dell'Antico Egitto* and
Testi Religiosi Egizi.

The University of Chicago Press, Chicago 60637
The University of Chicago Press, Ltd., London
© 1997 by The University of Chicago
All rights reserved. Published 1997
Printed in the United States of America
06 05 04 03 02 01 00 99 98 97   5 4 3 2 1

ISBN (cloth): 0-226-15555-2
ISBN (paper): 0-226-15556-0

Originally published as *L'Uomo egiziano*, © 1990,
Gius. Laterza & Figli.

Chapter 1 is published from the author's original English-
language version, with editing. All other chapters are edited
translations of original versions in the following languages:
Italian (introduction and chapters 3, 5–9), French (chapter
2), Russian (chapter 4), and German (chapters 10 and 11).
Chapter 11 is new to this volume.

Library of Congress Cataloging-in-Publication Data
Uomo egiziano. English.
    The Egyptians / edited by Sergio Donadoni ; translated
by Robert Bianchi . . . [et al.].
        p.   cm.
    Includes bibliographical references and index.
    ISBN 0-226-15555-2. — ISBN 0-226-15556-0 (pbk.)
    1. Egypt—Civilization—To 332 B.C.   I. Donadoni,
Sergio.   II. Title.
DT61.U6513   1997
932—dc21   96-44074
                                                        CIP

⊗ The paper used in this publication meets the minimum
requirements of the American National Standard for
Information Sciences—Permanence of Paper for Printed
Library Materials, ANSI Z39.48-1984.

CONTENTS

INTRODUCTION

Sergio Donadoni

It is no easy matter to travel back through time, to worlds whose often superficially familiar appearance hides such profound differences that a failure to take them into account would falsify all understanding. The rift dividing ancient Egypt and the modern world must therefore be borne in mind from the outset.

There must be some explanation for the fact that people were no longer able to decipher texts expressing the stubborn, indomitable desire of one generation to pass on the sum of its experiences and memories to the next. Well before the last hieroglyphs were sculpted, during the final period of the Roman Empire, the vigor of Egyptian civilization had turned into a weary struggle for survival, a gradual drift into the margins of history toward a bloodless, mythical idealization.

Our civilization is therefore confronted by an Egypt that is less a solid reality than an idealized site on which to construct images that sometimes praise and at other times deplore the Egyptian world—a site, in other words, for conceptions that do not originate in Egypt itself: sometimes wise, sometimes cruel; opulent or tyrannical; impious, superstitious, and knowing; infantile or politically exemplary; pious or cynical. For the classical world (and even up to the Enlightenment), Egypt often provided food for thought. Understanding of it, however, was fundamentally thwarted.

Obviously, Champollion's brilliant deciphering work, at the beginning of the Romantic era, transformed the situation. The ability to read documents and inscriptions ensured that the Egyptian world benefited even more from that interest in nonclassical civilizations

so typical of the period. (We have only to think of the particularly
long letter that Champollion wrote to von Humboldt, introducing his
system and describing his first results.) As a result, it became easier
to subsume the civilization of the Nile into a historicist framework.
In his initial encounters with the monuments whose voice he was
the first to understand, Champollion enjoyed the unraveling of a
chronology, a social structure, and a language. He began a process of
recovery that is still flourishing and that, one hopes, will continue to
do so. The abovementioned rift between ancient Egypt and our ability to understand it now appears to be bridged by a reading of previously denied texts, which now reveal their message.

However, a closer look shows that this is not the case. Other
historiographical worlds, such as those of Rome, Greece, and the
Middle Ages, form part of a long tradition whose organic unity has
been constantly and repeatedly tested by interpreting facts and data
that have been deliberately selected at one time or another for their
specific value, reconsidered, refuted, and reinterpreted. This tradition adopts the methods of different, coexisting, viewpoints. It offers
a basic scenario to which reference can be made (whether positively
or negatively) in order to establish a specific new area of research or
historical account.

This reassuring (and stabilizing) foundation is not available to
those who turn to Egypt or to other civilizations whose accessibility
has certain analogies with that of Egypt. There is no underlying organic design extending to the present and forming part of an entire
historiographical tradition. Rather than gradually maturing over the
centuries, an initial attempt was made to produce a reasonable over-
view from new facts and data that were collected, not according to
previously made decisions, but, in a sense, by pure chance. Everything that is genuinely known about ancient Egypt has been provided—in a real physical sense—by Egypt itself. Its earth is so
fertile archeologically that it has preserved objects to an extent impossible in most other countries. What interests us here is the survival of documentation, including texts written on papyrus. Authentic texts exist at every level, from private accounts to royal edicts and
literary texts.

It is not without significance that the historiographers of the classical world have discovered new themes and investigative techniques since excavations first began in Egypt, when papyri from the

Greek and Roman periods came to light. These discoveries of documentary material have also been important for historians of ancient Egypt. They have taken advantage both of the longer experience of classical historians and of the opportunity to compare the results obtained from the most recently discovered evidence with the traditional data (data that, in this case, range from historical accounts and literary texts to the great collections of legal documents).

Inserting newly discovered documentation into a traditional framework, however, becomes more difficult when we turn to the distant past of ancient Egypt. The inscriptions, papyri, and visual arts of this period of ancient Egypt have survived in a far more fragmentary and casual way. It was chance alone that preserved them up to the moment of their discovery. A papyrus survives, not because it was kept in an archive, but because it was not buried in a damp layer of earth, because no one used it to light a fire, because it was never nibbled by a passing goat, and because the person who found it used the appropriate techniques to preserve it. There was no ulterior motive for its survival. It was never intended to fulfill a specific documentary purpose. This is also true of inscriptions, which provide us with a wealth of information about kings and private individuals. It is obvious that the information provided by these inscriptions should be read bearing in mind their underlying ideology. Frequently, however, the reference point needed to evaluate their purport is not available. Far too often, this kind of uncertainty has led modern historians to accept as literal fact accounts of regal exploits and other apparently narrative texts. An Egyptian reader, on the other hand, would have been instinctively (or, rather, culturally) equipped to appreciate the greater symbolic and typological significance of the text, rather than the relative insignificance of the specific facts it contains, which offered no more than the occasion, or even pretext, for writing it.

The temptation to describe society, to theorize about its structure, and to gather together its historical and legal heritage rarely—if ever—existed in ancient Egypt, despite ancient Egypt's uncontrollable need to write. On the contrary, these elements are hidden in a dust cloud of specific, personalized facts, the organization of which it is our duty to attempt. As a result, we possess a more intimate knowledge of Egypt than we do of other classical civilizations, a knowledge that binds their world to ours by a series of vivid details.

At the same time, the overall picture is extremely uncertain, its vague contours redrawn according to successive—and contrasting—historiographical conventions.

These preliminary caveats should, in theory, discourage all attempts to approach the world of the Nile, restricting our understanding of it, at the most, to its more timeless values, an artistic experience divorced from historical context. This, however, is insufficient, as anyone with even the smallest amount of experience in Egyptology knows.

The sheer quantity of ruins left by Egyptian civilization has significance in itself. For almost thirty-five centuries, the residues and deposits of events were linked by an identifiable common thread, sometimes extremely evident and at other times less so, but always discernible. As we follow this thread—or threads, since naturally there are more than one—the past world of Egypt begins to make sense, revealing behavior patterns and allowing us to identify new issues.

Two different approaches exist to the problem of evaluating this past world. First, concepts expressed in a language that is now dead need to be translated into our own living language, with all the problems this entails. Second, subtle differences in the significance attributed to even the most apparently obvious facts must not be overlooked. It is not a question of choosing one or the other of these contrasting approaches but of seeing what results each of them produces in specific cases. This brings much-needed life to something that would otherwise be no more than two-dimensional documentation.

Certainly, the Egyptian world appears to be strikingly modern in many ways. The family was loosely organized (basically composed of parents and children), in contrast to the weight of a tribal structure linking distantly related individuals by blood and thus imposing automatic solidarity. The inheritance system divided estates up into more or less equal parts among the surviving partner and children. In private law, an intention that was freely expressed and documented had independent value, and the legal status of women allowed them to leave wills and act as witnesses without the intervention of a guardian. The notion of personal vendetta did not exist (nor did the word to describe it), and even mythical conflicts between gods were settled in court. Other elements that make Egypt seem so familiar include the territorial basis of the state's structure, its potential as a universal empire, the attention to detail of its clearly organized administrative hierarchy, and the importance of collective civic life (including strikes to defend one's rights). However, because we can understand these features with such ease, we tend to lose sight of what makes them peculiar to Egypt.

Let us consider one feature: the centrality of the state in Egyptian society. This was behind the potential equality between men and women, the absence of a tribal mentality, the existence of great collective building projects, the organization of agriculture on a national scale, the importance of the law in settling disputes, linguistic and cultural unity, and so on. These elements define a world that would appear to be translatable into our way of thinking. Not to take account of this fact would be not only unjust but also mistaken. At the same time, however, we must not forget that the "state" in Egypt was, in effect, identified with the "Pharaoh." The concept of the state, in other words, had a mythical value in addition to, or, rather, affected by, its rational significance. The need to respond to both values, the generically rational and the characteristically mythical, is equivalent to the experience of those who translate from a foreign language. Translators must certainly be aware of the actual meaning of the text in order to translate it; but, above all, they must respond to the value and expressive autonomy of the original language. When we study Egypt, we are confronted by two opposing but equally vivid needs that oblige us to recognize a single reality. From outside, we see what this reality might mean; from within, we see what it is.

Constantly underlying (or, according to one's viewpoint, overhanging) this problem of understanding and interpreting, however, is the mass of documentation. Readers of the essays in this volume will discover documents that are fragmentary, disparate, found by chance, and out of context, often without even the reassuring flourish of restoration. They will realize that the value of these documents varies, and they will also discover to what extent, and for what purpose, the documents can be trusted.

It is clear that it would be arbitrary to deduce a history of events from trivial details, although we constantly find ourselves doing so in a spirit of equivocation. Facts such as Amenophis III's toothache, revealed by the autopsy on his mummy, or a letter from the boy king Pepi II describing his joy at the news that a dancing dwarf is about to arrive from Africa are nothing but fragments, modest extracts from longer stories. These, and the many other curious details or remarkable pieces of information that continue to emerge, cannot be woven into a coherent history. This is equally true of descriptions of victories and exploits appearing in celebratory autobiographies, which, as we have seen, go beyond mere narrative, since their aim is not simply documentary.

Nevertheless, these apparent limitations do not mean that we cannot trace and interpret an alternative history based on structures, many of which are organic. Modern scholars are increasingly convinced that to write this history is both feasible and rational. The Egyptian world, made up of personal expressions and testimonies, thus tends to become choral, for the safety and serenity of historians. This is the price that must be paid in order to rise above a history of anecdotes, which may be amusing, and are often stimulating, but ultimately are restricted in their import.

The titles of the essays in this volume display a conscious intention to examine types rather than individuals. If we look more closely, however, we discover that, taken as a whole, the essays depict different facets of a single reality, and one that was by far the most significant in Egyptian civilization: the framework of the state. We ask the figures of the essays' titles to tell us, not who they are, but what they do. The activities of peasants, craftsmen, scribes, bureaucrats, priests, soldiers, and slaves are fundamentally complementary. Each person carries out a task necessary to the working of the social structure of which he or she is a part.

What we present in this volume, therefore, is a single historiographical reality that necessarily excludes many of the most profound aspects of ancient Egypt: art, religious speculation, and moral experience will be glimpsed only in passing. Emphasis will be placed on the guiding thread that identifies how rationality and secularity (if such words can be used in this context) influenced social relations in the ancient valley of the Nile. Although this approach pays only passing attention to the more complex reality, it should discourage the wilder imaginings of readers. The aim of this collection is to explain ancient Egypt as clearly as possible in terms of our own cultural world, without losing sight of the disparate perspectives that make it, at the same time, both similar and different.

As editor of the volume, however, I must add that I also had in mind another subtle educational experience. The contributing historians are of different origins and ages. Their range of academic backgrounds, their varied use of the same material, even their idiosyncrasies, may distort an image that the reader imagines to be unified. But why should we hide the fact that our discipline does not reduce research to a single perspective, and that each historian brings to his or her research concepts, reasons for inquiry, and passions that inevitably influence it? This is even more true in Egyptology than in many other fields, where long maturation of a common language has codified at least some general features.

By the end of this collection of essays, the reader should have a fairly clear idea of Egyptian society in its development as a complex of individuals whose ideal was to act together. At the same time, he or she will sense that other things can be found by examining this distant reality more closely, and that these new aspects will reveal the rich vitality of that world. After all, contradictions and uncertainties are more fruitful, and true to life, than the security of perpetual unanimity, provided, of course, that we seek to resolve them. That is the true task of the historian.

CHRONOLOGY

Early Dynastic Period	1st–3d Dynasties	ca. 3100–2630 B.C.
Old Kingdom	4th–8th Dynasties	ca. 2630–2213
First Intermediate Period	9th–11th Dynasties	ca. 2213–1991
Middle Kingdom	12th Dynasty	1991–1783
	13th Dynasty	1783–after 1640
Second Intermediate Period (Hyksos Period)	14th–17th Dynasties	1640–1540
New Kingdom	18th Dynasty	1540–1293
	19th Dynasty	1293–1190
	20th Dynasty	1190–1070
Third Intermediate Period (Libyan Period)	21st–24th Dynasties	1070–712
Late Period	15th (Ethiopian/ Nubian) Dynasty	780–664
	26th (Saite) Dynasty	664–525
First Persian Period	27th Dynasty	525–404
	28th Dynasty	404–399
	29th Dynasty	399–380
	30th Dynasty	380–343
Second Persian Period	31st Dynasty	343–332

Macedonian Dynasty	332–304
Ptolemaic Period	304–30
Roman Period	30 B.C.–A.D. 337
Coptic Period	337–641
Arab Conquest	641

1. PEASANTS

Ricardo A. Caminos

Peasants are all those who live on the land by their own labour.

SIR WALTER A. RALEIGH

From time immemorial down to the present day, Egypt has been, first and foremost, an agricultural country. Husbandry has always been the foundation of Egypt's economy, the country's welfare and prosperity being at all times in its long history dependent on the produce of the soil. It was farming, or, in the last analysis, the constant, persevering, backbreaking, unacknowledged, often despised, and always ill-rewarded toil of the tiller of the land, that made possible all the achievements that gave Egypt a leading position among the nations of preclassical antiquity. The Giza pyramids, Theban rock-cut tombs, colossal statues, obelisks, and massive temples that amazed ancient Greek and Roman visitors, as they continue to amaze tourists today; the skillfully wrought jewels, fine linen, furniture, and trinkets of all sorts now scattered among scores of collections throughout the world; the wealth and comfort of Egypt's upper classes; its military conquests, commercial expansion, and influence and prestige abroad; indeed, Egypt's entire legacy to humanity: the sweat of the peasant's brow was at the bottom of it all.

During the three millennia of Egypt's history under the Pharaohs, peasants were the backbone of the nation. And yet our knowledge of them and of their class is patchy, imperfect, and one-sided. We know nothing about them directly, that is, from records emanating from peasants themselves. This is regrettable but not surprising. Quite illiterate, they left no written accounts of the essential aspects

1

of their lives and persons, their aspirations and hopes and what they thought of their humble condition and unhappy lot. They were the lowest members on the social scale, the vast mass of the rank and file that constituted the bulk of Egypt's population. They struggled through a life of penury, privation, and physical toil, and passed away leaving no trace in this world; their dead bodies were abandoned on the fringe of the desert or, at best, dropped into shallow holes in the sand, with not even the poorest gravestones to bear their names.

What we know of Egyptian peasants is derived from epigraphic sources, literary and nonliterary writings, and archeological finds. The epigraphic documentation consists of iconographic and inscriptional records—paintings, reliefs, texts—preserved for the most part in the tombs of their masters and of the wealthy, dating from the Age of the Pyramids down to Greco-Roman times.

Passages bearing on peasant life and circumstances are scattered in a number of Egyptian literary compositions, mainly from the Middle and New Kingdoms, and also in the classical authors, principally the Greek writers Herodotus, Diodorus Siculus, and Strabo, who in their works touched upon many particulars of the rural activities performed along the Nile. Although the classical works reflect conditions of late times when the Pharaonic civilization, then almost three thousand years old, was only a shadow of its long-past heyday and was tottering to its end, they are still of considerable value. Nonliterary records written on papyrus also have much to tell us about the way of life and activities of the Egyptian field laborer. Of particular importance in this category of source material are the Demotic (the successor to the Late Egyptian language) and Greek papyri, of which large numbers have been vouchsafed to us. They deal, of course, with events of the time of the Ptolemies and the Romans, yet the situations of country life they document can with confidence be projected back into the past, even into a remote past, as we shall presently discover.

Likewise of great value is the archeological evidence. It includes agricultural implements such as seed baskets, hoes, plows, sickles, and winnowing scoops, the very tools the Egyptians used for work on the land. Related household utensils, such as ropes, baskets, and sieves, have also come down to us in great variety and from various periods, as well as small-scale wooden models, stuccoed and painted, which reproduce with quaint realism diverse activities of rural life.

Admittedly, the sources at our disposal are very unequally distributed in time and locality; this circumstance notwithstanding, it seems possible to present a relatively coherent picture of various aspects of peasant life that, it is hoped, may prove to be not too wide of the mark. The reader should bear in mind that the Egyptians were on the whole a very conservative people, and that agricultural pursuits and the peasantry are surely, and have always been, by far the most conservative and slow-changing elements in any society. With respect to Egyptian agriculture and the life of the people engaged in it, what is true of one period holds good, in many essentials, for others. The simplest rural implements, once developed, continued to be used with hardly any modification for centuries; farming operations depicted in the tomb of Petosiris, which dates from the second half of the fourth century B.C., differ but little, if at all, from the representations of farming work in Old Kingdom mastabas built some twenty-three or even twenty-four centuries earlier. The hard life, circumstances, cares, and daily chores of the Egyptian peasant appear to have barely changed from one end to the other of the long Dynastic Period, and even afterward until our own days, when the introduction of improved methods of irrigation and of electricity and, above all, the completion of the Saad el-Ali, or High Dam, near Aswan in 1972 began to alter the traditional pattern and rhythm of farming throughout the land. It is also because of that conservatism and, so to speak, immutability of Egyptian husbandry that the writings of Arab historians like Mowaffaq-Eddin Abd el-Latif (1162?–1231) and Taqi ed-Din el-Maqrīzī (1364–1442), the accounts of Europeans who traveled in Egypt in the seventeenth, eighteenth, and nineteenth centuries, and, last but not least, the works on the manners and customs of the modern Egyptians by keen observers like the savants who accompanied Napoleon's expeditionary forces to Egypt in 1798 and, in recent years, professional anthropologists and ethnographers like Winifred Susan Blackman and Nessim Henry Henein also advance in no small measure our understanding and knowledge of the peasantry in Pharaonic times.

From birth till death peasants were unescapably tied to the land they toiled upon, whoever its owner was. The system of land tenure changed from time to time following the political vicissitudes of the nation, but it is highly doubtful that such changes altered either the quality of their lives or the nature and manner of their labors to any significant extent. Whether they worked on Pharaoh's Crown lands, on fields owned by temples, or on the estate of some great landlord, it was, by and large, all very much the same to them—except that peasants in the service of certain temples could hope to be exempted from corvée (we shall discuss this issue further on).

What did vitally affect the field laborer and in fact the entire nation was the annual flood of the Nile, which both irrigated and fertilized the land. The flooding came and went with unfailing regularity during the summer months. The result of heavy rainfalls in subtropical Africa and the melting of the snows in the Ethiopian highlands, the flood made its appearance at Aswan in June and, unchecked by either barrages or dams, rolled steadily on, reaching Memphis about three weeks later. At first it penetrated the arable lands insidiously, so to speak, by a slow process of infiltration which filled hollows and marshes and soaked the soil from underneath. In mid-July the level of the stream began to rise rapidly, and the waters, overflowing the riverbanks, covered the land to a depth of two meters or more. From mid-August to mid-September the entire valley was flooded, giving the impression of a long, winding, narrow lake punctuated by the villages and towns built on higher ground. Then the inundation gradually subsided, and by the end of October it was gone, leaving the soil well soaked and upon it a layer of silt or muddy sediment rich in organic detritus and mineral salts, natural nutrients of the land in no way inferior to the best modern fertilizers. It also left behind pools of water scattered over the fields, which were supplemented by a complex network of man-made dikes, sluices, and canals to form a system of irrigation, called basin irrigation, already attested in the Protodynastic Period and used uninterruptedly in Egypt long afterward: it was still used in Upper Egypt in the 1960s.

Herodotus and Diodorus marveled at the Nile flood and its beneficial effects on the country's agriculture. Wrote the Father of History:

> No men in the whole world obtain the fruits of the earth with so little labour. They have not the toil of cutting up furrows in the ground with the plough, or of hoeing, nor of doing any of the tasks which all other men must perform to secure a crop. The river rises of its own accord, irrigates the fields, and after irrigating them it sinks back again. Then each man sows his plot of ground and lets pigs into it to tread down the seed, after which all he has to do is

to wait for harvest time. The pigs serve him also to thresh his grain, which is then carried to the granary. (2.14)

Diodorus declared that the Nile surpassed all the rivers of the world in its benefactions to humanity, adding that the floodwaters, coming with a gentle flow, brought fresh fertile mud and soaked the fields, making the tasks of the farmer both light and profitable. As soon as the waters receded, the peasants began to work on the soil, which was left soft and moist by the inundation; sowing and harvesting were all fairly effortless:

> The majority merely scatter their seed, turn in their herds and flocks upon the fields, and use them to trample down the seed; after four or five months the peasants return and harvest the crop. Some peasants apply light ploughs to the land, turn over no more than the surface of the soaked soil, and then harvest large quantities of grain without much expense or exertion. Speaking generally, every kind of field labour among other peoples entails great expense and toil, but only among the Egyptians is the harvest gathered in with very slight outlay of money and labour. (1.36)

Their rose-colored view of things agricultural in the country of the Nile, though wrong, is explicable. Herodotus and Diodorus came from countries where the harshest toil was required to wrest a meager crop from a reluctant rocky soil, and they were impressed by what they saw in Egypt: fertile lands irrigated by a mighty stream, a good climate, abundant harvests, a diversity of crops. To them Egypt was an agricultural El Dorado. It was not. Any ancient fellah (and a modern one too, for that matter) could have undeceived them.

The natural phenomenon of the rising and falling of the Nile occurred with predictable regularity—every year and always at the same time. What was not always the same was the volume of the flood, and thus the height of the inundation, which was crucial, for it brought either blessing or disaster. Too little water, a "low Nile," or too much water, a "high Nile," meant bad years for the whole country. Failure of the river to rise to the required minimum height and irrigate all the cultivable land meant that insufficient ground would be prepared for the next season's crop, and hunger and hardship, what the Egyptians referred to as a "year of famine," almost inevitably followed. An excessive flood was even more disastrous, wrecking as it did the network of irrigation dikes and canals and often causing heavy loss of human life, crops, and beasts; in addition, as Pliny the Elder observed (5.10.58), an excess of water took much too long to recede and left little or no time for sowing, germination, and harvest before the next flood came. The peasants were quite aware of all this, as they were the first to suffer from the vagaries of the Nile. Even if the level of the inundation had been optimal (they called it a "great Nile"), reaching the height known by experience to be productive of the best possible results, farming could not be left to chance. Hapi, the divine incarnation of the river in flood, had been bountiful and had brought bliss to the land, and it was all very well to sing hymns of praise and thanksgiving to him. But his bounty and favor alone could not make crops grow. Arduous human toil was required too. *Dii facientes adjuvant.* The Egyptian peasants were more aware of this than the wisest in the land, for while others shouted orders and issued directions, they did the work.

The weeks that followed the recession of the flood were a very busy time for the peasants. Canals, dikes, and water sluices clogged with mud, damaged, or altogether washed away by the flood had to be put in good repair or replaced by new ones, as they were essential to the proper functioning of the system of basin irrigation. In making the system fit for use again, peasants had to exert themselves vigorously and move fast, because the operation had to be completed as speedily as possible, before the land dried out. The work of the hoe and the plow, which, along with the sowing, came next and completed the first stage of the agricultural cycle, was vastly easier when the earth was still muddy and soft. It did not remain so for very long under the hot Egyptian sun.

The typical Egyptian hoe consisted of a flat piece of wood, which was the blade, tied transversely to the end of a wooden handle with twisted rope, the whole crude tool shaped like an **A** with one limb shorter than the other. There were also one-piece hoes, hewn from forked tree branches. Derived from the hoe, the plow was no less clumsy than its predecessor, and there is good reason to think that originally it was no more than a large hoe drawn through the ground, at first by a man with a rope and later by oxen. The normal plow of the Egyptian peasant, which remained virtually unchanged throughout the Dynastic Period and long afterward, was already in use in the Old Kingdom. It consisted of a share made of wood and sometimes sheathed in metal, which cut into the ground. It was attached to the lower end of a long wooden shaft that bore at the opposite, or front, end a wooden yoke in the form of a transverse bar lashed to the horns of the oxen with a rope. Occasionally, however, the backbreaking job of pulling the plow forward was done by men. An upward continuation of the rear end of the share was in some cases the plow handle, though more frequently there were two handles fixed to the lower end of the shaft. Whether single or double, the handle appears to have been used to press the share down into the ground rather than to control the direction of the plow.

The peasant seldom plowed alone. Nearly always he was helped by someone who guided the oxen and urged them forward with a stick or a whip and with shouts. Meanwhile, others were busy preparing the land for planting by breaking up the heavy clods of black earth with hoes. The sower also was there, scooping out handfuls of seed from a bag or wicker basket slung over his shoulder and broadcasting it onto the moist soil in a continuous stream. If the sower walked in front of the plow, the plow's oxen trod it in and the plowshare sank it deeper. When the sower walked abreast of the plow or followed it, the seed was trod in by a flock of sheep or goats driven over the freshly sown fields, enticed to move on by a peasant holding some green grass or a handful of grain to their noses, while another urged the whole bleating troop forward with a whip. Oxen and donkeys were rarely used for that purpose; Herodotus saw swine treading in seed in the Delta.

The tomb scenes that so vividly portray the peasants' labors also show the tomb owner, who might have been Pharaoh's bailiff supervising the activities on Crown lands, the steward of a temple estate, or a private landholder. He is, at any rate, always depicted much larger than the men and beasts sweating under his eye. He either stands there with a dignified, almost majestic bearing, a model of deportment, or sits at his ease in a kiosk, shaded from the sun, while a nearby booth is a well-provided larder from which a servant fetches him food and drink. The tomb inscriptions state that he has come either to inspect and supervise or merely to see what goes on in the fields. He is the *grand seigneur.* We can be sure that he never put hand to plow in all his life.

The scenes are also frequently enlivened by short texts which reproduce, or pretend to reproduce, remarks bandied about by the peasants at work, orders and gibes to one another, comments on the condition of the land or the weather, or threats and exhortations to their animals. "Push hard!" a man bawls to the yoked oxen he is guiding, and "Turn round!" when they reach the end of the field. And to the plowman, "Press the plow down; press it down with your hand!" A plowman warns his wearied mate, who shuffles on ahead of him, "Hurry up, leader, forward with the oxen. Watch out! The master is standing by and looking on."

Four men drawing a plow with ropes right in front of the master, who has bidden them for no apparent good reason to speed up their work, mutter among themselves, "We do work, look at us. Do not fear for the fields; they are great!" The young peasant who walks behind them casting seed responds, "The year is good, free from want, rich in all kinds of plants, and the calves are better than anything." The aged plowman signifies his approval, "What you say is quite right, my son."

A hoeing peasant bent to the earth in the same angular posture typical of his descendants today boasts, "I will do even more work than the master wants." The one next to him is not so eager. "My friend," he tells him, "hurry up with the work so we can get back home in good time."

Like the modern fellahin, the ancient Egyptian peasants sang at their work. A group of men engaged in planting the crop chant:

> Let us for the master toil!
> fair is the day and one is cool,
> away the oxen draw,
> the sky conforms to our wishes,
> let us for the master toil!

Work in the fields was incessant, and farming operations succeeded one another, varying in difficulty and intensity but with neither interruption nor end. After the crops had been sown and the ripening process had begun, the land away from the Nile might need further irrigation as the soil dried out, and for that purpose use was made of the water collected in basins, either natural or man-made. The basin water was directed to the fields as needed through ditches or narrow channels that branched off from larger canals directly fed by the water in the basins. The course and volume of the flow were regulated by sluices and dikes. The system demanded sustained attention and hard work. Even when the water ran freely through well-kept canals, it would not flow uphill, and the irrigation of higher ground had to be done by the peasants, carrying the precious liquid in cumbersome clay jars borne upon their shoulders. This they did for centuries, for it was not until the New Kingdom that a simple mechanical water-lifting contrivance was invented, the shadoof, first attested in the fifteenth century B.C. and constantly used in Egypt since.

The shadoof is made of two pillars, each about two meters high, joined near the top by a short wooden beam. Over the beam a long slender pole is balanced, which has at one end a vessel to hold water and at the other a large heavy lump of mud that acts as a counterpoise. A man standing at the water's edge dips the vessel down into the river or a canal and then lets the counterpoise lift the filled container up to the trough or feeder channel that carries the water to the fields. The shadoof served its purpose well enough, but it was painful, unwholesome toil to fill and empty the vessel again and again, all day long, day after day, the operator standing ankle deep in mire and bespattered with mud from head to foot.

The noria, or waterwheel, *saqqiah* in Arabic, did not appear in Egypt until the Ptolemaic Period; it came late, but it came to stay. Made to revolve slowly, groaning and creaking, by an ox, a cow, or sometimes a camel, hooded and driven round and round by a man or a child, the *saqqiah* is a typical feature of the Egyptian rural landscape even now.

The peasant had other worries while the crop was growing. The biblical Book of Exodus tells of sudden storms of thunder and hail in Egypt that would destroy the ripening grain, followed by swarms of locusts that would then "eat all that the hail had left" (Exod. 9:22–25, 10:12–15). Against the ruthless elements and the voracious insects the peasant was impotent, though surely he was not often visited with them, and never, we think, with the utterly devastating storms of the kind old Jehovah is said to have unleashed upon the land of Pharaoh. The marauding birds that hovered over the fields and gardens looking for seeds, grain, and fruit to devour were, however, a constant nuisance. But at least the peasant could cope with them more or less successfully. Men and children scattered over fields and gardens would scare the birds away with cries and slings and by waving sticks and rags; spring traps and net snares would be set up against birds that alighted either singly or in flocks. Another constant threat during the ripening and harvest periods was the incursions by foraging cattle from nearby pasturelands. Either straying into a field by themselves or led into it by a knavish herdsman belonging to some neighboring farm, the animals would wreck the crop as they trampled and fed. To prevent such incursions the peasant would patrol his field himself, helped perhaps by fellow laborers and children on the lookout here and there. Such measures were effective sometimes but did not always provide total security.

As the ears of grain began to turn golden yellow and harvesttime drew near, another pest, certainly not the least thorn in the long-suffering peasant's flesh, appeared on the scene: the inescapable tax inspectors, with their retinues of surveyors, scribes, and servants, who came round to measure the fields and reckon the yield of the crop in order to assess the tax the peasant would have to pay to the owner of the fields he cultivated: whether the Crown, a religious foundation, or a private landholder.

Then came the harvest, the busiest time of the year for the peasant. The chief crops were wheat, emmer, barley, and flax. The grain crops were particularly important, for cereals were used for making bread and beer, the basic elements of the Egyptian diet and the staples of the country's economy. Flax provided fiber and seed for a variety of uses.

The grain stalks were cut near the top with a short-handled sickle, which was originally made of a curved piece of wood inset with short, serrated flints to serve as a cutting edge. Sickle blades were made of bronze in the New Kingdom and were gradually superseded by sickles made of iron in the Late Period. With one hand the reaper, standing almost upright, grasped the stalks; with the other he hacked them just below the ears. The cut-off ears were laid on the ground, and the peasant moved on. The stubble was left standing high above the ground, quite possibly to be collected later and used as cattle fodder or for brickmaking, basket weaving, and fuel (there seems to be no evidence of what was done with it). The grain cutters were followed by the gleaners (in tomb paintings and reliefs the gleaners are women and children), who picked up the ears from the ground and took them to one end of the field, there to be stuffed into bags or baskets or large nets, which were promptly carried away to the threshing floor either by the farmworkers themselves upon their shoulders or on the backs of donkeys.

Probably situated near the village, the threshing floor was a more or less circular area of beaten earth on which the ears of grain were spread out and trodden by the hoofs of oxen or donkeys or beaten with pitchforks and whips to separate the grain from the husks.

Winnowing, the next operation, was also done on the threshing floor. The trodden grain was scooped up with shallow wooden bowls and tossed into the air; the grain fell straight down onto the ground, and the lighter chaff was blown away by the wind.

At this point in the process the inevitable scribe arrived again with his palette and writing tablet to take careful note, for tax purposes, of the amount of the yield of the harvest, which was measured in his presence, before the clean grain was carried away in sacks to be stored in the granary.

Flax culture was second in importance to the staple grain crops of wheat, barley, and emmer. It was harvested at different times, depending on how it was going to be utilized. Flax for making fine linen thread was best when still underripe, with darkish-green stems topped by red flower heads, because at that stage the fibers were supple and soft. When the plant was fully ripe, of a brownish yellow color, the fibers were tough, good for making strong, coarse fabrics, baskets, ropes, and mats.

The flax harvester did not cut the plant but pulled it out of the ground whole: head, stalks, and roots. The roots were trimmed off on the spot, and the long stalks, tied up in bundles, were taken away to be combed and further treated to serve one purpose or another. To separate the seeds from the stalks, the flax was drawn through a toothed, comblike implement (a ripple) set at an angle upon the ground. Part of the seed was reserved for sowing the next crop, for medical prescriptions, and also possibly to make linseed oil. But the overworked peasant was not done with the flax yet. He still must soak the stems to remove the woody parts from the fibers and then beat, scrape, and once more comb the fibers to leave them clean and flexible, ready to be spun.

And now, before we take leave of him, let us again listen to his voice as he doggedly toils away at harvesttime.

Men reaping corn sing what is described as an "answering chant," like the response of a choir:

> Fair is the day dawning upon the land,
> a cool breeze is rising from the north,
> the sky conforms to our wishes,
> with steady hearts let us toil on!

Shouts of ox and donkey drivers urging their charges on with good reason or from sheer force of habit, "Move on, fast as you can!" "Hurry up, straight on, don't turn round!" rang in the Egyptian fields

at harvesttime and do not tell us very much—they are timeless and
may be heard from the mouths of animal drivers all the world over.
A field hand goads a heavily laden donkey with shouts and repeated
applications of the stick, and his fellow laborer, who follows him driving a small pack of donkeys, seems well pleased with what he sees and
exclaims, "Heigh, heigh, hearty young fellow, you are great, great,
my comrade!"

An elderly peasant is combing flax with a will, or so it seems, for
he boastfully calls out to the young man who brings him another
sheaf, "Bring me 11,009 bundles if you like, I will comb them all!"
The youth replies, "Hurry up, don't talk so much, you bald old man
of a laborer!"

We have already overheard field-workers grumbling about the
unfairness of their master. Here there is again some sotto voce grumbling. Peasants are loading barges with barley and emmer which they
bring from the granaries in sacks upon their shoulders. Their master, watching them, urges them to hurry up. They complain among
themselves, "Are we to spend the whole day carrying barley and emmer? The granaries are already so full that heaps of grain run over
the brims. The barges are heavily loaded too, bursting with grain.
And yet we are still ordered to make haste. Are our hearts of iron?"

Now we walk back to the threshing floor and listen to a boy who
is singing while keeping the oxen moving round and round; his whip
flicking rhythmically over their backs marks time in pleasant fashion
for the oxen's heavy treading and the young driver's song:

> Thresh for your own good,
> thresh for your own good,
>   oxen,
> thresh for your own good.
> The chaff you shall eat,
> for your masters is the
>   corn.
> Do not tire, it is quite cool,
>   oxen, thresh on.

A melancholy song, which hints at the peasant's resignation to his
unhappy lot: for with grain and chaff so disposed of, what is left to
the young ox driver?

The vast majority of the Egyptian peasantry were engaged in the
cultivation of the country's cash crops, mainly cereals but also flax.

But there was another agricultural pursuit that occupied not a few. Many fields, large and small, were devoted to viniculture. The vine had been known and cultivated in Egypt from the earliest times. The principal vineyards were in the Delta and in the western oases of Kharga and Dakhla, though vines could also be found in small estates and gardens. Vineyard scenes are often depicted on tomb walls, particularly on those of the New Kingdom. They show our peasant harvesting, treading, and pressing the grapes, pouring the juice into pottery vessels, in which the fermentation took place, and shouldering the heavy jars of wine off to the cellar.

At harvesttime, in August and September, the bunches of ripe grapes were handpicked and carried in rush baskets to a long trough made of wood or stone, where they were trodden by five or six men. The juice flowed out through holes in the trough into a collecting vat. The mushy residue of skins, pips, and stems left on the bottom of the trough was then raked up and put into a stout sack, which was wrung to squeeze out the remaining juice. The juice was then left to ferment and clarify, which it did naturally, in large open vessels of clay. It was finally transferred to tall jars with pointed bottoms which were sealed, labeled with the place and year of the vintage, and stored, unless the wine was intended for immediate consumption. And here, once more, the detested scribe, who had already counted the baskets of grapes brought from the vineyard by the pickers, could be seen writing down the number of jars of wine for the benefit of the tax collectors, to the peasants' mute dismay.

We shall now touch upon other outdoor occupations in which peasants engaged to earn their living. While the privileged, including Pharaoh himself, went to the fens and swampy areas to fish and fowl for sport, the poor peasant fished and fowled in the marshlands to keep body and soul together and to fill the larders of his betters with the produce of his toil. He occasionally fished with a line or harpoon, but he found it far more rewarding to fish with a weel (a bottle-shaped basketry trap weighted with stones) or with a roughly conical net hung from a triangular wooden frame that he could manage single-handed. For even better results, a trawl net operated by several men was used. Part of the catch was sent at once to the nearest market, and part carried off to be presented to the landlord, but most was dealt with on the spot: split open, gutted, flattened out, and hung up on stakes to dry. The dry-cured fish were then stored away and used during the closed season.

The wealthy disdained the fisherman's crude tackle and would only use a spear to catch fish. By the same token, when the rich man went fowling, which he did purely for sport, he used a throwing stick, or boomerang, which he, gracefully posed on his light papyrus boat, hurled at his prey with ever unerring marksmanship, if one is to believe the depictions in his tomb. But here again, the humble fowler, who must keep his master's board well supplied with game birds, caught them in a less elegant but far more efficient fashion. Small gins were sometimes used, but more frequent were large clap or draw nets. Spread out upon the swampy ground where the birds were expected to alight, the clap net required six to twelve men, strong and quick of action, to make it work. A score or two of large birds, mostly geese, could be trapped in a single operation. They were removed one by one from the net, and most were crammed into square cages and sent off to the village market or to the master's poultry yard, while others were at once killed, plucked, trussed, and carried away to the landlord's cookhouse.

In the damp stretches of land bordering the marshes, the grass grew wild, and there cattle were bred and tended by rustics who doubtless lived the harshest life of all the country's peasantry. They were uncouth, ungainly, awkward-looking fellows, some bald, some with unkempt hair and matted beards; ill-nutrition had made some of them paunchy, some pinched and haggard. All were worn out with constant toil, bad food, and the dank air of their habitat. The herdsman lived near the marshes with his cattle. He had no settled home, a miserable, lonely reed hut sheltered him at night and held all his worldly goods: a rush mat to sleep on, a clay water jar, and a basket for his bread. He moved from place to place to graze his herd and had to keep a close watch all the time, for should anything go wrong—an ox stolen, a cow diseased, a calf stillborn—it was always his fault and he was brutally thrashed, if indeed he did not suffer worse.

In the foregoing paragraphs we have looked at Egyptian peasants almost exclusively in the light of the epigraphic and archeological documentation mentioned at the beginning of this chapter. We must now turn to the literary evidence, the writings of their contemporaries that have been preserved, and see what they have to tell us of the peasants and their circumstances. Not much. The reader must not expect anything even remotely resembling Hesiod's *Works and Days*. Literary sources relevant to our subject are scanty in the extreme, and, with the exception of a short tale told by a cashiered

priest turned peasant, of which more later, all of them are biased to
the last degree: they belong to the genre called "purpose literature"
or "tendency literature," namely, writings composed with a tacit but
quite definite purpose. Their unexpressed purpose was to extol to
the skies the scribal office and disparage all other pursuits as an incentive to the young pupil to be diligent at school and gain for himself the title of scribe as the reward of his efforts.

To that genre belongs The Satire of the Trades, which dates to
the Middle Kingdom or perhaps even earlier. A certain Duaf or
Duaf-khety is taking his son to the capital to place him in the government's school for scribes, and during the voyage he describes to him
the wretched life of those engaged in occupations other than that of
scribe. Of the sufferings of the countryfolk that concern us here, he
speaks to his son in these terms:

> The peasant is wailing all the time,
> his voice is hoarse like the croak of a raven.
> His fingers and arms fester and stink to excess.
> He is tired out standing in the mire;
> his clothes are rags and tatters.
> He is well as one is well among lions;
> ill, he lies down upon the swampy ground.
> When he leaves his field and reaches home in the evening,
> he is quite exhausted by the march.
> . . . .
> The fowler suffers exceedingly
> whenever he is on the lookout for birds.
> When the flocks fly past over him,
> he keeps saying, "Had I a net!"
> But god gives it not to him,
> and he is angry with himself.
> . . . .
> Let me tell you about the fisherman too;
> his calling is the worst of all.
> He toils on the river, surrounded by crocodiles;
> he is forever uttering lamentations.
> And yet he cannot say, "There is a crocodile there!"
> for fear has made him blind.
> Coming out from the swift running waters,
> he exclaims, "Such is the will of god!"

The picture is certainly overdrawn, but even allowing for a good amount of rhetorical exaggeration, there is in it, no doubt, a still larger amount of truth. It reveals, at all events, Duaf's unsympathetic turn of mind toward the peasantry, his utter contempt for the poor creatures whose endless, crushing toil kept him, his people, and the whole nation flourishing. There is good reason to think that his callous feelings were shared by his equals and his betters (Duaf was only middle class), for the condition of the ancient peasant was much the same as that of the modern fellah, who until the overthrow of the monarchy in 1952 was looked down upon by his masters and superiors, who put him on a level with his cattle and treated him on the same principle.

There have come down to us from ancient Egypt a number of papyri containing consecutive collections of didactic texts used in the New Kingdom for the instruction of scribes. They deal with miscellaneous topics and often harp on the advantages of the scribal career and the woes and trials of other trades and professions. Relevant to us now are those effusions that forewarn the trainee scribe against the miseries of peasant life. Work in the fields was hard toil indeed, pests ate the crop, and the plow oxen died of overwork or bogged down in the mire; but the tax was still collected, inexorably. Let us listen to an old pedagogue:

> Be a scribe. It will save you from toil and protect you from every kind of work. It will spare you from bearing hoe and mattock, so that you will not have to carry a basket. It will keep you from plying the oar and spare you all manner of hardships.
>
> Let me remind you of the plight of the peasant when the officers come to estimate the harvest tax, and snakes have carried off half of the grain and the hippopotamus has eaten up the rest. The voracious sparrows bring disaster upon the peasant. The remnants of grain left on the threshing floor are all gone; thieves have taken them away. What he owes for the oxen he hired he cannot pay, and as for the oxen, they are dead from excessive plowing and threshing. And just now the scribe lands at the riverbank to estimate the harvest tax with a suite of attendants carrying sticks and Nubians with rods of palm. They say, "Show us the grain!" But there is none, and the peasant is mercilessly beaten. He is then tied up and cast head foremost into a pool, where he gets thoroughly soaked. His wife is bound in his presence; his children are in shackles. But

the scribe commands everyone. He who works in writing is not taxed: he has no dues to pay. Mark it well.

Another schoolmaster drones on monotonously in the same vein:

> Let me also explain to you how it fares with the cultivator, that other tough occupation.
>
> During the inundation he is wet through, but he must attend to his equipment all the same. He passes the whole day making and repairing his farming tools, and the whole night twisting rope. Even his midday lunch hour he spends doing farming work. He equips himself to go out to the field as if he were a warrior. Now the land, free from the floodwaters, lies before him, and he goes out to get his team of oxen. When he has been tracking the herdsman for many days, he gets his team. He then comes back with it and makes for it a clearing in the field. At dawn he goes out to look after the team and does not find it where he left it. He spends three days searching for the oxen and finds them stuck in the bog, dead; and there are no hides on them either: the jackals have chewed them up!
>
> He spends much time cultivating grain, but the snake follows him and eats up the seed as soon as it is cast upon the ground. And that happens to him with three sowings of borrowed seed.

Notwithstanding the distinctly tendentious nature of these texts, they cannot be dismissed as mere scribal-training propaganda wholly divorced from reality. A peasant's life was one of unremitting labor, poverty, sickness, and extreme uncertainty. Peasants were at the mercy of forces they could not possibly control, much less understand: excessive or deficient floods, invasions, internecine wars, political changes. Last but not least, they were at the mercy of their lords and, worse still, of their lords' agents, who, like many of their class then and now and everywhere, were apt to act tyrannically over their subordinates—the following New Kingdom letter is much to the point.

A bailiff writes to his lord Amenemope, who is the administrator of some Crown lands, and informs him of what is being done in the fields at harvesttime. The letter is worth quoting in extenso: not only does it show how an overzealous and malicious agent could, and did, ride roughshod over the peasants, but it also offers fresh and welcome glimpses of the tasks field laborers were called upon to perform on a large country estate and how they went about them.

The writer begins by professing devotion to his master and eagerness in the execution of his charge and then assures him that the whole farmstead—the house, the land, the people, and the animals—is in flourishing condition, purposely implying, no doubt, that this happy state of affairs is due to his good management.

> I am carrying out with extreme zeal and the hardness of iron every commission with which my lord charged me. I shall not let my lord find fault with me. The house of my lord is well, his servants are well, the cattle out in the field are well, and the oxen in the cattle-stall are well; they eat their fodder daily, and the ox-herdsmen bring grass to fatten them. The team horses of my lord are well, and I see to it that their allotted measure of grain is mixed before them daily, while the grooms bring to them the best grass from the marshes. I assign grass to them every day and give the grooms ointment to rub them down once a month; and the stable foreman trots them every ten days.

That is only the introduction. The writer proceeds with the tacit encomium of his own abilities:

> The harvest of the Crown land of Pharaoh which is under my lord's authority is being reaped with the utmost diligence and good care. I write down the ass-loads of grain reaped daily and shall give instructions for transporting the grain from the field to the threshing floor. The threshing floor has already been laid out, and I shall arrange for a level area for 400 ass-loads of grain to be made ready. Meanwhile, at midday, when the grain is hot, I put all the men who are reaping to glean, with the exception of the scribes and weavers, who carry away their daily quota of grain from the gleanings saved from former days.

And he closes with, again, some transparent words of self-praise:

> I am giving bread-loaves daily to all the men who are gathering the harvest, and I am giving ointment oil to them three times a month. No one among them could denounce me to my lord concerning food or ointment. This letter is for my lord's information. *Vale.*

In those days, needless to say, there was no "collective bargaining" to fix the terms of enployment and the relationships between master and worker. The peasant was therefore totally in the power of the lord, who might or might not have developed a sense of responsibility and humanity toward his social inferior.

Humane and responsible was Amenemhet, who for a decade governed the Oryx Province in Middle Egypt in about 1950 B.C. and was a blessing to all those under his sway—if we can trust the message he left to posterity carved on the walls of his tomb at Beni Hasan:

> I was gracious, benign and ever loved, a ruler adored by his subjects. There was no common man's daughter whom I affronted, no widow whom I oppressed, no peasant whom I repulsed, no herdsman whom I turned away. There was no pauper in my community; no one starved in my time. When years of famine came, I had all the fields of my province plowed as far as the southern and the northern boundaries, and I kept the people alive, provided them with food, and no one was hungry in my province. I gave alike to the widow and to the married woman, and made no distinction between the great and the small in what I gave. Then came great Niles, bringers of barley and emmer, rich in all good things, but I did not exact the arrears of the harvest tax.

We hear men in positions of authority pride themselves for having given "bread to the hungry, water to the thirsty, clothes to the naked," and for having been "a brother to the widow, a father to the orphan, a man beloved of all his subjects." One dignitary declares, "I ferried the boatless in my own boat."

But to what extent should we believe such professions of benevolent and charitable behavior? We do not know. We shall never know. Let us give them the benefit of the doubt. The good intentions of a conscientious, benevolent lord could, however, be frustrated by his agents and overseers, who would fawn on their superiors and lord it over their inferiors. Amenemope's bailiff was such a one.

The peasant's wages were paid him in kind, for metal currency was not in use in Egypt until the arrival of Greek coinage. His pay was a mere pittance, subsistence wages: a little grain, doled out by a parsimonious hand, and perhaps also occasionally a small measure of oil. He might count himself very lucky if he also got a jar of beer on a festival day once in a long while. "A tiny sheaf a day is all I get for my work," says an old peasant as he plies his sickle over the grain stalks. With such paltry wages, peasant families always wavered between abject poverty and utter destitution, and of course it was entirely impossible for them to build up any reserve, let alone improve their squalid living conditions. And yet they were expected to lay aside some of their painfully earned grain to pay taxes. No wonder they were unable to meet their fiscal obligations more often than not.

The tax collectors manhandled the peasant in arrears viciously. He was beaten, tied up, and ducked; even his family fell prey to their brutality. The punishment of tax defaulters is depicted on tomb walls again and again. The hapless peasant is stripped and stretched out on the ground or bound to a whipping post and then lashed within an inch of his life, literally. Adding poignancy to the scene, his wife may be there too, vainly imploring mercy on her knees.

The extremes to which tax collectors could go in their cruelty is described by an eyewitness in the early days of the Roman domination:

> A short time ago a certain person was appointed to serve as collector of taxes in our own district. When some of the tax debtors who were in arrears obviously due to poverty took flight for fear of the deadly consequences of unbearable punishment, he took by force their wives and children and parents and their other relatives and beat up, trampled, and subjected them to every kind of outrage and contumelious treatment in order to make them either tell him the whereabouts of the fugitive or pay up his debt themselves. But they could do neither the first because they did not know, nor the second because they were as penniless as the fugitive. And so the tax-collector continued to chastise them and twisted their bodies with racks and instruments of torture, and finally killed them off with newly contrived methods of execution. He filled large baskets with sand, and having hung these enormous weights round their necks, put them in the middle of the market-place in the open air, in order that while they themselves dropped dead under the cruel stress of the accumulated punishment, the weights suspended on them, the wind, the sun, and the shame of being seen by the passers-by, the spectators of their punishment might suffer by the anticipation of the tortures that lay in store for them. Some of these, whose souls saw facts more vividly than did their eyes, feeling themselves ill-treated in the body of others, hastened to

take their lives by means of the sword, or poison, or the halter, considering that in their evil plight it was a great piece of luck to die without suffering. The others who had not seized the opportunity to kill themselves were aligned, as is done in the awarding of inheritances, first those who stood in the first degrees of kinship, after them the second, then the third, and so on, and they were put to death in that order.

And when there were no relatives left, the severe punishment spread even to their neighbours, and sometimes even to villages and towns, which soon became desolate and emptied of their inhabitants, who abandoned their homes and scattered to places where they thought they might escape detection. (Philo Judaeus, *On the Special Laws*, 3.30.159–62)

The writer, Philo Judaeus of Alexandria, may have exaggerated, but his statement is not all sheer invention. The shocking cruelty of many tax collectors to the innocent, defenseless relatives, often women, children, and elderly people, of debtors they could not lay hands on is well attested by a substantial body of records of the Greco-Roman Period. In fact, it was already known in the New Kingdom; see the text advocating a scribal career quoted earlier.

But taxation was not the last straw for the peasant. There was also the corvée. The corvée was a system of forced, unpaid state service exacted of the peasants (and to a far lesser degree of nonagricultural laborers also), who could at any time be conscripted for specific tasks such as the construction and maintenance of roads, irrigation canals, dikes, and sluices, the erection of large buildings, temples, pyramids, and even army duty and work in quarries and mines when extra manpower was needed. In operation at the very dawn of history, the corvée was used in Egypt uninterruptedly and was imposed with unabated rigor until it was abolished (at least on paper and not out of humanitarian considerations but entirely for reasons of political convenience) in A.D. 1889.

The only peasants, and indeed laborers of any kind, who were exempt from corvée duty (in theory, not always in practice) were those in the service of certain temples that, by royal charter, had been granted special privileges and immunities: exemption of their staffs from corvée duty was one of them. Immunity decrees were issued by Pharaohs of the Old Kingdom (beginning with Snofru [Snefru], the founder of the Fourth Dynasty, ca. 2600 B.C.), the First

Intermediate Period, the New Kingdom, and the Late Period. But such royal charters were frequently not enforced, and their dispositions for the safeguarding of temple personnel, peasants many of them, against taxation and corvée service were infringed, even, all too often, by officials and commissioners of the Crown.

One of the objectives of a decree of King Haremhab (ca. 1300 B.C.) was to put an end to the arbitrary, illegal, high-handed behavior of court agents and army officers who, for their own benefit, would unlawfully exact taxes and requisition freemen for corvée duty in the name of the king. We have not the slightest idea as to what extent the decree was implemented—it might have become a dead letter almost as soon as it was signed for all we know.

When excessive fiscal demands, constant requisitions for corvée service, ruthless masters, miserable wages, and appalling living conditions became intolerable, the peasant, in utter despair, would lay down his tools, forsake family, home, and field, and run away. *Anachōrēsis*, or *secessio*, the flight from the fields and abandonment of agricultural work, was the last refuge of the overburdened Egyptian cultivator. It can be traced back to the early Twelfth Dynasty (ca. 2000 B.C.) and was resorted to during the New Kingdom and Late Period with varying frequency according to the circumstances of the times; it increased under the Ptolemies and reached alarming proportions in Roman Egypt, when the population of some rural communities dwindled to a small number of persons, mostly old people, women, and children, hardly able to replace the fugitives and till the land; some villages were entirely deserted. The concerned administration, on both the national and the local levels, repeatedly resorted to negotiation and violence to combat the *anachōrēsis* and repeatedly failed to suppress it. The government's concern was fully justified. Such flights were a severe drain on Egypt's labor force, and abandoned fields meant uncultivated, unproductive tracts of otherwise good, tillable land: the consequences to the country's economy were very serious indeed. The *anachōrēsis* also had grave social repercussions. Some of the fugitives sought shelter in the swamps and the desert or tramped from village to village begging for a crumb. Others, not a few, joined or formed roving bands of brigands that preyed upon unprotected lonely villages and wayfarers, especially in sparsely populated areas of the country. Many runaways gravitated to the cities and large towns, hoping to lose themselves in the vast anonymous mass of the fallen and the dispossessed always to be found in such urban centers, where they very likely soon became ragged mendicants, and where we too lose sight of them for good.

It is well at this point to take a look at the place and the people, *his* people, the harassed runaway peasant left behind. He might have lived in the manner of herdsmen, alone in a rickety little shanty of rushes on the desert edge by the land he labored on. More likely, however, his home, like that of the majority of his fellow workers, had been a tumbledown house made of mud or crude sun-dried bricks in a small squalid village, lying, perhaps, as so many such villages did, at a considerable distance from his field.

All peasant villages were much the same and undoubtedly differed little from those in Egypt in our own day. Each was a cluster of gray, mean houses huddled together without any attempt at order or arrangement, crisscrossed by a maze of narrow, crooked, dismal lanes and blind alleys. To call them houses is, however, hyperbolical, for they were no more than sordid hovels, one-storied, with frowning doorways and no windows. Most of them consisted of one small room; only a few had two rooms, which opened directly into each other. The roof, made of palm leaves and palm branches, or of reeds and straw, was so flimsy and so low that a man of medium height, rising incautiously, would make a hole in it with his head. There was no flooring proper, but only the beaten earth, very seldom dry, permanently filthy, and tainting the air with a loathsome stench, for a good number of men, women, children, and cattle, all jumbled up together, cluttered the confined, foul hovel at night—Herodotus (2.36) was struck by how people and animals shared the same shelters in Egypt.

There was no furniture to speak of in that cell of a house, no chairs or beds, no table, but only one or two straw mats to sleep upon, an earthenware water jar, some coarse pottery, and a basket for bread and grain to keep them safe, not always successfully, from the swarms of mice and rats that infested the house and the whole village. That was all the peasant needed, or rather all he could afford, and all of it so valueless that the door, if there was one, was left open day and night—the very poverty of his worldly goods discouraged burglars quite effectively.

A stone slab set upon the floor in one corner of the rear wall was the hearth; a hole in the roof above it let the smoke out. The floor was strewn with reeking refuse and cattle ordure, and human feces too, if we believe Herodotus's remark that the Egyptians relieved themselves indoors. All that sickening fetid filth attracted clouds of flies, though quite probably they did not bother the villagers any more than they do the fellahin today. The overworked housewife, in any case, could not always stop in her daily rounds to gather up the floor rubbish and dump it by the door on the narrow street outside, but whenever she did, she would save the dung of her livestock to use as fuel before she threw the rubbish out.

In the winding lanes and murky alleyways, strewn with every kind of vile refuse, with puddles of putrid muddy water here and there, heaps of rubbish and filth everywhere, you would rarely see a dunghill. The droppings of donkeys, oxen, cows, and sheep in the streets were picked up while still warm, damp, and reeking by the village children daily. Plastered all over with dung, they moved along, scooping it up with their hands and putting it into a dripping basket balanced upon the head, all done with great skill and expedition. Herodotus must have seen them and might perhaps have had them in mind when he wrote that the Egyptians "took up dung with their hands" (2.36). Animal ordure is hand-collected in the streets by children in exactly the same fashion, including the basket perched upon the head, in Egypt even now. The dung from home and that brought by the children from outside were mixed, whisked, and made into a paste, and the paste was hand-molded into cakes, which were placed in the sun to dry—the dry cakes were the peasant's fuel.

No village was without a pond, the ever present *birkah* of Egyptian villages nowadays, a muddy pool of stagnant, gray-green, foul-smelling, thoroughly polluted water, from which the cattle drank and the women drew water. Near at hand there was always a dump, heaps of dank refuse haunted by hawks, vultures, dogs, and pigs, pecking and nuzzling in search of problematical food.

In such conditions, lacking the most elementary sanitary arrangements, the villages were loathsome cesspools of infestation. The many endemic diseases, which affected even the well-off classes, exacted a much heavier toll of the Egyptian countryfolk. The peasants were a ready prey to disease, for their systems were sorely weakened by hard toil, bad nutrition, and constant anxiety, by their bitter struggle for survival, their unwholesome hovels, and the squalid villages in which they lived.

Ophthalmia was rampant among the peasants, fostered by the fine sand and dust in the air, the fierce glare of the sun, swarms of flies, the pervading filth, and the absence of even a minimum of personal hygiene. The village was full of the bleary-eyed, the one-eyed, and the blind, with inflamed and festering eyelids, of all ages.

Also endemic was bilharziasis (schistosomiasis), a disease the peasant caught by wading through mire, pools, and the sluggish water of canals, which always teemed with species of water snails that are the carriers and transmitters of the infectious worms. The disease causes chronic ill health, anemia, and a variety of serious complications. In the 1950s, 95 percent of the fellahin suffered from it, and there is little doubt that the percentage was even higher among the peasantry in Pharaonic times, who knew nothing of personal hygienic care and sanitation.

Hepatitis (inflammation of the liver) was common. This condition depletes the sufferer of elements essential to vitality and vigor, reducing him to a state of almost constant prostration and making him, by lowering his natural defenses, an easy target for all sorts of diseases.

Also frequent was dracunculiasis (guinea worm disease), caught by drinking water infected with water fleas and producing worms as long as 80 centimeters that lodge just beneath the skin and cause painful blisters and a multitude of secondary infections.

Yet another scourge was amoebic dysentery, which since antiquity has never ceased to afflict the rural and urban population of Egypt to this day. It has also been shown that among the ancient Egyptian peasants, who went about unshod all the time, there was a high incidence of foot injuries and ailments.

The staple, indeed almost the only, food of the peasantry was bread. The flour from which it was made was unevenly ground and coarse and contained a considerable amount of dust, wind-blown sand, and other kinds of grit. The peasant did not chew his bread but rather ground and crunched it with much action of his jaws, like cattle. The abrasive impurities got the better of the strongest teeth in the long run, and many old men had worn their teeth down to the gums, like horses.

Space forbids us to go through the whole somber catalog of the ailments that plagued the cultivator and his fellow laborers—it is much too long.

There are some indications that gangs of workers employed in state mines and quarries occasionally included a healer, even at times a "specialist" in the treatment of scorpion bites. But there is not one jot or tittle of evidence that anybody in a position of authority, from

Pharaoh down to the village headman, ever even thought of providing the peasantry with the least form of medical care. Although the *argumentum ex silentio* is notoriously unreliable and fragile, we venture to suggest that nothing at all was ever done in that direction, and that when the field laborer was taken ill or had an accident, he had to shift for himself. Quite probably, in most cases, he would leave nature to take its course, for better or for worse. Or he might resort to one of those traditional cures of unknown origin which, like superstitions, were then, and still are, handed down from generation to generation by word of mouth. Or if he managed to scrape together enough to pay the fee, he might consult the local healer or an itinerant one—quacks both of them. One or the other, after consulting his leech book, would prescribe smearing a purulent ulcer with an infallible ointment which included caraway seeds and cat's dung in its composition, or drinking a potion made from the urine of a scribe and ox bile. He would reassure the credulous peasant, who, like today's fellah, loved prescriptions, that the efficacy of the medication had been successfully tested a thousand times.

The trials and tribulations of the peasantry are succinctly described in a tale cast in letter form and composed toward the end of the New Kingdom, about 1100 B.C. It deals with the wanderings and vicissitudes of a discharged Heliopolitan priest, Wermai by name, who is both the professed author of the letter and the hero of the tale. After being stripped of his office and banished from his town, Wermai roves around the country until he settles in a forlorn, poverty-stricken rural community in the Great Oasis, west of the Nile, where he earns his bread cultivating a poor plot of land bordering upon the waste. The place is dominated by an unscrupulous mayor (the *omdah*, or headman, of Egyptian villages in our time) and his ruthless staff. The local peasantry lead a hard, miserable life; many of them starve. The writer himself has not seen one grain of corn for a whole month. Whoever comes near the mayor with a request is promptly turned away; and if anyone dares to complain, the mayor's myrmidons placate him with blandishments and cajolery. The mayor himself does not hesitate to make empty promises to stop complaints. Restrictions of all kinds are imposed on the population. Wages, paid in kind, are low; and the authorities squeeze the villagers further by doling out grain rations and weighing those rations with a false measure. Wermai tells of a measure that was conspicuously "short," being no less than one-third smaller than it should have been.

Taxation is unbearably oppressive, and those that fall in arrears are thrown in jail. Wermai himself was in trouble because he had found the tax much too onerous and had failed to pay it on time. The wicked mayor brought him to the local court of magistrates and caused him to be fined for failure to pay the tax when it fell due. The situation grew hopeless, and in their despair the peasants left the grain crops untended, deserted even the best arable lands, and took to their heels. The mayor was powerless and at a loss to find a way to check the flight and make "the folded hands" take up the plow again.

It is possible that there were times of social unrest when the destitute working classes, always oppressed and neglected, could no longer contain their grievances but gave vent to them in a wave of violence and rapine, wreaking havoc in the country and reversing the condition of the poor and the rich.

> Behold, the Nile overflows, but none plow for it,
> everyone says, "We do not know what has happened in the land."
> Behold, hearts are violent, pestilence sweeps the land,
> there is blood everywhere, death is rampant.
> He who had no property is now a wealthy man;
> he who could not afford sandals is now the possessor of riches.
> Nobles lament; the poor men are full of joy.
> He who had no yoke of oxen now owns a whole herd.
> Every town says, "Come, let us get rid of the mighty among us."
> Behold, everyone has lost his hair,
> and a man of rank can no longer be distinguished from the pauper.

If that distressing picture is not sheer literary fiction, as has been maintained, then it may be reasonably supposed that the peasantry joined in the general upheaval and cast in their lot with the rebels. Nevertheless, such eruptions, if they ever did occur, must always have been as ineffectual as the last desperate struggles and plashings of a drowning man. In due course, the status quo ante would prevail, with all its grim features as harsh as ever, and the peasantry would continue in the same miserable life of yore.

Incessant arduous toil, paltry wages, want, destitution, hunger, chronic ill health, sordid living conditions, overbearing masters, onerous taxation—each of the woeful circumstances besetting the peasants from the cradle to the grave was by itself severe enough and hard to endure. In the aggregate they broke the peasants utterly, body and soul, and made of them the equal of the tamed ox, submissive, patient, cowed, dull. The peasants were aware that they had to struggle and work strenuously to live, and suffer much. That was their lot. They knew no better. Beyond this destiny they had no prospects, and they sought none. Had anyone tried, he would have run his head against a wall.

Payed a pittance for their labors, they never had the means, or were given the opportunity, to ameliorate their condition, find better ways of gaining their daily bread, and change their humble station. To live without the least hope of better days, inexorably chained to the very bottom of the social scale, shackled for life, that was the most distressing circumstance of their tormented existence—but did they ever in the least perceive it? Born peasants, they were stigmatized so, and so they remained to the end of their days: humble, half-starved drudges without a will of their own—ordered about, pushed around, beaten up to their last—despised by all, pitied by none.

Bibliographical Essay

Fernande Hartmann provides a general background for the study of ancient Egyptian peasantry in his *L'agriculture dans l'ancienne Égypte* (Paris, 1923). A masterly presentation of the life and occupations of the peasants is in Adolf Erman, *Ägypten und ägyptische Leben im Altertum* (Tübingen, 1885), chap. 17, "Die Landwirtschaft," reproduced virtually unchanged in Hermann Ranke's revised edition of 1923. It was, and still remains, a seminal study, the pattern of all subsequent treatments of the subject. Among these are, in chronological order: Pierre Montet, *La vie quotidienne en Égypte au temps de Ramsès* (Paris, 1958); T. G. H. James, *Pharaoh's People* (London, 1984); Franco Cimmino, *Vita quotidiana degli egizi* (Milan, 1985); and Laura Donatelli's contribution, enhanced by admirable illustrations, to A. Donadoni Roveri, ed., *Civiltà degli egizi: La vita quotidiana* (Turin, 1987). These works deal with the Egyptian peasantry before the commencement of the Ptolemaic dynasty. For Greco-Roman Egypt, Michael Rostovtzeff, *The Social and Economic History of the Hellenistic World*, 3 vols. (Oxford, 1967), and Michael Rostovtzeff, *The Social and Economic History of the Roman Empire*, 2d ed., 2 vols. (Oxford, 1957), are fundamental, with full references to sources, articles, and books on the subject and with excellent indexes. Gommaire L. Dykmans, *Histoire économique et sociale de l'ancienne Égypte*, 3 vols. (Paris, 1936–37), discusses husbandry, cattle breeding, fishing, fowling, and the status of the peasantry with great acumen and offers a wealth of valuable references to source materials and to the literature of the subject up to the date of publication.

For the tomb reliefs and paintings illustrative of rural activities, the following books are recommended: Luise Klebs, *Die Reliefs des Alten Reiches* (Heidelberg, 1915); Luise Klebs, *Die Reliefs und Malereien des Mittleren Reiches* (Heidelberg, 1922); Luise Klebs, *Die Reliefs und Malereien des Neuen Reiches* (Heidelberg, 1934); Pierre Montet, *Les scenes de la vie privée dans les tombeaux égyptiens de l'Ancien Empire* (Strasbourg and Paris, 1925); Jacques Vandier, *Manuel d'archéologie égyptienne*, vols. 5–6 (Paris, 1969, 1978); Yvonne Harpur, *Decoration in Egyptian Tombs of the Old Kingdom* (London and New York, 1987).

Much can be learned about the Egyptian peasantry in antiquity from the study of their descendants in the Middle Ages and modern times. The relevant works of the Arab writers mentioned above are available in French: Abd el-Latif, *Relation de l'Égypte* (Paris, 1910), translated and fully annotated with lucid erudition by Silvestre de Sacy; Taqi ed-Din Maqrīzī, *Description topographique et historique de l'Égypte* (Cairo and Paris, 1895–1920), translated by U. Buriant. The monumental *Description de l'Égypte* embodies the result of the observations and researches of the savants attached to Napoleon's military expedition to Egypt. The second part (*État moderne*) contains numerous monographs of considerable significance to our present study; only two of them will be mentioned here: the "Mémoire sur l'agriculture, &c." by P. S. Girard, and the "Essai sur les mœurs des habitants, &c." by De Chabrol. The former is in pt. 2, vol. 1, no. 17, pp. 491–711, and the latter is in pt. 2, vol. 2, no. 6, pp. 363–524, of the original edition (Paris, 1809, 1812). In the second, or Panckoucke, edition, Girard's "Mémoire" is in vol. 17, pp. 1–436, and De Chabrol's "Essai" is in vol. 18, pp. 1–340 (Paris, 1824, 1826). On the fellahin in the twentieth century, see Winifred S. Blackman, *The Fellāhīn of Upper Egypt* (London, 1927), which includes a chapter on "Ancient Egyptian Analogies"; Henry Ayrout, *Fellahs d'Égypte* (Cairo, 1952); and Nessim Henry Henein, *Mārī Girgis, village d'Haute Égypte* (Cairo, 1988).

On the shouts, calls, and talk of peasants at work in the fields, see W. Guglielmi's article "Reden und Rufen" in W. Helck and W. Westendorf, eds., *Lexikon der Ägyptologie* (Wiesbaden, 1983), vol. 5, cols. 193–95, with copious references. The quoted speeches and songs have for the most part been culled from the Sakkarah Expedition, *The Mastaba of Mereruka* (Chicago, 1938), vol. 2, pls. 168–70; and particularly F. L. Griffith, *The Tomb of Paheri* (bound with Naville, *Ahnas el Medineh* [London, 1894]), pl. 3.

On the Satire of the Trades, see Edda Bresciani, *La letteratura e poesia dell'antico Egitto*, 2d ed. (Turin, 1969), pp. 151–57; and Miriam Lichtheim, *Ancient Egyptian Literature* (Berkeley and Los Angeles, 1973), vol. 1, pp. 184–92. The pedagogue's admonition is a conflation of three parallel texts; see Ricardo A. Caminos, *Late-Egyptian Miscellanies*, Brown Egyptological Studies, 1. (London, 1954), pp. 51, 247, 315–61; Bresciani, *Letturatura e poesia*, p. 307. For the schoolmaster's description of the peasants' sufferings, see Caminos, *Late-Egyptian Miscellanies*, pp. 389–90; Lichtheim, *Ancient Egyptian Literature*, vol. 2, p. 170.

The letter to Amenemope from his bailiff can be found in Caminos, *Late-Egyptian Miscellanies*, pp. 307–8. Amenemhet's account of his governance can be found in Miriam Lichtheim, *Ancient Egyptian Autobiographies Chiefly of the Middle Kingdom* (Freiburg and Göttingen, 1988), pp. 138–39. For the professions of charitable behavior, see Bresciani, *Letturatura e poesia*, p. 131; on the wages of the elderly harvester, see Gustave Lefebvre, *Le tombeau de Petosiris* (Cairo, 1923), vol. 3, pls. 13 (upper center) and 14 (upper left). A translation of Pharaoh Haremhab's decree can be found in Jean-Marie Kruchten, *Le décret de Horemheb* (Brussels, 1981), pp. 193–201.

The *anachōrēsis* has been the object of numerous studies. Only three references will be given here: Claire Préaux, *L'Économie royale des Lagides* (Brussels, 1939), pp. 500–502, 613 s.v. *grève*; Rostovtzeff, *Social and Economic History of the Roman Empire*, vol. 2, p. 758 s.v. *Anachoresis;* for further bibliography, see Ricardo A. Caminos, *A Tale of Woe from a Hieratic Papyrus in the A. S. Pushkin Museum of Fine Arts in Moscow* (Oxford, 1977), p. 63 n. 1.

For brief surveys of the medical issues touched upon here, see Warren R. Dawson, *Magician and Leech* (London, 1929), chap. 6 ("Ancient Egyptian Medicine") and chap. 7 ("Drugs and Doses"); Gustave Lefebvre, *Essai sur la médicine égyptienne de l'époque pharaonique* (Paris, 1956). Those who wish to go deeper into this subject will do well to follow up the multitude of references and cross-references in the articles "Heilkunde und Heilmethoden" and "Heilmittel" by W. Westendorff in *Lexikon der Ägyptologie*, vol. 2, cols. 1097–1101.

Wermai's story of the ills of an Egyptian peasant community under misrule is translated in Caminos, *A Tale of Woe*, pp. 70–72. Quotations herein have been excerpted at random from the Admonitions of an Egyptian Sage; see Bresciani, *Letturatura e poesia*, pp. 65–82; Lichtheim, *Ancient Egyptian Literature*, vol. 1, pp. 149–63.

2. CRAFTSMEN

Dominique Valbelle

The birth of craftsmanship, even more than that of art, in any given culture is revealed to an archeologist by a culture's material remains and to the historian by the manifestation of a social structure supportive of a particular set of craft circumstances. Those crafts in ancient Egypt that our modern sensibilities identify as possessed of artistic value attained a high quality of execution at a very early date, and this perceptible quality indicates that each craftsman specialized exclusively in only one activity. Prehistorians are, therefore, in accord in interpreting such data as suggesting that there already existed at that time a rigorous division of labor within that society. Such a strong division of labor then indicates that the individuals engaged in specialized craft activities enjoyed a considerable amount of free time, or leisure. The system of time spent laboring at craft specialization interspersed with free time was already established in Egypt well before the creation of the Egyptian state at the beginning of the First Dynasty.

From these early periods one can gain some idea about the workshops of these craftsmen by examining the remains of professional installations such as those in which stone vessels were carved, flint was flaked, pottery was made, and so on. That information can be augmented by studying the finished craft products themselves, as well as by examining the tombs of craftsmen, which can be identified by the tools found in them.

Information about craftsmen increases for the First and Second Dynasties. This period provides evidence for groups of craftsmen, more numerous and more heavily concentrated than in the preced-

ing periods, working in large urban work sites limited to several great
craft centers. These urban work sites include Memphis (the capital),
Hierakonpolis and Buto (in Predynastic times, the capitals of Upper
and Lower Egypt, respectively), Elephantine, Edfu, Elkab, Abydos,
and many others. These work, or construction, centers belong to the
very dawn of Egyptian history, as does the creation of canals, which
irretrievably determined the economy of the country. As a result, the
work sites, like the canals, similarly reveal only blurred or indirect
traces of the men who worked in them. The dwelling places of the
subsequent generations of craftsmen, particularly from the Fourth
Dynasty on, suggest the first indications of the organization of the
labor forces and the quality of life of the individuals who built the
pyramids. Gradually, the nobles of the Fifth and Sixth Dynasties
elected to have the craftsmen in their employ depicted at work, particularly in the scenes on the walls of their tomb chapels. These depictions of craftsmen are often accompanied by inscriptions providing information about their social and professional settings. These
nobles also liked to include depictions and inscriptions on their tomb
walls recording the missions which they successfully fulfilled on behalf of Pharaoh. These missions include their responsibilities for architectural projects as well as their expeditions to mines or quarries,
which are frequently described in detail. These expeditions, either
within Egypt or to the neighboring deserts, are also known from the
traces of the actual stoneworking operations left in the living rock at
many of those sites, from the archeological remains of the huts of the
craftsmen, and from an occasional contemporary graffito.

In period after period of Egypt's history, the sources already cited
are enriched by new categories of information. For example, during the Middle Kingdom, one can add to the ruins of monuments
and the dwellings and workshop scenes of craftsmen depicted in the
tombs of their employers the data obtained from graffiti and the information gleaned from the archives of a few work sites. Their contents vary, but are often related to either a free or a slave labor force.
To these sources can be added the funerary stelae that portray the
employees along with their employers. Furthermore, the accounts
given of expeditions also mention the specialized craftsmen, laborers, and management involved. The administrative records, the representations in tomb chapels, the number of worker villages, both
permanent and temporary, the ethnographic evidence, and that

derived from popular devotions such as ex-votos in sanctuaries are more numerous and diverse during the New Kingdom.

The transformation and the progressive increase in one's data about craftsmen are simultaneously the results both of the hazards of preservation of the evidence and of a social evolution perceptible in the literature and the funerary rites in Egypt from the middle of the third to the beginning of the first millennium B.C. The clearest manifestation of these tendencies can be seen by taking into account certain texts from the Middle Kingdom on, in which certain categories of craftsmen, as well as the means of expression by which certain individuals can be identified, are indicated. No information coming from one particular period, however, can fill a documentary lacuna in another period. For this reason, my approach to each major aspect of this chapter's themes—society, work, lifestyle, artistic expression— cannot completely avoid the constraints of a chronological narrative.

Nevertheless, the weight of institutional permanence and of cultural particularism inherent in Egyptian civilization does articulate differences in such a significant way that one may give precedence to a thematic presentation. Such a presentation has its limitations, some of which are imposed by our actual state of knowledge, whereas others are deliberately chosen for explication by their authors. Two aspects of Egyptological research currently in progress bear in a significant way upon this chapter. The first is continuing archeological excavation of worker villages, and the second is those academic studies which focus on the administrative structure of Egyptian society in general. Each season in the field archeological missions uncover new elements in diverse contexts, whereas the studies transform with each passing year our still very incomplete, if not imperfect, vision of the nature of Pharaonic institutions.

One must now, therefore, define the three words used in this chapter: "laborer," "craftsman," and "artist." The first, "laborer," as it is applied in this chapter, designates a manual laborer in general, regardless of personal qualifications. The term "craftsman," on the other hand, emphasizes above all else an individual's mastery of a particular technique or craft over his ability to exercise a manual task on its own account. Although the first term applies to an important part of the situations to be enumerated below, the activities of certain other functionaries are encompassed by the second term, that of "craftsman." The modern notion of "artist" did not exist in ancient

Egypt. The identity of the individual responsible for any given craft-work is made known only on rare occasions, and even rarer are the mentions of individuals whom Pharaoh has singled out from among the ranks of the craftsmen for special recognition. One does, how-ever, recognize artistic achievement in the handiwork of craftsmen on the basis of two criteria that were valued by the ancient Egyptians themselves: the skill of the craftsman and the subsequent satisfac-tion of his employer with the resulting handicraft.

Men and Society

The individuals whose identity we wish to discover and their milieu vanished with the disappearance of Pharaonic civilization some three thousand years ago. It may, then, perhaps appear to be a futile task to attempt to exhume a precise and specific profile of those men from a cultural record that is for the most part extremely limited and that has come down to us from a land which has been perennially the prey of treasure hunters from the beginning of its history. Neverthe-less, it is precisely those "treasures" and their accompanying inscrip-tions, be they decorated architectural elements from tombs or the precious or mundane objects found within, that provide the most ancient and direct indications of the individuals we seek to identify. The tomb in Egypt concentrates on the primary elements of an in-dividual's personality. The weight and emphasis placed on the eter-nal afterlife at the expense of a temporary present makes the tomb the privileged instrument of commemoration. An individual's face perpetuates itself through the heads of sculpted images; one's name, functions, and titles are inscribed on the tomb's doors and walls as well as on articles of funerary furnishings. Other evidence about these craftsmen is indirect. It may be contained in the monu-ments of a second person, an employer or a parent, who thus serves as an intermediary between the craftsman and the present-day scholar. In either case, the individual so commemorated becomes the privileged ambassador of his craft. Usually only his occupation or his socioprofessional status is noted. On occasion, however, the crafts-man is also named. Direct evidence, given or ordered by the subject, occasionally becomes more lengthy. An autobiographical recitation may comment on the episodes of a craftsman's career, may specify the nature of the responsibilities entrusted to him, and may place him within his own family setting, which individual representations elsewhere may also depict.

The dwelling, although provided with fewer inscriptions and furnishings than a tomb, nevertheless displays with eloquence the place of its occupant(s) in Egyptian society at the time. Houses often do not, however, retain explicit traces of their owners' occupations, or indeed even of specific occupants. One frequently, therefore, gathers from such dwellings only some very general indications of the milieus involved. Nevertheless, such data have the advantage of being the intact expression of reality, unlike evidence from tombs, which represents the arbitrary choice of an employer and the wish to appear to posterity under the most flattering guise, in possible defiance of the real facts, which one rarely has the opportunity of controlling through other sources. The archives from institutions or patron foundations also present guarantees of objectivity, albeit from a somewhat different but nevertheless complementary perspective. These sources take into account, with varying degrees of precision, the geographic and social origins of the craftsmen, their expenses, and so forth. These sources list the tasks prescribed for everyone. They also detail wages according to function, privileges, and compensations, and forcefully evoke punishments for failure to fulfill an obligation.

In short, one might know everything there is to know about ancient Egyptian craftsmen if one only had access to more than the smallest percentage of the innumerable registers which accumulated, month after month, year after year, in the offices of the Egyptian scribes throughout the land. However, in antiquity, such scribal archives were hardly ever kept for more than a decade. Some of the papyri on which those records were written were erased and recycled for new records. Others were used to light fires, as is amply attested by the clay sealings from papyrus scrolls that have been found in abundance in the cinders of ovens. The documents that have survived have escaped destruction by accident alone. Some scrolls were forgotten and have reemerged in the ruins of their depositories. Others were placed, for reasons inexplicable to a modern, in tombs of high functionaries. Some fragments have miraculously been recovered from rubbish dumps of both towns and temples. Fortuitously, scribes seem to have been as untiring as they were omnipresent. Not merely content to keep minute accounts of craftsmen and labor, some of the scribes devoted themselves further to exercises in compilation, with either didactic or encyclopedic pretensions. In these compilations, or onomatica as they are called, and in different "chosen extracts" serving as models to train new generations of scribes, titles and functions are indexed according to an order which, without being rigorously followed, suggests certain general groupings and affinities of data. Taken as a whole, this body of evidence confirms the existence of social classes in ancient Egypt.

The Early Dynastic Period and the Old Kingdom

The further back in time one goes, the more infrequent and fragmentary the indications for craftsmen are. Before the use of a standardized system of hieroglyphs became common during the First Dynasty, tools are the only reliable evidence for craftsmen. When these implements are sufficiently specialized, they reveal the profession of their user. Craftsmen ordinarily had placed in their tombs the tools which sited them within their respective social strata. One can, therefore, identify among the graves which accompany the kings' mastabas of the First Dynasty sepulchers of craftsmen who were known to specific kings and in whose company those kings desired to be in eternity. So, for example, one learns the name of an individual called Bekh from the inscriptions on two copper adzes and of an individual called Kahotep, whose name is preserved on the blade of an axe. These two craftsmen remained in the service of Pharaoh Djer after their deaths. This practice was widespread in the royal necropolises of Abydos and Saqqara during the entire course of the Thinite Period.

From the Second Dynasty at the site of Helwan, south of modern Cairo, and during the entire course of the Third Dynasty at Saqqara, the titles accompanying the names inscribed on various elements of funerary furniture either replace the tools of the earlier periods or state the craftsman's function more precisely. The men distinguished in this way are either master sculptors or masters of naval construction, and they are known from stelae, stone vases, and/ or statues. During the reign of Pharaoh Djoser, of the Third Dynasty, the most luxurious private tombs imitate the mastabas of the Thinite sovereigns. Built of baked or sun-dried brick, the superstructures of these tombs are only rarely inscribed with the names of the deceased on false doors, stelae, stone statues, or sculpted wood panels. However, within the tomb, an ever more precise identification of the deceased included his name, title(s), effigy, and the like—all of which are guarantors of eternal life. The construction of private tombs seems to have been a privilege of high officials and of only a few, select craftsmen. These individuals were probably considered to be among the most highly valued craftsmen of their time, but they are no longer buried exclusively near the royal tomb. During the Fourth Dynasty, this practice becomes clearer, especially in the necropolises of Giza and Saqqara. The number of represented occupants becomes more diverse, but the individuals most often occupy positions of responsibility. Their titles include "master sculptor of the two administrations," "director of all the works," "director of the armory," "director of textile manufacturing," "director of the funerary workshop craftsmen," "director of the miners," or "director of the masons." One also encounters some simple craftsmen. However, the most appreciated of these individuals have been immortalized at work by virtue of having been depicted in the scenes in the funerary chapels of their employers. Such is the case for the sculptor Inkaf who appears among the scenes in the chapel of Queen Merseankh III and among those of her son, the vizier Nebemakhet, as well as for the painters Rahy and Smerka. A few other craft professions are anonymously evoked. But it is not, evidently, these men who inhabited the great worker cities at the foot of the pyramids at Giza or Abusir or the small, three-room houses which are extant at the south of the causeway of Pharaoh Mycerinos (Menkaure). Of the obscure Egyptians who lived there and whose number may possibly have included laborers as well, one knows very little.

During the Fifth and Sixth Dynasties, one can confirm the style of the iconographic theme of the craftsmen at work and extend it to the provinces where the nomarchs, or provincial governors, who were at that time more powerful and more independent than in preceding eras, delighted in detailing the activities carried out in their workshops and ultimately in declaring the presence among their craftsmen of masters belonging to the workshops of Pharaoh. From the Fifth Dynasty come the protagonists, employers and employees alike, who provide the evidence for more varied initiatives which help to site them somewhat better within the social strata of their times. Thus, on one wall of her tomb, Lady Wepemnefert is depicted in a vignette in which she directs the drafting of her will in favor of her son. This scene is accompanied by representations of witnesses, among whose number one can identify two physicians, a steward, a policeman, two clerics, and various craftsmen and building workers. Despite the fact that the information provided by this vignette and its accompanying inscriptions is not very specific about the respective places of each of these witnesses within society, their juridical rights are, nevertheless, indubitably documented. These men are, for the most part, employees of Lady Wepemnefret, and they are again depicted in scenes in the lower registers of the same wall performing their habitual tasks. Interestingly enough, these individuals are not named in any of the inscriptions accompanying their representations; they are captioned only by the name of their respective professions.

It is, then, to the private monuments of the craftsmen, more numerous in this period, to which one must now turn at last in order to become acquainted with some of them. Even individuals on the lower rungs of the social ladder—the masons, carpenters, fullers, smiths, metalworkers, and sculptors—have left their names on certain architectural elements of their tombs, as well as on offering tables, libation basins, and statuettes. Many of these objects are today dispersed in various museums and collections worldwide. One may cautiously suggest that it was their contemporaries who lived in the stone huts of one or two rooms that were built opposite the mines at Wadi Maghara in the Sinai, where deposits of copper and turquoise were exploited, because the miners no longer figure in the lists of members of these expeditions.

At Giza or at Saqqara the foremen and the supervisors are set to manage those tombs which are somewhat larger than expected and which are more extensively provided with decorative panels sculpted in stone and equipped with statues, the inscriptions on which preserve not only the identity, the specific craft, and the priestly functions of the deceased, but also those of their parents and children. The directors of the work and of the workshops often combine technical responsibilities and various missions of trust. Although voluntarily represented performing a manual skill, in which they were probably masters, their family antecedents as well as their personal merits destine them to high functions, which they mention with pride in the inscriptions on the walls of their tombs. Such individuals belonged to an elite recognized by the court. They lived and had themselves buried near the capital, Memphis, although they were subject to being summoned to supervise work and expeditions in the provinces or even abroad.

The Middle Kingdom

The profound changes undergone by Egyptian society during the troubled times of the First Intermediate Period are probably not unrelated to the changes one observes in the nature of the documentary sources. The sources take more interest in the humbler population groups than earlier ones did, notably the anonymous laborers, to whom the Old Kingdom seems to have avoided the slightest allusion. Neither work site archives (which are available prior to the Middle Kingdom) nor tables of service nor books of wages naming workers have been preserved. What have survived, however, are the Reisner Papyri. In their present state of preservation, there are four documents. Three come from management registers of various construction centers, particularly that of a temple, whereas the fourth relates to a tool repair workshop of the royal navy work site located at the city of This (Thinis) in Middle Egypt. The men employed are natives of the region of Coptos, about 150 kilometers south of This. The identity of each is expressed by recording his name, sometimes preceded by that of his father and occasionally by that of a grandfather. The bonds of kinship between brothers are also indicated. Many labored as farmworkers shuttling between two different work sites. These are designated by the term "*mnyw*," which closely corresponds to the term for "laborer," or by "*ḥsbw*," emphasizing their status as "ones listed [on a census]." Their wages cannot be given an absolute value because they received the basic part of their income in loaves of bread, the numbers of which are known but the weight(s) and/or shape(s) of which are not. The average ration is eight *trsst*-loaves, but this ration can vary for the same individual from one work period to the next.

Various other contemporary documents propose a scale of salaries for defined work sites. The bread unit remains undetermined, but one does learn about the relative bread payment of each category of worker. So, for example, for the management of a private tomb, the 96 *fḳȝ*-loaves furnished daily are allocated in the following way: each accountable (supervisory) person receives 10; equipment (tool) foremen, from 2 to 5, depending on category; the designer, 6; the sculptors, 2–3, depending on category; the quarrymen, 2; the laborers, perhaps 1. The differences are clearly noted, even for small groups of 47 individuals. These figures are yet more striking in the framework of an expedition of 18,741 men who were sent to bring back from the quarries in the Wadi Hammamat, in the Eastern Desert, stone for 60 sphinxes and 150 statues. The head of this expedition, who was assigned by the central administration, received 200 loaves of bread and 5 measures of beer daily, whereas his assistants received anywhere from 30 to 100 loaves of bread and from 1 to 3 measures of beer daily, according to their rank. On the other hand, the sculptors received 20 loaves of bread and one-half of a measure of beer, their assistants being allocated 15 loaves of bread daily and one-third plus one-fourth plus one-fifth (or 47/60) of a measure of beer. The 17,000 "ones listed [on a census]," who composed the army of men-of-all-work each received only 10 loaves of bread and one-third of a measure of beer daily. If one considers salary as a social criterion, the above distribution of payment in kind speaks for itself.

A glance at the dwellings of the pyramid town of Sesostris II at El-Lahun in the Fayyūm confirms the differences between workers, craftsmen, and their foremen, on the one hand, and the high officials responsible for the great construction and rebuilding projects, on the other. The town, built for the management of the Pharaoh's funerary complex, that is, for the administration and maintenance of the funerary cult celebrated there, was divided into two unequal districts separated by a surrounding wall as thick as that enclosing the town as a whole. The more modest district of this town, which occupies less than one-quarter of the area of the other, is composed of dwellings for laborers each consisting of between five and seven rooms. In contrast, the largest of the elegant villas in the other district of this same town consists of seventy rooms, and these dwellings are separated from a central water channel by paved streets. This marked contrast between the size and location of the dwellings in the same town is not due to a progression over time in which its inhabitants moved from a lesser to a better standard of living in the form of more spacious dwellings. Quite the contrary, this difference is due solely to the fact that these two contemporary districts reflect an intentional social stratification, the administrators enjoying greater benefits, commensurate with their exponentially higher daily rations, than those in the lower strata of society. Such social stratification, rarely discernible in excavated sites from the Old Kingdom, becomes increasingly more detectable in the archeological record from the time of the Middle Kingdom onward.

From other remains one can now add several complementary observations which permit one to gain a broader picture of the situation of craftsmen during the Middle Kingdom. Whereas in previous periods the private monuments belonging to these socioprofessional categories were rare, restrained, and restricted to the context of the tomb, the democratization of funerary practices henceforth afforded an opportunity for more modest individuals to erect monuments in their own names. Some of these individuals made a pilgrimage to the Upper Egyptian city of Abydos, where they erected either stelae or small shrines on the terrace of the temple of the god Osiris there. The genealogical information contained therein, when studied in association with contemporary inscriptions from other sites in Egypt which were home to these pilgrims, provides a wealth of documentary information. The stability of such dedications, over several generations within the same family, clearly reveals, even upon a cursory examination, the identification of the craftsmen's specialization. One notes, however, perceptible variations in the levels of responsibility entrusted to each, and in spite of the professional concentrations suggesting the preservation of a family tradition, one notes the practice of techniques or distinct crafts by certain elements of the group.

About thirty of these professions are mentioned in the onomasticon which the scribe Amenemope wrote at the end of the New Kingdom, although he probably employed an older model. Although it is difficult to recognize a deliberate hierarchy in his presentation, the avowed nature of this compilation is that of a didactic survey which attempts to be exhaustive. The section of interest here, because it does stipulate rather precisely the profession with which this chapter is concerned, lists positions and professions according to a scale of contemporary values, summarily classed from the most prestigious (Pharaoh) to the most humble (farmhand). The order followed by the scribe is not, however, always evident to the modern reader, and the collection remains very incomplete. One can, nevertheless, recognize a certain number of coherent groupings. Of the 162 headings, 31 concern craftsmen or laborers. The list of 162 headings begins with the royal family, the court, and those near Pharaoh. Then follow categories concerning military responsibilities and religious functions. Among these one may note the presence of a "great one of the masters of work of He-who-is-south-of-his-wall" (= the god Ptah), a key post in the world of craftsmen, over whom Ptah is patron. The passage on the crafts and techniques is preceded by a section on the professions of food provisioning and is interrupted by a brief allusion to the clothing professions. The occupation of policeman follows the list of crafts and introduces the last section, which is the most eclectic, dealing with such sundry categories as administration, agriculture, commerce, and the like. Within the passage of immediate interest for craftsmen, the crafts themselves are organized by their interrelationships. Thus, one finds gemwork, leatherwork, armory, elaborate jewelry, architecture, and pottery—categories in which certain correspondences of material and vocabulary have created an association.

The New Kingdom

The history of craftsmen communities is dominated in the Eighteenth Dynasty by the great work sites on the west bank of Thebes. These are then followed chronologically by those at Amarna and, finally, in the Ramesside Period, by the institution of "the Tomb." These three groups provide a wealth of complementary data on the craftsmen who labored on the funerary temples and the tombs of the monarchs of the New Kingdom.

The ostraca (either limestone flakes or pottery sherds, which served as a ready source of writing material) found near the two different tombs of Senemut, the vizier of Queen Hatshepsut, and in front of the temples of that queen and her relative, Tuthmosis III, at Deir al-Bahri mention works in progress by workforces rather than individual craftsmen by name. Moreover, several mentions of the origins of some of these workforces shed light on their social milieu. The workforces of these various work sites were composed of employees attached to the service of the sovereign, the vizier, and various nobles as well as of individuals sent from the cites of Esna, El-kab, El-Matanah, and Asfun (all south of Thebes) or from Neferusi (in Middle Egypt). One notes with equal interest the presence of Nubian and Palestinian workers. If the dwellings of these men have survived scarcely better than those of the first worker village founded several decades earlier by Tuthmosis I at Deir al-Medina, the furnishings excavated in the tombs of the neighboring cemetery constitute some of the oldest direct evidence for the quality of life of this category of craftsmen, whose qualifications, in the absence of any textual evidence, remain uncertain. The furnishings include chairs and straw-bottomed stools, "studio beds" strung with cords or hides as mattresses, tables, matting, and pottery. Taken as a whole, this collection of furnishings resembles quite closely the furniture of poor farms in France at the end of the last century. At the south of the funerary temple of Tuthmosis IV, a huge house, contemporary with the temple's construction, must have sheltered the superintendent of the work center and his family for a number of years. This dwelling covers an area of about 200 square meters and consists in plan of a central nucleus of seven rooms sharing a peripheral corridor. A large amount of good-quality pottery confirms the impression of a comfortable lifestyle. Whether or not such dwellings are preserved at other work sites, the location of this residence relative to the temple permits one to suggest that such homes for administrators of royal architectural programs were erected near the construction sites.

The situation regarding the dwellings of the craftsmen and laborers at Amarna is quite different. Within the city proper, several of the most luxurious villas have been identified as belonging to the master sculptors and master craftsmen in the service of the king and his court. These individuals were recognized as the best at their respective crafts during their lifetimes. They directed the most important workshops. One also finds evidence of other master craftsmen elsewhere in the city, and at least one was buried among the dominant personalities of the capital. Other, more humble dwellings were inhabited by craftsmen probably employed in the workshops of the palace. However, at some distance from the city proper, in a little desert valley midway between the city of Amarna and the Arabian plateau, was constructed a laborers' village, with shrines, cemeteries, and dependencies. As at Thebes, the qualifications of the men and the nature of their daily tasks remain imprecisely known to scholars because of the lack of inscriptions. Nevertheless, the similarities between these two different communities at Thebes and at Amarna and the numerous traces of craftsmen's activities recovered from their dwellings do not permit any doubts whatsoever about their function. The regularity of the plan of the village, its surrounding rectangular precinct wall, and the dimensions of its dwellings recall the laborer district of El-Lahun, which was likewise segregated from the elegant parts of town. In the village outside Amarna, a hierarchy is also perceptible. The larger, eastern sector consists of forty-eight dwellings, and the western district consists of twenty-six. This latter area contains the largest dwellings, several of which were probably multistoried buildings, including that of "the foreman of equipment (tools)." Outside this precinct, traces of subsidiary agriculture have been found. Pigs were raised, and some patches of land were cultivated, both activities indicative of regular food contributions in addition to the grain rations that each family must have received from the state. Still farther off, near the cliffs, a second laborers' village, smaller and built of stone, has been provisionally identified, but it has yet to be excavated. As for the dwellings in Amarna's neighboring alabaster quarries at Hatnub, these take the form of stone huts, usually of one or two rooms, features these dwellings share with others found at desert sites inhabited on a seasonal or occasional basis. One has here, then, concentrated in an area of several square kilometers, four contemporaneous groupings of dwellings, representing different craft and laborer environments, from the simplest to the most elegant.

Data are more numerous after the creation by Pharaoh Haremhab at the end of the Eighteenth Dynasty of the institution known as "the Tomb," the intention of which was to ensure the sovereigns of a permanent supply of specialists reserved for the management of their tombs in the Valley of the Kings, and of lesser numbers of kings' relatives in the Valley of the Queens. We can identify the origins of the men employed, define the roles filled by members of their families working outside this institution, determine the relative quality of their lives, and deduce their relationships to the inhabitants of the region as well as to the high officials of the kingdom, including in some instances the monarch himself. It is even possible to follow closely the evolution of their fate from the end of the Eighteenth Dynasty to the beginning of the Third Intermediate Period. There are remarkably few differences between the dwellings assigned to the men at Deir al-Medina by Tuthmosis I and those of the laborers' communities of the Middle Kingdom. These dwellings are found in a walled village of up to sixty-eight individual dwellings constructed of stone and unbaked brick. Each dwelling consists of two main rooms and from three to four secondary rooms and occupies an average area of some 72 square meters (the largest is 120 square meters, and the smallest only 40 square meters). The wages in grain and other revenues in kind are known from numerous registers, although they cannot be readily compared to those of other institutions or work sites for a number of reasons. Nevertheless, these registers reveal that a simple craftsman received on a monthly basis 150 kilograms of wheat and 56 kilograms of barley. In other words, the daily ration of these two cereals amounted to 5 kilograms of wheat and 1.9 kilograms of barley, amounts that permitted the worker to feed his family amply on bread and beer. Moreover, a corps of auxiliaries supplied him regularly with water, fish, vegetables, fruit, pottery, and fuel for his hearth. That was not all. The funerary temples of the west bank of Thebes or the Treasury itself supplied this worker on occasion with rarer products such as certain kinds of bread and cakes, meat, honey, and oil. Not content with these revenues, which were delivered on a regular basis when the country's economy did not go adrift, the craftsmen augmented their resources by undertaking small commissions of their craft specialties for private clients.

The quality of their lives depended, in part, on the health of the state's finances. Fiscal health affected the regularity of the salary-in-kind flow to the state's labor force. At the time of the creation of "the Tomb" the men recruited had worked first on various earlier Theban monuments such as the temple of Amun at Karnak and the funerary temple of Tuthmosis IV. Some had labored in other areas of the country, such as at Elephantine to the south. The positions they had previously occupied are often mentioned alongside their new functions on the walls of their tombs or on other private monuments. The relationships they maintained with their native towns may be gauged with some assurance by the religious inscriptions in which the people are named. At the beginning of the Nineteenth Dynasty, the apogee of the Ramesside Period, one finds an abundance of information about craftsmen and laborers in the material culture of the craftsmen's village of Deir al-Medina, which had been founded by Tuthmosis I. These men together with their foremen and supervisors are characterized by a certain number of external signs of wealth, among which are the possession of several servants and the ownership of buildings outside the village and of fields and beasts. Later, such privileges become scarce. However, assignment to "the Tomb" continued to be viewed as a sinecure by which individuals attempt to benefit the greatest number of their children. Those children not so enrolled were generally entrusted to various other institutions or entered the army. The inhabitants of the village of Deir al-Medina thus had family members throughout the entire region, with whom they could remain in steady contact. The small commissions that they performed on their own account also put them in contact with all sorts of other individuals, in particular with notables, whom they win over with their services of varying importance. The "Men of the Tomb," by the very nature of their work, therefore, interacted with the greatest men of the kingdom. The vizier, responsible for the work on the tomb of the reigning Pharaoh, regularly spoke with them. Additionally, these men sometimes had the opportunity of seeing and exchanging messages directly with Pharaoh.

They received material or honorific compensation from Pharaoh, which they considered, rightly or wrongly, to be a bond of familiarity with him. The essential role in the central administration played by their foremen at the end of the New Kingdom was exceptional. As deputies of a waning power, this group of men, assisted by circumstances, seem to have attained a destiny beyond that of their fellows.

The Craft Professions

As this rapid survey of the most significant sources shows, important disparities existed during all these eras among the social situations of (1) supervisors and foremen of work sites, workshops, or expeditions, (2) craftsmen, and (3) laborers. Deriving from three widely separated classes, they pursued their respective careers, professions, or tasks within their own milieus. Without being a caste society in the strictest sense of the phrase, Egyptian society was, nevertheless, very hierarchical from the beginning of its history, and it remained conscious of social stratification throughout its long history. The barriers existing between the lowest and the middle social strata were, in the New Kingdom at least, more permeable. The settling of foreign prisoners of war within autochthonous communities, for example, leaves no doubt, whereas the reverse process, passage from a lower into a higher status according to the requirements of the job, indicates a flexibility in the status of the craftsmen and laborers and was not undertaken without causing major modifications in the daily lives of the men concerned. From high to low in the social scale, craftsmen appear to have been registered, bracketed, and controlled in their activities by an omnipresent and usually efficient administration. The vizier Rekhmire prides himself on having been registered during the reign of Tuthmosis III. The governing staffs of each sector of activity bear a uniform title, that of *imy-r* or *imy-r pr*, "director" or "director of the department," used in all the registers of life and accompanied by the name of the department. At the lower levels, *shd*, "inspector," *hrp*, "foreman," and *rwdw*, "controller," are common titles in even the most diverse domains.

In the Old Kingdom, the highest ranks in the area of craft achievement were *imy-r k3t nsw*, "director of the king's work," and *mdh kd nsw*, "royal master of the masons." These two functions were

sometimes assumed by the same individual. Tradition holds that this
was the case with Iyemhotep the Wise, the architect of the Step Pyramid of the Third Dynasty Pharaoh Djoser at Saqqara. The title "vizier" is not yet attested at that time. Later, in the Fifth Dynasty,
examples multiply. One can follow during the reigns of Pharaoh
Asosi (Isesi) and Pharaoh Unas the stages of the career of one of
Iyemhotep's successors to the helm of government, namely Senedjemib, in the autobiography which he had carved on the walls of
his tomb at Giza. The recitation is authenticated by the citing of
archival documents and the mention of dates. He is first presented
as a "director of the double house of silver, director of the king's
cabinet, director of the arsenal, and director of all the offices of the
Residence and of the southern domains." These multiple responsibilities, economic as well as secular, allow Senedjemib to distinguish
himself and serve to have him decorated and promoted to the ranks
of "vizier, director of the scribes of royal acts, and director of the
king's works." In this supreme honor, the state's highest office after
that of sovereign, Senedjemib presents himself clearly as the chief
architect of the prestigious construction programs entrusted to him
in turn by the two monarchs under whom he served. These monuments occupy a choice place in the royal chronicles of the period and
are mentioned on the Palermo Stone, along with victorious campaigns, religious foundations, and commercial expeditions. Their
place of honor in this document underlines the importance given to
these architectural programs as durable evidence of a reign's success.
It is for this reason that such endeavors were habitually entrusted to
the most important men of the realm.

Other courtiers, from the earliest periods of Egypt's history, are
charged with certain of these works or missions related to the search
for indispensable precious materials. If one later consults the cir-
cumstantial reports of the Middle Kingdom about such expeditions
sent to the mines and quarries, one will find that they were habitually placed under the authority of high officials belonging to the central administration, notably the Treasury when mining operations
were concerned, whereas the high priests of Amun, in the moments
just before they seized control of the government in Upper Egypt
during the Third Intermediate Period, took over the exploitation of
the gold mines of Wadi Hammamat.

The great construction work sites of the Pharaohs of the Middle
Kingdom are particularly evoked in official texts in which Pharaoh

expresses himself in the first person. However, from the beginning of the Eighteenth Dynasty, the work on temples and royal Theban tombs is described by those who were in charge of those endeavors, usually in long narratives which they have left in the chapels of their own tombs. The oldest such inscription is that of Ineni, "director of the storehouses [granaries] of Amun," who took an active part in directing the rebuildings ordered by Amenophis I and his successors in the temple of Karnak and in the management of the tomb of Tuthmosis I. Although he continued to be honored under both Hatshepsut and Tuthmosis III, other men favored by these new sovereigns seem to have picked up the torch. Senemut and Amenhotep bore the title "great steward of the queen," doubtless because they both undertook architectural projects for Hatshepsut at Karnak, Hermonthis, Deir al-Bahri, and Luxor. Djehuty was "director of the double house of silver" and "director of the double house of gold." He seems to have discharged the same duties as Puyemre, whose only title appears to have been the less elevated "divine father." Hapuseneb already occupied the position of vizier when Queen Hatshepsut appointed him to the work site of her tomb, a task that, save for this glaring exception, was the prerogative of the prime minister during the course of the entire New Kingdom. These courtiers received for the occasion new titles such as "director of all crafts" (*ḥrp ḥmwt nbt*), "he who gives instruction to the craftsmen" (*swbȝ-ḥr n ḥmww r irt*), "he who reveals the secrets" (*wn-ḥr sšȝ m irwt*), and "foreman/director of works" (*ḥrp/imy-r ḳȝwt*). Their responsibilities extended from furnishing the primary materials necessary to complete the work (monolithic blocks of stone for the erection of obelisks; gold, silver, and electrum for the facings of the obelisks or of monumental doors; exotic woods; and so forth) to the actual direction (*sšm*) of the work and its regular inspection (*mȝȝ*). These were the same areas of responsibility that Rekhmire, the vizier of Tuthmosis III, assumed as foreman of the workshops of the domain of Amun.

The masters of works—foremen of tools, scribes—were often simple craftsmen promoted from the ranks. However, some of these officers were habitually chosen from certain families of craftsmen. Such families seem to retain their rank from one reign to another. For example, of the twenty-eight known "foremen of equipment (tools) of the Tomb," no fewer than twelve were sons of a "foreman of equipment." When one is not dealing with a permanent work site, such as those for the royal tombs of the New Kingdom, one still finds indications (if not a systematic transmission of responsibilities within the same family) of recommendations favoring the recruitment of the brother or the son of a man already valued for his ability in his craft. These candidates were often preferred over others without these familial connections.

In general, there is very little information about craftsmen who were particularly noted for their specialized skills, and in those rare instances when such individuals can be identified, the associated data do not mention their familial connections. The only craftsmen to have lifted the veil of their own anonymity are those whose autobiographies celebrate the esteem in which their respective sovereigns held them, those whom their employers judged highly enough to honor on the walls of their tombs, or those who have, more or less directly, signed their works. Such individuals are frequently painters and sculptors; occasionally they are architects. The favor they enjoyed was worth material advantage, and often a rich tomb, where the gifts of satisfied high personages were piled, was their reward.

Thus, the Scribe and Director of Works Kha possessed in addition to a superabundance of funerary furnishings, which may nevertheless have been commonplace in the Eighteenth Dynasty for a man of his station in life, several precious objects, including a cubit rod plated with gold, two vases of bronze and silver, a scribe's tablet, a game, and two carved staves, each bearing Kha's name. The deluxe cubit rod and tablet are objects suitable to be interred with a competent craftsman, and the staves are emblems of authority appropriate to his rank and status.

Sometimes Pharaoh recompensed one of his courtiers by sending him some of his best employees. At other times a prince or high official assigned his private team to one of the royal work sites.

Although our data do not permit the identification of other illustrious craftsmen such as Kha, there must have been a surfeit of accomplished, albeit anonymous, craftsmen of his caliber to judge from the marvels which fill museums throughout the world. One knows the value accorded to these individuals even by the earliest kings of Egypt from the siting of their burial places in close proximity to royal tombs at places such as Abydos. These craftsmen can be grouped into three categories. The first are those who work with resources obtained from mines and quarries. They are primarily cutters of fine flint, polishers of hard stone, makers of vases of alabaster and breccia, and the like. The second group comprises those individuals whose craft specialization requires the utilization of several materials and/ or technologies and includes goldsmiths, jewelers, the crafters of ebony and of faience, and the like. The third includes those who worked on architectural and sculptural projects sculpting, designing, and painting under the direction of the great specialists.

In the periods in which the workshops and royal work sites functioned through the length and breadth of Egypt, numerous craftsmen and laborers capable of quality workmanship could be found at court and in the provinces. These individuals, from the most unskilled laborer to the most accomplished craftsman, strove to be as competent as possible in the performance of their task or craft specialization. One might, therefore, state that objects of dazzling refinement, linking technique with harmony of color and form, are manifestations of periods of political stability and economic expansion. Conversely, objects from periods of political decentralization and foreign occupation often exhibit a naïveté and lack of accomplishment.

Directors of work, masters of work, craftsmen, and impressed laborers drafted from the corvée all have a status close to that of a functionary. And yet, social, upward mobility was not at the individual's disposal. That mobility depended on the employer. From the Old to the New Kingdom, the sovereign, the great proprietors, and the temple hierarchy—in short, those in positions of authority—disposed of the services of their employees according to need. The great Pharaonic programs, like private ones, often necessitated long and repetitive tasks, the most exceptional interventions, and the search for and procurement of particular materials.

Talents were exercised in permanent and in temporary settings. Certain craft communities offered the security of permanent employment for workers and their children and also the assurance of regular work in the neighborhood of their village. Less fortunate families were reassigned from place to place, and certain members had to undertake dangerous missions. These disadvantages affected more than just those populations of Egypt that were subject to the corvée, or forced labor. One example will suffice. Some men were sent, when the harvest was over, to build a temple 150 kilometers away from their homes. The officials responsible for the architectural programs and their best specialists had to travel not only to the work area but also to the sources of the different materials needed for the construction. Unis, who successively occupied positions at the royal palace and in the provinces in addition to having juridical responsibilities, recounts:

> His Majesty sent me to Ibhat to bring back the coffin of the living [ones] "Lord of Life," with its lid and the precious and august pyramidion intended for the pyramid named "Merenre-appears-in-his-perfection," my sovereign. His Majesty sent me to Elephantine to bring back the granite false door with its threshold, the jambs and lintels of granite, to bring back the doors and the granite flagstones for the upper chamber of the pyramid "Merenre-appears-in-his-perfection," my sovereign. I had them brought down to the Nile to the pyramid "Merenre-appears-in-his-perfection" in six barges and three boats . . . [?] in a single expedition [. . .] His Majesty sent me to Hatnub to bring back a great offering table in alabaster of Hatnub [. . .] (Roccati 1982, p. 196)

The lapidaries traveled to the turquoise mines of Sinai, where they presumably provided some measure of guidance to the miners in searching out the best deposits. In like manner the expeditions to the quarries of Egypt and Nubia included sculptors, who chose the blocks of stone and worked them on the spot. Jewelers and goldsmiths occasionally accompanied prospectors of gold to the Wadi Hammamat. At Sarabit al-Khadim, in the Sinai, the numerous molds collected near the ore deposits show that copper was smelted as soon as it was extracted. The way of life of the most sedentary craftsmen was very different from that of those who were moved from one work site to another. Such assignments affected every classification of craftsman and laborer from the highest on the social scale to the lowest. Moreover, men perpetually attached to a specific work site like that of "the Tomb" were often called on to move, perhaps within the same area, perhaps outside Thebes, as the stela of Merenptah (Merneptah) at Gebel Silsileh attests.

Remains of stone huts and shrines can still be seen at numerous quarries and mines from Wadi Maghara to Hatnub. At Gebel Zeit, for example, the installations are rudimentary, but they do adhere to an overriding town plan. They must have accommodated small groups at certain times and at other times many hundreds of people. One notes little difference in the buildings capable of reflecting the rank and social status of the inhabitants. Discoveries of dwellings

near a work site utilized for short or medium stretches of time—
between several weeks and several years—are too sporadic in the
landscape to allow for fruitful comparisons of the conditions of those
dwelling there.

Whereas the men of "the Tomb" seldom went far from their village on those occasions when they were sent to other locations to
work, the high officials, craftsmen, and laborers who participated in
expeditions, even for long periods of time, were separated from their
wives and children, as was everyone else charged with a mission.
The Egyptians traveled much more both within their borders and
without than they would have liked. Numerous preserved letters
bear witness to this annoyance, which the Egyptians resented. They
lived, in these circumstances, as a group, sleeping in dormitory-like
barracks or with several other individuals in the huts at their disposal.
At a construction site where the architectural program might take
two or three years to complete, such as might have been the case for
the great Theban funerary temples, the architect could often arrange
for a villa in the neighborhood. It is likely, therefore, that the architect of the temple of Tuthmosis IV was surrounded by his family in
the house made for him south of its precinct wall. If one takes this
case as a model, one may state that in general homes for those in
command were usually segregated from the homes of those responsible for the execution of the work. The most stable and regular jobs,
located near a reasonably good official's house, were much sought
after. That competition tended to provoke the darkest of intrigues
between craftsmen and laborers vying for such desirable postings.

In closing, one should mention that there are very infrequent
mentions of women among the ranks of craftsmen, and there is little
evidence to link any particular craft exclusively to women.

Individual Expression in Daily Life

This chapter began with the observation that a concomitant benefit
to craftsmen occasioned by the vigorous division of labor into craft
specializations was a certain amount of leisure time in which their
private lives might unfold. The topic of the "daily life" of craftsmen
is worth exploring, although admittedly the information is somewhat
limited because most of their daily routine was so subject to administrative organization and to a communal lifestyle that any time left for

individual initiative seems initially to have been very limited indeed. Nevertheless, from at least one site, that of Deir al-Medina, where the craftsmen attached to "the Tomb" lived, one can document their daily lives because of the chance preservation and discovery of a number of written, personal records which chronicle the personalities of some of those men and provide a window into their secret thoughts. These archival documents recount episodes in some of their lives, episodes that are as fresh today as if they had only just happened. The craftsmen's material needs were, on the whole, provided by the authorities: their houses, funerary grants, food, work clothing, and the like. Whatever their conditions of life were, these men organized their lives, beginning with their work. Although these men were expected to give priority to their work on the tomb of the living Pharaoh, be it as designer, painter, sculptor, or simple quarryman, each of these individuals nevertheless developed small, associated skills which allowed them to supplement their monthly allowances. They made baskets, furniture, statues, sarcophagi, and the like, not only for each other but also for clients residing outside the town of Deir al-Medina. These subsidiary activities took on greater or lesser importance depending upon the attitude of the authorities, who sometimes benefited from them.

These talents, applied in their own homes or tombs, contributed as well to the diversity of both. As a result, the town of Deir al-Medina, originally conceived in accordance with a regular plan, gradually took on a more whimsical configuration because of repeated rebuilding and enlargements which began in the Nineteenth Dynasty. Many of these alterations are attributed directly to the idiosyncrasies of the craftsmen themselves. One man might join two adjacent houses, another might add a room to his house, and a third might extend a kitchen into the street. The cemetery, on the rise behind the town, became so overcrowded during the two and a half centuries of its continued use that burial vaults from different tombs became interconnected, and this commingling of sepulchral chambers at the end of the Ramesside Period resulted in a rash of lawsuits, many of which are preserved in the archives from Deir al-Medina.

The variety of foodstuffs named in these archives or found preserved on the site and uncovered by archeological excavation demonstrates that, in addition to the usual rations of grain, fish, fruit, and common vegetables, the craftsmen found the means to obtain other victuals to improve their ordinary diets. Their menu was, nonetheless, restricted for the most part to bread, fish, beer, water, and some fresh produce, according to the individual's financial circumstances. Despite the fact that names of breads, cakes, and other sweetened preparations are abundant, no true recipe, however simple, has come down to us from Deir al-Medina, or from elsewhere in Egypt for that matter. This absence stands in marked contrast to the medical preparations, whose recipes have survived, revealing that they used common foodstuffs.

Dining must have been an important social act for the Egyptians, if one is to judge by the prominence of place given to funerary banquets. On this subject, however, the craftsmen of Deir al-Medina are no more communicative than their fellow countrymen. Conviviality, if not a daily occurrence, is at least on all special occasions and particularly on village holidays evoked by the preparation of offerings that were presented and consumed at these times. The furniture, the musical instruments, and the clothes whenever preserved suggest, in their design, social customs and a certain taste for public demonstrations, which are echoed in the texts from one era to another. This care in representation also finds its expression in the modest goods and furnishings and in the lands and servants which the men of "the Tomb" made every effort to acquire when they did not inherit them from their parents. In their ability to acquire goods they were considerably more fortunate than most of Pharaoh's workers. Most often surplus was expended on burial and funerary furnishings. This reflects a very widespread ambition among the Egyptian population, but here again craftsmen had specific advantages. They had access to funerary texts, and they did not stint in reproducing them on the walls of their own tombs. They knew how the work should be done. Whenever they did not possess the requisite skills themselves, they turned to one of their colleagues. In other cases they shifted for themselves as best they could. The results at those times are understandably uneven. Part of their estates were devoted to funerary furnishings, sometimes for the manufacture of specific sets of furniture. The remainder was divided among their heirs, many of whom perfunctorily discharged their obligations toward the deceased relative.

These employees, whose main obligation was after all to Pharaoh, benefited from the rights due to the Egyptian people as a whole. These rights manifested themselves not only in contracts, bequests, divorces, and the like but also in a judicial framework. A local tribunal, consisting of men "of the Tomb," rarely of women, dealt with minor misdeeds and internal dissension. The oracles of the local cult statue of the deified Amenophis I intervened to decide in difficult cases.

Devotions held an importance akin to that evidenced throughout Egypt and, as elsewhere, took specific popular forms, the result of regional and professional contexts as much as the origins of the men employed at these work sites or in these workshops. The multiplicity of cults and holidays is one of the most striking aspects of their daily lives. In addition to the deities who ruled in the Hereafter and over the Theban mountain, such as Hathor and Meretseger, those who protected the town, like the deified Pharaoh Amenophis I and his mother, Ahmose-Nefertari, and those who were patrons of craftsmen, like the god Ptah, the community adopted deities from all of the provinces of Egypt and even some from abroad. Some deities were adopted for personal reasons, and the adoption of others followed nationwide trends. The people's beliefs, to which one must add as well the worship of the dead, or ancestors, and fertility cults, gave great importance to images, including processional statues and household deities (which for convenience are termed lares, after the Roman practice). Sacred animals also played a role. As in the practice of medicine, magic was essential, particularly in the areas of repentance and fertility. The goodwill of the deities was paramount.

Legal proceedings are not the only documents that inform us about the system of ethics that flourished in Deir al-Medina. All sorts of notes, occurring in the "Journal of the Tomb," in other reports, in preserved correspondence, and in the inscriptions of the stelae of the blind entreating the goddess to give them sight in exchange for an act of sincere contrition, help to sketch a portrait that is representative of behavior. One man complains about another of bad character in the following way: "What does it mean, that you set yourself to act as you do, when no word penetrates your ear, except your extre[me] vanity. You are not a human being. You do not behave playfully to a woman, like your fellow [man]." In another passage, one reads, "You are very rich and you give nothing to anyone" (Černý 1973, pp. 212–13). Another denounces the innumerable exactions of the man occupying the post that he himself coveted, the foreman of equipment, named Paneb, by citing the corruption of the vizier in the profaning of sanctuaries and tombs, the dishonoring of many village women, the various acts of violence against his colleagues, thefts and embezzlements, perjuries and death threats.

Feelings other than hatred or envy, however, become apparent, such as that of friendship:

> But what? What wrong have I done you? Am I not your old companion in eating bread? [. . .] What will I do? Write to me concerning the wrong I committed against you; (send it) by Bes the policeman. Otherwise, write to me (whether it be) good or bad. Oh, these (?) evil times! I will ask nothing at all from you. It is pleasant [for] a man who is with his old table companion. When my letter reaches you, you will write (to me), by the policeman Bes, about your health. Explain to me the state (of your health) today. Do not have them say that I cannot enter your house and not to make (my) way within the walls and flee from the town! (Černý and Posener 1978, p. 16)

One might profitably compare these sentiments to those of love expressed by the scribe Butehamun toward his dead wife on an ostracon that he probably placed in her tomb so that it could be his spokesman to her.

> O venerable coffin of Osiris, the singer of Amun, Akhtay, who reposes in you! Hear me and transmit (this) message. Ask her, since you are near her: "How are you? How do you feel?" You will tell her: "What sadness that Akhtay is no longer living!" So says your brother, your companion. What sadness, you so beautiful, without equal. One could find nothing ugly in you. I call (you) constantly; answer [him who] [calls] you. (Valbelle 1988, p. 96)

Artistic Expression

If the craftsmen of Deir al-Medina were occasionally aware of creating masterpieces (e.g., when they decorated the tomb of Sethos [Seti] I), they remain silent on the subject. They attached great value to the commissions which they successfully executed but describe their talent in terms of skill, even of love (for the Pharaohs). The magnificence of the monuments they created is but a visual demonstration of their devotion to the gods and to Pharaoh.

The Pharaohs are scarcely more explicit on defining the idea of art. Nevertheless, Pharaohs did discriminate between craftsmen. Whenever a Pharaoh entrusted a specific individual with a task he particularly valued, whenever he elevated that same craftsman above his social station in life, Pharaoh raised that artisan to the level of an "artist," although the Egyptian language does not have an equivalent word for such an individual. The anonymity of most works helps erase the concept of individuality in craft enterprises, where the result, taken as a whole, counts more than the details considered individually. A handful of the craftsmen of these monuments, however, did manage to add their signatures, either directly or, by availing themselves of an opportunity elsewhere, indirectly. Nevertheless, the name that primarily occurs on a monument is virtually always that of the employer and not of the craftsmen or laborers. And one knows the importance the ancient Egyptians accorded to their names, which were their only promise of survival.

It is, then, a remarkable social constant that effaces the craftsman in favor of his employer. Art is, nevertheless, neither an exclusive privilege of the deities nor a royal monopoly. From the most distant of times, not only is art practiced for the sake of private patrons, but it is universally found throughout the population. In more or less modest form, everyone makes for himself or for his relatives an object—a bouquet, a necklace, a statuette. No one, from the humblest to the most fortunate, is deprived of this blessing. One is, therefore, faced with a paradox: art is one of the commonest expressions of daily Egyptian life, but only a handful of craftsmen's names have survived. Of that number, those craftsmen who were famous in their own time were rarely remembered by subsequent generations.

This impression that ancient Egyptian craft specialization was practiced by anonymous craftsmen is accentuated by the lacunae in our data. That impression can be somewhat tempered by the realization that there is evidence for the existence of at least one craftsman whom a modern might term an "artist." This remarkable individual is the sculptor Djehutymose, one of the high officials of the kingdom who lived at Amarna during the reign of Pharaoh Akhenaten (Eighteenth Dynasty). Djehutymose possessed a vast villa which adjoined his workshop in the very heart of the capital city. Within that workshop a group of extraordinary images was excavated that has contributed to the art historical fame of the so-called Amarna Period. Although none of these images is signed, in keeping with the ancient Egyptian tradition of the anonymity of craftsmen, there is no doubt that these statues, more than any others, express the personality of Djehutymose rather than the personalities of the individuals represented by them. At this particular moment in history, an Egyptian craftsman, Djehutymose by name, sought to superimpose, with simultaneous finesse and intensity, his temperament onto his creations. In so doing he gave free rein to his artistic sensibilities. The resulting images can best be characterized as humanistic variations of the prevailing Pharaonic ideology of the Amarna Period and find their closest parallels in contemporary literary compositions with their emphasis on nature. That ideology evidently permitted Djehutymose a degree of artistic license that enabled him to set aside the conventions of craft specialization so that he might practice his sculpting in a way that approaches a modern's definition of an artistic temperament.

Bibliography

Allam, S. *Das Verfahrensrecht in der altägyptischen Arbeitsiedlung von Deir el-Medineh*. Tübingen, 1973.

Bogoslovsky, E. S. "Hundred Egyptian Draughtsmen." *Zeitschrift für Agyptische Sprache* 107 (1980): 89–116.

Borchardt, L., and H. Ricke. *Die Wohnhäuser in Tell el-Amarna*. Berlin, 1980.

Bruyère, B. *Rapport sur les fouilles de Deir el-Médineh*. In *Fouilles de l'Institut Français d'Archéologie Orientale*, vols. 1/1, 2/2, 3/3, 4/3, 5/2, 6/2, 7/2, 8/3, 10/1, 14, 15, 16, 20, 21, 26. 1924–53.

Černý, J. "Papyrus Salt 124 (BM 10055)." *Journal of Egyptian Archaeology* 15 (1929): 243–58.

———. "A Community of Workmen at Thebes in the Ramesside Period." *Bulletin d'Égyptologie* 50 (1973).

———. *A Community of Workmen at Thebes in the Ramesside Period*. Cairo, 1973.

———. "The Valley of the Kings." *Bulletin d'Égyptologie* 61 (1973).

Černý, J., and G. Posener. *Papyrus hiératiques de Deir el-Médineh*. Vol. 1. Cairo, 1978.

Chartier-Raymond, M. "Notes sur Maghara (Sinai)." *Cahiers de Recherches de l'Institut de Papyrologie et d'Egyptologie de Lille* 10 (1988): 13–22.

Davis, W. "Artists and Patrons in Predynastic and Early Dynastic Egypt." *Studien zur Altägyptischen Kultur* 10 (1983): 119–39.

Drenkhahn, R. "Die Handwerker und ihre Tätigkeiten im alten Ägypten." *Ägyptologische Abhandlungen* 31 (1976).

Gardiner, A. H. *Ancient Egyptian Onomastica.* 3 vols. Oxford, 1947.

Hayes, W. C. *Ostraca and Name Stones from the Tomb of Senenmut (n. 71) at Thebes.* New York, 1942.

———. "A Selection of Thutmoside Ostraca from Der el-Bahari." *Journal of Egyptian Archaeology* 46 (1960): 29–52.

James, T. G. H. *The Hekanakhte-Papers and Early-Middle-Kingdom Documents.* Oxford, 1962.

Kemp, B. J. *Amarna Reports I–IV.* London, 1984–87.

Midant-Reynes, B. "Contribution à l'étude de la societé prédynastique: Le cas du couteau 'ripple-ware.'" *Studien zur Altägyptischen Kultur* 14 (1987): 185–224.

Petrie, W. M. F. *Kahun, Gurob and Hawara.* London, 1890.

Roccati, A. *La littérature historique sous l'Ancien Empire égyptien.* Paris, 1982.

Saleh, A. "Excavations around Mycerinus Pyramid Complex." *Mitteilungen des Deutschen Archäologischen Instituts, Kairo* 30 (1974): 131–54.

Schiaparelli, E. *La tomba intatta dell'architetto Cha nella necropoli di Tebe.* Turin, 1927.

Simpson, W. K. *Papyrus Reisner.* Vols. 1–4. 1962–86.

Smith, W. S. *A History of Egyptian Sculpture and Painting in the Old Kingdom.* Oxford, 1946.

Stadelmann, R. *Syrisch-Palästinensische Gottheiten in Ägypten.* Leiden, 1967.

Steinmann, F. "Untersuchungen zu den in der Handwerklich-kunstlerischen Produktion beschäftigen Personen und Berufsgruppen des Neuen Reichs." *Zeitschrift für Ägyptische Sprache* 107 (1980): 137–57; 109 (1982): 66–72, 149–56.

Valbelle, D. "'Les ouvriers de la Tombe,' Deir el-Médineh à l'époque ramesside." *Bulletin d'Égyptologie* 96 (1985).

———. *La vie dans l'Égypte ancienne.* Paris, 1988.

Ventura, R. *Living in a City of the Dead.* Göttingen, 1986.

Vercoutter, J. "The Gold of Kush, Two Gold Washing Stations at Faras East." *Kush* 7 (1959): 120–53.

Wilson, J. A. "The Artist of the Egyptian Old Kingdom." *Journal of Near Eastern Studies* 6 (1947): 231–49.

3. SCRIBES

Alessandro Roccati

Is there any here like Hardjedef? Is there another like Iyemhotep? There have been none among our kindred like Neferti and Khety. I recall to you the names of Ptahemdjehuty and Khakheperre-sonbe. Is there another like Ptahhotep or Kaires? (Chester Beatty Papyrus IV, 3.5)

Thus begins a famous passage containing a list of writers. These writers might be described as classical, since they all lived centuries before the composition in which they are mentioned was written (thirteenth century B.C.?) and wrote in the ancient tongue, which was substantially different from the language (Late Egyptian) that had entered into use by that time. The passage's unknown author uses the list to reaffirm the idea that writing is as long-lasting as the stone that was used to build the pyramids. Indeed, anyone capable of adopting writing is safer than the mummies enclosed in their luxurious tombs.

Although this attitude was widely shared in the last quarter of the second millennium B.C., when sophisticated palace culture was at its height, a number of indications suggest that it was not always true. Above all, who were the illustrious authors mentioned in the passage, to most of whom surviving works were attributed? Hardjedef was a son of Cheops (Khufu) who never reigned. However, a lesson reputed to be his work was widely read during and after the Ramesside Period. Only fragments of the text have survived. Nothing has been preserved, however, of the writings of Iyemhotep, vizier of the Third Dynasty Pharaoh Netjerikhet-Djoser, buried in the (first) Step Pyramid of Saqqara. Iyemhotep's fame as an architect, writer, and doctor (he was compared to the Greek Asclepius) was so well established up to (and, above all, at) the end of the Pharaonic era that he became the object of popular veneration, almost prefiguring Christian saints.

The Twelfth Dynasty prophecy attributed to Neferti, a magician-seer from the remote past, suggests that Pharaoh Snofru, father of Cheops and founder of the Fourth Dynasty, anachronistically possessed the ability to write, recording the words of Neferti with his own hands. A famous catalog of trades (the so-called Satire of the Trades, which we shall examine more closely below) is attributed to Khety (Duaf-khety), who lived at the beginning of the Twelfth Dynasty. The catalog's main aim was to ridicule all other activities when compared to that of the scribe. Yet Ptahhotep's Instruction, perhaps the longest and most well known text of its kind, dating back to the Fifth Dynasty and surviving intact in a number of manuscripts from the Twelfth Dynasty on, makes no mention of scribes.

It is not a paradox to observe that, during the period of the theocratic state known as the Memphite monarchy or Age of the Pyramids in the third millennium B.C., Egypt attached more importance to reading than to writing. In other words, the composition of texts appears to have been of secondary importance. The idea of the scribe as one who created, invented, and perfected the writing system remained primary throughout the third millennium. If we exclude the administrative use of accounting, which required limited skill, the competence of the scribe consisted in his ability to create, not so much the text of the composition, but rather its graphic representation. One of the Pyramid Texts (funerary texts written on the interior walls of the Saqqara pyramids) describes the Pharaoh as he who "is scribe of the divine scroll; he speaks that which is (read), and brings into being that which is not (written)" (1146c). The manipulation of writing, particularly in religious texts (the principal written texts during the third millennium, apart from administrative registers, letters, and decrees), required not only linguistic competence but also an understanding of the world of signs and symbols traced in the text.

From a linguistic viewpoint, above all, the scribe was the figure capable of transforming linguistic "confusion" into a single written text. In the third millennium B.C., writing faithfully reflected the world, not only in its graphic symbols (hieroglyphs) but also in the words of which it was composed. Each written thing necessarily corresponded to something real. When this was not so, the formulation of the word was sufficient to constitute a creative act. In this sense, writing coincided with the official language of the state (or, rather, the temple, from which the state emanated) and was, by definition, the only "true" language. In comparison, all the other languages spoken within the vast and anything but homogeneous area watered by the Nile were "obscure." Nor could it be considered in the same way as the languages of other civilizations, which were deliberately ignored. In Egypt, unlike in Mesopotamia, it was never necessary to replace the original language with a different one based on written culture, creating the need to unite the two systems. One might even claim that, in Egypt, not only spatial but also temporal changes were suppressed as "not true." To possess writing was also to possess the only language. Together they formed an unbreakable bond.

Associated in this way, language and writing were then submitted to the ritual needs produced both by religious practices and by the taboos connected with the values and functions of elements adopted as graphic symbols. The unknown author of the Pyramid Texts, which differ in their organization from funerary complex to funerary complex, is revealed in this light as a genuine scientist. Moved by the need to provide answers to ritual and linguistic problems, he considerably advanced the understanding of writing as a product of the phonetic and semantic content of the language it presented. For example, in the pyramid of Teti, it was decided to remove all signs connected to living beings from the graphic symbols. The written words were transformed in such a way, however, as to remain sufficiently intelligible. In other places, it was a question of indicating as precisely as possible the phonetic content of complex pictographic signs making up a word. It was usual to add all possible "phonetic complements" in order to remove any doubt. During the following millennium, practices of this kind led to the existence of a graphic instrument that could become pure "message," that is, a perfected means of communication.

It is obvious that, during the third millennium, the care that went into writing texts was matched by an equal concern for the way in which they were read. Reading aloud was not specifically intended for an audience but had an essentially ritual value. The reader possessed a special title, literally translated as "bearer of the ritual (book)" or, commonly, "ritualist" or "lector priest" (*ḥri-ḥb*). He was an essential figure in activities surrounding the recitation of sacred texts (as well as of the Pyramid Texts themselves), being the exclusive possessor of the title to that role. Among other things, this exclusiveness derived from his capacity to avoid the dangers and deleterious effects inherent in the written text, at both the graphic and the linguistic level.

The title of "lector priest" assumed the skills of the "scribe" but was considered superior because of the ritual function its holder performed. In the biography of Ptahuash (Fifth Dynasty, ca. 2400 B.C.), there is a reference to the "dean of doctors," who is also a "lector priest." This "dean of doctors," Niankhsekhmet, famous for his funerary shrine, on which the decision made by Pharaoh Sahure to donate the shrine is inscribed, emphatically does not receive the title "scribe," even though he was clearly able to write. The same can be said of Uni, another "lector priest," who rose to supreme command and was summoned to write the records of a trial involving the Pharaoh's harem. He also declined to display the title of "scribe." Clearly then, one must assume that the administrative title did not, in itself, entitle its holder to high rank, nor did it include all those who wrote or made use of writing, as we can see in funeral registers down to the Roman Period: "each *pure* priest, each scribe, each learned man, [. . .], each expert in hieroglyphics."

The inscription in the tomb of Bia, near the pyramid of Unas, also distinguishes between the "scribe," who will read the inscription, and Bia's rank as "lector priest," allowing him to express his gratitude: "whichever scribe passes near to this my tomb and reads this inscription (on the entrance lintel), I shall be his support in the courtroom of the great god, because I am a capable and genuine lector priest." In other places, the expression "capable lector priest" (*ḥri-ḥb iqr*) seems to be replaced by "capable scribe (who knows the rituals)" (e.g., on the tomb of Izi at Saqqara, beside Bia's tomb). This title allows its holder to refer to himself after death as a "capable spirit," differing from other dead people just as the scribe differed from ordinary mortals during his lifetime. We should also note that all the expedition leaders buried in the necropolis of Qubbet el-Hawa at Aswan possess the title "lector priest," while that of "scribe" does not appear in their inscriptions. Official graffiti, left increasingly frequently in mining areas during Sixth Dynasty expeditions, refer, however, to the constant presence in the teams of a scribe, who was clearly responsible for carrying out administrative duties. We can infer that the farthest-ranging expeditions undertaken by the travelers who were buried at Elephantine (Aswan) required the presence of someone with a special ritual (and magic?) understanding, as well as administrative capabilities (Roccati 1982).

Tradition has preserved the figure of the "lector priest" above all in that of the "magician." This latter term was used to translate the former into Babylonian (*asipu;* see Edel 1976) at the end of the second millennium B.C., during the Ramesside Period. The magician Djedi, who was almost certainly a "lector priest" and who enlivens one of the delightful stories of the Westcar Papyrus, is well known. In the story, Djedi is described as "small" (*nds*), the term used to identify the modest economic and social status of one who is not self-sufficient. Nonetheless, Djedi is exceptionally robust and, at the age of 110, continues to consume 500 loaves, a leg of beef, and a 100 tankards of beer each day. He is summoned from his tranquil village to court by Prince Hardjedef himself, in order to amuse the despotic Cheops, the infamous builder of the Great Pyramid, with his marvels. As he embarks on his journey to the palace, Djedi requests not only another boat for his children but also transport for his books. As with Neferti, mentioned above, an atmosphere of hyperbole surrounds the fabulous Djedi. Nonetheless, the equipment of a colleague who lived at almost the same time as that described in the story has survived. It is contained in a chest discovered in a tomb dating back to the seventeenth century B.C., in the birthplace of the great Ramesses II. The chest contains a series of scrolls called today the Ramesses Papyri. Among them is the scroll bearing, on one side, the Story of Sinuhe and, on the other, that of the Eloquent Peasant. But the chest also contains rituals, hymns, and over a dozen collections of spells partly familiar from other sources. Apart from these texts, other objects in the chest include four magic wands, an amulet of Osiris, a statuette of a monkey, and one of a masked woman holding two snakes, probably used during performances (Gardiner 1955).

The title of "lector priest" was frequently accompanied by another title, *ḥri-tp*, which was transformed from its original meaning of "leader" to such an extent that it was used to describe the figure of the "magician" in the Bible (the Hartummim of the Old Testament; see Gardiner 1938). The tomb of Djau at Abydos (end of the Sixth Dynasty) helps us to distinguish the different levels at which writing was adopted and understood. Djau was a scribe of divine scrolls, the director of the scribes of kingly acts, lector priest, and "leader" (*ḥri-tp*). The first and second titles probably referred, respectively, to the ability to produce hieroglyphic (iconic and sacred) and hieratic (aniconic and utilitarian) writing. The titles "lector priest" and "leader" derived from the first title and allowed Djau to use hieroglyphic texts for ritual purposes. The inscription on the Memphite tomb of Khentika, from the same period, explicitly refers to "this secret (or "reserved") writing of the hieroglyphs specific to the art of the lector priest," "being instructed in all the writings of the house of the divine writings (library of hieroglyphic texts)."

It is clear that when an official like Kaaper, who lived during the Fifth Dynasty (ca. 2400 B.C.), styled himself with a series of titles referring to his position as scribe ("scribe of the administration, scribe of the pasture of pied cattle, scribe of the documents department [archive?], inspector of the scribes of State, scribe of the acts of State, scribe of the royal expeditions [in various countries]"), he was simply indicating his ability to produce hieratic writing, the only form used for accounting during the Memphite age. A fine example of hieratic writing is the important archive of Abusir, dating back to the Fifth Dynasty Pharaoh Asosi (Isesi). This archive reveals the existence of numerous scribes organized into hierarchies (on the model of other, more modest administrative structures) according to the increasingly specialized nature of the duties performed. Not only writing was valued. The ability to calculate was also considered very important. It should not be forgotten that, among these scribes, there were probably people responsible for the economy, recording income, sorting out produce, and redistributing resources. During this period, however, there were also scribes who seem to have been employed as officials and priests, positions that did not require the use of writing. This can be seen from a saying in the Coffin Texts (on the Coffin Texts, see below): "their officials (magistrates) rise for you and their scribes who are on their mats before you tremble for you" (I 14b–c). In the Pyramid Texts, the work of the subordinate scribe is described: "he opens his (administrative) boxes of papyri, he breaks the seal of his decrees, he seals his papyrus scrolls, he sends his untiring messengers" (490–91). This is reflected, in the Coffin Texts, by the spell "to become the secretary of Thoth and to open what his book contains: I open the chest of the Great One, I break the seal [. . .], I open what the boxes of the God contain, I lift out the documents" (992) (Schott 1954).

The titles listed in the papyri of Abusir seem to refer exclusively to the need for documentation and to the use of hieratic administrative writing. This reveals the extent to which writing was adopted at that time in administration, according to a tradition that can be traced back to the dawn of the Pharaonic state (Posener-Kriéger 1976). The same range of administrative duties is revealed by inscriptions found in the tombs of the vast necropolis of Memphis, which housed the remains of the centralized state's accountants (Junker 1929–55).

A distinction, however, was made between, on the one hand, a "scribe of the archive" and, on the other, a "scribe of the archive of the divine scrolls," probably written in hieroglyphs and thus with a different content, and the related figure of the "scribe of the divine scroll," which was written in hieroglyphs. The goddess Seshat was the tutelary deity of the "archive of the divine scrolls." A scene from the temple of Sethos I at Abydos clearly shows the connection between this goddess, in the act of "writing the fate" of the Pharaoh, and the power of hieroglyphs, by attributing the following words to her: "My hand writes his long existence, like that which issues from the mouth of Re (thus identifying the spoken and written word); the pen is eternity, the ink time, the inkwell innumerable jubilees."

People holding these titles, such as Djati, "provost of the secrets (of the secret writing of the archive) of the divine words (hieroglyphs)," or Ti, "provost of the secrets of the secret words of the divine words (hieroglyphs)," or Nefer, Ptahuash, Kaenra, and Ptahhotep, "scribes of the divine scroll," were all "lector priests" as well. They lived during the Fifth Dynasty (ca. 2400–2300 B.C.), preceding the lector priests mentioned above.

The polyvalence of the scribe's role was naturally projected into the characteristics of the tutelary deity. This figure inevitably played an indispensable social role in the divine world. Every aspect of the intellectual sphere was governed by the moon god Thoth: he created languages and writing, above all hieroglyphic ("words of god," *mdw-ntr*) but also hieratic writing (*md't*, "[writing of] papyrus"), as well as everything reflected in language and writing, such as science and magic, not to speak of those positions to which knowledge gave access. In the later period, the figure of the baboon, sacred to Thoth, was used to represent the word "scribe." Thoth is the scribe of the gods and their "lector priest," the author of books (especially on magic). But he is also the divine vizier. The two roles are typically emphasized in an important story from the Ramesside Period describing episodes from the myth of Horus and Seth and in the god's presence in the scene from the Book of the Dead in which the heart is weighed. As a social type, Thoth is contrasted with the god Ptah, the ancient patron of crafts and guilds. Guilds were also an essential force in state organization and were equally distinct from the producing mass of the population. The Theban deity Khonsu, who was also a moon god, probably derived his role as patron of writing from Thoth.

The importance of the scribe during the Memphite age led to the creation of a special iconography in reliefs and statuary: the seated scribe, the only trade to be marked out as noble in this way during the third millennium. The scribe was presented sitting on the ground, knees bent, with an unrolled papyrus on his lap and, on occasion, a pen in his right hand. Along with a hint of plumpness, these details indicated the importance of the role and demonstrated that the scribe was the person who actually wrote in ink on the papyrus. He was not a theoretician of writing, who was more likely to have been the "lector priest," nor did he, normally, carve epigraphic inscriptions in hieroglyphics. There are cases, nonetheless, of scribes who wrote on the tomb for "my father and his beloved wife." And, on one occasion, tomb inscriptions were "made by her husband, the scribe of the royal acts," whose abilities thus included both hieratic and hieroglyphic writing.

Naturally, one of the functions of the scribe was to interpret the sculpted word for the majority of people, who could neither read nor write. At the entrance to certain tombs from the later part of the Old Kingdom we can read: "He is loved by the king, by Osiris presiding over the Westerners and by Osiris the lord of Busiris: each scribe who reads (aloud), each man who listens, each pure priest who observes (i.e., reads silently) (while) saying, 'praise Osiris and glorify Anubis who stays on his mountain, lord of the holy land, Senetites, the vindicated'" (*Catalogue général des antiquités égyptiennes du Musée du Caire* [hereafter abbreviated Cairo CG] 20017).

This proves that writing was no longer an end in itself, nor did it generally express the personal opinion or beliefs of the writer. It had become a product aimed at those who received its message. Toward the end of the third millennium, therefore, the step to the dramatic transformations of the Middle Kingdom was brief. The process of change accelerated during the second millennium. A well-to-do cultured class developed, and education, the use of writing and books, and the training of clerks were all greatly encouraged. It had become the custom for important people to be accompanied on their journey beyond the tomb, as a kind of viaticum, by coffins completely covered with texts (the Coffin Texts), whose reading or recitation might help the deceased, who was enclosed in a genuine magic casket.

Not only religious texts, however, were written and stored with care. A kind of literature that, despite its subtly edifying nature, was intended to be read for pleasure was promoted by the royal palace, leading to the written production of gnomic works and narratives of considerable stylistic accomplishment. The scribe now moved on from being an "inventor of writing" to being an "inventor of texts." In their turn, these texts were rigidly codified. The Prisse Papyrus, containing the complete text of the Instruction of Ptahhotep, and the papyrus in the Hermitage containing the Tale of the Shipwrecked Sailor, perhaps the oldest surviving literary manuscript, both bear a final annotation stating that they are exact copies of what was "found in writing," that is, in another papyrus. They were not, therefore, simply transmitted by memory, as must have been the case earlier.

At this point, texts began to multiply, not only in number but also in variety. Manuals (on medicine, geometry, astronomy, theology, etc.) and illustrated scrolls (maps; games; religious, satirical, and comic illustrations) appeared. By the second millennium B.C. at least, there is no doubt that writing had become essential for scholarly research, both in theology and for those concerned with what would become known as the "exact sciences." Increasingly integrated with oral teaching, it permitted investigative techniques and data gathering that would not otherwise have been possible (Derchain 1988). Apart from the documents already mentioned, the chest discovered near the Ramesseum (the funerary temple of Ramesses II at Thebes) also contained a papyrus known as the Onomasticon of the Ramesseum, the forerunner of a prominent genre from the New Kingdom to more recent times. This primitive dictionary is not organized according to words but according to the things to which the words refer, grouped by different associative criteria. The encyclopedic intention of the work clearly indicates a desire to emphasize possession of the extralinguistic world by revealing its underlying linguistic formulation.

The scribal profession became highly regarded. Scribes were

much in demand by the administration, which was organized into a series of departments that ranked scribes alongside officials. During the Memphite age, the palace's orders had been transmitted orally by diplomats (known as "messengers") with decision-making powers. Later, however, coordination of interests was increasingly entrusted to the written word, if only as a backup to oral communication, and the use of written messages became widespread. Scribes were organized into an even more rigid hierarchy than before, and the skill of the scribe supplemented activities that sometimes conferred special prestige. Officials and priests needed to be able to write, as can be seen from a coffin-shaped block, now at Avignon, whose definition of "scribe" is quite different from that in the passage from the Pyramid Texts quoted above: "O living on the earth! Each scribe, each magistrate, each priest, each sage who knows how to hold a pen (to write), each sage who knows how to read."

The scribe did not belong to the highest social class simply by virtue of his profession; he could not, however, be compared to the artisan. Even though scribes had no autonomous means of support but worked as salaried members of the administration, the rhetoric of the time insisted that, unlike all comparable occupations, that of the scribe was subordinate to none. This, at least, is the argument of a propagandist work known as the Satire of the Trades. In order to convince his son, who is just about to start school, that the scribal profession is better than any other, Khety describes the ridiculous and unpleasant aspects of twenty other trades. Since these are the humblest trades in Egyptian society, the implication is that the position of the scribe was also modest.

Scribal training was, however, a preliminary for more elevated careers. It was also the only kind of education that was strictly scholastic ("capable scribe, skillful with his hands, with clean fingers"), as well as being, at the outset, available only in the capital. In the Satire of the Trades, Khety takes his son from Sile to Memphis. Furthermore, scribal training required a certain maturity. Given the difficulty of the writing system, it was unlikely that training would begin at a very early age (probably not much before the age of ten). The family therefore needed to possess not only cultural inclinations but also sufficient means of support. These needs, combined with the privileges that scribal training brought, tended to restrict it to a single professional circle.

Being a scribe was not simply a profession. Other, more personal and intellectual aspects were often involved. We have seen that some scribes became famous posthumously as authors. We have no evidence that these writers existed or convincing attribution of the works to which they have been linked. References to historical figures, ideally of a certain prestige, were intended to make a story more realistic, and thus believable, or to increase the impact of an example, particularly when the text contained moral maxims. It should be noted, however, that these *authors* are no longer described as "scribes." Their prestige derives either from their noble rank or from the function they performed. It is not until the New Kingdom that we find authors who worked habitually as scribes (such as the authors of the eponymous maxims Ani, Amenemope, and Amennakhte, only the beginning of whose Instruction has survived). Within the largely anonymous society of third- and second-millennium B.C. Egypt, there was a clear tendency to link specific individuals, initially, to the composition of texts and, subsequently (during the Ramesside Period), to their codification and transmission.

Furthermore, there were certainly private collections of books, since the temple and palace libraries, such as the one mentioned above, existed to preserve, rather than to diffuse, knowledge, a state of affairs that continued through the Middle Ages. From the second millennium B.C., we begin to find the figure of the learned and enthusiastic collector of precious works. His existence is borne out by private inscriptions in necropolises, many of which contain not only stylistic flourishes but also deliberate references to the most famous compositions. Summaries of some of these compositions can be seen on the stela (Cairo CG 20538) dedicated at Abydos to Sehetepibre, who died during the reign of Pharaoh Amenemhet III (ca. 1800 B.C.). Although not very large, it has the same shape as a memorial stone, and its four sides are covered with inscriptions. Much of the moral and biographical profile duplicates that on the monument to the vizier Mentuhotep (Cairo CG 20539), also at Abydos and erected during the reign of Sesostris I (ca. 1900 B.C.). Also on the Sehetepibre stela is a text describing the festival of Osiris, a text also found on other stones in the area. But the revealing text is a literary composition copied onto the opposite side of the stone, the identity of which was recognized as the Loyalistic Instruction after Posener's reconstruction of the original (Posener 1976). Although the stela of Sehetepibre bears a shortened text, it is undoubtedly the oldest surviving version of this unusual Twelfth Dynasty political tract, which, during the Ramesside Period, became a classic for apprentice scribes. The originality of Sehetepibre's monument lies precisely in its combining of different works, some of which are known today. Copies of these works were evidently among his possessions, although, like others among his contemporaries, he probably restricted himself to quoting from moral or religious texts, suited to the environment of the tomb. "Scribe" and "lector priest" do not appear among Sehetepibre's many honorific and professional titles. He was an official, commissioner, and treasurer and must have possessed some familiarity with writing. We can clearly recognize him, therefore, as someone who read, and valued, books.

The selection of works used to decorate Sehetepibre's stela stands out as atypical. It should, however, be considered within the context of numerous other anthologies of texts which the wealthy took with them to their graves during the Middle Kingdom. These anthologies are known as the Coffin Texts, since they were used to decorate the interiors of mummy cases. They imitated the ancient religious texts covering the walls of royal Memphite pyramids from the Fifth Dynasty on. However, whereas the Pyramid Texts were still markedly epigraphic, the Coffin Texts displayed the influence of the papyrus prototypes on which they were certainly based. They can be seen as books of prayer—precursors of the Book of the Dead—that the deceased would read as consolation against the perils of the Beyond. Apart from their utilitarian purpose, these texts clearly belonged to a social class accustomed to reading, whose members could personally select texts from the manuscripts possessed by local temple libraries and, possibly, could import them from other sources. Similar spells were quoted in coffins from necropolises far apart in space and centuries apart in time, revealing careful preservation of precious religious literary material.

Some people made use of nonreligious texts as well. Buau, who lived in Thebes during the middle of the Twelfth Dynasty, included in the burial anthology of his coffin (T 9 C) an extract from a tale, The Shepherd Who Saw a Goddess, associated in a contemporary papyrus with strictly literary compositions. The coffin was found in a tomb in the Deir al-Bahri area in Thebes that had been usurped by Mentuhotep, who added his own name only on the outside of the tomb.

From the New Kingdom on, a vast range of hymns, above all to the sun, are included in the decorations of private funerary chapels. Their presence, which can be attributed to the same erudite tastes, adds considerably to the information we have from papyri.

At the end of the fourth century B.C., a Theban priest and scribe named Nesmin, who held numerous positions without ever becoming a member of the upper hierarchy, took with him to the tomb some of his own books instead of the more usual Book of the Dead, as we can see from their colophons. Although the books still reflect a religious and funerary purpose, the texts they contain are remarkable for their rarity. The longest papyrus described as the "secret book of the Treasure, which no one has seen," is known as the Bremner Rhind Papyrus. It is preserved at the British Museum in London and contains separate books such as the Songs of Isis and Nefti, the Ritual for Transporting Sokar, and the Book for Bringing Down Apopi, all of which are copies of texts dating back to at least the New Kingdom. Two other papyri, both palimpsests of Demotic administrative documents, transcribe rituals connected with the "Festival of the Valley" and the "Glorification of Osiris." These have also been referred to in other documents (Heykal 1970). Nesmin may have been the father of another scribe of Amun, Shepmin, the lid of whose splendid coffin can be seen in the Egyptian Museum in Turin. Shepmin's character is well summed up in the funeral elegy written by Haronnofri, one of his colleagues: "provost of the secrets of the words of the god (hieroglyphs), expert in every box (of papyri) of the House of life, [. . .] head teacher of the sons of the priests [. . .], scribe of the sacred books" (Habachi 1971, p. 70).

Although it was very unusual, educated individuals sometimes wanted to take with them beyond death works that did not reflect a funerary mood, sometimes in versions of no intrinsic value. In the intact tomb of an artisan of Deir al-Medina, Sennedjem, and his family (thirteenth century B.C.) a gigantic ostracon was found. Now in the Cairo Museum it contains most of the Story of Sinuhe. Nothing is known about the discovery of most literary manuscripts, but it is likely that they were preserved by being buried in tombs, as was the case of the anonymously owned chest mentioned above, found in the area of the Ramesseum. Written during the Saite Dynasty (the Twenty-Sixth Dynasty), the Vandier Papyrus describes the misadventures of the magician Merira. The text has been preserved because the other side of the papyrus was used to write the Book of the Dead. Toward the end of the Middle Kingdom, Neferhotep, the scribe of the great harem had buried with him an accounting scroll, discovered in his tomb at Dra Abu n-Naga, part of ancient Thebes, in 1860 (Boulaq Papyrus 18). The Prisse Papyrus, one of the best-preserved literary texts, is believed to have come from the same area. It contains the Instruction of Kagemni and the Instruction of Ptahhotep.

Because of the numerous inscriptions in their tombs, the necropolises of ancient Egypt became the most immediately available public archive. This gave rise to the figure of the "discoverer of (precious) texts":

> Beginning of the anthology of cures for illnesses, found in ancient writings in a casket beneath the feet of Anubis at Letopolis during the times of His Majesty King Hesepti (of the First Dynasty), the vindicated [. . .] This scroll was then taken from his feet and sealed by the scribe of the words of god (hieroglyphs) and dean of those able doctors that satisfy god; when the scroll was made, a servant of Aten made an offering of bread, beer, and incense on the flames in honor of Isis the great, Harkhentekhtai, Khonsu, Thoth, and the gods that are in the members. (Luft 1973, pp. 110–11)

Legend has handed down to us the exploits of a learned man who tracked down these literary texts, Prince Khaemwese, the fourth son of Ramesses II and high priest of Ptah at Memphis (thirteenth century B.C.). Khaemwese was responsible for restoring the pyramids and rebuilding the temple of Ptah. There is no doubt that he also produced catalogs of libraries. The discovery of chapter 167 of the Book of the Dead is attributed to him. He became famous to posterity as a "magician," equal to the legendary Djedi of the Westcar Papyrus, although with connotations that seem to prefigure a Faust-like character (Pieper 1931).

Holding the position of priest in an elevated temple hierarchy certainly opened the doors of archives to Khaemwese and to others like him. These archives contained ancient texts, the understanding of which required special training. The results of scholarly investigations sometimes appear in tombs. That of the second prophet of Amun, Puyemre (during the reign of Tuthmosis III, fifteenth century B.C.), is a good example. He was "provost of the secrets of the sacred words (hieroglyphs) in the temple of Amun (at Karnak)" and filled his tomb with designs and erudite quotations from writings of the

Middle Kingdom. People like this were the true representatives of culture in the world of the Pharaohs. It is probably to them, more than to any other group, that we owe our image of that world.

The "House of Life" was the part of the temple, near the "House of Books," that was dedicated to teaching and to the storing and copying of manuscripts. Its priests sometimes recorded the discovery of rare ancient texts. They examined the state of preservation of the texts and wrote "discovered damaged" if the original was beyond repair. The priests also produced forgeries whenever they felt it necessary or adapted the ancient texts to new needs, following the same principle as that adopted by the restorers of buildings. In a sense, the first glimpses of philology can be seen in their activities. During the Ramesside Period, the "chief of works" (palace architect), Ramessenakht, was also "scribe of the sacred writings in the House of Life." This meant that architects also had access to the temple archives, according to whose precepts they must have been obliged to build. In this sense the House of Life at Heliopolis seems to have been regarded as a model architectural school for a considerable period of time. Bubastis, Abydos, and Sais were considered the best centers for the study of medicine (Habachi 1971).

The scribes appointed to such a prestigious institution as the House of Life were therefore also entrusted with delicate areas of investigation. During the Ramesside Period, at least, they were called upon to judge the ritual significance of materials brought back from expeditions, a task that had previously belonged to lector priests:

> His Majesty ordered the scribe of the House of Life, Ramesseashahab, the scribe of the Pharaoh, Hori, and the priest of the temple of Har-Min and Isis at Coptos, Usermaranakht, to investigate works at the Seat of Truth (the Theban necropolis) around the site of the *bekhen*-stone, after having discovered the existence of large and wonderful monuments. (Gardiner 1938, pp. 162–63)

Erudite people who became famous did not come only from the most illustrious families, nor did they belong only to the highest class. This is exemplified by the career of Amenophis (Amenhotep), the son of Hapu. He has left a sketch of his life, which, among other things, allows us to see the stages through which a "manager" passed. Born at Athribis, probably while Tuthmosis III was still on the throne (Tuthmosis died around 1450 B.C.), Amenophis was initially appointed to the low-ranking position of "royal scribe." He was initiated into the sacred book, saw the power of Thoth, and knew his secrets to such an extent that he was able to resolve all difficulties and give advice in all circumstances. At the age of about fifty, during the reign of Amenophis III, he was promoted to the position of "high-ranking royal scribe": more precisely, "royal scribe (as) military scribe." This elevated rank allowed him to act as "overseer of all the works (head architect) of the king." He was employed in the mining of materials at Gebel Ahmar near Heliopolis, in the building of the Pharaoh's funerary temple and a number of other structures in the sacred area of Karnak, in the erection of the king's statue, and, finally, in the creation of a temple dedicated to himself. His prestige was so great that he was venerated as a saint by the Romans, who attributed to him the discovery of the Book of the Secrets of Forms, probably preserved from the Book of the Dead (Louvre 3248; Erman 1877).

A scribe's training thus opened the way to considerable knowledge and gave access to positions of the highest rank. "Knowing how to write" now indicated an educational level rather than a specific professional or social position (like the term "doctor," which could also be equivalent to "scribe"). During the second millennium, anyone could learn to write, as long as he or she did not belong to the mass of the population involved directly in production. In the Story of the Eloquent Peasant, the main character, despite his extraordinary eloquence, is quite incapable of using "paper and pen."

Although at the end of the Old Kingdom knowledge of writing was certainly required at the highest positions, this knowledge was not necessarily equated with the profession of scribe, just as a sage ("someone who knows things") was unlikely to have been literate. As time passed, however, an awareness of caste among those who belonged to the consortium of scribes increased, especially among those who descended from educated and lettered families. The privilege of rank tended to be preserved within the same circles, even more so when it was linked to the transmission of certain skills or bodies of knowledge. Families of scribes, covering several generations, existed. In other cases the role of scribe alternated from one generation to another with that of priest or official. Often the same person occupied more than one position. It was common for a priest to be a scribe of the sacred offerings in the temple as well.

In the New Kingdom scribes were not concerned merely with administrative needs, as had been the case during the Middle Kingdom. Scribes became a genuine intellectual class, no longer necessarily producing culture on behalf of the palace but also producing it for their own privileged "caste." "Being a scribe," at this point, acquired precise social connotations, and it has been observed that the authors of maxims during this period (Ani, Amennakhte, Amenemope) all bear the specific title of "scribe." Amenemope, in fact, in the prologue to his work, confirms that his role was that of administrative scribe. Enene and Pentuere, calligraphers of important literary texts, were Treasury scribes, while Qenherkhopshef, a collector and copier of manuscripts, was scribe to the artisan community of Deir al-Medina. Scribes could keep a statue of their patron god Thoth beside them and dedicate special acts of devotion to him. As a sign of the scribe's status, scholastic compositions criticized the "high-spirited" behavior of youngsters who neglected school and clearly referred to the advantages of an administrative career over the hard life of a soldier, however attractive a military existence might be in other ways. It is impossible to assess statistically the ratio of literate people to the illiterate masses, although scribes were clearly concentrated in palaces, in administrative centers linked to royal residences, and in temples, where the number of people able to write was probably extremely high. Throughout the rest of the country, however, most of the population was completely illiterate. A saying from the Coffin Texts, already five hundred years old, was still valid: "I was scribe for the multitude" (II 176f). The scribe was no longer simply the reader of tomb inscriptions. By this point he had begun to write and read written correspondence, which had replaced oral messages, as well as to prepare reports and draft legal documents.

However, the scribe's new importance did not go unchallenged. It has been shown that, from the middle of the Eighteenth Dynasty (ca. fourteenth century B.C.) the number of scribes working in military administration began to exceed the number in civil service. The skills of the scribe, which had enabled people to reach the supreme rank of vizier, were now providing the army with many of its leaders. Generals such as Tjaneni (who wrote the war diaries describing the expeditions of Tuthmosis III), Thoth, Maia, Amenhotep, Paatenemhab, and Nakht were all originally military scribes. Butehamun, a necropolis scribe known to us from many texts written toward the end of the Twentieth Dynasty (ca. 1100 B.C.) and the final descendant of a family of seven generations of scribes, had also worked in military administration. In the literary text the Satirical Letter,

sent by Hori to a certain Amenemope, the latter is identified as a
military scribe. Hori, in the colorful list of honorific titles that describes Amenemope's ability, simply transposes military expressions
into the peaceful field of letters: "artisan of the words of god (hieroglyphs), without ignorance, *valorous of victory in the art of Seshat*, servant of the lord of Hermopolis (Thoth) in his room of books, master
of clerks in the department of books [. . .] *rapid* in the copying
of manuscripts." This presumes a rivalry between scribes in different administrative fields; more specifically, between the traditional
class of civil servants and the new class, which owed its fortune to
the army.

The Ramesside Period was marked, in fact, by its awareness of
radical social change. The spoken language of the time (Late Egyptian) differed from the ancient codified language of the temple and,
later, the palace, while texts, whose variety and range of genres reflected a wider and more varied public, began to be written in a more
cursive script. In a society undergoing profound transformation, the
cult of ancient books became stronger. These books were preserved,
read, and copied, however, without necessarily being understood.
Numerous remains of anthologies of ancient texts, copied onto papyrus, or potsherds and limestone flakes known as ostraca, have been
preserved at the community of Deir al-Medina, the home of the artisans who decorated the royal tombs. The writing of certain scribes,
such as Qenherkhopshef, is well known, making it possible to recognize autograph documents. Qenherkhopshef lived during the reign
of Ramesses II and died during the reign of Siptah. Other members
of his family, down to the time of Ramesses IX (late twelfth century
B.C.), were also scribes. But he is most significant for having system-
atically collected manuscripts for private use. His library, from which
the Chester Beatty collection of papyri comes, contained as many as
forty volumes, some of them of extraordinary interest, such as the
Tale of Horus and Seth and the Book of Dreams (Pestman 1982). An
anxious letter has also been preserved suggesting that some of these
papyri should be spread out in the sun to dry after a downpour.

Other people took with them into their tombs copies of ancient
works, such as the previously mentioned Sennedjem, a craftsman
who did not possess a copy of the Book of the Dead but chose instead the Story of Sinuhe, copied onto an enormous ostracon. In the
microcosm of Deir al-Medina, as in the country as a whole, it was
already possible to see how things would develop, with literary

scribes specializing in the writing of books and literate clerks responsible for administrative registers, written in an increasingly cursive,
though less elegant, script. This new reality can be seen in the ever-
wider gap between the two kinds of writing. Administrative script
becomes more cursive and more simplified, so full of abbreviations
and specialized signs that it could be deciphered only by trained
people. Literary writing, on the other hand, although still hieratic,
was fairly regular and easily read.

In any case, copies of literary texts were, by this time, signed by
those who produced them, not only indicating that the work had
been copied in its entirety but also, since the copyist was a scholar
of some prestige, guaranteeing its quality. The names of two scribes
working in Memphis during the thirteenth and twelfth centuries
B.C., Enene and Pentuere, are linked to some magnificent manuscripts. Enene, Treasury scribe and subordinate to the Treasury
scribe Kageb, produced five scrolls of scholastic miscellanies that
have survived, as well as a single manuscript, the D'Orbiney Papyrus, containing the Tale of the Two Brothers. Pentuere was responsible for a manuscript copy of the Poem of Kadesh, in honor of
Ramesses II, most commonly found in epigraphic versions. The
holder of the post of Treasury scribe could become rather wealthy.
Minnakht, scribe of the Double Treasury during the reign of Tuthmosis III, was so important that statues in a number of temples were
dedicated to him. He also possessed a tomb at Thebes and a ceno-
taph at Silsila (Silsileh).

Temples also contained workshops (Houses of Life) capable of
producing exceptionally fine manuscripts, such as texts of the Book
of the Dead for splendid burials. These presupposed a sufficient
knowledge of hieroglyphic script, at least until the end of the New
Kingdom. After that, hieratic script was also introduced for sacred
texts, in line with the choice of this rapider writing style for communicative purposes regardless of the nature of the text. During the
Third Intermediate Period, in fact, attempts to use hieroglyphs for
the Book of the Dead reveal clumsy, unpracticed hands. From the
New Kingdom on, it became easier for scribes to obtain manuscripts
for funerary use. Over fifty copies of the Book of the Dead belonging
to scribes from a variety of positions in the hierarchy, from that of
General Nakht, mentioned above, to those of more humble clerks,
have survived.

The word used to describe the work of the scribe is related to the primary meaning of "to paint" (*sš*). In Russian too, the verb "write" (*pisat'*) is etymologically linked to "paint." The term refers to the manual activity, probably on lightweight surfaces to begin with and then extended to cover monumental epigraphy, even though the latter is described more correctly as "engraving with script." The scribe can thus be grouped with other artisans such as painters and designers. In the Middle Kingdom, a handmaiden who made up her mistress was sometimes referred to by the feminine version of the title "scribe." In any case, the figurative character of Egyptian script, at least that used on monuments, required not only the ability to write but also experience in drawing and, often, painting. In this context the social position of the scribe was essentially the same as that of the salaried craftsman.

In the New Kingdom we must suppose that the scribe also acted as a mediator and interpreter. During this period Egypt was extremely open to the civilization of Syrian and Palestine, which was increasingly under the sway of Mesopotamian culture. At Tell el-Amarna, during the reigns of Amenophis III and Amenophis IV (fourteenth century B.C.), some people were conversant with important languages such as Babylonian, Hittite, and Khurrite, and some scribes were able to read the languages written in cuneiform and to understand, more or less competently, diplomatic phraseology. Among these scribes are those known as "scribes of letters" (*sš š 't*; Babylonian *shakhshikha*). Halfway between the large temple and the small temple at Tell el-Amarna, Amenophis IV's capital, was a small building containing an archive of foreign correspondence.

The discovery of a fragment of the Mesopotamian Epic of Gilgamesh reveals that the scribe's apprenticeship involved the study of demanding works of literature, undoubtedly with the guidance of foreign teachers. This was followed by attempts to write in other languages using Egyptian script. However, it would be anachronistic to regard "translating" as part of scribal activity during this period, just as it would be, for the most part, for the first millennium B.C. There was certainly both interest and curiosity in the literature of other languages, but its content was, at the most, transferred into Egyptian literature by means of free adaptations and reelaborations to make it suitable for its new environment. This process was exclusively oral, just as it was in other countries. The more precise activity of literal translation can only be found in an international legal context, as in the drafting of treaties such as that stipulated by Ramesses

II with the Hittite king Muwatalli. Some Egyptian scribes were expert in cuneiform script and able to compare it with their own and to be influenced by it.

In any case, knowledge of the graphic and lexical Egyptian heritage already required considerable erudition. It is significant that skilled scribes attributed to themselves epithets that described them in terms of their ability: "intelligent when he penetrates things (or "writings" or "knowledge")" or "expert in that which is not known," an allusion to the mysterious and occult nature of Egyptian texts. In the later period the ancient title of "provost of secrets" referred specifically to the initiate whose knowledge of myths and rituals allowed him to enter the faith. In the same way, the epithet "scribe of the House of Life" became, like the ancient "lector priest," a way of describing a magician (in Coptic, *sphransh*). In his turn, the "lector priest" became an embalmer, since the primitive meaning of "magician of writing" no longer had any significance.

The recovery, or pseudorecovery, of ancient texts reached its peak when the Nubians conquered Egypt in the middle of the eighth century B.C. and settled there as the Twenty-fifth Dynasty. This dynasty, founded by an extremely different people speaking a different language, adopted not only the script of Egypt but also its language and literary tradition. In an attempt to retrieve past glories, one of the greatest Nubian kings, Taharqa, copied what was left of a worm-eaten papyrus onto a basanite slab. The text, chosen because of the importance it seemed to possess, is known as the Memphite Theology.

The Saite Dynasty (Twenty-sixth Dynasty) witnessed the revival of erudite research. Knowledge of Egypt's remote past was increased by gathering quotations from ancient monuments, by collecting rare works, and by recovering and reproducing ancient models. This required special skills: a knowledge of the ancient language and its script had to be combined with that of the contemporary language and some, although not necessarily all, of its scripts. Demotic script, which spread throughout the country during the Twenty-sixth Dynasty (seventh to sixth centuries B.C.), remained essentially administrative until the Ptolemaic Period, while hieratic (uncial) script continued to be used in the production of manuscripts of religious and literary texts (as it had been since the Ramesside Period). The increasingly obsolete hieroglyphic script was cultivated mainly by priestly circles, where its symbolic properties were studied: "O all you pure priests who penetrate the words of the gods (hieroglyphs) and are expert in writing, intelligent in the House of Life, and who have discovered the ways of the gods, who have penetrated the archives of the House of Books and know how to interpret the difficulties of the 'Ba di Ra' (the sacred books), you who are expert in the work of our forefathers and know what is on the walls, who engrave tombs and interpret their difficulties" is the appeal of Peteharpocrate on a stela now in the Louvre (C 232; see Gardiner 1938).

It was probably during this period that the myth of the ancient sages developed. Figures such as Iyemhotep and Prince Khaemwese, mentioned above, became, respectively, an object of worship and the hero of a number of tales. The profound and well-documented knowledge that some dignitaries possessed can be clearly seen from the range of texts used in the decoration of their tombs. Erudite people's knowledge of the past during the Late Period was aided by the preservation of the hieroglyphic tradition. Although this script was falling into disuse, the study of ancient texts and their language gave it renewed vigor.

The ability to use a variety of scripts—hieroglyphic, hieratic, and demotic (the latter two being used for different types of texts for a considerable period)—was certainly necessary and was explicitly demanded of priests. Abnormal hieratic script (a southern variant of the hieratic used for administrative texts) was used at Thebes until the Twenty-fifth Dynasty and was replaced by demotic (the northern variant) with the arrival of the Saite Dynasty, but there is no evidence that single scribes were competent in both abnormal hieratic and demotic.

When the Macedonian occupation firmly established Greek culture in Egypt, a process of osmosis with indigenous traditions began. Central figures in this process were the *hierogrammatèis*, as scribes of Egyptian documents were then known. The importance given to written documentation in Greece after the fifth century B.C. was also felt in Egypt and led to the diffusion of demotic script for all uses of the Egyptian language. This did not only mean that documents and other works were written in the two main scripts, demotic and Greek. The literary heritage of the two linguistic groups also came into contact. Equally significant was the fact that the indigenous scripts were influenced by more modern forms of writing, such as the Greek alphabet. This alphabet would later become the model for the Coptic writing system. As a result, the duties that had been assigned to the role of scribe since the earliest times continued to remain alive. Even the Library and Museum of Alexandria can be seen as magnified versions of the ancient Houses of Life.

In the southern city of Pathyris a certain Diogenes was paid two and a half *kite* to translate a Greek document into demotic (Kaplony-Heckel 1974, p. 239). Other Greeks, such as Hermapion, devoted their spare time to the study of Egyptian writing. Later, during the reign of Emperor Hadrian, an Egyptian called Ashaikhet made a collection of hieroglyphic, hieratic, and demotic papyri, including the Papyrus of Signs and a geographical papyrus, in his home at Tanis in the Nile Delta (Griffith 1889). Even later, a Coptic monk of Deir al-Medina was buried with a hieratic papyrus bearing the maxims of Ani, a hieratic papyrus containing prayers for the twelve hours of the night, and a demotic papyrus with the Tale of Setne Khaemwese. The manuscripts, in a wooden chest along with Coptic texts from the nearby monastery, provided the monk throughout eternity with arcane evidence of his native land, even though the ancient texts were probably incomprehensible to him.

On a statue in the Museum of Alexandria in Egypt, Hor is described as a "man of faith in the counsels of the god, who fills that which has been found destroyed (in the inscriptions) in the temples, who mummifies their sacred Ba (sacred inscriptions)." The times were ripe for the production of treatises on hieroglyphics, such as the one in Greek which has reached us as the work of the significantly named Horapollo. Understanding Pharaonic writing, no longer an instrument of state, had become the object of individual study and research. In a world made uniform by Greek culture and open to new horizons, the written remains of the ancient Egyptians concealed a body of lost wisdom and thus exercised an exotic and occult attraction. The curse against the scribe and his tools invoked by a Pyramid Text (476) had been carried out: "Scribe! Scribe! Destroy your palette, break your brushes, tear your papyri to shreds."

Bibliography

Albright, W. F. "The Egyptian Correspondence of Abimilki, Prince of Tyre." *Journal of Egyptian Archaeology* 23 (1947): 190–303.

Bresciani, E. "Testi lessicali demotici inediti da Tebtuni presso l'Istituto Papirologico G. Vitelli di Firenze." In *Festschrift E. Lüddeckens (Grammata Demotika)*, pp. 1–10. Würzburg, 1984.

Chassinat, E. "Un interprète égyptien pour les pays cananéens." *Bulletin de l'Institut Français d'Archéologie Orientale* 1 (1901): 98 ff.

Derchain, P. "Encore le monothéisme." *Chronique d'Égypte* 63 (1988): 77–85.

Devauchelle, D. "Remarques sur les méthodes d'enseignement du démotique." In *Festschrift E. Lüddeckens (Grammata Demotika)*, pp. 47–59. Würzburg, 1984.

Edel, E. *Ägyptische Ärzte und ägyptische Medizin am hethitischen Königshof.* Opladen, 1976.

Erman, A. "Amenophis Sohn des Paapis." *Zeitschrift für Ägyptische Sprache* 15 (1877): 147.

Gardiner, A. H. *Chester Beatty Gift.* Hieratic Papyri in the British Museum, 3d ser. London, 1935.

———. "The Mansion of Life and Master of King's Largess." *Journal of Egyptian Archaeology* 24 (1938): 83–91.

———. "The House of Life." *Journal of Egyptian Archaeology* 24 (1938): 157–79.

———. *The Ramesseum Papyri.* Oxford, 1955.

Griffith, F. L. *Two Hieroglyphic Papyri from Tanis.* London, 1889.

Habachi, L. "The 'House of Life' of Bubastis." *Chronique d'Égypte* 46 (1971): 59–71.

Heykal, F. *Two Hieratic Funerary Papyri of Nesmin.* Brussels, 1970.

Helck, W. *Der Einfluss der Militärführer in der 18, ägyptischen Dynastie.* Untersuchungen zur Altertumskunde und Geschichte Ägyptens, 14. Leipzig, 1939. Reprint, Hildesheim, 1964.

———. *Die Beziehungen Ägyptens zu Vorderasien im 3. und 2. Jahrtausend v. Chr.* 2d ed. Wiesbaden, 1971.

Junker, H. *Giza.* 12 vols. Vienna, 1929–55.

Kaplony-Heckel, U. "Schüler und Schulwesen in der ägyptischen Spätzeit." *Studien zur Altägyptischen Kultur* 1 (1974): 227–43.

Kitchen, K. A. *Ramesside Inscriptions, Historical and Biographical.* 8 vols. to date. Oxford, 1968–.

Koenig, Y. "Notes sur la découverte des papyrus Chester Beatty." *Bulletin de l'Institut Français d'Archéologie Orientale* 81 (1981): 41–43.

Luft, U. "Zur Einleitung der Liebesgedichte." *Zeitschrift für Ägyptische Sprache* 99 (1973): 108–16.

Pestman, P. W. "Who Were the Owners in the 'Community of Workmen,' of the Chester Beatty Papyri?" In *Gleanings from Deir el Medina*, ed. R. J. Demarée and J. J. Janssen, pp. 155 ff. Leiden, 1982.

———. "Lo scriba privato Amenothes, figlio di Panas: Tre documenti provenienti dall'archivio di Totoes." *Papyrologica Lugduno-Batava* (Leiden) 23 (1985): 167–97.

Pieper, M. "Zum Setna-Roman." *Zeitschrift für Ägyptische Sprache* 67 (1931): 71–74.

Posener, G. *Littérature et politique dans l'Égypte de la XIIème dynastie*. Paris, 1956.

———. *L'Enseignement loyaliste: Sagesse égyptienne du Moyen Empire*. Geneva, 1976.

Posener-Kriéger, P. *Les archives du temple funéraire de Néferirkarê Kakaï (les papyrus d'Abousir)*. 2 vols. Bibliothèque d'Étude 65. Cairo, 1976.

Roccati, A. *La littérature historique sous l'Ancien Empire égyptien*. Paris, 1982.

Schlott, A. *Schrift und Schreiber im alten Ägypten*. Munich, 1989.

Schott, S. *Die Deutung der Geheimnisse des Rituals für die Abwehr des Bösen*. Wiesbaden, 1954.

Sethe, K. *Die altägyptischen Pyramidentexte*. 4 vols. Leipzig, 1908–22.

Simpson, W. K., ed. *The Literature of Ancient Egypt*. New Haven and London, 1972.

4. BUREAUCRATS

Oleg Berlev

The Story of Joseph

Long before a brilliant Frenchman deciphered the hieroglyphs, the world became aware of Egyptian bureaucrats and Egyptian bureaucracy of the era of the Pharaohs thanks to the last chapters of the biblical Book of Genesis, which contains a marvelous historical tale from the time of the Nineteenth Dynasty. Joseph, the hero of the tale, is a Jewish foreigner descended from shepherds, a milieu especially unpleasant to Egyptians (due to a religious taboo). Nevertheless, because of both exceptional circumstances and his exceptional abilities, Joseph becomes the virtual head of the Egyptian administration, the second man, so to speak, in the Egyptian government. His career was so remarkable that it is a fitting end to a book of Holy Writ that is dedicated to deeds and events of gigantic scope—the creation of the world and of humanity, the universal flood, the formation of peoples and kingdoms, the covenant with God—because the Egypt of this period was not simply another Middle Eastern state but surpassed all others in power, wealth, and territorial extent. But Joseph's career interests us here only in what it can tell us about the Egyptian bureaucracy. That bureaucracy is depicted as a colossal force, capable of withstanding an unrelenting nature and of radically transforming the socioeconomic structure of a people of many millions. Understandably, the author of the biblical tale presents it as the deeds of an extraordinary individual. It is clear to any objective reader, however, that it is not the individual personality alone which is at work in the story of Joseph but also his position—the particu-

lar job and its connections and relations. He is a bureaucrat and is
supported by a whole hierarchy of bureaucrats, and all his deeds are
totally realistic.

Joseph, wielding bureaucratic power, enabled his country to
withstand a catastrophic seven-year famine. But such achievements
were expected from the Egyptian bureaucracy. Who is unfamiliar
with Strabo's famous utterance on the effectiveness of the Egyptian
administration? Pointing out the country's dependence on the height
of the Nile's floodwaters, which were measured each year, and that
a high Nile meant abundant harvests and a low Nile meant famine,
Strabo notes (17.1.3) that when there was a good administration (in
Strabo's story, in the person of the Roman governor of Egypt, Petro-
nius), there was no famine even if the Nile waters were low. The
structure of the bureaucracy with which ancient writers were acquainted was believed by the Egyptians themselves not to have developed naturally but to have been introduced from above, as the
result of reforms attributed to a period much more ancient than the
Nineteenth Dynasty, and because of the Egyptians' ideology, they
did not attribute the reforms to a bureaucrat, no matter how highly
placed, but to a king, Sesostris I of the Twelfth Dynasty.

A good administration! Has any other bureaucratic hierarchy of
the ancient world, and not only the ancient world, deserved such an
appellation? Obviously not. Because only in Egypt did the bureaucracy really preserve the people from famine, really act as a productive force. A simple compilation of data about famine years (Vandier's
[1936] is the most complete) shows that famine years were unknown
in the so-called beneficent periods of Egyptian history, when the
central power was absolute (a good administration). I have identified
the well-known famine of year 25 (the king's name is not indicated)
with the low waters of the Nile during the reign of Sesostris (Berlev
1979), but this is merely the exception that proves the rule.

In periods of poor administration (a weak center) individual administrators themselves were forced to take measures to counteract
the forces of nature, and their writings (autobiographies) are valuable
in that they tell of the whole arsenal of measures which a good administration should have undertaken. The method of laying in supplies, which Joseph chose, is only one. In general, it is interesting to
note that the predominance of private philanthropy (mentioned in
the autobiographies of bureaucrats, who are immortalized in their
tombs) over state philanthropy is an index of the "lack of prosperity"

of a given historical period, a testimony to the fact that the administration was poor. This is comparable to reportage from the front on the superhuman heroism of soldiers when there are no military victories to boast about.

There is no doubt that the biblical reflection of the dialectics of "the good administration" is correct. It was difficult for the people to bear it, in spite of all its beneficial aspects. This is one of the reasons why good administrations were replaced in due course by poor ones and the power at the center weakened.

Indeed, good administration under Joseph brought the Egyptians a major evil: by saving them from death by starvation, it put them in bondage by creating an enslaving structure that turned people into slaves of the king. The sharpened sense of reality of the author of the last chapters of Genesis suggested to him the possibility of using the story of Joseph to explain the structure of Egypt, one so different from what the Jews had at home and observed in neighboring countries. He claims that such a structure arose in catastrophic conditions and that the administration used a natural catastrophe to the Pharaoh's advantage. Meanwhile, it was well known that the structure was definitely created by the Egyptians themselves and, moreover, not as a result of a natural catastrophe. Thus, the author on the whole greatly underestimated the Egyptian administration.

This structure was consistent with the absence of metals circulating as money. All prices in the least sizable were quoted in silver but in reality were paid in kind (in the Bible this is explained by the fact that all silver was given over to the Treasury). Given that the people lacked their own cattle and land (both were also rendered to the Treasury in famine years), there was general equality based on the Egyptians' universal status as slaves of the Pharaoh (a sort of self-sale in years of famine; in the story of Joseph only the priesthood is treated differently).

In addition to the ancient Hebrew, biblical version of the seven-year famine, there was an Egyptian tale, recorded under the Ptolemies. This tale of a seven-year famine is written as a royal decree from Djoser, Pharaoh of the Third Dynasty, to the nomarch of Elephantine, concerning the allocation of 12 Egyptian miles as a gift for Khnum, the god of the sources of the Nile floodwaters. This tale, however, is of little interest for the history of the bureaucracy. In it the seven-year famine is not only not prevented but has already been

survived by the populace. It supplies the reason for Pharaoh's interest in what god presides over the flood time. The Egyptian Joseph,
Iyemhotep, appears in this tale not as a bureaucrat (although he was
one, and was in charge of the construction of the famous Step Pyramid complex of the Pharaoh) but as a priest-ritualist, which is what
he has chiefly remained in the national memory. Moreover, his title
of lector priest links him with our subject inasmuch as such a priest
has access to the sacred books and knows them. In them he finds the
answer to the question concerning the god of the flood time, which
is perfectly confirmed by the Pharaoh's dream: the god appears to
him and promises mercy.

It would hardly be worth lingering over this story here, were it
not that the addressee of the rescript is a nomarch. The fact is that
we encounter the administrative division of the country into so-
called nomes for the first time under Djoser, and it was those very
nomarchs who in the time of Joseph were the chiefs of cities and
large villages (compare the Onomasticon of Amenemope, no. 101;
more on this document below) and who created the supply stocks
in the seven years of abundance, since the supplies were collected,
according to the biblical text, for (or "gathered into") the cities. This
is the most ancient dated mention (the nineteenth year of the reign
of Djoser) of the local administration, although it is a post factum
mention. The titles of the offices held by the nomarchs, however,
are attested on vases from Djoser's pyramid complex, although they
are undated and without the name of the Pharaoh.

A Textbook of the Hierarchy

What was this all-powerful bureaucracy like? To answer this question, let us consult the appropriate "textbook," which is what Maspero called the work he published a century ago on the one copy
then known of the Hood Papyrus. Soon after this edition was published, a much fuller and the most informative of the copies known
at present was found: Golenishchev Papyrus III (so called in accordance with the Egyptological custom of naming a papyrus after the
discoverer or first owner and numbering papyri of the same owner
in the order of their discovery or publication: Golenishchev I is a
mathematical papyrus purchased in 1888; II is the Report of Wenamun; IV is the "literary letter"; II–IV were purchased in 1891; V is
the Hymn to Diadems). Over a half century later the text of the work

was published by Gardiner (1947) based on eight copies (the ninth, in the British Museum, could not have been taken into account by him) and dedicated to V. S. Golenishchev, who had presented the papyrus he had discovered to him for publication. This work is an Egyptian encyclopedia or, more accurately, a glossary or onomasticon. This onomasticon is not the most ancient (fragments of onomasticons from the end of the Middle Kingdom are known), but it is, without doubt, the most complete, although it, too, has not come down to us in its entirety.

The onomasticon, and this is a rare case in Egypt, has an author. He is the scribe of sacred books, Amenemope. Not one of the copies is older than the beginning of the Twenty-first Dynasty. The composition of the work is dated to the end of the Twentieth Dynasty. The part of Amenemope's onomasticon that Maspero designated "the Textbook of the Hierarchy" is fully preserved in the Hood Papyrus and in Golenishchev Papyrus III, and partially in other copies. It is extraordinarily valuable because it is the only document of its kind that we have from the epoch of the Pharaohs. The first part (the upper hierarchy) of the Textbook corresponds so closely to a listing of ranks greeting Ramesses II in his third year inscribed on the Luxor temple (on the southern wall of the front court) that the latter can be assumed to be the prototype of the corresponding part of the Textbook.

The correspondence is so great that it allows us to correct a major error that crept into the interpretation of the first published editions of the onomasticon. In contrast to the general rule of the onomasticon (one term—one article), the titulature of the heir to the throne comprises five simple titles (article nos. 72–76). However, these must be considered as one title. This invalidates the accusation that the compiler of the onomasticon repeated some titles and included obsolete, independent titles, as well as the accusation that he did not place the titles strictly by rank and that bureaucratic titles occurred "above" the rank of heir apparent. In fact, the bureaucratic titles begin his titulature.

The Textbook, which by Gardiner's count covers articles 72–229, presents a whole spectrum of ranks, titles, and names of professions, and so on, ranging from the heir to the throne (preceded by a list of the members of the royal family, without connection to the administration) to farmworker, gardener, farmer, vegetable gardener, and tender of (livestock) stalls. Bureaucratic ranks are given only at the beginning of the Textbook and are followed by military, priests, artisans, and farming ranks.

It is impossible not to conclude that these titles, ranks, and professions, only some of which are bureaucratic, must have been thought to be related in some way. And indeed, after the Textbook of the Hierarchy an entirely new section begins, entitled People, and after it one entitled Man. In the section People are included both the corresponding collective noun (no. 230) and the traditional designations of the Egyptian people and the names of neighboring countries and peoples (nos. 231–94). The section Man (nos. 295–311) lists designations for people according to sex and age and ends with the concepts of "slave" and "female slave," the absolute limit of the human species, the perfect *non plus ultra*.

But if the sections People and Man are divided so naturally in the composition of the onomasticon, how are we to understand what Maspero called the Textbook of the Hierarchy? There can be but one answer: this is the "House of the King," a mysterious institution that the texts are full of, but always in such monotonous and, as a rule, impenetrable contexts that it is difficult to glean from them what the concept means. It designates the palace of the king and his household, more in the sense of final products (income), and at times it even means the government administration itself.

And here is the essential point: this whole section on the House of the King is juxtaposed to the sections People and Man, and consequently, the House of the King is not people. But that is as it should be, since the Pharaoh is definitely not a man but a god. It naturally follows that the members of the House of the King, constituting the material expression of his divine power, must be conceived in their sum as the body of the king-god, similar to the way in which the Egyptians could view their entire pantheon as a unity, as the body of a single god, the sun god.

The hierarchy is interesting also in that the servants of the House of the King differ from those who do not enter into this House. This means that there were such people. Moreover, each constituent part of the House of the King, each article, we could say, can also be considered outside this context. Then it is described in categories from the section Man, which has no direct linkage to the section on the House of the King. In such a case the following conclusion is interesting and even important: the concepts "slave" and "female slave" have no relation to the section on the House of the King, there are not and cannot be "slaves" in the House of the King, the servants in the House of the King are all on a similar social level in that they are all "nonslaves." The concepts "slave" and "female slave" appear in the section Man because they are considered categories characterizing the concept "human." The concept "slave" is not juxtaposed in the onomasticon to "free," no matter how the latter concept might be conceived. Rather, "slave" is contrasted with "nonhuman." "Slave" and "female slave" are included in the section Man as parts of a man's private household. It is interesting that the professions associated with production that are most typical for private households are also included in this section. The building of boats is one such profession, which is understandable in a country where the river and canals were the main routes of communication and where crocodiles and poisonous water snakes proliferated. The possession of a boat, even one made only of papyrus, was essential.

But is this in truth what the House of the King is? Amenemope does not title his subsections, and readers must orient themselves using their knowledge of Egyptian life and context. But what else can the House of the King be if not the only institution that can be juxtaposed to every private house and household? In the House of the King there are bureaucrats, military men (retainers), priests, artisans, and agricultural workers. The presence of priests may surprise us because of the frequent royal prohibitions against plenipotentiaries of the House of the King interfering in temple affairs. Be that as it may, temples definitely were part of the House of the King. The proof of this is the stela of the early Twelfth Dynasty in Turin (no. 1612 of the *Catalogo generale del Museo Egizio di Torino*).

Thus, we have before us a staff list for the House of the King, of which the group of bureaucrats occupies about one-third. The number of bureaucratic titles exceeds the numbers for each of the other four groupings of the House of the King: military men, priests, artisans, and agricultural workers. (These last four groups are mentioned in the inscription in the tomb of the military scribe Tjeneni, who lived during the reign of Tuthmosis IV and is depicted compiling lists of such functionaries.) The purpose of the onomasticon is to present the terminology, the names of positions, not to order the categories in a hierarchy. And the titles of the positions only give a general sense of what the positions entailed. It is important to point out that the highest priestly positions of the three major Egyptian gods—Amun, Re, and Ptah—are given as bureaucratic positions; that is, they were definitely viewed as bureaucratic.

The Principle of Hecateus

Having established that the term "bureaucracy" refers only to those people who work for the House of the King, and having clarified that along with the other positions in the House, they represented, so to speak, the powers of Pharaoh—who was a god, second in importance in the cosmos, "the beautiful god," the son of the Sun (Re), second only to his father, the creator of the world—and, consequently, that in this sense the bureaucracy as a whole was a divine force, we cannot but recall the principle of Hecateus, expounded by Herodotus (2.143). (The details of the story that are irrelevant to the present discussion are omitted here.)

Hecateus of Miletus, one of the first travelers to describe Egypt, boasted to Egyptian priests of his ancient and noble lineage, which he traced back through many generations to a divinity. The priests then showed him pictures of the more than three hundred generations of the high priests of Ptah, which, if one counted four generations per century, made this priestly family unbelievably old. Each high priest was named son of the previous one. But this clan did not trace its lineage back to a deity. The priests thus showed to Hecateus that no human clan could trace its lineage to a god, and least of all the Greek clans, who did not "shine" with any special antiquity.

This is no contradiction of the principle of Amenemope, that is, his principle of the divinity of the House of the King as a whole, inasmuch as each article of the staff list was filled with mere humans sharply juxtaposed in the ideology of Egypt to the Pharaoh—god as his subjects, who in no way whatsoever approached his status. The only strange thing is that the priests, in demonstrating to Hecateus a teaching about the sharp delineation of the divine/royal and human/subject that undoubtedly existed among the Egyptians, neglected to mention a relevant tradition. As it happens, the clan of the high priests of Ptah did trace its lineage to the god Ptah himself. This is demonstrated by the pedigree of these priests preserved on a fragment of a chapel in the Berlin Museum that, as has become clear, lists not only priests but also viziers and other highly placed functionaries. The vizier Rahotep served under Ramesses II. According

to the testimony of a descendant living during the Twenty-seventh
Dynasty, this vizier declared (made a "declaration"; literally, "a
voice"; something like a juridical affidavit) that he was descended
from Iyemhotep, a contemporary of Pharaoh Djoser. When Hecateus
and Herodotus traveled to Egypt, Iyemhotep was considered the son
of the god Ptah. True, tradition also indicated the names of his human parents: his mother, Herduanka (I omit the variant spellings),
and his father, Neferkhnum, who appeared on the monument shown
to both Greek travelers. Nevertheless, the priests could not have
failed to know that Iyemhotep was believed to be the son of Ptah.
And still they considered him a man, since they mentioned no exceptions.

Bureaucrat-Gods

Strictly speaking, the priests were correct, although this would have
been difficult to explain to foreigners. Iyemhotep was a god of a particular kind, the kind that Egyptian bureaucrats of high rank became
after their deaths. In ancient Egypt, especially in the time of the
most ancient dynasties, most of the tombs were built for bureaucrats.
Only someone buried in a tomb could become a miracle-worker, inasmuch as depictions of the deceased, detailed inventories of his
titles, and even biographical data were necessary. According to the
Egyptian understanding, because the tomb owner was depicted on
the tomb walls, he could see his own tomb (specifically, the cult
place, on the walls of which were pictures and texts) and read the
texts recorded on the walls and thus recall who he was and his rank.
The owner of a tomb becomes "bright" (in Egyptian, *ikh*), that is,
"sighted," "rational," able to enter into contact with people (as a
rule, in writing, in the form customary to the bureaucrat). Because
of his high position in life, which he retains in the otherworld, the
bureaucrat could help people. Certain "bright" ones were especially
effective and were revered as miracle-workers. The Egyptians called
them gods, but gods of a special kind. After all, they divided the
other gods into classes, too. From the common host they separated
off the sun god Re, who was a senior god (literally, "big"), the creator
of the world/Egypt, and the father of "the beautiful god" (the king
of Egypt/the world). The Egyptians counted the miracle-workers
from the tombs among the class of "living gods," that is, active, effective. (Of course, the worshipers of the miracle-worker could omit

the epithet "living" and in no way offend the god thereby.) For example, the residents of Edfu revered Izi, a nomarch of this region (Second Nome of Upper Egypt), who lived during the Fifth or Sixth Dynasty. "God Izi" and "Izi God" are both attested in their inscriptions. But the word "god" here had approximately the same meaning in this context as did the bureaucratic title of miracle-worker. Thus, they called the miracle-worker Hekaib, who lived in the second half of the Sixth Dynasty, simply *orpais*, that is, "nomarch," in this instance meaning "god."

Inasmuch as miracle-workers, without exception, had been bureaucrats in life (which did not prevent them from also holding priestly posts), the question arises: was not this whole idea of miracle-workers connected with the idea of the divinity of the House of the King, to which they were assigned after death eternally or, more exactly, for as long as their tombs remained standing? A second question also arises: was not the very aspiration in the House of the King to immortalize its positions, mainly bureaucratic ones, in tombs (i.e., the tomb cult in its essence) the result of this principle?

Especially popular miracle-workers whose fame survived for centuries, such as Iyemhotep, could be proclaimed the sons of the gods of their ministries. Some bureaucrats called themselves "sons" in this manner, at least when they were not prevented from doing so. Neheri, for instance, a nomarch of the Fifteenth Nome of Upper Egypt who lived during the Tenth Dynasty, and his two sons each called himself not only the son of the local god Thoth but also the son of Thoth's female counterpart in the Ennead (a grouping of nine divinities). And they did this while still naming their biological mothers and fathers. Consequently, the divinity of the position is manifest.

Of course, expressions of this sort could enter into the tradition. Thus, when his daughter became queen regent for the underage king Pepi II, the nomarch of the Sixth Nome of Upper Egypt, Khui, who lived during the early Sixth Dynasty, was exalted by the fact that a specific kinship term was included in his purely bureaucratic titulature and was raised to the rank of vizier. The queen regent was believed to have had conjugal relations with Re after the god had assumed her husband's body. The term "father of the god" appears to be the description of a person who is not that in fact but whose body Re used to engender the king of Egypt. The case of Khui is one of the most ancient usages of a kinship term linking him to a divinity via a daughter's status.

It was also deemed mandatory to give the divine title of *nebet* to the queen regent. The term "mother of the god" was, for one reason or another, not used. Later, it was used twice, in the Twenty-second and Twenty-third Dynasties (the stela of Harpeson), as the title of the mothers of those dynasties. In the Sixth Dynasty, wives usually took the title of their husbands, *orpais* (a ruler, in particular a vizier or nomarch) or *topais* (by the Sixth Dynasty, as a rule, the head of a region or city). Both these titles, however, can begin the titulature of a highly placed bureaucrat (e.g., of the vizier). These titles had feminine correlates (similar to the Russian words *general'sha*, "wife of the general"; *minister'sha*, "wife of the minister"). The following titles are attested: "woman-*orpais*, daughter of Geb" (Geb was *orpais* in the world of the gods); "woman-*topais*, daughter of Merhu" (Merhu was god of herds), corresponding to the nomarch in charge of the nome's herds; and "woman-vizier, daughter of Thoth" (Thoth was a vizier in the world of the gods).

However, in subsequent centuries when the view of the consort of Amun was elaborated definitively, she received Upper Egypt from her god-husband as a kind of dowry for her maintenance (in Egyptian, *sansh/shansh*). The title Nebet (lady, mistress) became standard for the wife of Amun (e.g., on the statue of Amun's wife Ankhnesneferibre, from the Twenty-sixth Dynasty). Here, too, bureaucratic titles are easily correlated with the gods and interpreted in the framework of filial relations with the gods.

As for the status of a living god, that is, the bureaucrat who became a miracle-working saint after death, we may note that a bureaucrat's suicide had no effect on his role as a god. According to Manetho, because of the ascent to power of maimed ones/lepers (*lelobèmenoi* in Manetho and *shelkēt* in Egyptian, the correspondence in the Apophthegmata Patrum Aegyptiorum) at the end of the Eighteenth Dynasty (i.e., Akhenaten and his flunkies, who were depicted by the new Amarna art as if they all suffered from severe physical ailments), the advisor of Amenophis III, who was also named Amenophis (son of Hapu), committed suicide. This advisor's cult survived until Greco-Roman times. Like the cult of Iyemhotep, it spread to all of Egypt. In Thebes a temple was erected for him while he was still alive, a very special grace granted by Pharaoh during a man's life.

Education

The author of the historical tale at the end of Genesis makes only one serious miscalculation, that of Joseph's lack of education. No amount of success in the interpretation of dreams could replace an education. A bureaucrat had to be able to read, write, and perform mathematical operations such as calculating square footages and volumes. He also needed a certain knowledge of engineering. He had to be able to carry out any task and do it well; otherwise, there could be serious, at times extreme, consequences.

The tendency in the didactic literature to glorify bureaucratic careers grew particularly strong in the Nineteenth Dynasty. In effect, education was equated with bureaucracy. It was worthwhile to get an education, for in that way a bureaucratic career was guaranteed. In fact, an education was needed in other spheres also. Suffice it to mention here artisan scribes (who transferred the contours of inscriptions onto stone for sculptors and for those who painted in the hieroglyphs) and priests, especially those who performed rituals, whose profession was connected to that of copyists of sacred books.

In the bureaucratic milieu children (including girls?) could receive primary education at home, although data about such training are practically nonexistent. I can only refer to the Thirteenth Dynasty stela in Vienna (no. 71) on which a "domestic servant–teacher of writing" is immortalized along with a bureaucratic family. One cannot, of course, exclude the possibility of help from relatives within bureaucratic families, but there is no definitive information about that either.

The possibility of education in the "House of the King's Offspring" at court is attested as early as the Fourth Dynasty. Clearly, this was a palace school (naturally, only for boys) where the sons of highly placed officials could study and learn together with the king's sons. In the palace school, for which we have information extending through the Tenth Dynasty, students learned to write, "sang" the writings in chorus, and also learned to swim, a skill very important in a country bisected by a river and crisscrossed by a network of canals.

It is clear that instruction in the palace school provided education to a certain class and a more successful start for individual careers. It could determine a child's fate and affect his life beneficially. It is known that kings visited this House and could certainly take note of the schoolboys. In one case this resulted in marriage to the king's daughter (Fourth Dynasty), which virtually defined the life trajectory of the fortunate man. He was later one of the two high priests of Ptah, the god of crafts, the main god of the capital.

Studying with the king's son and heir could offer many opportunities for his classmates, even save their lives. King Achtoy advised his son not to kill those with whom he had sung the sacred writings. Apparently, a natural spirit of school camaraderie came about that lasted throughout the lives of the alumni.

The palace school taught more than writing, counting, and swimming. It also taught literature, eloquence (oratory), and a lucid and rich image-filled literary style. The Story of the Eloquent Peasant is evidence of this. Its author dates its action to the Ninth Dynasty. King Achtoy Nubkaure shares a passion for a euphuistic literary style with Rensi (let us call the latter his minister), who has the honor of discovering the unusual oratorical gift of the peasant when the peasant comes to him complaining of a theft. He is so eloquent that the minister forces the man to pronounce more and more speeches, until their number reaches nine. In this way, a cycle, a complete literary work, is created.

Where the palace school is concerned, we cannot overlook the example of a very young king, Pepi II, who ascended the throne at the age of six. Two or three years later (the dating system adopted in the Fourth to Eighth Dynasties suffers from a certain ambiguity, the resolution of which requires a chronological aid for the individual reigns such as the chronicles of the Palermo Stone), he was able to write or at least dictate an outstanding letter to the nomarch of the First Nome of Egypt, Herkhuf. It is hardly possible to assume that anyone edited or reworked the text of a king's letter, even of such a youthful king.

It goes without saying that the palace school could not supply the country with enough educated people. There must have been educational opportunities in the provinces also. However, if provincial schools are likely, the following circumstance comes to mind. Throughout the country there was a more or less unified and definitive standard for cursive writing. And it remained in force for millennia until the revolution of year 19 of the reign of Ramesses XI, when the separate development of Upper and Lower Egypt, which lasted half a millennium, began. Toward the end of this period, Upper Egypt was already clearly considered part of the dowry of the Spouse of Amun, the "worshiper of the god" in Thebes, a priestly title, which at that time was conferred upon the daughters of the kings of Libya and Ethiopia and of the Saite kings. The Persian conquest, which put an end to "Amun's dowry," unified the country and the writing system once more. The demotic script, a cursive script developed in the north for business writing, became the sole form of writing and pushed out the southern script, the so-called anomalous hieratic.

According to Manetho, a revolution at the end of the Eighth Dynasty put an end to the ancient monarchy, which dated "from the creation of the world." In essence, this was one megadynasty, although Manetho counted up to eight dynasties from Menes. Transitions from dynasty to dynasty, however, were so painless that one is compelled to conclude that power remained in one family of kings. Still, there is no basis for considering Menes the founder of the royal line. It is possible that its roots lie in the early phases of the Aeneolothic or even the Neolithic.

The revolution, if it did not destroy the ancient bureaucratic class, dealt it a powerful blow to say the least. Those of that class who remained viewed themselves as an elite and the new bureaucratic class "as urine."

This simile is historically significant in the highest degree since it proves that the revolution which overthrew the Eighth Dynasty was the first in Egyptian history, the first post-Neolithic revolution. We could say that for the Egyptians it was the first revolution after Re created the world, and it undermined faith in the perfection of the creation and in the omnipotence of Re. The urine about which the bureaucrats of the Ninth and Tenth Dynasties write is an effluvium from Re. All rational creatures in the world originated as liquid effluvia from the body of the sun god: gods from his sperm, among them the gods of the sky and earth; people from his tears; taste and perception from two drops of blood from a cut. From his urine, apparently, emanated second-rate human beings, and are they really humans after all? Some sort of riffraff!

Overcoming a crisis that lasted centuries, the first kings of the Twelfth Dynasty, the restorers of the old regime, were forced to take measures to reinstate the old bureaucracy. It is precisely at this time that we first hear of a special school for bureaucrats and one that is far from elementary.

This is definitely not a palace school, where the students are mainly princes, but a school for the children of bureaucrats. And its students are not small children learning the basics but adolescents capable of exercising judgment, who can benefit from lengthy instruction that would obviously be above the head of a small child. This school is in the capital. In that epoch it was definitely located in the city of It-towi, an abbreviation of the Pharaoh's name, Amenemhet It-towi, the last part meaning "seizer of the two lands (the two lands = Egypt). It-towi was a fortified residence near present-day Lisht. In the time of the Roman Empire "Lisht" was the Egyptian name for Rome.

It is interesting that from this time nothing is heard about the palace school. However, if the titles "ward of the king" and "scholar of the king" are to be taken literally, then the palace school must have continued to exist along with the bureaucratic one in the capital.

Be that as it may, precisely at the beginning of the Twelfth Dynasty a need was discerned (a need that the Neolithic—or, if you wish, the first monarchy to appear after the creation of the world—had not felt at all) for a bureaucracy. Inasmuch as there can be no bureaucracy without an educational system, the publicists of the period promoted the advantages of education, its attractive aspects, and the career it opens to a young man.

Something along this line had been attempted in the Ninth to Tenth Dynasties (Book of Kemit), but it was a certain Khety who managed to cast it in the perfect form of the detailed teaching of a sort of ideology in a work called the Satire of the Trades. If he is the same Khety mentioned in the famous literary passage in Chester Beatty(?) Papyrus IV, verso, who authored another great didactic work of the period, the Instruction of Amenemhet I, written, as is clear from the papyrus, during the reign of his son King Sesostris, then it is logical to assume that Khety was charged with writing the king's Instruction on the basis of his earlier literary achievements. If this is true, the earlier didactic work, which glorified the bureaucracy and education, must have been written under Amenemhet I. But the very inclusion of the literary passage in the Chester Beatty Papyrus and in such a prestigious monument of the writers and poets of Egypt as the Monument of Daresi (Nineteenth Dynasty) presumes an authority more significant than a mere shadowy role in writing an Instruction in the king's name (according to Posener 1956).

In his Instruction Khety underlines the openness of the capital school even to residents of other cities and to the children of nonbureaucrats. The title of Khety's position, indicated in the Instruction, serves to emphasize this. Unfortunately, we know the Instruction only in copies from the Nineteenth to Twentieth Dynasties, when the title was already difficult to interpret. Originally, it was, obviously, a military title, as appropriate for this writer as Don Quixote's well-known phrase to the effect that the lance never dulls the pen. In the Nineteenth to Twentieth Dynasties the title could indicate that the author was from the far eastern part of Egypt.

My aim here is not to trace the complex system of ancient Egyptian education. It naturally changed over the course of millennia (this subject is treated in greatest detail in Brunner 1953). Let us note, however, that in the Nineteenth Dynasty there was an upsurge of interest in professional bureaucratic didactic literature. Not only was the ancient Instruction of Amenemhet read and recopied anew, but original works were created in that uncommonly motley mixture of genres characteristic of the Nineteenth and Twentieth Dynasties. The reason for this increased interest is clear: the most frequent contrast in this system of didactic contrasts is the opposition of a bureaucratic career to a military one, the latter being understandably attractive at a time of ceaseless victorious campaigns, which, although difficult and dangerous, promised considerable booty.

The revolution of year 19 of Ramesses XI put an end to the professional strain in didactic literature. And not only to that—but this is a subject for a separate study since that revolution so far has not been fully recognized for what it was.

Temple schools are also known from the Nineteenth to Twentieth Dynasties (e.g., the temple of the Ruler of the Sky—or Heaven—at Karnak), and there was a school for the artisan-scribes who painted the inscriptions on the royal tombs. Numerous examples of the work of the alumni of that school are extant.

The Crisis of the Bureaucracy

In this brief chapter, I cannot even outline the history of the bureaucracy, since it would take us too far afield. Yet I must treat the period of crisis in that history. I speak not of the first Egyptian revolution in the Eighth Dynasty, nor of the period of foreign rule during the Second Intermediate Period or of the only revolution from above to occur in Egypt (Perepelkin has termed it a "coup"), which took place during the reign of Akhenaten and shook the foundations of all aspects of Egyptian life. Whatever loss these shocks inflicted on the bureaucracy, it recovered its powers comparatively quickly. At any rate, there was no question in those periods of replacing the bureaucracy with something else.

Quite different was the situation in the revolution of year 19 of Ramesses XI, which led to the creation of a new type of state previously unknown in Egypt. This theocracy, or, more precisely, the state of Amun, is totally comparable to the religious state of the ancient Hebrews. Ramesses XI was not dethroned and was mentioned in dates until his death, even in Upper Egypt, which had long since been out of his control. (We have no dates from the period from Lower Egypt.) Moreover, he was so revered that even a century later people boasted of connections to him. This notwithstanding, the monarchy collapsed politically and ideologically in year 19. At that time the new regime in Upper Egypt had become so manifest a reality that it made sense to break openly with the monarchy and to recognize a new state.

This was symbolized by the creation of a new chronological system, which counted periods from the revolutionary year. The new era was called the Repetition of Births. In Upper Egypt they sometimes collated this system with the years of the reign of Ramesses XI; sometimes they used only one system. In any case, by year 5 of the new era the new regime was firmly established, the country was divided into two parts, and in both, though in unequal degrees, Amun was acknowledged king. The actual plenipotentiary ruler of Upper Egypt considered himself merely the supreme priest of the god-king and even when he resolved to usurp the royal titulature, he wrote this priestly title on his coat of arms.

We simply do not know much about Smendes, the founder of the Twenty-first Dynasty. It is notable that already in year 5 he had a residence in Tanis and that the founding of Tanis as capital was associated by the Jews with the founding of Hebron (Num. 13:22), yet another divine state. The era of the Repetition of Births is by and large the era of Tanis. In this connection we should note that Hebron was founded in year 12 of Ramesses XI. Moreover, Smendes and his wife Taamun were called at that time "the founders of the earth," to whom Amun gave Lower Egypt (Golenishchev Papyrus II, 2.35). It is assumed that Smendes assumed his royal title only after the demise of Ramesses XI, although there are not sufficient grounds to convince us of this. In any case, he did not include his priestly title in his royal one, if indeed he had a priestly title before becoming king. Of his successors, only Psusennes I did this, but not on a regular basis.

In the south there were claimants to the kingly title also. Herihor was guilty of making such a claim, as later was Pinodjem I, who in the end directly appropriated the kingly title. His descendants no longer did this, although his son Menkheperre appropriated the king's coat of arms from time to time—however, sans kingly titles. Since the successors of Smendes all bore the kingly title and the successors of Herihor (except for Pinodjem I) all had a priestly title only, we conclude that the southern kingdom acknowledged the suzerainty of the northern kings, especially because, apparently in connection with the death of Ramesses XI, the system of Repetition of Births was abandoned, and all Egypt resumed counting years according to the reigns of the individual kings, now based in Tanis (Twenty-first Dynasty). But one can consider this another way, that is, that the idea of a theocracy had taken hold in the south more than in the north, where the principle of the pontificate was not accepted. The north retreated to the traditional monarchy, with its accustomed dating system. In the south, with its millennium-old cult center of Amun in Thebes, the idea of Amun's divine state was stronger. Dating according to the reigns of northern kings could be simply an eponymous phenomenon. Be that as it may, the revolution of year 19 led to a situation in which a king who had not been formally overthrown and had retained all his divine-royal titles was officially acknowledged to be, not god, but a mere man, albeit the man with the highest rank in the state.

In the famed Report of Wenamun, who traveled to Byblos, this is stated unambiguously (Golenishchev Papyrus II, 2.53). In general, the Report was undoubtedly proffered as the manifesto of the new ideology. It is emphasized that Wenamun serves god and not man, that the king of Byblos, Zakar-baal (cf. Janssen 1976, no. 72071), is obliged to comply with Wenamun's wishes because the latter is the envoy not of a man but of a god, Amun. More precisely, he accompanies the true ambassador, the god, that is, the statuette of Amun in his hypostasis as "Amun of the Way."

Wenamun was not a bureaucrat, because then he would have been the representative of the powerless human king. Rather, he bore the title of a temple servant, similar to that of the temple gatekeeper at Karnak. This title in itself testifies to the fact that Egypt had experienced a revolution, that the country of yesterday and to-day were totally incompatible. Something unheard of had occurred. The "gatekeeper of the temple" had emerged in a diplomatic role. This has no parallel in Egyptian texts. Before the revolution of year 19 such a thing was simply unthinkable. Zakar-baal says that the earlier kings of Egypt used to send to his predecessors on the throne of Byblos requests for wood, which was dispatched for considerable sums of money. There can be little doubt that bureaucrats accompanied such envoys, as well as military leaders or servitors of the court, but not "gatekeepers of the temple."

Soon after Wenamun's trip, stability was regained in Egypt and the monarchy was restored, in the north in any case. It is therefore possible that in the Twenty-first Dynasty (after the death of Ramesses XI) such a mission was again rendered an impossibility. Still, we see the idea of a theocracy propounded quite consistently in the Report of Wenamun. In a human, nondivine state such as Egypt had been, the king acted through his servitors, the bureaucrats; in a divine state, their place must be taken over by servitors of the god. Wenamun is just such a servitor. He acts on the authority of the personal decree of Amun, given, apparently by an oracle, and of the letter of the supreme priest of the god which confirms this decree.

The state of affairs described in the Report is even more interesting: Wenamun's embassy, which was a divine embassy, made the trip only because a previous embassy sent for the same reason (to acquire wood for Amun's sacred boat), but in the king's name while the monarchy still existed, had failed. As Wenamun sees it, this was because the embassy comprised humans dispatched by a human king, to whom naturally no one was obliged to give any consideration, especially since the king was unable to pay the sum demanded. Wenamun names this king in an abbreviated form, Kamose, without the royal coat of arms. This did not, however, imply disrespect. From the age of Akhenaten and perhaps before, kings were often referred to by shortened names, and these names were usually not accompanied by the coat of arms: Waenra (Akhenaten), Mehi (Haremhab), Mesu (Amenmesse), Sesu (Ramesses II), Heqamaat (Ramesses IV), Kamose (Ramesses XI). In essence, the direct naming (without coat of arms) of the rulers of the northern and southern kingdoms—Smendes and Herihor—in the Report points to their status as sovereign rulers. Such people bore names that required no explanation, be it a title, patronymic, or place of origin or residence.

The envoys of Ramesses XI dispatched to Byblos were seized by Zakar-baal and spent seventeen years in prison, where they died. It was deemed important for Wenamun to be shown their graves. In general, the juxtaposition of Ramesses' human envoys and the divine one shows that the mission of the embassies was the same, although the purpose of the first one is not made explicit in the Report. Wood for the special sacred boat of Amun was the concern, not of just anyone, but of kings. See, for instance, the drawing of this boat in Brooklyn Papyrus no. 47.218.3 from year 4 of Psamtik I. The boat is inscribed with the name of the latter's predecessor, the Ethiopian king Taharqa.

The situation seems to have been as follows. While the envoys of the first mission were still living, a second one could not be sent. The second one was dispatched immediately upon news of the demise of the members of the first. The period of seventeen years in which they languished in prison in Byblos allows us to fix the date of their mission to year 7 or even 6 of Ramesses XI. This event must be included among the chain of events in Egypt leading up to the introduction of the era of the Repetition of Births: the suppression of Amenophis, high priest of Amun, the rebellion by Panehesi, the viceroy of Kush, and, finally, the appearance of Herihor and the declaration of the era of "renaissance" in year 19. In the north Smendes set up his capital of Tanis, possibly in year 19, although we have no mention of him until year 24. The dastardly acts Zakar-baal perpetrated on the royal mission testify not only to the weakness of Egypt but to much more. The king could not supply wood for the boat of Amun; consequently, he clearly was not pleasing to Amun, who through the oracles could concern himself with the life and property of literally everyone, including people of the most modest station, deciding all sorts of matters for them, even the most petty.

A king was not able to acquire the wood, but Wenamun, the envoy of Amun, managed to do it. Of course, Wenamun paid for the wood, but he received it only by constantly reminding the king of Byblos that he was a divine envoy, that refusal to comply would offend the god, and that Zakar-baal had taken revenge on the first embassy only because it was from a king who himself was only a man. The last point is the only such acknowledgment in all the writings of ancient Egypt. And it was possible only as the result of a revolution.

Wenamun's embassy was unique, possibly, because after the

death of Ramesses XI, the monarchy was restored, at least in the north, after reincorporating the southern kingdom of Amun. Nevertheless, the theocracy had powerfully undermined the prestige of the bureaucracy and advanced the priesthood to the fore. The priestly class was unquestionably the aristocracy of the last ten Egyptian dynasties. The priestly class emphasized in every possible way the antiquity of individual clan lineages in which priestly rank was transferred from generation to generation. Aspiration toward remunerative priestly positions, which had been characteristic of the bureaucracy in all epochs, was now modified. Hereditary bureaucrats considered themselves first and foremost hereditary priests. As in the abovementioned genealogy of the high priests of Ptah, in whose clan there also numbered highly placed bureaucrats, the representative of each generation begins his titulature with the priestly title "father of the god." Naturally, about each of them one could say "so-and-so, the father of the god," inasmuch as in effect he was a vizier (the head of the Egyptian administration) or the nomarch of Memphis or a holder of some other prominent bureaucratic position. And thus, "the father of the god Ankhsheshonqi," author of a well-known Instruction and, according to the narrative preamble to his maxims, involved in a conspiracy against the Pharaoh, did not necessarily have to be a priest only. It is more likely that he was also a bureaucrat.

Groupings within the Bureaucracy

The narrator of the story of Joseph intentionally emphasizes his humble beginnings so that the reader, having learned what heights Joseph achieved, could appreciate how exceptional Joseph's path had been. Meanwhile, from the Egyptian point of view, there was nothing exceptional here at all. The Egyptians were particularly fond of discovering talent (and Joseph undoubtedly is depicted as talented) in the most unexpected places. Thus, Ptahhotep, author of a well-known didactic work and vizier during the second half of the Fifth Dynasty, says that a witticism is worth more than an emerald and yet one can find it behind a female slave's millstone. The same idea lies behind the "Story of the Eloquent Peasant," which we discussed earlier: an uneducated man who spent most of his time in the desert far from people and moreover hailed from a region where, according to Herodotus, people even consulted an oracle to learn if it was fitting for them to consider themselves Egyptians turns out to be blessed with such a gift of eloquence that the highly cultured king of Egypt (who, before the revolution of year 19 of Ramesses XI, was considered a god, not a man) and his minister take supreme pleasure in his speeches and order them to be recorded and preserved for posterity. The same Egyptian attitude toward talent is also found in the legend of Pharaoh Amasis. His exceptional gifts as a ruler stand out all the more when one considers his lowly origin, his tendency to drunkenness, and even his lack of respect for others' property.

Lowly origin, therefore, was not an impediment to a bureaucratic career, at least in theory. Moreover, we see in practice that in the scribes' school where the children of bureaucrats studied, nonbureaucrats could also place their children and such placement was not at all uncommon.

The king of Egypt was master in his own house and therefore every person in the king's household, from the heir apparent to the overseer of the stables (Onomasticon of Amenemope, nos. 72–76, 229), could be replaced if the king so chose. Nevertheless, in all periods of Egyptian history, except for the most ancient, the most widespread good wish was "May you leave your position to your children," in all imaginable variations. There is certainly no contradiction here. Inheritance was the order of the day, but deviation from it was entirely possible if the holder of a position died without heirs, committed a crime, incurred someone's displeasure, fell out of favor with the king, or the like.

At the same time it is clear that effort was made not to disrupt the normal order. However, it is proved that from the Twelfth Dynasty and possibly earlier, and continuing to the end of the Twentieth Dynasty, there existed in Egypt a system of "reviews" or "determination of loss" that was used to determine the staffing deficiencies and inconsistencies on all levels and at all points of that unique institution called the House of the King. This system also made it possible to arrange for the employment of the younger generation of males, according to specific age categories listed in the section Man in Amenemope's Onomasticon. The section Man is thereby related to the section on the House of the King specifically through the age categories and moreover through the categories characterizing human work capabilities negatively—the blind person and the crippled person (absent in the Onomasticon) are listed in the "reviews" correlated to professional-social categories, of which there are five in all:

military men, priests, artisans, agricultural workers (all of these are listed by the military scribe Tjeneni, Eighteenth Dynasty), and bureaucrats. The "reviews" could be local or could apply to all of Egypt. They could have only the aim of arranging the staff in groups; that is, in essence, they could be just inspections. But they could also be linked to the mobilization of military or labor groups for the royal work projects; that is, they could be mobilization reviews.

Of course, bureaucrats were less straightforwardly included in the system than agricultural workers, the basic population of ancient Egypt, or military men, which meant basically all youth fit for military service who could be easily mobilized without depleting the other four groups too extensively. It was not without reason therefore that the military scribe Tjeneni, describing a pan-Egyptian review, mentions and discusses only four groups, completely ignoring the fifth, the bureaucracy. Nor is it surprising that almost all the evidence about these reviews derives from the war-torn epoch of the Eighteenth and Nineteenth Dynasties and is related to military recruitment. In the information that has come down to us, bureaucrats are mentioned only once in the reviews (the sample letter for students to copy contained in Anastasi Papyrus IV, 4.8–9; other copies of the letter are also extant), and in a strictly local review at that. Mobilizational reviews, which could have some effect on the bureaucracy, concern specific, more or less short-term tasks and are beyond our purview here. In fact, the bureaucrat was exempted from the system of reviews. This is obvious from the very essence of the professional didactic literature: according to Khety's Satire of the Trades, getting an education exempts one from military service, apprenticeship in a trade, and farmwork. The alternative is expressed with utmost clarity: either the fifth group or one of the other four. It is interesting that the professional didactic literature even includes priests in the undesirable four groups on the basis that priests are first and foremost associated with grain production in the country.

The peculiarity of the position of the bureaucracy in the system of reviews was explained, of course, by their career preparation. They share this in some measure with the priesthood and those artisans specializing in the immortalizing work of writing inscriptions and, finally, with the elite bureaucrats. Their small numbers compared with other categories also no doubt contributed to the special treatment.

A review inspection obviously confirmed categorization of positions into separate groups. Appointments and removals, when they were called for, could be done during a review, but in the sources bureaucratic appointments are treated regularly without relation to reviews. The same can be said of the hiring of youth in the bureaucratic group as described in Khety's Satire of the Trades. And bureaucratic careers are described without allusion to the reviews. The inheritance of positions stands outside this system, but in principle it does not conflict with the system and harmonizes with it.

Over millennia the transfer of bureaucratic positions from father to son and from relative to relative remained very stable because it was a way of providing for the bureaucrat in his old age. In Egyptian law this institution was called "the shepherd's crook of old age." Yet this succession was less explicit in some periods and more marked in others. This might be explained by the peculiarity of the epoch in question and the availability to scholarship of sources from it.

The classic case of transfer of a bureaucratic position from father to son, of course, is that of the clan of the supreme priests of Ptah, which made such an impression on Hecateus of Miletus and Herodotus. This clan descended in a direct line from Iyemhotep, under King Djoser, to Psenptah, who died (or was killed) on the day Augustus's troops entered Alexandria, after which a lateral branch of the clan was promoted, seemingly for a very short time.

This clan's monopoly of the supreme priesthood lasted almost as long as the Egyptian monarchy (including the Ptolemies, whom the clan did not outlive and who were Pharaohs with greater rights than the pagan Roman emperors). According to Hecateus and Herodotus the supreme priests of Ptah composed a direct father-to-son line for over three hundred generations. The Pharaohs provide an interesting contrast: they could not boast of such a smooth, stable succession. They spanned more than three hundred generations, but they belonged to different families, possibly related ones in some cases. (Although some families ruled concomitantly with the rulers of the Pharaonic succession, these families did not generate long-lasting dynasties.) The genealogy of the priests of Ptah turns out to be more reliable than the chronology of the Pharaohs. Although our subject is the bureaucracy, let us recall that the Textbook of the Hierarchy includes the high priests of the supreme deities of Egypt in the bureaucratic staff listings of the House of the King.

L. Borchardt's discovery and publication of the famous Berlin genealogy confirmed the correctness of Hecateus's and Herodotus's descriptions. The genealogy depicts the representatives of the clan of high priests of Ptah, each of whom is the son of his predecessor. The titulature of each begins "father of the god," which, as we saw earlier, was also a term of kinship in the sphere of sacred marriage, in which Re fathers the Pharaohs. As mentioned above, in sacred marriage the term designated the spouse of the mother of the future king, whom Re made to conceive through her spouse's (human) body. If this man were a king, he could be called "King So-and-So," and the term "father of the god" was superfluous. But for the father of a king who was not a king himself, this kinship term was the highest rank that a human subject of the king could achieve. Thus, a kinship term was converted into the specific title for the founder of a royal dynasty, the sire of gods. This title made perfectly clear that the father of the god (i.e., the father of a king) was not a god himself but was a man. And that is exactly how the Egyptians translated the title for Hecateus: "a human, son of man," who was "the father of the god" (plus the name of his position) so-and-so, the son of "the father of the god" (plus the name of the position) so-and-so, etc., dozens of times. We learn this from the passage in Herodotus which quotes the corresponding Egyptian word *piromi*, "person," in its Greek form, *peromis*.

Many, but not all, representatives of the clan are portrayed on the monument in Berlin. The genealogy continues only to the epoch of the Twenty-second Dynasty. It is preserved on only one wall of the chapel. The generations are arranged in order from top to bottom and right to left, beginning with the one who erected the monument, tracing the lineage backward in time to ancient ages. The genealogy continued to at least one other, nonextant wall. This makes it impossible to determine how many generations were represented. It is clear, however, that they are far fewer than on the monument Hecateus and Herodotus describe.

Not all representatives of this clan were high priests of Ptah, which disagrees with the evidence of the Greek writers. Among the clan members were viziers, administrators of Memphis, and other prominent bureaucrats and priests. High priest of Ptah and vizier, however, were the most typical positions held in the clan. High positions (especially high priest of Ptah) were held occasionally by members of other clans, but this lineage always recovered them, as if family members attempted at the first opportunity to regain the positions.

It is not impossible, of course, that the purity and continuity of the lineage is "doctored" a bit here and there. Certainly not all the parallel genealogies of the clan and the data on the monuments agree. Despite this, the existence of a bureaucratic clan claiming high positions in Egypt over three millennia is very impressive.

We do not know to which tribe the man who founded the chapel traced his lineage, but the vizier Rahotep depicted there, who lived during the reign of Ramesses II, definitely traced it to Iyemhotep (Third Dynasty). At a later time, Iyemhotep was unarguably considered the son of Ptah, which determined the upper boundary of his genealogy.

This family is, of course, unique, but genealogies also come down to us from other bureaucratic, especially priestly, families. As a rule, they come from the epoch of the last ten dynasties. Inclusion of ten or twenty generations is not at all rare. In more ancient times, however, there are few genealogies, but monuments and documents of the epochs allow us to reconstruct a great deal.

Not all can be discussed in this short essay, but we must mention the remarkable story of the family of nomarchs of the Sixteenth Nome of Upper Egypt. It was written in the name of the nomarch Khnumhotep (mid-Twelfth Dynasty). It is a short tale spanning little more than a century, but marvelously told. It is the only such history of a family from ancient Egypt with which one can partially compare the history of the bureaucratic-priestly family from Dhuty (Twenty-sixth to Twenty-seventh Dynasties) found in a judicial complaint (Rylands Papyrus IX). In the latter family the position of nomarch was handed down not only through the male line but also through the female.

We must also mention the picture gallery of ancestors in the tomb of Ahkhotep, the nomarch of the Fourteenth Nome of Upper Egypt during the reign of Amenemhet II. The tomb contains sixty portraits of men of the rank of *topais* (at this time the title of the nomarch or mayor) and their wives without indication of their kinship relations or their relations to the owner of the tomb. Since it was not the custom at that time to depict in tombs all the relatives of the person buried in the tomb, especially distant relatives, those depicted had to be ancestors, but not necessarily by a direct line.

From the epoch of the Thirteenth to Seventeenth Dynasties, despite the complex circumstances of this period, during which only slightly fewer kings ruled than in all the other twenty-five dynasties combined, monuments allow us to compile the genealogy of a bureaucratic family that included two queens, several viziers, and the line of nomarchs of Elkab (the Third Nome of Upper Egypt). The position of nomarch was so hereditary in this family that they considered it their property and sold it for 60 *debens* of gold (paid, naturally, in goods) to another family member. In the whole history of the Pharaohs, this is the only known case of the sale of a nonpriestly position.

There are frequent indications in autobiographies of bureaucrats that they began their careers very early, when they were infants only knee-high, still nursing, etc. Such declarations must be understood to indicate the hereditary nature of the positions. It is, moreover, important to note that the new bureaucrat did not have to wait for the position to be vacated: he could be appointed as an aide to his father or other relative holding the position. Thus, under Psamtik I, Petesis, who discharged Joseph's position as administrator of the harvest in the country and was the officer in charge of boat transport, asked Pharaoh to appoint his relative of the same name as his helper, but with the same title. This relative would assume the job in fact, sending his superiors reports. The large number of similar cases of two or more persons in the same position forces us to differentiate official holders of positions from those who do the real work. In the Sixth to Eighth Dynasties, the differentiation is made either by adding the epithet "true/genuine" to the name of the position or by indicating that the executor acts only as a deputy.

The epitome of the treatment of bureaucratic positions as property was the concept of "the proprietary position." It is mentioned only once (stela British Museum 101), but in a context that makes clear that it is a common phenomenon throughout Egypt. In an address to the living to utter words of well-wishing to the master of the monument (a frequent request in tomb inscriptions, on desert rocks and stelae, and later on statues) are listed those who are next in line for the position, who should express their good wishes. But the words are addressed first and foremost to priests and bureaucrats. And this is always the case from the Fifth Dynasty on. The version "proprietary position for children" found on the abovementioned stela is the general case.

Research on the term "property" (by Perepelkin) shows that the Egyptians understood it much more diffusely than we do. For example, petty bureaucrats earning extra money in the households of highly placed people or of those in the king's favor were considered the "human property" of their masters.

It goes without saying that all these "rights" to a position were relinquished in an instant if the king required different dispositions. Thus, the family of the high priests of Ptah naturally had to yield when Amenophis III desired their hereditary position for his son Tuthmosis, and when Ramesses II and III desired it for their sons, who were both named Khaemwese. When the king was dissatisfied with a bureaucrat and removed him, he was unlikely to appoint that bureaucrat's son to the post. When Amenemhet III replaced the vizier Akhtoy, whom he found unsuitable, he believed it necessary to give detailed instructions to the new apprentice on how to execute the office. Such a thing would have been unnecessary were the new apprentice Akhtoy's son or relative. The king's censure, even in mild form, was terrifying for a subject, all the more so since the kings often lavished favors. It is interesting that this was the only Instruction for the first eighteen dynasties. Otherwise, it would be difficult to understand why the viziers of the Eighteenth Dynasty reproduced it on their tombs as the most authoritative document guiding them in the discharge of their professional duties. However, we do know of other viziers falling into disfavor before Akhtoy.

It should be noted that during the Third to Sixth Dynasties, when the "first vessel" still existed, that is, the direct descendants of the "first people," sculpted by the god of creative powers, Khnum (rather than being created from the urine of Re, a belief that replaced the earlier one in the Ninth to Tenth Dynasties; see above), who were undoubtedly a nobility and clearly a bureaucratic nobility occupying high positions in the capital and nomes, all official seals were anonymous. In later epochs official seals indicating bureaucratic position disappear almost completely (sometimes seals with a special ornament or with the names of the ruling Pharaoh were used as official seals), although in the late Twelfth Dynasty and especially in the Thirteenth, personal seals appear in the form of scarabs and indicate not only the position but also the name of the holder, as if a personal link with the office was then perceived as more stable. Personal seals appear again in the Twenty-fifth and Twenty-sixth Dynasties, as if an observed peculiarity of the more ancient epoch had been reborn.

We constantly hear about demotions and punishments of bureaucrats in royal decrees and in inscriptions of the bureaucrats themselves. This threat always existed—trials and caning, physical mutilation, as well as execution. Often we encounter the threat of depriving fined bureaucrats of their social standing, such as relegation to the status of farmworker. However, actual execution of this punishment (of a priest, not a bureaucrat) is found only in the well-known Golenishchev Papyrus IV, published first by Korostovtsev and later, perfectly, by Caminos (1977). The events described in the papyrus refer to the end of the Twentieth Dynasty (see Fecht 1962).

Provisioning of the Bureaucrats

We can assume that a bureaucrat working in the House of the King was supposed to be supplied provisions, although we have no actual records of disbursement of provisions. Mentions of more or less regular distributions of grain from the granary, of clothing and utensils from the Treasury, and meat directly from the palace are found in the texts of the Fifth to Sixth Dynasties and other epochs. In the Instruction of Khety (Twelfth Dynasty) it is stated that any bureaucrat can take provisions from any "place" (by which is meant something close to our "ministry"), including from the capital, here in the sense of the House of the King, of course. Food was delivered directly from the palace to the house of a bureaucrat residing in the capital only in cases of special favor and for elderly bureaucrats (Sinuhe, the author of a famous Twelfth Dynasty story; Ineni, nomarch and builder during the Eighteenth Dynasty).

Akhenaten speaks directly about his distributions of food to bureaucrats but does not dwell on how he does it. Along with constant supplies, which are not listed in detail, small, one-time distributions could also be made from the royal *shenu* (the place where food was prepared and stored according to Perepelkin) in the capital and when the court traveled about the country. To receive several loaves of bread and a vessel of beer (the usual proportion was 10 to 1) was a great honor even for a vizier. One-time distributions directly from the king's palace are attested in at least one detailed document, Boulaq Papyrus 18, from the early Thirteenth Dynasty.

On the whole, however, the king gave the bureaucrats something more than one-time distributions of food rations or even than the regular official allowances of provisions. In the Fourth through Eighth Dynasties, large private economies made up of many villages, staffed by numerous servants, and containing thousands of head of cattle are depicted on the tombs of highly placed bureaucrats and of those in the king's favor.

After the revolution in the Eighth Dynasty, such large private landholdings seem to disappear, but in the Eleventh and especially the Twelfth Dynasties, they are apparently reborn, although on a lesser scale than before. A further change is noted: villages are no longer in private hands. However, it is directly stated that the king grants a private farm to a bureaucrat. This, it would seem, was a form of remuneration for the labor of the bureaucrats. In the Loyalistic Instruction (early Twelfth Dynasty) it is declared that loyal and effective service to the king is remunerated by the gift of people, "slaves of the king," whereas the king's disfavor deprives a man, and a bureaucrat especially, of slaves, that is, of economic well-being.

The brother of the master plays no small role in the private farm. It is possible that, owing to the multiple meanings of the word "brother," it is used to indicate one of the master's male relatives in general. The "brother" can run the farm of his relative, be in charge of all accounting, or control this or that branch of the operation. He is called "proprietary brother" (see Perepelkin 1986). It is important to note that this term is known from the stelae from Helwan which date to the Second Dynasty. Therefore, it is quite probable that large private landholdings existed much earlier than the Fourth Dynasty.

In the Twelfth Dynasty the "proprietary holdings" of a major bureaucrat were divided clearly into two parts: his official property and his patrimony. When the Egyptians say that private property is granted by the king, they mean property that is attached to a bureaucratic office. This division is seen long before the Twelfth Dynasty, precisely, in the Fifth, but it may go back to the Second Dynasty. The "patrimony" is a concept comparatively close to our notion of "private" or, at least, "personal" property though the Egyptians included property that came with their bureaucratic position in the concept "private holdings."

It is noteworthy that priestly positions are included in the patrimony. Their holders' rights to them were greater than rights to bureaucratic positions, although the latter were also considered property. The kings had reserves of priestly positions that they could award to bureaucrats for services rendered. The concentration of priestly positions, and in the Fourth through Sixth Dynasties of positions on pyramid-building staffs, into few hands was sometimes pro-

nounced, as shown by the Abusir papyri of the epoch of the Fifth
to Sixth Dynasties (marvelously published by Posener-Kriéger and
Cenival and studied by Posener-Kriéger). All these duties really had
to be performed. Even if we take into account that some priestly
duties had to be performed only three months out of the year, it is
hard to understand how people who held numerous positions coped
with all the duties involved unless we assume that some of the duties
were actually carried out by others, for example, by relatives.

Bureaucrats and Egyptian Culture

The material contribution of this social group to Egyptian culture is
most visibly expressed, of course, in the extraordinary monuments
of ancient Egypt that have survived. Their erection was administered by the bureaucrats. It is hardly possible to attribute the artistic
design of these monuments to bureaucrats, even when a bureaucrat
declares that he personally built that or another one, as occurred with
respect to the Khontamenti temple (Osiris) in Abydos at the time of
its initial construction under Sesostris. The vizier and head of the
Treasury, Mentuhotep, undoubtedly was in charge of the works.
However, a certain Meru claims "authorship." Judging by his title,
Meru was a construction specialist. The architectural part of the
work was certainly the responsibility of Meru. Yet it is also clear that
the organization of the project (laborers, tools, supplies, transport)
was in the domain of the treasurer.

Similarly, in the places where valuable alabaster and graywacke
were mined, it was not the bureaucrats who carved the obelisks and
statues of kings and high-ranking bureaucrats; rather, the supplying
of labor and transport for the monuments was their responsibility.

In literature whole genres owe their appearance to the bureaucrats: the autobiography and the didactic work. The first of these
arose from the enumeration of bureaucrats' numerous titles on their
tombs, through which they wished to assert their nobility in the
world beyond the grave and call the attention of the visitors of the
tombs in this world to themselves as examples for emulation. The didactic genre records the advice of such individuals to the younger
generation based on their personal experience. The same proclaimed
principles from the autobiographies are here transformed into practical action. Sometimes it is even difficult to pinpoint which of these

two genres we have before us, but works of an unquestionably didactic nature, a genre especially appreciated by Egyptians, were written for a thousand years by viziers. Iyemhotep himself was a vizier and apparently the originator of the genre and father of the vizier Kagemni (end of the Third Dynasty) and ancestor of the famous Ptahhotep (Fifth Dynasty) and Mentuhotep (early Twelfth Dynasty). In the same category with these viziers was the king's son Djedefhor (Manetho's Thampthis; this connection has been made from a comparison of the list of kings of the Fourth Dynasty in Wadi Hammamat with Manetho's list; the king's son was apparently placed in the list of kings by mistake), who had the same amount of authority as a vizier. It is true that Iyemhotep is not called a vizier on the monuments built in his lifetime (e.g., inscription on the statue of King Djoser and the graffito from King Tosertasis's pyramid complex), but tradition considers him one. The vases from the Djoser pyramid show that the title existed at that time. Iyemhotep is not called a vizier on the vases; however, a certain Menka, apparently his predecessor, is so called on the vases. Mentuhotep, the last vizier to author a didactic work, wrote the Loyalistic Instruction. Although his name does not appear on any of the known copies of this work, part of a titulature is preserved that matches only his titulature out of all those of the viziers of the Twelfth Dynasty. Subsequent didactic works are sharply lower in stylistic tone, and there are no sons of kings or viziers among their authors. Nevertheless, Ani and Amenemope (the similarity of the latter's Instruction and the Proverbs of Solomon has been noted) were prominent bureaucrats.

We are indebted to bureaucrats for the world's oldest scholarly books: the books on mathematics preserved in Golenishchev Papyrus I and Rhind Papyrus. The scribe Akhmes was the copyist of the Rhind Papyrus (which is dated to the Fifteenth Dynasty). The inventor of the clepsydra (water clock) was a contemporary of Akhmes and was a bureaucrat. His name, Amenemhet, is the most ancient in the history of physics.

Of course, it is impossible to list all the achievements of the ancient Egyptian bureaucrats, but one thing must be mentioned: the measurement of the length of Egypt from north to south in 106 so-called river miles. These figures were already known to Sesostris, in the twentieth century before Christ. Eratosthenes, the first to calculate the circumference of the earth, used the length of Egypt as his basic measure.

Bibliography

Berlev, O. D. Review of H. M. Stewart, *Egyptian Stelae, Reliefs, and Paintings from the Petrie Collection*, pt. 2, *Archaic Period to Second Intermediate Period. BiOr* 38 (1979): 318–19.

Brugsch, H. K. *Die Aegyptologie: Abriss der Entzifferungen und Forschungen auf dem Gebiete der aegyptischen Schrift, Sprache und Altertumskunde.* Leipzig, 1891.

Brunner, H. *Altägyptische Erziehung.* Wiesbaden, 1953.

Caminos, R. A. *A Tale of Woe from a Hieratic Papyrus in the A. S. Pushkin Museum of Fine Arts in Moscow.* Oxford, 1977.

Fecht, G. "Der Moskauer 'literarische Brief' als historisches Dokument." *Zeitschrift für ägyptische Sprache und Altertumskunde* 87 (1962): 12–31.

Gardiner, A. H. *Ancient Egyptian Onomastica.* 3 vol. Oxford, 1947.

Janssen, J. J., comp. *Annual Egyptological Bibliography 1972.* Leiden, 1976.

Perepelkin, J. *Privateigentum in der Vorstellung der Ägypter des Alten Reichs.* Tübingen, 1986.

Posener, G. *Littérature et politique dans l'Égypte de la XIIème dynastie.* Paris, 1956.

Posener-Kriéger, P. *Les archives du temple funéraire de Néferirkarê-Kakaï (les papyrus d'Abousir).* 2 vol. Publications d'Institut Français d'Archéologie Orientale du Caire, Bibliothèque d'Étude, 65/1–2. Cairo, 1976.

Posener-Kriéger, P., and J. L. de Cenival. *Hieratic Papyri in the British Museum.* 5th ser. *The Abusir Papyri.* London, 1968.

Vandier, J. *La famine dans l'Égypte ancienne.* Recherches d'archéologie, de philologie et d'histoire, 7. Cairo, 1936.

Vergote, J. *Joseph en Égypte: Genèse chap. 37–50 à la lumière des études égyptologiques récentes.* Louvain, 1959.

5. PRIESTS

Sergio Pernigotti

When Herodotus went to Egypt in about 450 B.C. to collect documentary material which he would later use in compiling the second and part of the third book of his *Histories*, the country was once again, after the long and glorious interruption of the Twenty-sixth Dynasty, under foreign control. For almost a century it had been a satrapy in that immense group of states composing the Persian Empire. As a result, Egypt had been, and continued to be, involved in the massive clash between the Persian "Great King" and the Greek world, and for the first time in its long history, the country's relations with the eastern Mediterranean, Greek and non-Greek, took precedence over its traditional contacts in Africa and the Near East.

Nevertheless, despite the foreign presence and wider political and cultural horizons, the basic structures of the state, which had been reconstructed and firmly reestablished during the Saite Dynasty, were still essentially intact, as were the lines along which the country's economic and social life, tried and tested over a 2,000-year period, developed. Government was entrusted to a satrap, while the most important decisions were made far from the Nile Valley, at the court of the Great King. Generally, however, after the stormy period encompassing the conquest and brief reign of Cambyses, nothing seemed to interrupt the flow of Egyptian life. The temples were open, the worship of the gods had not been disturbed, and intellectual life proceeded along traditional lines, as we can deduce from many clues despite the lack of explicit documentation. Furthermore, a fine series of freestanding statues reveals that Egyptian sculptors were influenced in only the most marginal ways by the presence of foreigners.

This is what makes Herodotus's observations, at least when they are dealing with his personal knowledge of the country, so invaluable now: the eye of such an attentive, educated foreigner as the historian from Halicarnassus allows us to see (and sometimes to assess) facts and situations that were often merely implied in earlier Egyptian documentation, since they were considered too obvious to be pointed out to people who would very probably know all about them already.

In the pages that the Greek historian devotes to Egypt, religion and the priesthood assume considerable importance. This is certainly also due to the interest of the narrator, but it is primarily a reflection of the significance that these aspects of Egyptian life had in the history of the country, something that the foreign visitor was acute enough to notice. The observations and judgments of Herodotus were followed by those contained in the works that later Greek historians devoted to the same subject. Together they provide us with a picture of Egyptian religious piety and the Egyptian priesthood that is, to some extent, unbalanced and unilateral.

On the other hand, when we consider the reticence of Egyptian texts, the information provided by classical writers becomes more valuable. The powerfully conservative nature of Egyptian society makes it likely that situations and types of behavior documented in the later period, up to the Ptolemaic and Roman ages, might be significantly related to those of much more ancient times.

"They (the Egyptians) are religious to excess, beyond any other nation in the world," affirms Herodotus (2.37). Returning to the subject later, he adds that "the Egyptians are meticulous in their observance of [...] everything [...] which concerns their religion" (2.65). Other classical sources exactly corroborate the Greek historian's judgment. In any case, visitors to the Nile Valley cannot fail to be struck even now by the number and size of the religious structures that have survived, signs of a culture that appears to have been deeply permeated by religious values. If it is the case that religious buildings have survived because they were built of stone, compared to the unbaked brick used for secular architecture, it is also true that what has been preserved is no more than a small fraction of the enormous number of religious buildings erected in ancient Egypt. These were the buildings that Herodotus admired during his visit, when the temples of the Ptolemaic and Roman ages, the largest and best preserved of those now surviving, had not even been built.

A country this rich in religious buildings—each divinity in the infinite Egyptian pantheon had his or her own temple or chapel within a temple dedicated to other gods—inevitably possessed a proportionate number of cult adepts. It is easy to imagine that the large number of priests scattered throughout the country must have played a significant role in Egyptian society, even though the scarcity of explicit documents requires a certain caution, especially when we are dealing with the more remote periods.

The fact that temples represented an important reference point from an economic and cultural viewpoint also meant that priests ended up by playing a significant role in the social and moral life of the country. The profound respect with which Egyptian priests were considered by classical writers, certainly exaggerated in terms of the merits attributed to them, was nonetheless a consequence, and distant reflection, of historical events and of a prestige matured over centuries and rooted in the remote past.

When Herodotus speaks of Egyptian priests he focuses his attention on their customs:

> The priests shave their bodies all over every other day to guard against the presence of lice, or anything else equally unpleasant, while they are about their religious duties; also, the priests wear linen only, and shoes made from the papyrus plant—these materials, for dress and shoes, being the only ones allowed them. They bathe in cold water twice a day and twice every night—and observe innumerable other ceremonies besides. Their life, however, is not by any means all hardship, for they enjoy advantages too: for instance, they are free from all personal expense, having bread made for them out of the sacred grain, and a plentiful daily supply of goose meat and beef, with wine in addition. Fish they are forbidden to touch; and as for beans, they cannot even bear to look at them, because they imagine they are unclean [...] They do not have a single priest for each god, but a number, of which one is chief priest, and when a chief priest dies, his son is appointed to succeed him. (Herodotus, 2.37.2–5; trans. Aubrey de Selincourt)

Many centuries after Herodotus, however, Porphyry concentrated entirely on the religious aspects of the Egyptian priesthood. His portrait is imbued with the greatest spirituality:

But these (philosophic priests), having relinquished every other
employment, and human labours, gave up the whole of their life
to the contemplation and worship of divine natures and to divine
inspiration; through the latter, indeed, procuring for themselves
honor, security and piety; but through contemplation, science; and
through both, a certain occult exercise of manners, worthy of antiquity. For to be always conversant with divine knowledge and inspiration removes those who are so from all avarice, suppresses the
passions, and excites to an intellectual life. But they were studious
of frugality in their diet and apparel, and also of continence and
endurance, and in all things were attentive to justice and equity
[. . .] Their walking was orderly, and their aspect sedate; and they
were so studious of preserving this gravity of countenance, that
they did not even wink, when at any time they were unwilling to
do so; and they seldom laughed, and when they did, their laughter
proceeded no further than to a smile. But they always kept their
hands within their garments [. . .] With respect to wine, some of
them did not at all drink it, but others drank very little of it, on
account of its being injurious to the nerves, oppressive to the head,
an impediment to invention, and an incentive to venereal diseases.
(Porphyry, *De Abst.* 4.6–8; trans. Thomas Taylor)

Porphyry describes the figure of a priest as a miraculous balance
between inner peace, the result of constant contact with the divine
world and of speculation about scientific matters, and outer decorum,
revealed by moderation of gesture, simplicity of lifestyle, honesty,
and discretion in his relationships with other people.

There is no reason to doubt that this picture largely corresponds
to the truth, at least during the period in which it was drawn. The
sources in our possession confirm that, even in the most ancient
times, priests existed in Egypt whose moral prestige came very close
to that described by Porphyry. Other documents, however, reveal
that Egyptian priests often led lives that were far removed from the
harmonious control of passions and constant dialogue with the divine
described above.

In practice, Egyptian priests appear to have been so firmly rooted
in the political and social realities of their land that its virtues and
vices were faithfully reflected in them. This is so true that it is often
difficult to know whether to attribute either virtue or vice to the
priestly state itself or to the person occupying the role. The expres-

sions of great admiration for the Egyptian priesthood that we find in classical authors effectively reflect the later stage of a tradition that had become even more narrowly normative and that concealed a progressive detachment from the more profound motives underlying religious life behind the formality of ritual. Religious practice had stiffened into a series of external gestures. Surrounded by mystery, these gestures were no more than a sign that the millennial tradition had become arid, unable to respond to the arrival of new needs and to a richer, more vital, new form of religious thinking.

Among the chorus of praise and the admiring tones, however, there are discordant voices. A single example is the scornful tone with which Juvenal, in his Fifteenth Satire, refers to Egyptian cults and their adepts:

> All the world, Volusius Bithynicus, knows what monsters are objects of reverence to the superstitious insanity of Egypt. One district adores the crocodile, another stands in awe of the snake-gorging ibis. The long-tailed ape, too, is a sacred being; its golden image glitters in the spot where the mutilated Memnon's wizard chords make music, and where lies in ruin ancient Thebes with all her hundred gates. In one part whole towns worship the cat, in another the fish of the river, in yet another the hound, albeit Diana the huntress has not a single votary. But to profane leek or onion with a crunching tooth, that is an abomination. Devout indeed must be a people that has such deities sprouting in its kitchen-gardens! (Trans. Alexander Leeper)

The tone is in marked contrast to the respectful admiration found in the work of Herodotus. There is no doubt that much of it can be attributed to the Roman world's basic lack of understanding of Egyptian civilization.

It is surprising to see how little space is dedicated to the figure of the priest in Egyptian sources from the Age of the Pharaohs. Not that documents are lacking. They might even be said to be unusually abundant from a certain point of view. Thousands and thousands of inscriptions carved onto statues and stelae, painted or engraved on the walls of tombs and coffins, and preserved in documents of all kinds contain, among the titles of their owners, mention of priestly positions. In some cases there is only one title, which indicates that its possessor was priest to a single god. Often, however, we find long sequences in which it is possible to trace the successive phases of a religious *cursus honorum* in the service of one god or of a number of gods venerated in the same place, if not in the same temple. Some individuals have long series of titles referring to the cults of a number of gods venerated in different places, sometimes linked by a network of religious relationships often of great antiquity.

Titles of religious positions also appear along with titles of civil or even military appointments. It is often impossible to interpret the relationship between one post and another. The titles might be arranged chronologically, in order of importance according to a career in which religious and secular positions followed each other in a precise order, or they might be cited in no particular order at all.

An examination of these sequences taken from different periods in Egyptian history might help to clarify the nature of the problem. Hapuseneb, an important figure who lived during the reign of Queen Hatshepsut (1479–1458 B.C.), held the titles of "noble, prince, chancellor of the king of Lower Egypt, first prophet of Amun," to which a statue preserved in the Louvre adds the post of "vizier." The association of an extremely high religious appointment (first prophet of Amun) and the most important secular position (vizier) would lead one to think that both secular and religious powers were united in the hands of the same man, whose weight in Egyptian political life would therefore have been considerable. It might indicate a direct policy to impose a kind of secular control over the powerful priest of Amun or, alternatively, a "priestly" incursion into civil life. Our ignorance of the relationship between the two posts in Hapuseneb's career makes it impossible to draw a conclusion.

A few hundred years later, in the transitional period between the Twenty-fifth and Twenty-sixth Dynasties, a figure named Montuemhet effectively possessed royal power in Thebes. Some of his many titles are the same as those of Hapuseneb—"noble, prince, chancellor of the king of Lower Egypt, only loved friend"—and have little historical interest. Two other titles, however, are always added to this list—"fourth prophet of Amun and prince of the city (Thebes)"— one of which is religious and the other secular. It is startling to see that a person with the rank of Montuemhet should hold such a modest religious appointment as fourth prophet of Amun. It might be the case that religious posts were so devalued during that period that the "prince of the city" had no interest in bearing an important religious title. Alternatively, he may have held the post of fourth prophet of Amun *before* becoming prince of the city. The former title would then be merely a record of the first stage of his ecclesiastical career, which then provided the basis for his secular career. His ecclesiastical career, however, was not abandoned, possibly for reasons of political expediency. Montuemhet was also, in fact, "superintendent of the prophets of all the gods of Upper Egypt," a post that gave him power over all the priests in southern Egypt.

A remarkable degree of complexity and, indeed, pomposity could be reached when listings of ecclesiastical posts and secular posts were combined with fragments of idealized autobiography. This can be seen in the list of titles held by Padineit, an Egyptian who lived during the Thirtieth Dynasty (380–343 B.C.) and whose tomb has been discovered at Saqqara. In the tomb inscription he describes himself in the following way:

The devoted servant of Ptah-Sokar-Osiris, the great god who re-sides in Shetat, (and of) Osiris, who presides in the West, great lord of Rosetau, noble, prince, only friend, beloved, great in knowledge, he who hides his thought, exempt from lightness, he who listens to the petitions of those who petition him, he who is prudent in his speech above all others, he who shows indulgence neither toward his nobles nor toward his great ones, he who is praised by the gods, he who is stable in the good name of the temples, he who does good things for all, he who guides the obedient with his praise, the provost of dominions, the great one of the five, the provost of the peacemaking of the entire earth, he who judges foreign lands as Egypt, the eyes of the king of Upper Egypt, the ears of the king of Lower Egypt, trusted by Horus in his palace, divine father and beloved of the god, *sem*-priest, prophet of Ptah and servant of Horus *wer-wagety, wab*-priest of the gods [...], prophet of Horus *menekh-ib*, prophet of Bastet consort of Anekh-taui of Hutka-Ptah, prophet of [...] who presides at Scen-su, prophet of (Osiris) *mer-itef* in the temple of Hathor consort of Mefekat, prophet of Osiris *res-wedja* and of Seshat, the great one who presides at the chapel of Pe and of Dep, prophet of the statues of the son of Re, Amasi, of Pe and Dep, great in the month of the first and third rows of Pe and Dep, prophet of Atum who presides at Mer, substitute prophet of Horus of Pe and Dep, of Uadjit and the gods of Pe and of Dep, great governor of Neteret and prophet of Horus of Pe, governor of the city, judge of the gate, and vizier Padineit [...]

Descriptions of this length are anything but uncommon in the Late Period. They demonstrate how certain political careers (such as that of Padineit, who became vizier) are solidly rooted in earlier ecclesiastical careers, out of which they seem to grow. The relationship between the two, however, is still not clear.

As we have seen, the titles held by priests and by officials holding ecclesiastical positions provide us with valuable information for reconstructing the organization of hierarchical structures in priestly and state administration. They also help us to trace the religious topography of certain areas of ancient Egypt. In many ways, however, they are sketchy and disappointing. They offer the skeleton of a structure without the biographical references that would allow us to reconstruct the status of priests in Egyptian society and to assess to what extent the picture preserved by classical writers corresponds to the historical reality of earlier periods.

This does not mean that we lack autobiographies. It is well known that, throughout all periods of Egyptian history, autobiography was a widely practiced literary form. Like all literary genres, it had its rules and conventions and was expressed in a largely formulaic language that reflected the moral concepts and worldview of its historical period, rather than the biographical events and spiritual development of the person whose life was narrated. In the best cases, we have a highly idealized portrait whose set expressions are shared by thousands of other examples of the period; in the worst, banal formulae that do no more than suggest a spiritual tendency to trace out a hierarchy of generally accepted values.

The close links between religious and secular office make it impossible to decide to which these self-glorifying texts refer. In most cases, it is very likely that the distinction we naturally make between the two fields was seen as irrelevant by the Egyptians, at least in the sense that a separation between religious life and the secular state was understood in a different way, up to the final stage of Egyptian civilization.

In this situation, the figure of the priest can be provided with precise historical connotations in two ways: by examining how the functions he performed in religious ceremonies were described and by consulting the few literary and nonliterary documents that explicitly refer to priests who played a historical role. It should also be said that the nature of the sources available makes it difficult to trace the historical development of the Egyptian priesthood because it is usually described as a constant and unchanging reality. The very slight changes to which reference is made are almost all undated. Even if we admit that very little changed from one millennium to the next due to the conservative nature of Egyptian society, an indisputable fact however we might wish to interpret it, there is no doubt that much of our view of Egypt is due to the extreme reticence of the documentation available.

We can find an example in the passage from Herodotus quoted above, in which the hereditary character of priestly appointments in ancient Egypt is explicitly stated: "when a chief priest dies, his son is appointed to succeed him." This was probably true of the period in which Herodotus visited Egypt. Furthermore, religious appointments were certainly considered hereditary throughout the Greco-Roman Period, at least partly justifying the image, undoubtedly false in some ways, of an Egypt divided into classes with no communication between them. The problem is to understand the situation in earlier periods and to establish when the process of social rigidity that eventually led to hereditary office began.

We know for certain that, theoretically, entry into the priesthood could only take place after nomination by the king (or his delegate), and that, nonetheless, the tendency in Egyptian society was to make all appointments, whether religious or not, hereditary. In the autobiographies of priests and officials, the desire that sons inherit their fathers' posts is frequently expressed. There is no doubt, however, that this tendency to make appointments effectively hereditary by keeping them within the family could be overridden by the king, who, in certain cases, chose to name the priest himself (usually choosing someone of rather high rank). This was done for practical reasons, perhaps to reward a faithful official with a good living, or for political purposes, when it became necessary to control the priests in a particularly important temple.

This formally perfect picture is, however, complicated by equally valid evidence which proves that in certain cases heirs could—and did—claim priestly appointments held by their fathers or other forebears that had been illegitimately denied them by people with no hereditary claims at all. This would suggest that at a certain point, hereditary appointments, previously limited by the direct intervention of the king, were replaced by a situation in which the Pharaoh must have been restricted to intervening as a judge in order to reestablish the violated rights of the legitimate heir. The state of our sources, however, allows us neither to establish the truth of this hypothesis nor to formulate a plausible chronology, since much of the indirect evidence on which it is based has no reliable chronological framework, at least for the period before the Greco-Roman era.

In order to understand the role and functions of Egyptian priests in their society, we must consider some general features of Egyptian religion, as well as the position held by the king in that religion and in the constitutional structure of the country.

When Herodotus accurately observed that in Egypt there was not a single priest for every god but that, on the contrary, each god was served by many priests, only one of whom was the leader, he focused on one of the essential features in the organization of the Egyptian priesthood, something that clearly distinguished it from the Greek world.

When an Egyptian priest entered the service of a god he became part of a rigid hierarchy, at the top of which was a "high (chief) priest." Although this title varied according to place and the god being venerated, the high priest was always at the top of the structure. A priest could begin at any stage in the hierarchy: at the lowest level, passing gradually up toward the top; at an intermediate level; or even at the highest level of all.

Whatever the fate of individual priests in this structure—whether they moved from bottom to top or remained in the lower or middle ranks of the hierarchy—the priesthood itself was a complete and entirely autonomous structure. Each temple, large or small, was organized as an independent self-governing church. It was subordinate to no other section of the priesthood, unless this had been specifically established.

The consequence of this is that we cannot speak of an Egyptian *priesthood*, but only of *priesthoods*, each of which was completely independent. It is thus pointless to present the Egyptian religious hierarchy, whether historically, spiritually, or politically, as something distinct from, and in contrast to, secular power. At most, there are individual cases in which a specific group within the priesthood was in clear disagreement—or agreement—with secular power. In other words, ancient Egypt never possessed anything resembling a church in the modern sense. Thus, there was no chance of the conflict between church and state that has played such a constant role in the history of the West, nor of a theocratic state whose religious doctrines could be transformed into political practice, and thus government, by means of state structures.

In Egypt, priests were at the service of a god who was worshiped in one place and in one temple. This is why, in Egyptian sources, priestly titles were always accompanied by details of the god being served; it was rare for someone to be referred to generically as "priest." It is quite true that a priest could serve more than one god, in more than one place, but this merely meant that he belonged to parallel priesthoods at the same time. This is confirmed by the fact that a priest's rank could vary according to the gods in question, even when they were worshiped in the same temple.

This closely reflects both the original features of Egyptian religion and its historical development. Ancient Egyptian gods were not arranged into a consistent hierarchy. Each town of a certain importance had its own gods, unrelated to those of neighboring towns (apart from later examples of syncretism or subordination, which often reflected the political situation). Throughout the country's long history, the gods of ancient Egypt were local deities: each city or village possessed its own god, whose worship often went back to protohistoric or even prehistoric times, paralleling the way in which the worship of other gods had developed in neighboring settlements.

During the various stages of territorial expansion that led to Egyptian unity at the beginning of the historical period (ca. 3000 B.C.), increasingly complex state structures developed. In this period, however, locally worshiped gods did not become subordinate to the gods of those centers that gradually assumed greater importance in the process of national unification. On the contrary, all deities maintained their independence. This created a polycentric system that helps to explain the exaggerated polytheism of Egyptian religion. The system does not, finally, appear to offer a consistent explanation of the universe by referring to a single informing principle. On the contrary, the system is the sum of an extraordinarily high number of parallel religions, barely moderated by the grouping of gods into triadic families composed of father, mother, and child, by the syncretist speculations of the main centers of religious culture, and by the effective prevalence throughout Egypt of dynastic gods.

The plurality of religious centers is reflected in the obvious plurality of priesthoods. It is true that, from the Eighteenth Dynasty on, some "imperial" deities, such as Amun-Re, became pan-Egyptian during certain periods due to a modest shift toward syncretism. This development, however, did not substantially change the situation described above, since it did not produce "national" priesthoods. It merely led to an increase, often enormous, in the importance of local clergy—in the case of Amun-Re, that of Thebes—sometimes accompanied by the worship of the god in other centers. This led to the creation of local cults with autonomous priesthoods, parallel to that in the original center.

In practice, this extreme fragmentation was resolved by the figure of the king. From the earliest periods of Egyptian history, Pharaoh possessed the double title of king of Upper and Lower Egypt. By the dawn of the third millennium B.C., the unification process linking northern and southern Egypt had culminated in a marriage between the two states into which the country had been divided during the Predynastic Period. Even though unification was brought about by the military conquest of the north by the south, the first king of the Dynastic Period—Menes, according to both classical tradition and Egyptian sources—did not incorporate the north into the south but united the two kingdoms in his own person by crowning himself king of both south and north Egypt.

An irrevocable link between the two kingdoms was thus guaranteed. It was then reinforced by transferring the figure of the king from this world into that of the gods. Despite doubts expressed by some authorities regarding the divine nature of the Pharaoh, there is no doubt that, at least in terms of dogma, the king was considered a god. He was invested pro tempore with the task of governing Egypt and destined after death to return to heaven, to be reunited with his brothers and sisters. After becoming one of the undying stars, he would then pursue his destiny as an astral divinity.

Since the king was himself a god, and thus shared their nature, he had a special, though not exclusive, relationship with the divine world. It was up to him to ensure concord between the order that regulated the life of the universe and that part of the created world, Egypt, which he had been entrusted to govern. This concord was known to the Egyptians as *maat*, a word with many meanings that, in this sense, described the balance between the visible world and that of the gods.

A central element in the concord was the benevolence of the overcrowded divine community toward Egypt. It was the task of the king to ensure this benevolence to the country over which he governed by means of cult activities and the presentation of offerings in the temples. Since he belonged simultaneously to both the world of humans and that of the gods, the king was the only figure with the authority to perform the delicate role, both religious and secular, of maintaining relationships with the gods and of guaranteeing that Egypt would receive their protection. He was thus the only priest available to the entire country, the only real holder of the priestly title. Because of this, he was high priest to all the gods, and just as he united the kingdoms of north and south in his person, so he brought the varied multitude of different cults together into one. Each priesthood was crowned by the person of the Pharaoh. It was, in fact, the king who delegated this function to the high priest of each temple, who was effectively no more than a stand-in for the ruler. This explains why the king could not only nominate people but also revoke their nomination, sometimes interrupting a father–son succession.

The fact that the cult was a royal prerogative is shown by the images inscribed or sculpted on temple walls. In these images, the relationship between the world of the gods and that of humans is entrusted almost exclusively to the king and, to a far more limited extent, to other members of the royal family, primarily to the queen. In scenes that are repeated with only minor variations in different cities and temples it is the king who performs cult acts, making a wide variety of offerings to the gods and receiving in exchange the protection and benevolence that would be felt throughout Egypt.

During the Amarna Period (1353–1336 B.C.), the exclusive relationship between the divine and human realms mediated by the king became even more accentuated when all private monuments, such as stelae and scenes in tombs, were forbidden from representing cult acts unless they were performed by the king or by some other member of the royal family. This clearly reaffirmed, on a figurative level, the principle that priestly acts were a royal prerogative.

The Pharaoh's central role in the constant exchange, and reciprocal influence, between the world of the gods and that of humans reaches its peak in the statue of Ramesses II (1279–1213) in the temple of Abu Simbel. The king is shown making offerings to himself as a god, seated as a fourth figure beside the triad to whom the temple is dedicated.

The information at our disposal, therefore, suggests that priesthood was a royal privilege, one of the channels through which the role of the king was expressed, the other being the government of Egypt. These two roles were so closely intertwined that they can be regarded as two sides of the same coin. The fact that the king delegated the right to perform cult acts to priests meant that they were not very different from other state officials, other than in the field in which they operated. They also seem to have fulfilled a secular role, in that they both worked for the state and represented it. In the final analysis, they played a specialized part in state structure. This also explains why kings sometimes entrusted temples with important economic functions. This was not a question of transferring state power to an autonomous and contrasting structure but a simple fact of organization within state structures.

It was only when the priesthood (or, rather, a single priesthood) attempted to supplant royal power and to deprive it of its prerogative that the system was severely tested. This occurred during the reign of Amenophis IV/Akhenaten (1353–1336 B.C.). The situation finally came to a head after a state of conflict was openly declared between the monarchy and the priests of the temple of Amun-Re at Thebes. After a series of vicissitudes, the conflict culminated, at the end of the Twentieth Dynasty (1190–1070), with the accession to the throne of the first prophet of Amun, Herihor. Nonetheless, despite the importance of this conflict, it was only a single episode in the thousands of years during which the role of the king as the only authority with the right to intercede with the gods was never seriously questioned.

The temple was the principal site for priestly functions. The role of the priest as royal delegate, a specialist in his contact with the divine realm, was only valid within the temple itself. Beyond its walls priests do not appear to have been obliged to behave in a particular way or to have been restricted in matters such as housing and clothes. Nor did belonging to the priesthood imply a specific training in theology or a period as a novice involving a process of moral preparation.

Since the Egyptian priesthood was defined by the *service* it offered to the god, its members were excluded from all activities not strictly connected to such service. It was not until the Late Period that priests became famous as practitioners of a refined and, to some extent, mysterious science, with complete control of their passions, evidenced in their external behavior and described with such admiration by classical authors. This idea developed during the final days of Pharaonic Egypt or in the Ptolemaic and Roman Periods and, as far as we can tell from the evidence available, did not reflect the situation in earlier periods, when a priest could be a person of great moral prestige, capable of elevated theological speculation, without this necessarily relating to the fact that he served a god.

The temporary character of at least some priestly appointments, combined with the fact that a single person could accumulate both priestly positions and secular administrative posts, meant that the life of the priest was not distinct from that of ordinary Egyptians. On the contrary, in modern terms, the religious and secular states were open and interchangeable, so that it was possible to pass from one to the other without difficulty. When an Egyptian priest gave up serving a god and reentered secular life, nothing distinguished him from the varied mass of officials also serving at his rank, whether high or low.

Priests were thus identified by their activities within the temple. Furthermore, the actual structure of religious buildings influenced the cult acts carried out inside their walls.

The Egyptian temple, as we know it from the beginning of the second millennium to the Ptolemaic and Roman Periods, was of a standard type, regardless of size. Whether large (in some cases, very large) or small, it always contained the same elements, linked to one another in an almost unvarying scheme. The temple was sited in a vast area surrounded by a wall of unbaked, and often impressively large, bricks. This wall sometimes enclosed less important religious buildings, as well as other structures, also built of unbaked brick, such as service facilities, warehouses, and the homes of the priests, other temple functionaries, guardians, and administrative personnel.

The temple itself was a long building composed of a series of sections in which the roof gradually became lower and the floor higher, until the chapel was reached. The chapel contained the tabernacle holding the image of the god to whom the temple was dedicated. Anyone entering the temple passed through the monumental gate at the same level as the first pylon, moving from the bright sunlight of the open forecourt, through the shadows of the hypostyle hall, and into the increasing darkness of the rooms leading to the sanctuary and of the rooms that sometimes surrounded it.

A structure of this kind is by its nature reserved for its priesthood, to the almost total exclusion of the faithful. The temple was home to the image in which a deity was pleased to reveal himself or herself. It was not intended to welcome anyone other than adepts of the cult. Seen from the outside, surrounded by a massive outer wall and punctuated by enormous stone pylons, the temple appeared to be fortified. Since it housed the deity to whom it was dedicated, along with the deity's family, the temple was intended to offer protection both from potentially hostile forces and from the indiscreet eyes of those who were not adepts in the deity's service. The temple was the house of the deity, not of the faithful, who were normally forbidden to see the god's statue. It was the god who temporarily abandoned his home on occasions such as festivals and periodic processions to show himself to the faithful.

It is clear, therefore, that access to the temple was reserved to a restricted group of specialists: priests and their auxiliaries. Everyone else was rigorously excluded from the sacred area, which could be entered only on certain occasions. The priest himself could not begin to serve the god unless certain conditions had been fulfilled. Access to the sanctuary could only take place when he had complied with a series of prescribed rituals, the first of which was the purification of his body.

Exceptions to this vision of the temple as the house of the deity, in which one passed from sunlight to the darkness announcing the divine presence, were the solar temples. In these temples, the sun was worshiped in its physical form, as a star shining high in the sky. It is clear that worshiping the sun in a temple such as the one just described, in which contact between priests and god could only take place in darkness, would have made no sense. The sun god crossed the sky each day, and everyone, not only the priests of his cult, could see him. He revealed himself daily to humans in the full light of day:

> Thou appearest beautifully on the horizon of heaven,
> Thou living Aten, the beginning of life!
> When thou art risen on the eastern horizon,
> Thou hast filled every land with thy beauty;
> Thou art gracious, great, glistening, and high over every land.
>   (Trans. J. A. Wilson, in Pritchard 1969, p. 370)

Thus sang Pharaoh Amenophis IV/Akhenaten to his god, Aten, who was none other than one of the forms the sun could assume in the eyes of the Egyptians: the sun disk considered in its physical form of a star, shining in the sky at the height of its heavenly path. The structure of the solar temple was completely different from that of temples dedicated to the cults of other gods. It took the form of an open courtyard, in the center of which was an altar, where offerings to the god were placed. The altar sometimes held a solar symbol such as an obelisk.

An extremely fine example of this kind of temple can be seen at Akhet-Aten, Akhenaten's capital and the site of the present-day Tell el-Amarna. Dedicated to Aten, the temple has the simple plan described above, with no obelisk, unlike the Fifth Dynasty solar temples at Abu Gurab, near Saqqara. Images depict the Pharaoh himself performing the ceremonies of the divine cult, a solemn reminder that priesthood is primarily a royal function. However, even Amenophis IV/Akhenaten had to accept that, in temples built outside the capital, his role was delegated to the local high priest.

As we have seen, belonging to the priesthood of a particular god meant becoming part of a hierarchy. We are relatively well informed about the structure of religious hierarchies, at least those of the most important temples. As far as the smaller temples are concerned, there is evidence, primarily from the strings of titles of people who had held posts as priests, that they were organized in a similar way to larger temples. The difference did not lie in the organization but in the number of people involved.

The many people working within a temple were, first of all, divided into two groups: those who formed part of the spiritual hierarchy, that is, the priests themselves, and the temple's administrative and technical staff, who were organized into a parallel hierarchy. Surviving documents suggest that membership in one hierarchy did not preclude membership in the other. In other words, a single person could be both priest and administrative official. Movement between the two career structures seems to have been perfectly normal. The distinction that we tend to make between the religious and the secular world might be artificial, in the sense that both priest and official served the god, the former in religious ritual and the latter by administering the god's wealth, which allowed his temple to operate.

Within the religious hierarchy a clear distinction was made between the higher priesthood, in charge of the cult and of decision making and discipline, and the lower priesthood, who performed purely auxiliary tasks. The two ranks were united, however, by their

need for ritual purification. The qualification of *wab* (*w'b*), "pure,"
was the common denominator between different ranks. It is no accident that the Coptic word *oueb*, which derives from the same root, is
used to describe a Christian priest.

At the summit of the temple's religious hierarchy was the "first
prophet," whose importance was in direct proportion to that of his
god. The first prophet of a god like Amun, Ptah, or Re was a very
high-ranking individual who, in certain periods at least, possessed
not only the prestige deriving from his religious position but also
considerable political power. As we have seen in the case of the
Theban high priest of Amun-Re, the first prophet could rival the
political power represented by the king. The title "first prophet" is
an incorrect translation, from Greek sources, of the Egyptian *ḥm-ntr
tpy*, "first servant of god," which expresses more clearly the idea
of *service*, a role that has been repeatedly emphasized as central
to Egyptian priesthood. Our own term "high priest," while not reflecting the exact sense of the Egyptian expression, comes closer to
describing the reality of the time.

The first prophet of certain deities was described in specific
terms that reflected, not his position in the hierarchy, but the function that he had performed, often in the remote past, in the god's
cult. The extremely powerful high priest of Amun at Thebes had
the modest title of "first prophet of Amun." The high priest of Heliopolis, on the other hand, was called "great in the vision of Re," a
reference to his privilege of having direct sight of the god, while his
equal in both rank and historical and religious importance, the high
priest of Ptah at Memphis, bore the curious title "great among craftsmen." This referred to the fact that crafts were under the protection
of the god-demiurge Ptah. His temple was therefore regarded as a
workshop in which the priests were "craftsmen" and the high priest,
as a consequence, was the master craftsman. In other cases, the high
priest was described by using an epithet of the god he served, which
thus passed from god to priest. For example, the famous Potasimto
of Pharbaithos, an important general during the reign of Psamtik
II (Greek, Psammetichos) (595–589 B.C.), bore the priestly title of
"great warrior, lord of triumph." This title had originally been a
simple epithet of Harmerti, the god of his natal city.

Moving down the hierarchy, we come to the second, third, and
fourth prophets. We do not know exactly how their functions differed from those of the high priest, although it seems very likely that

the second prophet acted as a deputy to the first. There is no doubt that each of these positions was occupied by a single person. They were, in other words, posts filled by individual priests rather than by collegial groups. The second, third, and fourth prophets must have had managerial responsibilities that supplemented those of the high priest. Even the lowest rank, that of the fourth prophet, had a certain importance, since the famous Montuemhet, who, as we have seen, in effect exercised royal power in the Theban nome between the Twenty-fifth and Twenty-sixth Dynasties, bore the title "fourth prophet of Amun and prince of the city." This startling combination, a religious post at only fourth place in the priestly hierarchy alongside an important secular position, suggests that the priesthood of Amun had lost much of its political influence, as we have already seen. However, despite the other possibilities considered above, it also confirms that the fourth prophet must still have possessed some prestige, since a figure of Montuemhet's rank would certainly not have been satisfied with too modest a religious title.

Below the prophets came the ordinary priests, whose Egyptian name hmw-ntr meant "servants of the god." There could be a considerable number, depending on the size and importance of the temple. These priests were organized into groups, now called phylae, from the Greek term $phylāi$. There were four phylae until the Ptolemaic Period, when a fifth was added. Unlike more important ranks in the hierarchy, these were rotating positions, with priests working in monthly shifts, so that each phyle served the god for only three months of the year. When the number of phylae was increased to five, it is likely that the system was reorganized, with each shift probably being reduced.

At the head of this category of priests was an "overseer of the prophets," who clearly had managerial power, although it is not clear how his role combined with that of first prophet. He was assisted by an "inspector of the prophets," whose function is sufficiently clear from the title, and by a "supplementary prophet," obviously a substitute who took over when one of the other priests was unable to carry out his tasks. Each phyle had a leader, or, to use the Greek term, "phylarch."

Immediately below the prophets came a group of priests known as the "fathers of the god," whose tasks are unclear. All we know is that they too belonged to the higher ranks of the Egyptian priesthood, as can be seen from numerous strings of religious titles in which the "fathers of the god" are constantly mentioned after the prophets. The title "provost of the mysteries" also referred to a high-ranking priest but, as in the preceding case, we do not know his exact role in the temple hierarchy. One hypothesis is that he conducted ceremonies celebrated before restricted groups of priests, or even before the king himself when he visited a temple and took part in its rites.

These were followed by a vast range of low-ranking priests. The largest group was made up of *wab*-priests, or "pure priests," distinguished by the simple fact of having been ritually purified. Whenever there were enough of them, they were grouped into four phylae, like the prophets. There is no doubt that these priests were also organized hierarchically. They were responsible for a wide variety of tasks (such as carrying the sacred barque in processions) that were not directly related to the cult but that nonetheless required a basic knowledge of ritual.

In this part of the hierarchy came the "lector priests," who were entrusted with the reading of the sacred texts during religious ceremonies (see chap. 3). Apart from being "lectors," they often bore the title of "magician" (*ḥry-tp* in Egyptian), showing the close link between the two functions. The "lector and magician" played an important role in certain circumstances. In order to appreciate the importance that a "lector priest and magician" could acquire in ancient Egyptian society, we need only remember that the largest tomb in the entire necropolis of Thebes was built for a certain Petamenofis, who held this position at court at the beginning of the Twenty-sixth Dynasty (664–525 B.C.).

The lower ranks could also include priests whose roles are not always easy to define. Those referred to with the Greek term *pastophóroi* carried cult objects. Others were responsible for selecting and sacrificing animals. The *onirocrítai* interpreted dreams.

This varied series ends with the so-called hour-priests, who were probably entrusted with establishing the exact moment at which cult acts should begin by observing the stars, and the *horoskópoi*, who had to identify which days were good-omened and which evil-omened.

The priesthood described so far was composed entirely of men. It is clear, however, that from the very earliest times, there were priestesses in Egypt. Nonetheless, with occasional exceptions, they never possessed power comparable to that of the men, and information regarding them is much more limited. Speaking generally, we might say that the role of women in Egyptian temples was *roughly* comparable to that of specialized personnel: first, because they were restricted to typically feminine roles; and second, because they carried out specialized tasks.

In the context of the former restriction, Egyptian priestesses were typically referred to as "brides of the god." This title indicated that the priestess was united with the male deity of the temple. In the Late Period, the "bride of the god" at Thebes had an importance equal or, sometimes, even superior to that of the "first prophet of Amun," and the title was reserved for daughters of kings. The arrival at Thebes in 656 B.C. of the daughter of Psamtik I, Nitocris, along with her splendid court of Saite officials, to be adopted as successor to the reigning priestess, Shepenupet II, is one of the most memorable moments in Egyptian history during the Twenty-sixth Dynasty. The role of "bride" went far beyond a mystic union with the deity. It involved far more concrete political and economic interests, as we can see from the troops of officials at the service of these princesses.

Apart from the "bride," temples could also include a harem of the god's "concubines." There is a clear parallel here between the structure of the temple and that of the royal palace, where the Pharaoh also had both a bride and a harem. It should be emphasized, however, that nothing resembling holy prostitution existed in Egypt. The god's relationship with his bride and concubines was purely spiritual, since all sexual acts within the temple were strictly forbidden. The fact that no exceptions were made to this rule is confirmed by Herodotus: "There is a similar story told by the Egyptians at Thebes, where a woman (the bride of the god) always passes the night in the temple of the Theban Zeus (Amun) and is forbidden, so they say, [. . .] to have any (sexual) intercourse with men" (1.182).

Specialized functions connected with music seem to have been performed mostly by women. Throughout Egyptian history we find dancers, singers, and musicians, and many women from the highest levels of Egyptian society, wives of priests and important officials, belonged to these categories.

Even though each temple's priests formed a separate world, independent of those in other temples, signs suggest that collaboration between different sections of the priesthood was not unknown, and that a basic "national" structure coordinating their activities must have existed. We know that in certain circumstances the priests of a temple met together in a synod, and larger synods comprising more, if not all, Egyptian priests have also been documented.

Furthermore, the existence of posts such as "superintendent of the prophets of all the gods of Upper Egypt" and "superintendent of the prophets of Upper and Lower Egypt" suggests that Egypt possessed something resembling a ministry of religious affairs, even though its real significance remains unknown.

Egyptian temples were also a focus for important economic activities. At the very least, they had to be supplied with everything they needed in order to operate. For this purpose, they possessed vast amounts of property, the income of which was used to pay for the temple's upkeep, above all the cost of the personnel. It should not be forgotten that priests did not serve the god for free. On the contrary, they received salaries that must have been rather enticing when one considers that priests tried to ensure that their posts were hereditary, not to speak of the interminable legal battles to establish their possession.

More funds were needed to cover the expense of religious ceremonies, such as offerings (of both plants and animals) made to the gods, and of temple maintenance. This included the cleaning and restoration of buildings within the sacred area and the replacement of furnishings and objects necessary for the cult.

All these activities, above all the administration of the temple's possessions, required a host of officials organized into a strict hierarchy, who produced a vast amount of administrative documents and accounts. These officials made up the temple's secular personnel. Although excluded in principle from priestly functions, the delicacy of the work they carried out meant that they played a role of considerable importance within temples, particularly in the wealthiest temples.

The main function of Egyptian priests was to serve the gods. Before being admitted to divine service, however, priests had to fulfill certain conditions of ritual purification, by bathing in the sacred lake of the religious precinct and removing all hair from their bodies. They also had to wear linen garments (wool was strictly forbidden), to protect their feet by wearing sandals, and to respect a series of sexual and dietary taboos, although it is extremely unlikely that generalized taboos existed throughout Egypt. Priests certainly had to abstain from eating the meat of certain animals as well as from certain plants. Juvenal's scornful remarks about priests who not only adored animals but refused to eat leeks or onions for religious reasons come to mind. In practice, dietary taboos were restricted to the animals and plants in which certain gods manifested themselves. The taboos relating to a specific god applied only to the priesthood and followers of that god. Taboos thus had a primarily local character, with no power outside the city or nome in which the god was venerated. It is probable that only the king—the high priest in whom all priesthoods finally converged—was bound by every dietary taboo. Since his purity had to be absolute, it extended to all cults in the country.

The temple was the house of the god, whose presence was made manifest by the statue in the sanctuary. The cult was thus composed of a series of essentially physical acts, intended to care for the statue. The ritual of daily worship involved the same stages in all Egyptian temples. The only differences lay in the richness of the offerings made to the deity, in the number of participants, and, finally, in the degree of pomp that surrounded the ceremony. The first stage of morning worship was to prepare animal and plant offerings, which had to be presented to the god. The priests in service on that day, after performing the ritual ablutions, which were an indispensable part of the ceremony, then formed a procession leading into the temple.

After the offerings had been placed on the altars and purified, the highest-ranking priest opened the doors of the sanctuary at the exact moment in which the sun appeared on the horizon, accompanied by hymns that were intended to propitiate the awakening of the god who lived within the temple. This marked the beginning of the most important and solemn phase. The priest entered the darkness of the sanctuary, barely lit by torches, and opened the door of the shrine containing the statue of the god. The deity then revealed himself to the eyes of his officiant, privileged by his sight of the idol in which the god allowed himself to be seen.

The laying of hands on the statue and the recital of prayers preceded the sacred meal. This was composed of the offerings that had been placed on the altars, the actual possession of which was "turned," as the Egyptians said, to the priests and other temple personnel, who used the food for their daily meals. The god received only that part which evaded the perception of the senses. The rest, composed of a denser physical reality, was for human consumption.

The next phase involved tending to the actual person of the god, that is, his statue, which was treated as though it were a human being. It was washed, made up, and dressed in new clothes, which replaced those it had worn the previous day. It should be noted that each of these acts was surrounded by precise ritual prescriptions, such as the offering of four strips of the finest-quality linen in four different colors: white, blue, green, and red. In certain circumstances the god was adorned with jewels and other symbolic objects connected to his typology. Finally, the priest who had opened the shrine and performed the entire ritual anointed the statue with oil and made an offering of grains of rice and resin. This was the end of the ceremony. All that remained was to close the door of the shrine once more and to reattach the seal, which would be broken the following day. While some final acts, such as the libation of water and burning of incense, were performed, darkness once again enveloped the shrine in which the statue of the god was kept.

Although this was undoubtedly the most important part of the daily ritual, temple priests were busy throughout the day. The next ceremony was at noon, a much simpler rite composed of libations and the burning of incense. A slightly more complicated version of the same procedure was repeated in the evening, although the shrine remained closed until the following morning. When night fell, the temple was closed and remained empty; only the astronomers and adepts at the calculation of time could be seen at work on the roof.

The "work" of Egyptian priests was not concerned merely with daily cult ceremonies. They were also responsible for the god's periodic trips outside the temple, when his statue was placed on a smaller model of the sacred barque and carried around the streets of the village on the priests' shoulders. More rarely, on the occasion of important religious festivals, the image of the god was carried in procession in a real barque that sailed on the Nile. The route taken was sometimes very long and was, in all cases, strictly defined by ritual.

Along with the "festive" aspects of the god's leaving his house, the procession was an important opportunity for contact between the god and his followers, an event in which the priest-god relationship was momentarily extended to those who were normally excluded from the sacred area in which the god lived—extended, but not interrupted. During the procession, the faithful had the chance not only to see their god but also to ask him questions about problems, both large and small. In their role as oracles, priests were inevitably intermediaries. They represented an irreplaceable link between the faithful and the god whom they alone served, the possessors of a privileged, if not exclusive, relationship with their deity.

The tasks of the priest, however, also involved other fields, whose boundaries are often difficult to define with precision. It is clear, for example, that they were responsible for something defined as justice "at the gates of the temples." Although there is no doubt that this was a judicial function, we do not know its exact significance. It is likely that people with minor legal disagreements went to the gate of the temple, where a priest, or priests, rapidly resolved the issue, so that it need not be taken before the normal seats of justice. This aspect of the priest's activity was probably connected in some way to his role as oracle and interpreter of dreams, which, in the final analysis, implied a direct relationship with the god.

Egyptian priests, however, could also perform far more important roles. The fame they enjoyed among foreigners as sages and scholars, repeatedly mentioned in classical sources, stemmed from the fact that they belonged to what the Egyptians called the "House of Life," a cultural, educational, and religious institution annexed to the temples that operated as a scriptorium and institute of higher education, similar in importance and function to modern universities. Priests belonging to the House of Life bore the title of "scribe of the sacred book." They were responsible for preserving and transmitting the cultural heritage entrusted to them in the temple libraries. They copied not only religious material but also scientific texts dealing with astronomy, mathematics, medicine, and magic. Naturally, since ancient texts were copied both by and for these schools, the temple and the House of Life became cultural circles, frequented by intellectual priests who not only produced original works but also, as teachers, transmitted the culture they had inherited to their pupils. This culture inevitably reflected the ideology of the ruling class. It was also, however, a "lay" culture, since not only religious works were studied in the schools. Secular texts, the classics of traditional Egyptian literature, formed the basis of the young students' education.

There was, finally, another group of priests, whose functions were very different from those described above; these were the adepts at funeral ceremonies (see chap. 9). In order to understand their importance we have to consider that in ancient Egypt funeral rites involved considerable expense. As a result, they were a significant source of income for priests and, more or less directly, temples.

Funerals did not involve ordinary priests, the "servants of the god," but specialized colleagues known as the "servants of *ka*" (*ka*, very roughly, means the "soul") of the deceased. They were responsible for the funeral itself, the rite of burial, and the funeral cult. The funeral cult might have been established by providing a small endowment for a priest, whose job it was to ensure that the deceased received the offerings and other ceremonies needed for survival in the otherworld. A considerable amount of wealth changed hands with the building of the tomb, the preparation of the objects buried with the deceased, his or her mummification, and the funeral itself. It is no surprise that priests ensured that a large amount of this wealth came to them.

Although it is relatively easy to enumerate the duties, list the titles, and reconstruct the genealogies of Egyptian priests, it is far more difficult to flesh out the bare skeleton with stories of actual lives that provide a human dimension to the abstract (or bureaucratic) role. Inevitably, the documentation available, which is neither abundant nor evenly distributed in time, offers only exceptions: priests whose lives were particularly reprehensible or, on the other hand, priests whose exemplary careers resemble those of saints in the Christian tradition. What we need, and do not have, is an account of priests immersed in the routine of day-to-day life, describing their relationship with the temple, the faithful, and the inhabitants of the city or village.

Egyptian priests were not expected to spread the faith. Nor did they preach conformity to a moral law according to which their own irreproachable behavior would serve as a model to those worshiping the god in whose temple they served. Deeply immersed in the life of their times, individual Egyptian priests might have constituted a moral example or, on the contrary, a model to be avoided, just as officials in other sectors of the state might have behaved in an exemplary or a dishonest manner.

Thus, when accounts available to us provide slightly more explicit proof of priests involved in all kinds of scandal, there seems to be little hint of disapproval that dishonest acts should have been committed by members of the religious hierarchy. Even though priests were not originally expected to set a moral example, however, it is clear that, by the later part of Egyptian history and the Ptolemaic and Roman Periods, they had begun to acquire this connotation. This might have been due to an increased stress on ethical values among the priesthood and to the fact that the concept of "purity" had extended beyond the cult into everyday behavior.

Even in the Late Period, however, this was not always the case, as has been amply shown in the striking document known to historians as the Petition of Petesis, contained in the Rylands IX Papyrus in Manchester. This important text, written in Demotic and dated at the beginning of the first period of Persian domination (Twenty-seventh Dynasty: 525–404 B.C.), is an official report made by a certain Petesis. He belonged to a family of priests of Theban origin who had moved to Teudjoi (present-day El-Hibe) in Middle Egypt during the reign of Psamtik I (664–610 B.C.). Addressed to the authorities of his nome, the report tells the story of a dispute, which had already been going on for over a century, between Petesis's family and the priests of a local temple dedicated to the cult of Amun. The dispute concerned the entitlement to a prebend that Petesis's ancestors had received. It is impossible here to follow the story through the complex maze of legal cavils that makes the affair resemble an adventure tale. It is sufficient to note that in the legal battle involving Petesis's family and the priests of Amun, the latter use all means at their disposal, legal and illegal, to defend their claims, from murder and armed aggression to arson and attempts to win over to their side important local and national government figures. We should not forget, of course, that we only have Petesis's side of the story, the last known descendant of the family. We do not possess the version of the priests of Amun. It is not impossible that they had a similar list of charges to make against Petesis and his forefathers!

Such violent and illegal tactics were not new during the Saite and Persian Periods. On the contrary, they were part of a long tradition, as we can see from the scandal that occurred at Elephantine in the Twentieth Dynasty, during the reigns of Ramesses IV and Ramesses V (1156–1145 B.C.), when part of the priesthood of the local god Khnum had set up nothing less than a criminal gang under the command of a certain Penanuqet: the theft of temple goods, physical aggression, and the corruption of state officials were only three of the many crimes committed by this gang.

It is difficult to say how frequent cases such as this were. They were probably limited, and it is comforting to know that Penanuqet and his gang were finally unmasked and brought to trial and that

Petesis was able to write the petition with which he requested justice, although it is by no means certain that he obtained it. These
facts seem to suggest that Egyptian society, and, in this case, the
priesthood in particular, were healthy enough to react to criminal
acts, which were even more serious when they were committed by
men in the service of the gods.

At the opposite pole is the high priest of the god Thoth at Hermopolis, Petosiris, who has left us his autobiography inscribed on the
walls of his tomb in the necropolis of Tuna el-Gebel. The tomb, in
the form of a small temple, was built during the early part of the
period of Greek domination in Egypt, during the reign of Philip III
Arrhidaeus (323–317 B.C.). The image that Petosiris has left of himself is that of a saint who chose to spend his entire life in submission
to the will of god, in observance of moral law. Death was accepted
with resignation but in the firm conviction that the god would reward
those who followed his commandments by doing good and shunning
all evil actions. Death was a necessary evil. But good people knew
that the otherworld offered them a reward that would make their loss
of life less painful.

This way of conceiving life and the fate that awaits people after
death provided Petosiris with the inspiration for a text of considerable moral power. It is justly famous for the vivid image it provides
of a dark period in Egyptian civilization, when individual destinies
were often inextricably linked to that of the country, fallen once
more beneath the domination of a foreign power:

> O you [who are still] alive [on earth and who come to this necropo-
> lis and see] this tomb, come [because] I will act in such a way that
> you are instructed in the will of god. I will lead you along the path
> of life, the good path of those who follow god. Happy is he whose
> heart leads him toward this path! Certain is the life on earth of him
> whose heart is steadfast on the path of god, and great is the joy on
> [this] earth of him in whose heart is a great fear of god!

This theme is returned to, and expanded, in the long autobiographical inscription, which should be considered at greater length:

> O all you prophets, O you *wab*-priests, O you sages who enter this
> necropolis and see this tomb, pray to god for its owner [. . .] be-
> cause I am one who is blessed by his father, praised by his mother,
> loved by his brothers [. . .] The West (the kingdom of the dead)

is the land of those who are without sin; praise god on behalf of a man who has reached it, and no one will arrive there unless his heart is sincere in the practice of justice. There, there is [no] distinction between rich and poor [. . .] I was faithful to the lord of Hermopolis (Thoth) from my birth; all his teachings were in my heart; [for this reason] I was chosen as administrator in my temple, because they knew that fear of him was in my heart.

What distinguishes the words of Petosiris is the tone of certainty deriving from a moral choice that could no longer be unmade. The priest did not exhaust his duties by carrying out the ritual tasks of divine service and by attending to the running of the temple. He was an example to those who were excluded from the temple and from daily contact with the gods, so that they could be inspired by a future life in which both rich and poor were rewarded for living blamelessly. In the final analysis, death was the place in which the infallible laws of the god were realized. It is no accident that the tomb of Petosiris is in the form of a temple.

This was the image of elevated morality, expressed in slightly preacherly tones, that Egypt presented to its new rulers when the Greeks arrived in the Nile Valley after the conquests of Alexander. The picture we have been able to assemble of the Egyptian priesthood during the centuries that followed, up to the end of paganism, is remarkably close to the portrait of the priest that we can reconstruct from the autobiography of Petosiris.

Bibliography

Donadoni, S. *La religione dell'Antico Egitto.* Bari, 1959.

Donadoni Roveri, A. M., ed. *Civiltà degli Egizi: Le credenze religiose.* Turin, 1988.

Gauthier, H. *Le personnel du dieu Min.* Cairo, 1931.

Kees, H. *Totenglauben und Jenseitsvorstellungen der alten Ägypter.* Leipzig, 1926.

———. *Der Götterglaube im alten Ägypten.* Leipzig, 1941.

———. *Das Priestertum im Ägyptischen Staat vom Neuen Reich bis zur Spätzeit.* Leiden-Cologne, 1953.

———. *Die Hohenpriester des Amun von Karnak von Herihor his zum Ende der Äthiopenzeit.* Leiden, 1964.

Leclant, J. *Enquêtes sur les sacerdoces et les sanctuaires égyptiens a l'époque dite "éthiopienne."* Cairo, 1954.

———. *Montouemhat.* Cairo, 1961.

Lefebvre, G. *Le tombeau de Pétosiris.* Cairo, 1923–24.

———. *Histoire des grands prêtres d'Amon de Karnak jusqu'à la XXIᵉ Dynastie.* Paris, 1929.

Moret, A. *Le rituel du culte divin journalier en Égypte.* Paris, 1902.

Otto, E. *Die biographischen Inschriften der Ägyptischen Spätzeit: Ihre geistes-geschichtliche und literarische Bedeutung.* Leiden, 1954.

Pritchard, J. B., ed. *Ancient Near Eastern Texts Relating to the Old Testament.* 3d ed. with suppl. Princeton, 1969.

Sauneron, S. *Les prêtres de l'ancienne Égypte.* Paris, 1961.

6. SOLDIERS

Sheikh 'Ibada al-Nubi

The oldest figurative artifacts in Egypt, palettes dating back to the Protodynastic Period, either illustrate or allude to war. Victorious Pharaohs appear on the facades of all Egyptian temples, and battle scenes are the theme of the great historical reliefs of the New Kingdom. This ostentatious interest in war, however, is reflected in neither general attitudes nor the meager descriptions of military experience in the many autobiographies produced by ancient Egyptians. In this volume, military structures are referred to a number of times, although merely in passing, when dealing with peasants, scribes, officials, foreigners, slaves, and—in another sense—kings. However, the soldier, and military qualities as such, play no part in the official picture that Egypt has left for us. It might be significant that, despite an infinite number of ways to define the "enemy" and a multitude of terms for battle and fighting, the Egyptian language did not possess a single precise term to define that particular legal, political, social, and economic situation known as "war."

This paradox is the result of clearly identifiable facts and concepts. The "insularity" of Egypt stemmed from the fact that its frontiers were clearly defined by deserts and the sea. These not only provided the country with almost total security but also encouraged it to become an organic and potentially self-sufficient unit. The need to face "others" only arose when the absolute nature of this unit was threatened. This happened at times, due to wider movements in Near Eastern society (and thus history). Normally, however, the "others" were on the fringes of the Egyptian cosmos, nomadic inhabitants of neighboring areas that supplied Egypt with special minerals and other materials. They were not part of the state but ethnic groups that, along with their role in the peaceful exchange of goods, could only be the protagonists, or victims, of raids. They were a disturbing element in the stable progress of the Egyptian world, and the king, as representative and official personification of that world, was obliged to keep them in check. Military action was therefore always regarded as an intervention against "rebels," or disorganized forces that compromised absolute order—in practice, Egyptian order. Just as the king ensured the divine cult by releasing individuals from their responsibilities to the deity, so he was entrusted with the protection of Egypt. Like his ritual functions, which were performed by the priesthood, his military tasks were delegated. Nonetheless, he remained the titular head of both worship and warlike exploits. It was extremely unusual, therefore, for religious or military themes to be presented in any other way than in ritualized and ceremoniously conventional documentation.

This generically abstract presentation adapted itself in many ways to developments in Egyptian society. Not only can we follow its differing forms, but we can also estimate the increasing importance of the military in the history of Egypt. This allows us to assess the true importance of the soldier, a figure rarely exhibited by Egyptian society.

Apart from allusions to victories found in graffiti (especially in Sinai) commemorating the arrival of Egyptian expeditions in search of valued minerals such as turquoise and malachite, some other data throw light on military activity during the Age of the Pyramids. It is impossible not to consider the organizational problems involved in the massive use and large-scale coordination of labor during this period. Egyptian society must have been able to create disciplined and structured groups of men, to provide for their subsistence, and to determine their tasks. In other words, the foundations for the characteristic feature of the Egyptian army—a punctilious attention to logistics—were established at that time. "Civilian" influence can also be seen in the structure and function of the army during that period. Military service was one of the many kinds of *corvée,* or unpaid labor, demanded of Egyptians and did not require specific skills. Soldiers were usually employed on missions to obtain valuable materials outside (or on the borders of) Egyptian territory. Troops had to protect the workers from nomad attacks and sometimes collaborated in technical operations. Typically, their task was to intimidate rather than to attack.

This was not all that soldiers did, however, as can be seen from a few eloquent documents, both visual and written. Two Fifth Dynasty reliefs—one at Saqqara, in the tomb of a certain Kaemheset, and the other at Deshasha, in the provinces, belonging to someone called Inti—provide us with the first two illustrations of military actions in process. Both reliefs show the siege of fortresses about to fall into Egyptian hands. The Saqqara relief depicts a fortified field containing men, women, children, and animals. The walls are being attacked by sappers digging at their foundations and, with considerably more vigor, by a group of armed soldiers climbing a ladder resting against the wall, against which it has been moved on wheels (wheels were not normally used in Egypt before the New Kingdom, showing that the ladder is a war machine). The relief at Deshasha is livelier and more incisive. The motif of the ladder (this time without wheels) and sappers reappears, but the realism of the scene is enhanced by what is happening inside the fortress. Some people are listening to the sinister noise as the wall is battered down; women are bustling around the wounded; their leader is desperate. Outside, different stages of the battle and scenes of hand-to-hand combat are portrayed, with the Egyptians bearing axes against their enemies, already pierced with arrows from the first encounter and dressed in what is clearly Asiatic costume. The picture concludes with a line of prisoners bound to one another, followed by a still-armed Egyptian soldier carrying a girl on his shoulders (a theme that will be repeated in a humorous sense in a much later period). It is difficult not to think that such exceptional images represent actual events. In any case, they are evidence of military activity beyond the Egyptian border and of officially recognized, though elementary, siege techniques.

The most explicit, and significant, document, however, is an unusually long autobiographical text. The text relates how the many talents of an official called Uni enabled him to rise through the ranks. During his extremely varied career, he was administrator, official, courtier, armorer, transporter, a judge in extremely delicate trials, and a general:

> When His Majesty took action against the Asiatic Sand-
> dwellers, His Majesty made an army of many tens of thousands

from all of Upper Egypt: from Yebu in the south to Medenyt in the
north; from Lower Egypt; from all of the Two-Sides-of-the-House
and from Sedjer and Khen-sedjru; and from Irtjet-Nubians, Medja-
Nubians, Yam-Nubians, Wawat-Nubians, Kaau-Nubians; and from
Tjemeh-land.

His Majesty sent me at the head of this army, there being
counts, royal seal-bearers, sole companions of the palace, chieftains
and mayors of towns of Upper and Lower Egypt, companions,
scout leaders, chief priests of Upper and Lower Egypt, and chief
district officials at the head of the troops of Upper and Lower
Egypt, from the villages and towns that they governed and from
the Nubians of those foreign lands. I was the one who commanded
them—although my rank was that of overseer of royal tenants—
because of my rectitude, so that no one attacked his fellow, so that
no one seized a loaf or sandals from a traveler, so that no one took
a cloth from any town, so that no one took a goat from anyone.

I led them from Northern Isle and Gate of Iyhotep in the district of Horus-Lord-of-Truth (Snofru) while being in this rank [. . .].
I determined the number of these troops. It had never been determined by any servant.

> This army returned in safety;
>   it had ravaged the Sand-dwellers' land.
> This army returned in safety;
>   it had flattened the Sand-dwellers' land.
> This army returned in safety;
>   it had sacked its strongholds.
> This army returned in safety;
>   it had cut down its figs, its vines.
> This army returned in safety;
>   it had thrown fire in all its mansions.
> This army returned in safety;
>   it had slain its troops by many ten thousands.
> This army returned in safety;
>   it had carried off many troops as captives.

His Majesty praised me for it beyond anything. His Majesty sent
me to lead this army five times, to attack the land of the Sand-
dwellers as often as they rebelled, with these troops. I acted so that
His Majesty praised me for it beyond anything.

Told there were marauders among those foreigners at Nose-

of-Gazelle's-Head, I crossed in ships with these troops. I made a
landing in the back of the height of the mountain range, to the
north of the land of the Sand-dwellers, while half of this army was
on the road. I came and caught them all and slew every marauder
among them. (Lichtheim 1973, pp. 19–20)

This account of warlike activities alone gives us the essential
elements of a soldier's life during the Old Kingdom. Above all, we
should note the presence of both Egyptians and foreigners, a typical
feature of the Egyptian army. Nubians are precisely identified by
their origins, proof of the constant contact that Egypt is known
to have had with Nubia during this period. Libyans (Tjemeh-land)
are also mentioned. These groups traditionally supplied mercenaries, who appear to have been led by "scout leaders"—Egyptian officials responsible for dealing with foreigners. Egyptian soldiers were
also controlled by secular and religious administrative personnel. Officials who were obliged to perform military duties automatically
took command, giving the impression that what counted most in this
varied army was the ability to organize. As general commander, Uni
also described his civil merits as a moderator of this mob of soldiers
(who, despite everything, undoubtedly stole a few pieces of clothing
and goats), but the account of the actual war takes the very literary
form of a hymn. This is the structural climax of the story, although it
lacks the bite and precision to be found in the rest of his account.

It is clear from the account that follows the hymn, describing a
plan to defeat the inhabitants of "Nose-of-Gazelle's-Head," that Uni
is no mere military dilettante. At the first, still vague, news of danger
("marauders"), Uni attacks in a complex pincer maneuver, with some
troops advancing by land and others by sea. This is another foretaste
of the kind of military activity that would develop fully in the New
Kingdom. It demonstrates the beginning of a tradition of "the art
of war."

There is evidence of Egyptian fortresses abroad from the earliest
times. At Elephantine, the island just downstream from the First
Cataract, which is still (and was even more so in the past) in Nubian
ethnic territory, a fortress named after Huni, the Third Dynasty king,
reveals the presence of the Egyptians. Other Old Kingdom fortresses
existed in Nubia, now hidden beneath forts built at a later date (such
as one at Buhen, at the Second Cataract). More than one interpretation of these data exists. They might have been no more than

agreed-upon fixed bases for trade and the many commercial missions in the region. Nonetheless, it is due to such contacts that the Egyptians began to employ soldiers from these countries as standing armies in Egypt. We have just come across such soldiers in Uni's composite army. They can be found elsewhere, described as "pacified (i.e., "subject") Nubians" or with the ethnic name of Medjaw (corresponding to the modern Bedja).

These troops were stationed in Egypt to maintain public order in general and were often no more than a police force. The Nubian soldiers, however, gradually became an integral part of the Egyptian sociological panorama. This explains the significance of lines from the Lamentations of Ipuwer (also known as Admonitions of an Egyptian Sage) concerning the fall of the Memphite monarchy. In the general subversion of values, which is the theme of the lament, the following question is asked: "How can a man kill his own brother? The troops that we have recruited for ourselves have become a people of the Bow (an enemy was traditionally referred to as the "Nine Bows") and have come to destroy." The fact that these troops, described shortly before in the text as Medjaw and Nubians, can now "destroy" is thus compared to fratricide, as evidence of universal subversion.

This subversion of values at the end of the Memphite Period influenced the entire later development of Egyptian civilization and had particular significance for the military. With the collapse of a central authority, the creation of various autonomous centers of power, and the rise of economic disorder, violence of an immediate, personalized nature broke out ("we go plowing with the shield"; "the strong man steals from the weak"; "if three men take the same road, only two will be found: the more kill the fewer"), as well as a more ceremonial state violence. The king had to oppose rebel princes, who, in their turn, fought among themselves. During this period (the First Intermediate Period), the terrible power of warrior princes began to be celebrated in a formulaic manner. This practice passed down to the Middle Kingdom pharaohs and, from then on, was strictly restricted to the ruler.

"I am one strong of bow, mighty with his arm, one much feared by his neighbors," declared Khety, a prince of Assiut. "I am the champion who has no peer," was the refrain to each of the texts illustrating the tomb of Ankhtifi, nomarch of Edfu, at Moalla. These princes described, and illustrated, their exploits with great vividness:

The chief of the army of Armant came to say: "Here, champion, go downriver to the fortress [of Armant]." So I went downriver, in the region to the east of Armant, and I found that Thebes and Coptos, in their entirety, [had stormed] the fortresses of Armant on the Hill of Semekhsen. This was why they had come to me. Then [my arms] were strong [against them] like a hook in the nostrils of a hippopotamus in flight. Then I went upriver to demolish their fortresses with the courageous troops of Hefat. Because I am the champion who has no peer.

This first-person account depicts a swift, energetic professional soldier. Like other autobiographical texts of the time, it enjoys presenting its subject's success. Another description in the same tomb narrates the same event with greater objectivity, or at least defines more clearly both its complex development and the personal commitment of those involved in the battle:

Having gone downriver with my courageous and faithful conscripts, I landed on the western bank of the Theban nome, while the first part of the fleet was at [the level of] the Hill of Semekhsen, and the last part of the fleet was at [the level of] the Estate of Tjemy. My faithful conscripts sought combat in the region to the west of the Theban nome, but no one dared come out for fear of them.

Having gone downriver once more, I landed on the eastern bank of the Theban nome, while the first part of the fleet was at the level of the tomb of Imby, and the last part of the fleet was [at the level of] the Field of Sega. They besieged the walls after the gates had been closed in fear. Then these courageous and faithful conscripts turned into explorers to the west and east of the Theban nome in their search for combat, but no one dared come out for fear of them. Because I am the champion who has no fear.

However, apart from these adventures outside the province, local militias fulfilled their daily role as keepers of the peace. "When night came, someone who was on the road thanked me, because fear of my soldiers protected him as though he were in his own house," said a prince of Siut (Griffith 1889, III, pl. 11, l. 10).

From the tomb of a nomarch of Assiut we have two very impressive groups of figurines, fixed on bases of wood, each representing a regiment of soldiers on the march. They are organized into four col-

umns of ten men each and probably represent a tactical unit. One
group shows Egyptians, wearing simple loincloths. They are holding lances, with tips shaped like bay leaves, in their right hands and
shields in their left. The shields, rounded at the top, are made of
wood covered with leather. The second group of soldiers bear only
bows and represent Nubians. These were the troops that fought in
the civil wars, during which the career of soldier became popular
and thus more common. Illustrations in the tombs of princes show
gymnastic exercises, warlike dances, and assaults on fortresses in
which both aggressors and victims are represented as a mixture of
Egyptians and Nubians. The fortresses are equipped with battle-
ments and sloping ramparts, while the other force has more complex
techniques for attacking the walls than in the past. They now use
mobile shelters, from beneath which they swing heavy battering
rams against the wall. Although there is no doubt that the Egyptian
army was still based on unpaid military service, or corvées, a professional element was clearly developing. This was particularly evident
among the Nubian forces. Representations of Nubians appear spo-
radically all over Egypt, but a large series of stelae at Gebelein, just
south of Thebes, records their presence as an organized complex.
They are represented in rustic style with their bows and arrows in
their hands, often accompanied by their dogs. This typology is quite
different from that used for Egyptians. The Nubians were a genuine
ethnic nucleus, inserted into the Egyptian context, operating in, and
on behalf of, Egypt, but without losing their character. This precedent would have considerable importance in later Egyptian history.

In the background of this restless feudal world we can glimpse
the presence of the king. His role, albeit limited, was nonetheless
essential. Some princes still recognized the king as their superior and
bore arms in his service. ("I had a fine fleet [. . .] the beloved of the
king when he came toward the south," said a prince of Assiut.) Others, however, opposed the king ("I saved my city the day of the sack-
ing before the terror of the royal house," boasted a prince of Hermopolis; in Hatnub 23.24). During this period, kings were constantly
fighting wars and were surrounded by armed men, both loyal and
rebellious. This had a decisive impact on political activity and the
role the monarchy had to assume.

Royal authority appears to have been particularly strong in the
northern part of the country, between Memphis and Herakleopolis
and in the Delta. A royal text of the period, the Instruction for Meri-

kare, attributed to Merikare's father, clearly describes the importance of armed forces to the monarchy: "Make your officials rich and
promote your warriors (*'ḥȝyw*). Give abundantly to the young troops
(*ḏȝmw*) of your retinue." A little earlier he had advised: "Raise up
your young troops (*ḏȝmw*), that the Residence may love you [...].
For twenty years the rising generation is happy in following its desire. As discharged men, they move into the reserve forces. Conscripts (*s' qyw*) called up for training will take their place." The text
clearly reveals the emergence of a specifically created full-time military class in Egyptian cities.

But the conflicts that wreaked havoc in Egypt as kings struggled
to maintain their supremacy over princes—whether allies or enemies—were not the only problem. Egypt's fertile lands, pastures,
and waters also had to be protected from invasion by nomads from
beyond the border. It was the monarch's task to block these foreigners. The Instruction for Merikare describes a series of fortresses
manned by Egyptian colonists in Lower Egypt. The colonists are
both "citizens" and soldiers, "who know how to bear arms." The
"Road-of-Horus" (Horus being the god personified by the king) was
a line of forts from the Isthmus of Suez to Minia (Minieh) in Middle
Egypt protecting the water supplies for the desert crossing. It was
difficult to cross this fortified territory, as we know from the Story of
Sinuhe. Set in a slightly later epoch than the one being considered
here, the story describes the risks of the journey, under the eyes of
sentries who watched each movement below their fortresses. In the
Prophecy of Neferti, a pseudoprophetic text celebrating the founder
of the Twelfth Dynasty, Amenemhet I, whose acts brought the feudal period to an end, the situation is described in the following way:

> The Asiatics will fall before the terror that you inspire, the Libyans
> will fall before your flame, the nobles will retreat from your anger,
> and your enemies from your strength. The walls of the prince will
> be erected to prevent the Asiatics from descending into Egypt.
> They will beg for water, for their herds to drink.

This vision of order imposed by threat brings the feudal period
to an end. The experiences of this period shaped Egypt's military
mentality and tradition (along with other aspects of Egyptian civilization). Bravery and courage in the field became positive elements
in assessing an individual. The army was linked to specific groups,
such as the armed colonies of the Delta, or princely troops. Attitudes

toward non-Egyptians clearly polarized. On the one hand, foreigners were incorporated (although not assimilated) into specific military contingents and assigned to specific territorial bases (e.g., the Nubians of Gebelein). On the other hand, they were identified as barbarians (e.g., the Instruction for Merikare gives a splendid picture of how, and why, Asiatics and Egyptians differed) who *had* to be kept at a distance by structures of state control. The soldier became a figure whose qualities could be praised and whose role was essential, because, as the Prophecy of Neferti says: "the right order must return to its place; wicked disorder must be thrown out."

The reunification of Egypt during the Eleventh and, especially, the Twelfth Dynasties took place as a result of a war in which the enemy included Egyptians themselves. Military methods developed during the preceding period were used unquestioningly. The language of the feudal period, which had described the courage of princes and the ability of their soldiers, now became official. A series of stereotypes depicted the king as an invincible hero. At the very beginning of the Twelfth Dynasty, Sinuhe praised his king in the following way:

> He is a god indeed, without peer [. . .] He is a champion who acts with his own arms, a fighter without anyone like him when he is seen attacking the bowmen and engaging the fray. He is one who bends back the horn and renders hands powerless, so that his enemies cannot muster their ranks. He is vengeful when he cracks skulls, and no one stands up near him. He steps wide when he annihilates the fugitive. There is no chance for the one who shows his back to him. He is upright of heart at the moment of contact. He comes again and does not show his back. He is stalwart of heart when he sees a crowd, and he does not allow cowardice around him. He is eager when he falls upon the retinue, and he is joyful when he plunders the bow-people. As soon as he takes up his shield, he strikes down. He need not repeat the act of killing, for there is no one who can deflect his arrow nor one who can draw his bow. The bowmen retreat before him as if before the might of a great goddess. He fights having foreseen the outcome, and he takes no care for the remnants. (Simpson 1972, pp. 61–62)

Sinuhe adds the important detail: "But he is well-favored and very gentle; through love he takes."

At the height of the period's military glory, a hymn honoring Sesostris III makes the equally hyperbolic claim that the king is capable of "slaying the bowmen without striking a blow / shooting an arrow without drawing a bow," and, later: "The tongue of Your Majesty restrains Nubia / and your words rout the Asiatics."

The monarchy succeeding feudalism had to find enough autonomous strength and vigor to oppose local princes effectively. The period was characterized by a methodical extension of the border to the south, the source of many valuable goods. The royal task of protecting Egypt from "barbarians," which had previously been entrusted to Uni, and about which the father of Merikare had later boasted, was now rationalized by creating specific positions such as "overseer of the Eastern Desert" and "overseer of the Western Desert." One of the people to hold the latter title described his activities in the following way: "I arrived at the western oasis, I explored all the ways, and I brought back the fugitives that were discovered there. The army was in good condition and suffered no losses" (Anthes 1930, p. 108). The tomb of an overseer of the Eastern Desert also depicts the arrival and checking of "37 Asiatic Bedouin," who had arrived with gifts and been allowed to enter Egypt. The "overseers of the hunters," who accompanied and protected caravans, were usually desert people, members of nomad tribes in the service of Egypt. By this time, the "Wall of the Prince," near the border of the isthmus, played the same role of policing and surveillance.

The attitude toward Nubia, however, was very different. Now that the boundaries were being extended, it was no longer merely a question of surveillance. Egypt had been expanding southward for centuries, incorporating regions along the border until it had reached the natural boundary of the First Cataract. This gradual process of peaceful assimilation now changed into a precise desire to extend Egyptian territory. From Amenemhet I on, there was war in Nubia. The Second Cataract, at Wadi Halfa, was finally reached under Sesostris III.

"I made my border to the south of that of my father and added to that which he had left me as my inheritance. I am a king who speaks and acts." These words come from a famous stela, found on the border at Semna. The language is that used by far less illustrious individuals during the feudal age to talk of their financial success in increasing the flocks inherited from their fathers, of having used, in other words, both their strength and their intelligence. This historical analogy unintentionally reveals the economic motives that lay behind extending the borders. Autonomous possession of the Nubian province—like the later acquisition of the reclaimed land of Fayyūm—gave the ruling house greater freedom from the local nobility. If we look more closely, however, we see that most of this freedom derived from the initial availability of an army. This can clearly be seen from the texts: "How joyful are the recruits (*dʒmw*), for you have brought them to manhood. / How joyful are your honored old folk, for you have made them young," declares the previously mentioned song in honor of Sesostris. Some of these soldiers were summoned to bear arms in certain cities; others lived in military quarters near the palace.

At the beginning of the dynasty, a nomarch of the Sixteenth Nome took part in Amenemhet I's Nubian expedition, as revealed in the inscription in his tomb at Beni Hasan. The Memphite system of contingents of drafted men led by individuals who had been responsible for choosing them, which we saw in Uni's inscription, was still being used. Later, a "first son of the king," in the role of "scribe of the army," went on a recruiting mission to Tini, calling up one in every hundred men (Erman 1900, p. 42). The vague title of "citizen"(*ʿnḫ n niwt*), frequently found in inscriptions, has been identified by Oleg Berlev as indicating a professional soldier. The technical terms "warriors" (*ʿḥ, wty*) and "companions" (*šmsw*)—members of forces in the direct service of the king—were also used. These selected full-time soldiers can still talk to us about the military activities that provided them with their livelihood. A "companion," Khusobek, describes his successes in the following way:

> His Majesty ordered me to carry out my military service with six men from the palace. Then His Majesty appointed me "companion of the prince" and gave me sixty head of cattle. [. . .] Then I defeated the Nubian [. . .] near my city [. . .] Then he appointed me "inspector of the companions" and gave me a gift of one hundred head of cattle.

Not all professional officers had the splendid career of Khusobek, of course. But there were roles for many people in the Egyptian garrisons, in the frontier posts, and in the numerous fortresses that punctuated the key crossing points of the Nile in Nubia. Some of the dispatches sent by the commander of one of these forts, that of Semna on the southern border, have been preserved. They give us a glimpse of the dull routine of day-to-day garrison life, with nothing to do but guard the frontier, a duty also described on a surviving inscription.

Egypt's military spirit is revealed elsewhere in the national literature when Sinuhe, having fled to Syria, describes his fortunate career in the service of the local prince with whom he had sought refuge and found favor:

> When the Asiatics became so bold as to oppose the rulers of foreign countries, I counseled their movements. This ruler of [Re]tenu had me spend many years as commander of his army. Every foreign country against which I went forth, when I had made my attack on it, was driven away from its pasturage and its wells. I plundered its cattle, carried off its inhabitants, took away their food, and slew people in it by my strong arm, by my bow, by my movements, and by my successful plans. I found favor in his heart, he loved me, he recognized my valor, and he placed me at the head of his children, when he saw how my arms flourished. (Trans. J. A. Wilson, in Pritchard 1969, p. 20)

This is the language that was used in the private autobiographies of the First Intermediate Period, expressing pride in achievement by using formulae now reserved, in Egypt, for the exploits of the king. But these events had taken place outside the Nile Valley. It was as a representative of his civilization that Sinuhe insisted on his military prowess. This can also be seen in the adventurous episode of the duel following the barbaric challenge of a "mighty" local man, a duel won by the Egyptian with an air of serenity:

> A mighty man of Retenu came, that he might challenge me in my [own] camp. He was a hero without peer, and he had repelled all of [the land of Retenu]. He said that he would fight me, he intended to despoil me, and he planned to plunder my cattle, on the advice of his tribe. That prince discussed [it] with me, and I said: "I do not know him. Certainly I am no confederate of his, so that I might move freely in his encampment. Is it the case that I have [ever] opened his door or overthrown his fences? [Rather], it is hostility because he sees me carrying out thy commissions. I am really like a stray bull in the midst of another herd [. . .]
>
> During the night I strung my bow, and shot my arrows, I gave free play to my dagger, and polished my weapons [. . .] Then he came to me as I was waiting, [for] I had placed myself near him.

Every heart burned for me; women and men groaned. Every heart
was sick for me [. . .] Then [he took] his shield, his battle-axe,
and his armful of javelins. Now after I had let his weapons issue
forth, I made his arrows pass by me uselessly, one close to another.
He charged me, and I shot him, my arrow sticking in his neck. He
cried out and fell on his nose. I felled him with his [own] battle-
axe, while every Asiatic roared. I gave praise to Montu (the Egyptian god of war), while his adherents were mourning for him [. . .]
Then I carried off his goods and plundered his cattle. What he had
planned to do to me I did to him. (Trans. J. A. Wilson, in Pritchard
1969, p. 20)

At the beginning of the Middle Kingdom Sinuhe could accom-
plish his military exploits in Syria, giving advice to the "princes of
the foreign countries" (ḥqȝw ḫȝswt). One of these princes is depicted
on the walls of a tomb at Beni Hasan, officially importing his animals
and the produce of his country into Egypt. This is one example of a
larger influx of Asiatics, who settled in the country as a group. Familiar to us from the literature and, now, from archeological discoveries
as well, they are none other than the Hyksos—the Greek term that
renders the Egyptian *ḥqȝw ḫȝswt*.

During the last few years, Bietak's Austrian mission has been
excavating Hyksos settlements in the Delta. They have revealed the
presence of a well-defined nucleus, which imported into Egypt materials and building techniques typical of the Syrian Middle Bronze
Age. If we remember that the characteristics of the Nubians had
been emphasized at Gebelein, we can see how the cultural difference of the Hyksos might stand out in the otherwise homogeneous
Egyptian panorama. They were foreign soldiers, summoned according to an ancient tradition to bear arms in a country whose peasant
inhabitants only fought on exceptional, and short-lived, occasions.

When Egypt's centralized power began to show signs of structural weakness at the end of the Middle Kingdom, these organized
soldiers, who had maintained their own culture, took control of the
country. It is significant that some of them adopted the name of
"general" (*mr-mšʿ*) as a royal title. As far as we can judge, this government of soldiers-turned-kings tended to adopt Egyptian ways, even
though later propaganda has painted their barbaric impiety in lurid
colors. This is not the place to examine the events of this period

(the Second Intermediate Period). We need only remember that the government's power was limited by the presence of a princely family in the south, established at Thebes and in control of most of Upper Egypt. This family also had its soldiers and its Nubian mercenaries. It was during this period that the latter left their typical burial structures at a number of places in Upper Egypt. Known as "pan graves" these have also been found, dating from the same period, in Nubia itself.

For a time, the two powers managed to coexist. Marriages were probably organized between ruling families, and economic interests and property rights outside the areas of strictly defined sovereignty were recognized. But when the equilibrium was disturbed and the princes of Thebes decided to unite Egypt once again, the country's military history acquired a completely new importance and character.

The war of liberation soon became a war of conquest, or, at least, of subjection, as the Hyksos were driven from the borders of Egypt as far as Palestine. An empire was created that stretched, at its height, from the Euphrates down to the Fourth Cataract of the Nile, in the heart of what is now Sudan. Control over such a vast territory was obviously entrusted to the army, and soldiers both created and defended new social demands linked to the flow of tribute and slave labor into the Nile Valley. The economy of the country, and the social structure itself, were profoundly altered as a result.

Representations of the king now became gaudily symbolic. During the Memphite era he had appeared as nothing more than a ritual sacrificer of foreigners, and in the Middle Kingdom, he had been celebrated in all his terrifying invincibility. The traditional presentation, reflected in the titles used to praise the king, was now embellished with his concrete achievements on the field of battle. He was transformed from victorious king into soldier-king. His royal training was described in this new context. On a stela, Amenophis II recalls his early training with horses:

> Now, when he was still a boy, he loved his horses and he took delight in them; he was happy in his heart to deal with them, being one who knew their nature, able in their training.
>
> This was heard in the royal palace by his father [. . .] It sweetened the heart of his majesty to hear this and he took delight in that which was said of his eldest son [. . .] His majesty said to

those at his side: "Let him be given the horses of his majesty's stables at Memphis, and let it be said to him: Take care of them, break them in, train them, heal them if they are ill."

After these things were done so that the son of the king might occupy himself with the horses of the royal stable—and Reshef and Astarte (two bellicose Semitic deities) took delight in him— doing all that his heart loved; in his training of his horses he had no peer. They were tireless when he held the reins and they did not break into a sweat during long gallops. He trained in Memphis in a wonderful manner and he stopped at the sanctuary of Harakhte.

In the tomb of an important official of the time, the future king is shown being taught how to use a bow by the official. Although the idea of teaching a king goes against Egyptian tradition, since a king was regarded as such from birth, the student later boasted of the ability he had acquired:

> He bent three thousand hard bows, to compare the work of their makers, to distinguish an expert from an ignorant worker. He came doing that which is placed before you; he entered his northern pavilion and found that four Asiatic copper targets, of the thickness of a palm, had been set up for him, and that twenty cubits (just over ten meters) separated one pole from the next. His majesty appeared on his horse like Montu (the god of war) in his power, took his bow, grasped four arrows together. Then he advanced, shooting at them, like Montu with his arms. His arrows passed to the other side; then he attacked another pole.
>
> No one else has accomplished this feat. It has been heard of no one that he shot an arrow against a copper target, that it penetrated it and fell to the ground, except of the strong and powerful king that Amun has made victorious, the king of the Valley and of the Delta, mighty as Montu.

As hereditary prince, the future king had control over the troops during this period and prepared himself in this way for his future role.

In the field, it was the king who convened the war council and discussed matters with his generals (and, according to a recurrent formula, proposed daring solutions in opposition to their more prudent suggestions). At the beginning of the war of liberation against the Hyksos, Kamose discussed matters with his generals in the following way:

> The great men of this council said: "Now, the Asiatics have [advanced] to Cusa [. . .] But we are satisfied with our [part of] Egypt [. . .] The best their fields can offer is grown for us [. . .] Spelt is sent for our pigs and our livestock are not taken away [. . .] He keeps the land of the Asiatics; we have Egypt [. . .]." But they were unpleasing to the heart of his majesty. "As for your counsel [. . .] [it is base. Now, I shall fight] the Asiatics. Success will come. When [I have won,] the entire earth [will proclaim me, mighty king] in Thebes, Kamose, the protector of Egypt."

This is obviously the background for the enthusiastic celebration of the successful exploit that followed.

In a much calmer tone, reflecting the precision of a specific situation, Tuthmosis III describes the events preceding the battle of Megiddo:

> Year 23, Ist month of the third season, day 16—as far as the town of Yehem. [His majesty] ordered a conference with his victorious army, speaking as follows: "That [wretched] enemy of Kadesh has come and has entered into Megiddo. He is [there] at this moment. He has gathered to him the princes of [every] foreign country [which had been] loyal to Egypt, as well as (those) as far as Naharin and M[itanni], them of Hurru, them of Kode, their horses, their armies, [and their people], for he says—so it is reported—'I shall wait [here] in Megiddo [to fight against his majesty].' Will ye tell me [what is in your hearts]?"
>
> They said in the presence of his majesty: "What is it like to go [on] this [road] which becomes (so) narrow? It is [reported] that the foe is there, waiting on [the outside, while they are] becoming (more) numerous. Will not horse (have to) go after [horse, and the army] and the people similarly? Will the vanguard of us be fighting while the [rear guard] is waiting here in Aruna, unable to fight? Now two (other) roads are here. One of the roads—behold, it is [to the east of] us, so that it comes out at Taanach. The other—behold, it is to the north side of Djefti, and we will come out to the north of Megiddo. Let our victorious lord proceed on the one of [them] which is [satisfactory to] his heart, but do not make us go on that difficult road!"

Then messages [were brought in about that wretched enemy and discussion was continued] of [that] problem on which they had previously spoken. That which was said in the majesty of the Court—life; prosperity, health!—"I [swear], as Re loves me, as my father Amon favors me, as my [nostrils] are rejuvenated with life and satisfaction, my majesty shall proceed upon this Aruna road! Let him of you who wishes go upon these roads of which you speak, and let him of you who wishes come in the following of my majesty! 'Behold,' they will say, these enemies whom Re abominates, 'has his majesty set out on another road because he has become afraid of us?'—so they will speak."

They said in the presence of his majesty: "May thy father Amon, Lord of the Thrones of the Two Lands, Presiding over Karnak, act [acording to thy desire]! Behold, we are following thy majesty everywhere that [thy majesty] goes, for a servant will be after [his] lord." (Trans. J. A. Wilson, in Pritchard 1969, pp. 235–36)

In the end, this soldier-king makes it clear that, after having decided on the plan of action himself, he also fought in the field. Immediately after the Megiddo council of war, Tuthmosis III took personal control over the difficult and daring campaign, which effectively led to victory. His son, Amenophis II, later described how he stood guard over an entire camp of prisoners, armed only with his battle-axe, after a day of battle.

The topos of the warrior-king continued throughout the subsequent dynasty. The speech made by Ramesses II after being surprised by the Hittite army when the bulk of his own troops were far away evidently suffers from a lack of objectivity. Nonetheless, the text provides us with a clear and authentic picture of what was expected from a king at war:

What about you, my captains, soldiers,
my charioteers, who shirked the fight?
Does a man not act to be acclaimed in his town,
when he returns as one brave before his lord?
A name made through combat is truly good,
a man is ever respected for valor [. . .]
Did you not know it in your hearts:
I am your rampart of iron!
What will men say when they hear of it,
that you left me alone without a comrade,

that no chief, charioteer, or soldier came
to lend me a hand while I was fighting?
I crushed a million countries by myself
on Victory-in-Thebes, Mut-is-content, my great horses;
it was they whom I found supporting me,
when I alone fought many lands.
They shall henceforth be fed in my presence,
whenever I reside in my palace.
                                        (Lichtheim 1976, pp. 69–70)

This new-style model of the king effectively depended on his army, which now assumed (with modifications between the Eighteenth and Nineteenth Dynasties) a much more obviously defined hierarchy. We pass from simple soldier (w^cw) to "chief of the Fifty." This was probably a sub-unit of the tactical unit comprising 250 men under the command of a "seal-bearer" ($t3y$ $srit$). Then there were superior officers (hry-pdt) in command of a fortress, and general officers, such as the "general" (mr $mš^c$), the "general of the cavalry" (mr $ssmt$), and the "scribe of the army" ($sš$ $mš^c$), who was probably also "scribe of recruits" ($sš$ $nfrw$). Ranking above all these was the general in chief (mr $mš^c$$wr$), usually a royal prince. Garrison commanders in occupied or controlled areas and the numerous contingents of foreigners (mercenaries or prisoners of war who had been Egyptianized and were used for military purposes) were not included in this hierarchy. Each army corps contained five thousand men. During the Eighteenth Dynasty there were two corps, although this number grew to three, and then four, during the Ramesside Period. The forces were divided into infantry and charioteers. For special tasks, there also existed a "navy" with armed vessels, although there is no evidence that sea battles were ever actually fought. The navy was more likely to have been used to transport troops as part of a general strategic plan based on the use of archers, infantry, and charioteers. We actually possess accounts of Egyptian battles based on journals kept by people delegated to make such records, which are, in a sense, technical. Tjeneni boasts in his tomb inscriptions of "having written of the exploits of His Majesty (Tuthmosis III), carried out in every foreign land: they were described as they happened" (*Urkunden* IV, 662). The development of the battle of Megiddo, conducted by this very king, has been reconstructed by Yeivin. It shows a battle plan that was worked out and, as far as possible, carried through to the end, a plan that did not depend on the actions of individual soldiers.

It is not the task of this chapter to describe the military structures of Egypt or the history of its conquests outside the national borders. It is, rather, to see how far this new climate affected individual lives (as far as we can) and to examine the extent to which individual cases were typical of the society as a whole.

Some autobiographies, written at the beginning of the Eighteenth Dynasty, are particularly valuable. They show how far it was possible for people to feel part of the history of the nation during this period and the extent to which personal lives were interwoven with that of Egypt. Here is the autobiography of a certain Ahmose, son of Abana (his mother):

> I speak to you, all mankind, that I may let you know the favors which have come to me. I have been awarded gold seven times in the presence of the entire land, and male and female slaves in like manner, and I have been vested with very many fields. The reputation of a valiant man is from what he has done, not being destroyed in this land forever.
>
> He speaks thus:
>
> I had my upbringing in the town of el-Kab, my father being a soldier of the King of Upper and Lower Egypt: Seqnen-Re, the triumphant, his name being Bebe, the son of (the woman) Ro-onet. Then I served as soldier in his place in the ship, "The Wild Bull," in the time of the Lord of the Two Lands: Neb-pehti-Re, the triumphant, when I was (still) a boy, before I had taken a wife, (but) while I was (still) sleeping in a net hammock.
>
> But after I had set up a household, then I was taken on the ship, "Northern," because I was valiant. Thus I used to accompany the Sovereign—life, prosperity, health!—on foot, following his excursions in his chariot. When the town of Avaris was besieged, then I showed valor on foot in the presence of his majesty. Thereupon I was appointed to the ship, "Appearing in Memphis." Then there was fighting on the water in the canal Pa-Djedku of Avaris. Thereupon I made a capture, and I carried away a hand. It was reported to the king's herald. Then the Gold of Valor was given to me. (*Urkunden* IV, 1 ff.; trans. J. A. Wilson, in Pritchard 1969, p. 233)

The autobiography of a certain Amenemheb has a similar tone. After listing, with great geographical precision, the sites of the battles in which he fought in Palestine and Syria, he records his victims and spoils on each occasion. Thus, near Aleppo, "I took thirteen Asiatics as prisoners of war, thirteen men; seven live asses; thirteen bronze lances, the bronze of which was worked with gold." He took more prisoners at Carchemish, Kadesh, and other places, handing them all over to the king: "Then my lord gave me the Gold of Valor. List: two gold necklaces, four bracelets, two flies, a lion (flies and lions were military decorations), a female slave, and a male slave" (*Urkunden* IV, 890 ff.).

Even more specific details exist. When the prince of Kadesh released a filly in heat in order to create havoc among the stallions drawing the Egyptian chariots, Amenemheb pursued the horse on foot and killed it. And when the king hunted elephant in the country of Ny (in Syria), and the largest animal in the herd attacked him, Amenemheb turned on the animal and cut off his trunk: "Then my lord gave me gold; he gave me [. . .] and three changes of clothes."

What emerges from these texts is the pride of veteran soldiers, the satisfaction of having played a part in the flow of historical events, the taste for honors through which the king invited them to share in his glory, no longer solitary, by giving them decorations that testified to their courage, and, finally, the discreet allusion to a direct relationship to the king, almost as though he were a brother-in-arms. During the festival of Opet following his coronation, Amenophis II saw Amenemheb rowing his boat. He recognized him and summoned him to the palace: "I know you from the time when I was still in the nest, when you were a companion of my father. I now appoint you lieutenant of the army, and from now on you will command the royal bodyguard" (*Urkunden* IV, 900).

We shall be returning to this intimacy between the king and his officers. First, however, we need to examine the more general situation. The military appears to have been a hereditary caste, with positions handed down from father to son and recorded in constantly updated lists. When a soldier retired, his son took his place and the benefits that went with it: the use of a piece of land, usually situated in circumscribed areas that thus became military villages, as well as any slaves he had been awarded from time to time for his acts of valor. Although, at least until the Nineteenth Dynasty, soldiers did not actually own this land, they did not work on it themselves but made others do it for them. They represent the birth of an intermediate social group, between the ruling class and those workers who did not possess the means of production. The "middle-class" tone of the Eighteenth Dynasty, which was proud of well-made objects displaying a simple good taste and a certain gaiety, is partly due to this nucleus of people exempt from daily work and with a modest, but sufficient, income.

In other texts, kings (Ramesses II and Ramesses III) boast of the fortune from which their soldiers have benefited. Despite the customary hyperbole, the basic truth of such a claim is proven by the numerous stelae dedicated by soldiers to Ramesses II as a god, in particular to his deified statues (the so-called Stelae of Horbeit [Pharbaithos], which are actually from the town of Piramesse).

The existence of a regular army thus profoundly modified the economic structure of the country by encouraging the long-term creation of small and medium-sized property owners, alongside the land owned by the sovereign, princes, and, above all, temples. Obviously, the economic situation showed most improvement at the higher ranks. We also know more about officers, since they were more likely to leave documents describing their activities and problems. They were responsible for the well-being and efficiency of the army and can be divided into two groups: combat officers and service officers. Although it is doubtful that the entire personnel was divided methodically between the two duties, one of the most striking features of the Egyptian army was the importance, and attention, given to its organization. Distances between cities were measured; ports for disembarkation were prepared; rations, duties, arms, and wages were distributed; and so on. Portrayals of an Egyptian camp at Kadesh, before Ramesses II's battle, show a rampart on which shields have been placed. Inside, tents contain stools and small tables, as well as equipment for cooking and other activities. People are busy washing themselves, asses are being unloaded, and so on. It is a small, well-organized city in which day-to-day life proceeds smoothly. But the fact that these "civil" aspects still have their place, in the middle of a risk-filled military campaign, reveals a considerable increase in the work of, and efforts made by, the army's auxiliary services.

The following school exercise, which clearly takes pride in using as many terms as possible (not all of which can now be translated with precision) in an ostentatiously rhetorical style, tells us what the quartermaster-general's branch might have taken on an expedition in Syria:

Apply yourself to cause to be ready the steeds of the team which is [bound] for Khor, together with their stable-masters as well as their grooms; their bags of hairy fabric filled with provender and finely chopped straw; their haversacks filled with *kyllestis*-bread; [every] single ass in the charge of two men; their chariots being of *brry*-wood, filled with all manner of weapons of warfare; eighty arrows in the quiver, the *ḥmyt*, the lance, the *ḥrp*-sword, the sword, the *ḳwt*, the *sk-ḥm*, the whip of *tjaga*-wood provided with lashes, the chariot club, the staff of the watch, the javelin of Khatti and the rein-looser, their facings of copper of sixfold alloy engraved with burin carving [. . .] Their cuirasses are laid beside them, the bows [. . .] to (?) their strings. Their wood has been tested in drawing; their leather *mšy* are of neat webbing(?); the pole is of *tjaga*-wood, [. . .], trimmed, leather-fitted, finished off, oiled and polished. (Caminos 1954, p. 431)

A classic example of this interest in organization can be found in a famous literary text, the Satirical Letter, a polemical letter written by an army scribe called Hori in response to a colleague, Amenemope, who had written to him in a way he considered offensive. Hori's letter, full of sarcastic courtesy, replies to his rival by asking him a series of questions designed to test his professional maturity. The questions deal with geography, accounting, assessing labor needs, and dividing rations. They are presented by someone who is not only lettered but also an official and, above all—as he makes quite clear—a soldier, because he goes on horseback, typical of his military status. A passage from the letter provides us with an exceptional example of what these officers did:

O acute, intuitive scribe [. . .] flame in the darkness before the army, to which you give light! You are sent on expedition into Phoenicia [(?) . . .] The troops that are before you number 1,900: 520 Shardan, 1,600 Qehaq (Libyan), 100 Meshwesh (Libyan), 880 Nubians, 5,000 in all, not counting their officials. A present is brought before you of bread, livestock, wine. The number of men is too great for you, and the victuals are insufficient for them [. . .] The soldiers are numerous and the victuals few [. . .] The army is prepared and ready. Register them quickly, each according to his troop. The Bedouin are watching furtively; "What a cunning scribe!" (in Syriac in the text) they say. Midday has arrived and the camp is hot. They say: "It is time to go. Do not anger the troop's officer! We have a long march ahead of us." But, let us say it, why is there no bread at all? Our night quarters are far away. Good lord, what does it mean to ill-treat us in this way? Yet you are an intelligent scribe. (Anastasi Papyrus I)

The preeminence given to organization and administration emerges from many other documents. Models of official letters given to school students during the Ramesside Period, apparently an anthology of authentic texts, speak of mistaken enlistments that had to be revised (young men destined for the priesthood who were taken away as soldiers; veterans included in lists of peasants, Bologna Papyrus 1094), peremptory invitations to respect the reciprocal duties of various officers (Anastasi Papyrus V, v.25.2 ff.), and frontier-post registers (Anastasi Papyrus III, v.6.1) of messengers carrying orders from Egypt to scattered garrisons in countries under surveillance. These garrisons were composed of small groups of soldiers under the command of an Egyptian officer. They were formally at the disposal of local princes in order to back up their authority, as long as this coincided with loyalty to Egypt. Chariot officers were also frequently given civilian duties, such as being sent as ambassadors to Syria, the country in which they had fought and with which they were thus familiar.

A clear sign of this administrative bent is the fact that the person who came immediately below the rank of "general" in the military hierarchy was the "scribe of recruits" (or "of the army"). He was responsible for maintaining the lists of sons of professional soldiers who took their fathers' places and of villages that had to provide army personnel as auxiliaries of various types, "according to their numbers" (*Urkunden* IV, 1007). Other constantly updated lists recorded slaves of war assigned to various administrative sections, from which they could be requested.

We know about a number of these scribes of recruits, a rank that included some remarkable characters. One was Amenophis, the son of Hapu, a scribe of recruits during the reign of Amenophis III. The fact that the army could be employed in civil works requiring manual labor as well as in military operations meant that scribes of recruits were linked to building activity at all levels. We find soldiers working, for example, in quarries or erecting obelisks, as Hori's polemical letter, mentioned above, describes. Thus, Amenophis was also "overseer of all the works of the king" and "overseer at the mountain of quartzite (Gebel Ahmar, near Cairo)." He was thus responsible for the impressive constructions that marked the reign of his ruler (who, among other things, built the temple of Luxor, the colossi of Memnon—out of quartzite—and the entire royal city of Malqata). Amenophis was so appreciated by the king that he was granted the right to build a funerary temple among the royal temples on the west bank at Thebes, and was soon deified. His cult, under the Greek name of Amenothes Paapis, survived through the Roman Period.

Toward the end of the Eighteenth Dynasty, another "scribe of the army" had an even more varied and brilliant career. Haremhab occupied so many important positions that he was able to take over the function of ruler when the dynastic line of succession came to an end.

Even when they failed to reach such exceptional levels, it was common for officers to take up positions of civilian command within the structure of the Egyptian state during periods of leave. Parenen, "overseer of the royal stable," was "scribe of the House of Life of the Two Lands" and was in charge of organizing the festivals of the god Osiris (Wien 906.51). Haremhab, who had been an officer under Tuthmosis III and Amenophis II, became "overseer of all the priests of Upper and Lower Egypt" during the reign of the latter's son, Tuthmosis IV. Under the same king, Mai became "prince and chief of the prophets of the Tenth Nome of Upper Egypt," "companion of His Majesty Tuthmosis IV in all foreign lands from Nubia to Syria [Naharin]," and "chief of the stable." Amenophis became high priest of Onuris at Tine during the same king's reign. Generals were often entrusted with the administration of land belonging to the king, the women of the royal house, or gifts offered to royal funerary temples. Scribes of recruits became "general administrators" (*mr-pr wr*). The autobiography of King Haremhab, on his statue at Turin, explicitly refers to the fact that officers replaced traditional priests after the Atenist heresy.

There was a constant process of osmosis, which is often documented in individual title strings. We can assume that the process was even more frequent than it now appears, since in many cases high-ranking officials omitted from their lists of titles previous military positions and included only their civilian posts. As a result, we only know by accident that many of these officials had also been soldiers. This indicates fairly explicitly that, in Egypt, the administration had more prestige than the army, even when the empire was at its height.

Nonetheless, the army must be recognized not only for having extended the boundaries of Egypt but for having permitted the creation of an urban middle class. Although, in many cases, an analysis of rhetorical inscriptions has shown that important officials were related to the Pharaoh by a "milk brotherhood," other genealogies reveal that some people in high office had parents with only modest titles or with none at all. The careers of these latter officials were connected to their wartime accomplishments or, at least, their participation in military campaigns conducted under the eye of the king, who promoted them in order to provide the traditional ruling class with tried and tested new blood. This process can be seen throughout the Eighteenth Dynasty. It came to an almost symbolic climax at the end of the dynasty with the three generals who occupied the throne: Haremhab, Ramesses I, and Sethos (Seti) I. The movement from army to administration had become quite normal by this point. It allowed the Pharaoh to sidestep the principle of heredity when choosing his officials.

The Ramesside Period now appears to be the time during the New Kingdom when the middle class matured; the sociocultural attitudes of officials and soldiers were revealed in all their variety. Scribes and soldiers had parallel careers and opportunities that culminated in a single social context. The tensions that this inevitably created, however, can be seen from certain details. These found literary expression in a series of texts that scribes delighted in recording in their exercise and study books. They update an old theme in scribal culture: the absolute superiority of the man who wields a pen. This is the subject of the Satire of the Trades, composed at the end of the feudal period, when the administration was reformed to provide a united power center at the disposal of the king. With impious verve, the text describes all the members of Egyptian society during the fatigue of their daily labor. It is worth noting, however, that the figure of the soldier is missing from the list, despite being an essential element in society both during the feudal period and later.

The exemplary text of the Satire was used in schools throughout the Ramesside Period. Its lack of references to soldiers was amply compensated by a series of other, similar, often parallel texts, which took perverse delight in underlining the difficulties, risks, and frustrations of military life. The following text is typical:

Come, let me describe to you the ills of the soldier, since his superiors are many: the general, the chief of archers, the *seket*-officer who is before them, the standard-bearer, the lieutenant, the [military] scribe, the commander of fifty men, the garrison chief. They come and go from the halls of the palace of the king and say: "Let them work."

He is woken in the early hours of the morning. They attach themselves to his ribs as to an ass, and he works from dawn to sunset, in the darkness of the night. He is hungry; his body is tormented; he is dead while still alive. He receives his ration of corn when he is released from his duties, but when it is ground it is no longer good.

He is recalled into Syria before he has rested. There are neither clothes nor sandals. The arms of war have been gathered together in the fortress of Tjalu.

His hill marches are long, he drinks water once every three days, and it is fetid and tastes of salt. His body is destroyed by dysentery. The enemy comes and surrounds him with arrows; life is far from him. They say: "Come on, brave soldier, win yourself a glorious name!" But he no longer knows who he is. His body is weak and his knee contemptible before [the enemy]. Victory takes place. The booty destined for Egypt is assigned to His Majesty. The foreign woman [prisoner] is taken by a fainting fit during the march and placed on the shoulders of the soldier. His shoulder bag is abandoned and taken by others, because he is loaded down by the prisoner. His wife and children are in their village. But he dies before reaching them.

If he survives, he is destroyed by marching. Whether in quarters or in the country, he is discontent. If he runs and goes away with the deserters, all his people are imprisoned.

When he dies at the edge of the desert, there is no one to perpetuate his name. For him both life and death are [equally] painful. When the hanging sack is brought to him, he no longer knows his place of rest.

Be a scribe, so that you may be saved from being a soldier, so

that you may be called and one says "Here I am!" so that you may
be freed from torment. Everyone tries to raise him: take note of
this.

The literary taste for exaggeration and the grotesque is evident.
The contempt displayed toward qualities that were officially prized
(the glory of courage, already praised, as we have seen, during the
Eighteenth Dynasty) is a feature of the genre. This can be seen in
the case of the female prisoner who, instead of being a desirable spoil
of war (as in the oldest military representation, dating back to the
Memphite Period, at Deshasha, mentioned above), becomes a la-
mentable and damaging encumbrance.

The immediacy of this picture becomes evident when we recall
the passage quoted above from the Satirical Letter of Hori, which
describes the distribution of rations with the Bedouin lurking in the
background. The context is that of one officer talking to another, but
the lively and demystifying tone is that of a writer who observes the
situation from the safety of his office.

Throughout the period, however, these repeated warnings to
young men not to be enticed by the fascination of horses and arms
were accompanied by an extremely effective military propaganda.
Visible to everyone, detailed images on the outside walls and fore-
courts of temples depicted each stage of the military exploits of the
king, who was represented, not as the solitary ritual slaughterer of
prisoners before his titular god, but as the leader of his troops. These
representations were copied at different times and in different
places. The battle of Kadesh, fought by Ramesses II, can be seen in
a variety of identical examples, all deriving from the same cartoon
and thus official. They show the battle's dramatic moments, the deployment of soldiers, the fallen, and the geographical features of the
battlefield. Similar images celebrate the Syrian exploits of Sethos I
in the Karnak reliefs and those of Ramesses III against the Peoples
of the Sea in his funerary temple at Madinet Habu. Victory, or that
which was accepted as such, is not simply taken for granted in these
reliefs. It is shown in detail, with inessential but telling features,
such as enemy shepherds frantically driving their beasts away from
the battlefield. These images are clearly more concerned with narrative than with history. The actual facts of the war are used to excite
the imagination. It was during this period, in fact, that military
events stopped being described in the matter-of-fact language used

by the Annals of Tuthmosis. Many different accounts of the battle of Kadesh exist, at various levels of literariness, from the bulletin to the poem. These became official school texts (alongside antimilitaristic texts!). Beyond officialdom, as part of the literature of entertainment that flourished during this period, historical figures from the past appeared in military garb. There was, obviously, General Sisene, with whom Pharaoh Pepi II had an ambiguous relationship. There was also Tuthmosis III, the celebrated hero of exploits in the distant past, and his general, Djehuty (of whom we possess monuments and proof of his brilliant military career). Texts describe his occupation of the city of Jaffa, where he surreptitiously introduced Egyptian troops, using a strategy that would later be adopted by Ali Baba. During this period, military exploits stimulated the Egyptian imagination.

In the account of the dramatic details of Merenptah's Libyan wars and in the representations of Ramesses III's battles against the Peoples of the Sea, new protagonists entered the history of the eastern Mediterranean and other parts of the ancient world. These peoples, threatening and disturbing, roamed the area in search of new lands. They destroyed the equilibrium of a number of different empires within the region, replacing them with new, more varied political situations.

In Egypt, these people are depicted as soldiers dressed in their typical ethnic costumes. The great decisive battles that had warded off invasions by these foreign peoples had also provided Egypt with very large numbers of prisoners, whose fate is described in a text written during the reign of Ramesses III: branded like beasts, they were held in forts, where their language was "overturned" and they were forced to adopt Egyptian ways. Their experience and military skills were exploited by turning them into soldiers. Thus, for a certain period, ethnic groups such as the Shardan and the Meshwesh were not only soldiers in the service of Egypt, as it extended and defended its borders, but also aggressive enemies, to be faced with decisiveness.

According to Egyptian custom, these foreign soldiers were kept together in special camps, similar to the fate of colonial contingents of European armies in recent times. Their ethnic character was thus maintained. According to regulations, however, these units were commanded by Egyptians (just as officers from the colonizing country were always in command of colonial troops). There were some exceptions to this: units known as "hunters," who patrolled the desert and were composed of nomad tribesmen who knew the area well, were led by members of their own ethnic group.

What was an exception during the Ramesside Period became the rule during the period that followed. When prisoners were replaced in the Egyptian army by imported Libyan mercenaries, the latter were led by their own princes. They did not adopt Egyptian names, as foreigners who had acquired importance in the past had done. They wore an ostrich feather, the characteristic decoration of their people, proudly on their heads. Distributed throughout the country in garrisons reserved for them, their generals assumed more power as the monarchy and the administration became increasingly uncertain. They became princes and official priests of the local gods, effectively taking over the king's prerogatives. Finally, one of their number, Sheshonq I, ascended the throne, initiating what is known as the "Libyan" dynasty. There is an obvious parallel with the Hyksos appropriation of the Egyptian throne. If the Hyksos culture was absorbed by Egyptian civilization, this process was even easier for the Libyans, who had already assimilated much of Egyptian culture. The Libyan Period was, in effect, marked by the refinement of a culture that exploited the experiences of the Ramesside Period. However, its originally military structure, deriving from the rise of a group of garrison chiefs of the same rank, provided Egypt with a new political model. The "kings" multiplied, with single cities becoming centers of power. The political homogeneity that had been the main feature and strength of the Pharaonic state, rarely threatened and always regarded as an ideal, was now shattered.

The artistic products of this period reveal a wealthy and cultured country, and there is certainly no sign of decadence. On the contrary, in an epoch that saw the imperialist ideology of the entire eastern Mediterranean in crisis after the passing of the Peoples of the Sea, the peaceful crumbling of Egypt into an articulated system of city-states was a change reflecting the spirit of the times, since the preceding system had clearly begun to lag behind the period when compared with the world around it. The process, however, was interrupted by the invasion of Ethiopians from the south, who reunited the Nile Valley from the confluence of the two Niles to the sea and who possessed a very different ideology. The Ethiopian kings were then defeated by the Assyrians, whose victory reduced Egypt to a province of a foreign power for the first time.

This does not mean that the history of Egypt came to an end.

The sudden end of Assyrian domination left the field open to Libyan dynasties and to those twelve "kings" who amused Herodotus. He saw them as a perverse multiplication of a monarchic ideal that he was unable to share. The re-created "Libyan" political world, however, was soon to succumb to the decisiveness and ambition of one of those princes, Psamtik of Sais.

Once again, soldiers were behind a shift in Egyptian history. Returning to the earlier practice, Psamtik called foreign soldiers to serve in Egypt. This time they were Carians from Asia Minor and thus were predominantly Greeks. With their help he strengthened his position as the only king, handing down to his successors a power base that enabled the star of Egypt to shine once more. We encounter these soldiers in the oldest Ionian inscription known to us, on the foot of one of the colossi at Abu Simbel. They left their signatures and named the king they were serving and the commander (an Egyptian) of their contingent of foreign soldiers. We also know where they were stationed in the Delta: at Daphnae, now Tell Dafanna. These Greeks appear to have succeeded the Nubians of Gebelein and the Hyksos of Tell Dab'a. An Egyptian-made statue of one of these Greeks has recently been found. It had been taken back to the man's city in Asia Minor. The Greek inscription records the honors he received in Egypt, both decorations (the Gold of Valor of Egyptian soldiers of the New Kingdom) and payment (a "city," whatever the value of that might have been).

Along with the many similarities with preceding times, however, there are some basic differences. The first has to do with information. Up to this point, our sources have always been Egyptian. They are now Greek, from Herodotus and Thucydides to Plutarch, with all the difference in viewpoint, and richness of detail, that this entails.

There is, however, another, more important difference. Ancient Egyptian soldiers, whether Egyptian or foreign, were entitled to the use of land, a practice that became known as the "cleruchy" during the Ptolemaic Period. Egypt thus became their country. It was in their interests to defend its borders, and it was the Egyptian political system that ensured their position. Greek mercenaries, however, wanted, not land, but money. It was for them that an Egyptian ruler finally made an exception and minted coins. The need to acquire money was thus created. As a result, it became necessary to structure trade with this end in view. A Greek trading city, Naucratis, grew up in the Delta, with its own constitution and laws, within a framework of obligations enforced by Egypt.

As soon as Greek mercenaries were paid off, they had no further links with the land they had served. They had fought for a wealth that would finally be taken out of Egypt, whereas the produce of the cleruchy remained and was subject to taxation. Finally, Greek mercenaries moved easily from one side to the other. The general who organized the defense of the isthmus against the Persian threat was the same man who showed the invading army the way through at the moment of conflict. There had also been tension on earlier occasions between Egyptian and foreign soldiers, which had led to the replacement of King Apries by Amasis.

The Persian conquest of Egypt was the beginning of a completely new era. During some periods, the country was a satrapy ruled by Persian interests. At other times, it was in rebellion against the foreign yoke, led by Egyptian kings who were sometimes short-lived but sometimes (as in the case of the two Nectanebos) able to rebuild, and revitalize, a great tradition. Military presence was an essential element in political and social life during this period as well. Whether as occupying troops or as supporters in the struggle for independence, soldiers were often at the center of events. The Persian government established its own garrisons in the traditional forts on the frontier. The most famous was the camp at Elephantine, on the southern border with Nubia. Aramaic papyri found there document the life of a Hebraic military colony, a rare and vivid picture of a world that in general we know only through the filter of biblical tradition. As Persian subjects, the Egyptians crossed their own borders, sending troops to fight in the exploits of the Persian "Great King." Some Egyptians made a career for themselves this way. A certain Glos was admiral of the fleet that defeated Evagoras of Cyprus in 381 B.C.

The situation was more complex, however, when Egypt became independent and a potential enemy of Persia. Hostility to Persia united Egyptian and Greek political interests. Although Greek soldiers had already fought alongside Egyptians during the Saite Period, Greek presence now took on an entirely new character. It adopted the form of official aid, with troops led by such notable figures as Agesilaus (a king of Sparta) and the Athenian Cabrias. Although they were under the formal control of Egyptian leaders, in practice these troops followed the orders that came from their native cities as policies toward Persia changed. Greek generals dictated their terms to local leaders, whose survival often depended on their presence and support, and interfered in Egypt's domestic affairs. It was Cabrias who obliged the monarchy to use temple treasuries to finance defense, something that predictably led to internal hostility. But it was also Cabrias who returned home on Athenian orders, leaving a country in which he had exercised an authority practically equal to that of a *sirdar* (the term used to designate the British resident who "advised" the Egyptian monarchy when Egypt was a British colony). The Greek conquest and the Ptolemaic Period, followed by Egypt's annexation to the Roman Empire, led to Egyptian soldiers becoming essential elements in the country's social life once again. The Ptolemaic cleruchy adopted the old model of stationing soldiers in agricultural colonies. The presence of Egyptian soldiers at the battle of Raphia (Rafa) was the first sign of a new vigor among the native element of Ptolemaic Egypt. During the Roman Period, service in the Imperial army assumed special importance when veterans returned to their home cities in Egypt, forming a link with the rest of the Roman world. But these issues need to be examined in another framework, on the basis of very different documentation. This is not the place to deal with them.

The traits with which we have identified, rapidly and, at times, maybe elliptically, the social and cultural significance of soldiers in Egypt's history should have shown that although they were among the least prominent figures of Egyptian civilization, they were nonetheless an essential component. At times, the soldier was at the center of critical moments in the country's history. It is typical, however, of Egyptian civilization that it should have concealed the importance of weapons (and their possession) behind ideals of peace and peaceful coexistence, and that—while knowing how to celebrate courage and valor—it should have continued to insist on the greater importance of wisdom and justice.

Bibliography

Anthes, R. "Eine Polizeistreife des Mittleren Reiches in die westliche Oase." *Zeitschrift für ägyptische Sprache und Altertumskunde* 65 (1930): 108–14.

Caminos, R. A. *Late-Egyptian Miscellanies.* Brown Egyptological Studies 1. London, 1954.

Christophe, L. A. "L'organisation de l'armée égyptienne à l'époque ramesside." *Revue du Caire* 39, no. 207 (1957): 387–405.

Curto, S. "Krieg." In *Lexikon der Ägyptologie,* vol. 3, cols. 745–86.

Erman, A. "Zwei Rekrutenaushebungen in Abydos aus dem Mittleren Reich: A. Ein Denkstein in Berlin." *Zeitschrift für ägyptische Sprache und Altertumskunde* 38 (1900): 42–43.

Faulkner, R. O. "The Battle of Megiddo." *Journal of Egyptian Archaeology* 28 (1942): 2–15.

———. "Egyptian Military Organization." *Journal of Egyptian Archaeology* 39 (1953): 32–47.

Griffith, F. L. *The Inscriptions of Siût and Dêr Rîfeh.* London, 1889.

Helck, W. *Der Einfluss der Militärführer in der 18. ägyptischen Dynastie.* Leipzig, 1939. Reprint, Hildesheim, 1964.

Kadry, A. *Officers and Officials in the New Kingdom.* Budapest, 1982.

Kruchten, J. M. *Le décret d'Horemheb.* Brussels, 1981.

Kuentz, C. *La bataille de Qadesh.* Cairo, 1928.

Lichtheim, M. *Ancient Egyptian Literature.* Vol. 1, *The Old and Middle Kingdoms.* Berkeley and Los Angeles, 1973.

———. *Ancient Egyptian Literature.* Vol. 2, *The New Kingdom.* Berkeley and Los Angeles, 1976.

Pritchard, J. B. *Ancient Near Eastern Texts Relating to the Old Testament.* 3d ed. with suppl. Princeton, 1969.

Säve-Söderbergh, T. *The Navy of the 18th Dynasty.* Uppsala, 1946.

Schulman, R. A. *Military Rank, Title and Organization in the Egyptian Middle Kingdom.* Berlin, 1964.

Sethe, K. *Urkunden der 18. Dynastie, historische-biographische Urkunden.* 4 vols. Leipzig, 1906–9.

Simpson, W. K., ed. *The Literature of Ancient Egypt: An Anthology of Stories, Instructions, and Poetry.* 2d ed. New Haven, 1973.

Stadelmann, R. *Die Abwehr der Seevölker unter Ramesses III.* Freiburg-Munich, 1966.

Wolf, W. *Die Bewaffnung des altägyptischen Heeres.* Leipzig, 1946.

7. SLAVES

Antonio Loprieno

Egyptologists inevitably feel a certain embarrassment when they are called on to discuss the figure of the slave in ancient Egypt, since the mere hypothesis that a classical form of slavery existed in the Nile Valley continues to be a subject of debate among social and economic historians. It is true that since biblical times received opinion in the West has imagined Egypt as a *bet abadim* (Hebrew, "house of slavery"), a civilization whose wealth was founded on the exploitation of forced labor. Nonetheless, Egyptologists cannot regard as merely accidental the absence of a legal codification of the status of "slave" in a society like that of Pharaonic Egypt, in which written documentation pervades the entire communicative sphere of individual and state alike. The abundance of written documents—epigraphic and on papyrus, literary and administrative, secular and religious—handed down by Egyptian culture is in marked contrast to the scarcity of information concerning the anthropological status (in the largest sense of the term) of this figure. As we shall see, documents show that many social groups described in royal decrees and administrative texts were subject to restrictions on their individual freedom. It is far more difficult to know to which of these groups—referred to at different times as *mrj.t*, "dependents," *d̠.t*, "personnel," *hsb.w*, "forced laborers," *bꜣk.w*, "workers," *ḥm.w*, "servants," *ḥm.w-nzw*, "royal servants," *sqr.w-ꜥnḫ*, "prisoners of war," *ꜥꜣmw.w*, "Asiatics," etc.—the term "slave" should be applied. Our sources need to be examined very carefully.

The problem facing us is, in part, one of pure terminology and could thus, at least potentially, be disregarded. To interpret the social structures or culture of one civilization by means of the paradigms of reference (including linguistic ones) of another is always, from a hermeneutic viewpoint, a spurious activity. It is inevitable, however, that scholars operate in the light of their historical experience when involved in intercultural analysis. Can one speak of the "city" in Pharaonic Egypt? Clearly, one can, since the opposition between *n'.tj*, "citizen" (or Egyptian), and *'ʒmw*, "Bedouin" (or Asiatic), is a frequent cultural topos in classical Egyptian literature. The famous passage from the *Prophecy of Neferti* is typical:

> A strange bird will be born in the marshes of the Delta, and a nest shall be made for it on account of the neighbors, for men have caused it to approach through want. Perished are those erstwhile good things, the fish ponds of those who carry slit fish, teeming with fish and fowl. All good things have passed away, the land being cast away through trouble by means of that food of the Asiatics who pervade the land. Enemies have come into being in the east; Asiatics have come down into Egypt. (Ll. 29–35; trans. R. O. Faulkner, in Simpson 1973, p. 235)

It would be extremely difficult, however, to discover an Athenian-style agora, even at Memphis or Thebes. Did Egyptian philosophy exist? Certainly, if we consider the frequency of the motif of "intellectual research" (*ḥḥj nj jb*) in the Middle Kingdom literary genre of "lamentations." Khakheperreseneb entitled his literary composition "The gathering together of sayings, the culling of phrases, the search for words by an inquisitive mind, which the *wab*-priest of Heliopolis, Seni's son, Khakheperreseneb, who is called Ankhu, wrote." But it is clearly impossible to discover in Egypt a metalinguistic analysis of the *sophia*, philosophy, in the sense intended by the Greeks. Many other examples of this problem could be found.

But there is a more important issue, which is central to our discussion. How can the fabric of Egyptian society be analyzed from within, and which historical developments can be identified? Scholars and modern readers often tend to treat Egyptian culture as though it were static, with no appreciable changes throughout the three thousand years of Pharaonic history. If we look at slavery, however, we shall see that the administrative texts of ancient Egypt make it possible to trace clear developments in the concept and practice of slavery, and to obtain an overall picture that converges with what literary sources reveal about the history of ideas in Pharaonic society. The dichotomy between "administrative texts" and "literary sources" should come as no surprise. More than any other ancient Eastern civilization, Egypt developed a series of formal elements that distinguish specifically literary discourse from documents serving a pragmatic purpose. Rigidly applied metrical, prosodic, and stylistic conventions and, above all, a different way of presenting the state and psychology of individuals or social groups were specific to literary contexts in the strict sense, principally in the two most representative genres: the "instructions" and the "tale." These are concerned with the "beautiful" (*nfr*) rather than with the "truth" (*mȝ'*) of religious texts or with the "royal" nature of administrative texts. This is why Egyptian documents need to be examined in the light of different interpretive filters, linked to the nature of the sources in question. The gods, kings, and foreigners documented in pragmatic texts do not always correspond to their fictional literary counterparts. We only have to think of the ironic presentation of the myth of Osiris in the Ramesside tale of the Contendings of Horus and Seth for the Inheritance of Osiris; or of the contrast between the divine state of the Pharaoh in religious texts and the flippant treatment of the ambiguous relationship between King Neferkare (Pepi II of the Sixth Dynasty) and Sasenet (Sisene), one of his generals, that became the motif of the fragmentary tale named after its protagonists; or, finally, of the wisdom of the Bedouin prince of Retenu and the Mitanni prince of Naharin, whose treatment of the Egyptian fugitives (respectively, Sinuhe and the Predestined Prince) was far removed from the barbarity generally associated with the cultural stereotype of the Asiatic. It is symptomatic of this that the portrayals of "Egyptian men" in literary texts, rather than in religious documents, were often those accepted by Western tradition, from Herodotus on. We only have to recall Herodotus's description of the wickedness of Cheops (2.124 ff.), undoubtedly stimulated by the surprise he felt as a Greek when confronted by the architectural majesty of the pyramids. He would inevitably have realized that they were the product of a powerful centralized authority. But such portrayals were also based on an indigenous literary tradition that portrayed Cheops as the prototype of the wicked king, as we can see from the Westcar Papyri, which predate Herodotus's narrative by a thousand years. We might also cite his descriptions of Pheros (2.111), the "Pharaoh" par excellence (probably Ramesses II), and Rhampsinitus (2.121 ff.) (probably Ramesses III), the protagonists of folklore motifs later taken up by other Near Eastern literary traditions.

The Slave and Textual Sources

A particular feature of the slave, when compared to other Egyptian figures, already begins to emerge. The existence of slaves is already mentioned in the oldest purely literary texts in Egyptian civilization, such as the Middle Kingdom Lamentations of Ipuwer. In these texts, the cultural evolution of society, as it passed from the Memphite state to the feudal age, appears to stagnate ideologically into a series of oppositions between golden past (the Old Kingdom) and tragic present (the First Intermediate Period): "Now even slave women (*hm.wt*) speak without restraint, / and when their mistress gives an order, the servants (*b3k.w*) show their impatience" (Admonitions of an Egyptian Sage 4.3).

The human condition of this figure (whether *hm* or *b3k*) is never, however, *narrated* at a literary level. A classic of Middle Kingdom literature, the Satire of the Trades (also known as the Instruction of Khety, after the name of the narrator), describes the advantages of the scribal profession over all others. In Egypt more than elsewhere, professions tended to correspond to specific social groups, since individuals were identified with the work they did. During the Middle Kingdom, the profession of the scribe became the vehicle for the values of the ruling classes, who were torn between fidelity to state institutions, represented by the king, and the affirmation of individualism, made possible by professional success. To the scribe, an individual's dependence on his own labor appeared to be more a measure of "servitude" than of "service."

This text is a classic of Middle Egyptian literature, and its antitheses regarding the way in which paid labor is perceived became paradigmatic as Egyptian culture developed. Khety was remembered six centuries later as one of the most important great learned scribes of the past in one of the most celebrated school texts of the Ramesside Period (thirteenth century B.C.):

Is there any here like Hardjedef? Is there another like Iyemhotep?
There have been none among our kindred like Neferti and Khety.
I recall to you the names of Ptahemdjehuty and Khakheperre-

sonbe. Is there another like Ptahhotep or Kaires? (Chester Beatty
Papyrus IV, 3.5)

The absence of any explicit reference to the condition of slavery in
the Satire of the Trades derives, in my opinion, from the fact that
slavery was never regarded by Egyptian culture as a clearly defined
human condition, with the status of an autonomous social group. On
the contrary, in Egypt, there existed a wide range of levels of subjection within the world of work. The philological proof of this is provided by the Satire of the Trades. The literary expression of various
forms of forced labor can be found in a number of instances in the
text: the fact of being "drawn to work" ($nhm.w \ hr \ b3k = f$) or "obliged
to work in the fields" ($mnj.tj$); the impossibility of a carpenter's family benefiting from his labors ($nn \ pnq \ n \ hrd.w = f$); a punishment of
fifty lashes received by a weaver for a day's "absenteeism" ($hwj.tw =$
$f \ m \ ssm \ 50$); and, possibly, the submission of a gardener to a yoke
($k3r.y \ hr \ jnj.t \ m3wd$). That these are not cases of actual slavery, however, is demonstrated by the fact that the term generally translated
as "slave" (hm) is used to describe two figures who appear during the
same epoch in another literary text, the Tales contained in the Westcar Papyrus, dated to the end of the Middle Kingdom:

> Boats were prepared for the king's son, Hardedef, and he sailed
> south to Ded-Snefru (place-name), the vindicated. After these
> boats were moored at the riverbank, he went by land. He sat in a
> carrying chair of ebony, its poles made of *sesnedjem*-wood and
> sheathed in gold leaf. When he reached Dedi, the carrying chair
> was put down, and he proceeded to address him (Dedi). It was
> lying down on a mat at the threshold of his house that he found
> him, a servant (slave) at his head massaging him and another wip-
> ing his feet. (Ll. 7.9–16; Simpson 1973, pp. 22–23)

It was not until the New Kingdom that the slave became part,
albeit indirectly, of the range of human types presented by the wisdom texts. In his Instruction, the first edition of which is dated to
the second part of the Eighteenth Dynasty, Ani advised: "Do not
take another person's slave (hm) if he has a bad reputation" (V.15).
Slavery had thus become an integral part of Egyptian ideology, and
it is well known that, in Pharaonic culture, ideological influences
played an extremely significant role both in guaranteeing social co-
hesion (e.g., the concept of *maat*, the basis of religious and political

life in Pharaonic society) and in affirming the individual (as can be seen in the rigid instructions provided by the wisdom texts for ensuring the survival of the *ka*, the part of the individual's soul that remained among the living to become the object of a funerary cult). As Georges Posener first noticed, throughout the long history of Egyptian culture, ideology was transmitted primarily by means of literature.

There remain, however, interpretive problems created, on the one hand, by indirect mention of slavery from the Middle Kingdom on, and, on the other, by the total lack of any ideological presentation of slavery. In order to resolve these problems, and to understand the anthropological role of slavery in Egypt, we need to leave literary material to one side and turn to historical and administrative texts. So-called historical Egyptian documents (autobiographies, decrees, annals, etc.) must always be read, however, by taking into account the difficulties of distinguishing between ideological "truth" (*mʒ'.t*) and the underlying historical "reality." Furthermore, before making use of administrative documents, which are fundamental if we are to reconstruct the day-to-day life of ancient Egypt, we need to consider two points. First, the quantity and quality of the documentation vary considerably from one archeological period and area to another. There is a limited amount of material for the Old Kingdom: a few royal decrees and the single archive of Abusir. The Middle Kingdom has provided us with more documents: the abundant archives containing the correspondence of Heqanakhte and the papyri of El-Lahun, as well as important administrative texts, such as the Brooklyn Papyrus. Even more material has survived from the New Kingdom, above all in the area of Deir al-Medina, the city that housed the workers of the Theban necropolis. A substantial number of texts, although with less to say about the problem of slavery, has also reached us from the entire Late Period. Second, the documentation is distinctly "empirical." In Egyptian literature, even individual figures fulfill a paradigmatic function (the authors of wisdom texts always have pseudonyms; Sinuhe is the model of the Middle Kingdom official torn between loyalty to the king and self-affirmation, Wenamun symbolizes Egyptian disappointment over the loss of centralized power, etc.). In the administrative texts, however, attention is focused exclusively on single episodes. Attempts to discover a legal code or economic decree, in the form such documents took during classical times, particularly in Rome, are doomed to failure. We shall therefore be obliged to base our comments on entirely inductive analysis, often generalizing from something suggested by a single document. We must rely on the fact that our knowledge of ancient Egypt, albeit fragmentary, is statistically fairly representative. A lack of written documentation regarding a certain aspect of Egyptian society probably corresponds to its absence—or relative irrelevance—in that society, whereas an abundance of documents generally reveals the considerable historical relevance of the phenomenon in question.

The Old Kingdom

To begin, let us briefly consider the structural features of Egyptian society at the onset of its documented history. In the so-called Decree of Dahshur (*Urkunden* I, 209–23), Pepi I of the Sixth Dynasty specifies the number of people and the amount of inalienable property destined for the "City of the Pyramids" of the Fourth Dynasty king Snofru and presents the ruling class of the Old Kingdom, composed of "queens," "nobles," and "officials" (*srjw.w*), in whose service "dependents" (*mrj.t*) work (210.14–17). During the Old Kingdom, therefore, the social opposition was seen as being between "officials" and "dependents"—an opposition that corresponds to the ideological distinction between "the nobility" (*pʿ.t*) and "the people" (*rhj.t*), and that was destined to survive in religious literature until the end of ancient Egyptian history. When the solar cult based at Heliopolis triumphed during the Fifth Dynasty, the "solar priesthood" (*ḥnmmw.t*) was added to these two categories. This ideal distribution of Egyptian society into three groups continued unchanged until the second century A.D., as is shown by the late Egyptian papyrus found at Oxyrhynchus, written in Egyptian using the Greek alphabet and with the addition of demotic signs: the "nobility," the "people," and the "priesthood," which constituted the three poles of Egyptian society in the Old Kingdom, still appear as, respectively, *pē*, *lhē*, and *ḥameu*.

None of these were closed social classes, however, in the way that Indian castes are. They were flexible divisions, within which individuals could improve their original status, as we can see from the autobiographical inscription of Henqu at Deir al-Gebrawi (Sixth Dynasty): "As for those who were dependent workers (*mrj.w*) in other centers at my service, their role became that of official (*srjw*)" (*Urkunden* I, 78.6–7). "Dependent" does not mean "slave." It refers to the mass of people, regularly employed in agricultural activities (the land being owned by the king or, in other words, the state) and, at times, recruited for compulsory service (*corvée*). These "dependents" were sometimes used as laborers in nonagricultural work. We only have to think of the work involved in building the pyramids of the Old Kingdom, the organization of which is mentioned, for example, in the first dated graffito at Wadi Hammamat:

> Mission carried out by the eldest son of the king, the treasurer of the god, the general of the expedition (*mš*, "army"), Djati, known as Kanofer, who had care of his men on the day of battle, who knew how to foresee the coming of the day of obligatory recruitment. I distinguished myself among the multitude and I carried out this task for Imhotep, with 1,000 men of the royal palace, 100 men of the necropolis, 1,200 pioneers, and 50 engineers. His Majesty ordered all these people to come from the Residence, and I organized this task in exchange for provisions of barley of all kinds, while His Majesty placed at my disposal 50 oxen and 200 goats for the daily victuals. (*Urkunden* I, 148.16–149.10)

At other times, they were employed as soldiers on long expeditions in Nubia and Libya, described by important dignitaries of the Sixth Dynasty, such as Uni and Herkhuf:

> When His Majesty took action against the Asiatic Sand-dwellers, His Majesty made an army of many tens of thousands from all of Upper Egypt: from Yebu in the south to Medenyt in the north; from Lower Egypt; from all of the Two-Sides-of-the-House and from Sedjer and Khen-sedjru; and from Irtjet-Nubians, Medja-Nubians, Yam-Nubians, Wawat-Nubians, Kaau-Nubians; and from Tjemeh-land. (*Urkunden* I, 101.9–102.8; Lichtheim 1973, p. 19)

"Decrees of exemption," such as the Decree of Dahshur mentioned above, also reveal that a relatively large proportion of the population was exempt from compulsory military service and corvée duty, being employed either in a royal funerary complex (the "City of the Pyramid") or in a private or religious foundation. In this case too, we are dealing with "service" rather than "servitude," since the same kind of social diversification that we have already seen also developed within this exempted group. People involved in such activities (a class that increasingly included also priests and officials, who derived economic benefits from being "exempt") bore the title of *ḥntj-š*, "those who govern the lake." Once again, "dependents" (*mrj.t*) were obliged to take orders from them:

> My Majesty has ordered the permanent exemption of these two cities of the Pyramid from carrying out any forced labor whatever for the Royal Palace, from performing any forced labor whatever for the Residence and from carrying out corvée duty according to that which has been requested. My Majesty has ordered the exemption of whatever *ḥntj-š* of these two cities of the Pyramid from all activities as messengers by river or by land, heading north or south. My Majesty has ordered that no field belonging to either of these two cities of the Pyramid should be plowed by the dependents of any queen, of any prince, of any noble or official, excepting the *ḥntj.w.š* of these two cities of the Pyramid. (*Urkunden* I, 210.7–17)

> I have ordered the exemption of this funerary chapel and of the personnel (*mrj.t*) and livestock, both large and small, that belongs to it. No claims can be made on them. As regards he who is sent on a mission to the south, My Majesty will permit none of the costs of the voyage to be charged to this funerary chapel, nor those of the people following a royal mission. My Majesty has ordered the exemption of this funerary chapel. My Majesty will not permit this funerary chapel to be taxed by any amount for the Residence. (214.2–17)

Already by the time of the Old Kingdom, the population of Egypt included foreign prisoners of war (*sqr.w-ꜥnḫ*, "bound for life"). From the epoch of Snofru, there is evidence of important military expeditions to Nubia to kidnap workers to be employed in the state economy. The ideological aspect of these raids is represented by the so-called execration texts, apotropaic spells inscribed on terra-cotta figurines of the foreign princes to be suppressed, as well as by the ritual of "killing the enemy" and the reliefs of prisoners of war with their arms tied behind their backs, which are found throughout Egyptian history on the walls of temples. From the Middle Kingdom on, prisoners captured during wartime and raids on occupied territo-

ries (initially in Nubia and later in Asia and Libya as well) formed
the largest group to whom the term "slave" was applied.

These wars and raids over the border were conducted by local
princes and nomarchs. Their rise to power led to the destruction of
the Memphite state, and their "provincial" attitudes led to the culture of the First Intermediate Period. The primary vehicles of expression for the values of this new ruling class were their autobiographical texts. These formed the literary genre from which both
wisdom texts and narratives would develop. They document a "mer-
itocratic" evolution that marked the emergence of an upper middle
class, destined to become the educated class of the Middle Kingdom
(the audience for a literature that achieved its formal perfection during that period). The new social fabric encouraged the creation of
forms of individual servitude (*Urkunden* I, 217.3–5): "I have also kept
for him (for the king) the accounts of his personal possessions for a
period of twenty years. I have never struck anyone until they fell
beneath my hand. I have never reduced anyone to servitude (*b3k*),"
announced the architect Nekhebu (Sixth Dynasty), indirectly revealing the existence of this type of coercion, despite using the term
b3k, which had previously defined a generic dependence on the
king, and thus applied to *all* Egyptians. One of the most frequent
rhetorical figures in the autobiographies of Memphite dignitaries was
that of being appreciated, praised, and loved by the king "more than
any other among his servants" (see ibid., 52.5, 81.6, 84.1, 99.4). The
previously quoted autobiographical text of Henqu at Deir al-
Gebrawi provides a visual image of this evolution in that the verb
b3k, "to reduce to servitude," is accompanied by a determinative (a
hieroglyphic symbol indicating the lexical class to which the term
belongs) of a seated man with a yoke around his neck: "I have never
reduced one of your daughters to servitude" (ibid., 77.4; see also Davies 1902, table 24.9).

This shift suggests that, at the end of the Old Kingdom, the beginnings of forced servitude were represented by state officials ille-
gally recruiting girls from among the common people. But an even
more decisive sign of social change is the contemporary emergence
of a term that Egyptologists normally translate as "slave": *ḥm*. In one
of its very rare first appearances, this term is accompanied by the
determinative of a seated man or woman holding a club, none other
than the phonogram (a hieroglyphic symbol standing for a sequence

of phonemes) of the word *ḥm:* "So much to each noble, to each official and to each dignitary that [...] will nominate one of my male slaves or female slaves, that [...] one of my funerary priests, who will conduct [...]" (Fischer 1958).

This determinative is similar to the one sometimes used during the Old Kingdom beside the words "servitude"(*bȝk*) and "dependence" (*mrj.t*) in connection with groups of laborers or soldiers, or beside the ethnic names of foreign peoples, such as "Nubians" or "Asiatics." This would imply that during the Old Kingdom, subjection had been a general feature of labor carried out by the mass of the agricultural population, in contrast to the world of the palace. However, the emergence, toward the end of the period, of a new social structure, the characteristics of which will be analyzed when we look at the Middle Kingdom, encouraged the birth of "slavery" as the most extreme form of forced labor. Even the Pyramid Texts, the first body of theological Egyptian texts to present the myths and rituals connected to the death of the king, indirectly document this social evolution. In Spell 346, the later versions of Merenre and Pepi II substitute the word "slaves" (*ḥm.w*) for "butchers" (*sšm.w*), which occurred in the earlier text on the pyramid of Teti (beginning of the Sixth Dynasty): "Spell to recite: The souls are in Buto, yes, the souls are in Buto; the souls will always be in Buto, the soul of the dead king is in Buto. How red is the flame, how alive is Khepri; be joyful, be joyful! Slaves, give me something to eat!" (Pyramid Texts, 561).

Approaching the problem in this way, we should also note that the term *ḥm* previously appeared only in compound names referring to religious (*ḥm-ntr*, "servant of god") or funerary (*ḥm-kȝ*, "adept of the funerary cult") functions; that it was first used with the new meaning (between the Fifth and Sixth Dynasties) in a royal context ("I have never said anything bad about anyone, neither the king nor his servants" in *Urkunden* I, 233.13–14); and that the first term in which it is possible to recognize the characteristics of the slave is the compound *ḥm-nzw*, "servant of the king" (see Davies 1901, table 16; Lepsius 1849, vol. 2, 107): "Sifting grain by the servants of the king." There is also the fact that after a brief appearance during the Sixth Dynasty, all mention of those people who were "bought" or "hired" (*jsw.w*) to perform the function of funerary priest disappears from documents. This indicates a society in which each individual's work was increasingly specialized. We can therefore establish that at the end of the Memphite Period, the figure of the "servant"—no longer an "adept in the service of" but a specific category, distinguished by its state of subjection—gradually began to emerge.

The Middle Kingdom

This evolution seems to have come to an end during the so-called First Intermediate Period (2213–1991 B.C.), a label used by Egyptologists to cover the period of Egyptian history between the Old and Middle Kingdoms. It was an epoch of profound religious change (with the rise of the moral dimension and theology of the *ba* in the Coffin Texts), cultural developments (with the growth of a genuine literature of dialectical confrontation, between individual conscience and social demands), political modifications (as power moved away from the rigid centralism of the Memphite Period to the provinces), and shifting economic patterns (as a series of insufficient inundations of the Nile led to a redistribution of wealth). The spectrum of social classes widened considerably during the period. For the first time, documents mention commercial transactions involving "workers" (*b3k.w*), with evidence that someone bought three "male workers" and seven "female workers" to add to those inherited from his father (Daressy 1915). Someone else even added twenty "heads" to his inheritance (Clère and Vandier 1948, n. 7). It is also important to note, however, that regardless of social differences, each Egyptian, even a servant, was now a "man" (*rmt*), an "individual" endowed with autonomous dignity, even when serving another person: "I bought oxen, I bought men, I bought fields, I bought copper" (Merer stela, MNK-XI-999, 7–8); or "The men at the service of my father, Mentuhotep, were born at home, the property of my father and mother. My men also come from the property of my father and mother, and apart from those who belong to me, there are others I have bought with my own means" (BM stela 1628, 13–15).

In the more complex social structure of the Middle Kingdom, there was a tendency to identify the individual with the work that he or she did. From this period on, the stelae erected by individuals normally bore the title of their craft or profession. The literary outcome of this trend is represented by the Satire of the Trades, discussed above. The average Egyptian was thus no longer a "dependent" (*mrj*), recruited from time to time for corvée duty, as he had been in the Old Kingdom. As an individual, aware of both his status and his abilities, he could now become a free commoner (*nds̲*) after serving for a period as a priest (*w'b*): "I did not let their water flood the fields of other people. I behaved like any efficient commoner, ensuring that my family had all the water they needed" (MNK-XI-999, 10–11).

There was another side to the coin, however, as we can see from the Satire of the Trades and from the following lines from the Instruction for Merikare. During the Middle Kingdom, anyone who was a simple field-worker or a craftsman dependent on a commoner was subject to forced labor or heavy taxation, whereas members of the tax-exempt ruling class were gathered together under the administrative definition of "officials":

> Its walls and its soldiers are many and the dependents (*mrj.w*) in it know how to take up arms, apart from the priests (*w'b*) of the camp: the region of Djed-esut totals ten thousand men consisting of free untaxed (*w'b nn bȝk.w = f*) commoners (*nds̲.w*), and officials (*srjw.w*) have been in it since the time of the Residence. Its boundary is established, its garrison is brave. (Merikare, 100–102)

That commoners were a typical part of Middle Kingdom society is also demonstrated by the way in which literary texts of the period anachronistically tended to project the figure into earlier epochs, when, as we have seen, it did not exist. We only have to think of the commoner Dedi of the stories in the Westcar Papyrus (see above), who appears in the narrative while being massaged by two slaves. There was a general social rise of the working class, not only of its free members but also of those who were dependent, or "bound" (according to the etymological meaning of the term *mrj*) to public service or as servants in private houses (when they were often called *d.t*, "service personnel," as in the papyri of El-Lahun, table 10.7 and 21). This was paralleled by an increasingly notable social division between the working class and a slave class, the latter being composed of "conscripts" (*ḥsb.w*), "deserters" (*tȝj.w*), and "royal servants" (*ḥm.w-nzw*), frequently mentioned in Middle Kingdom administrative texts. The first two terms refer to soldiers and field-workers conscripted to serve in the army or to labor in state building projects or agriculture. The most abundant documentation is offered by the papyri of El-Lahun and the Reisner Papyri, which mention conscripts being employed in quarries to excavate rock for the architectural achievements of the state (there are frequent "lists of the *ḥsb.w* who excavate stone for the pyramids": see the El-Lahun Papyri, tables 15.14 and 31.25). The administrative text of the Brooklyn Papyrus (see Hayes 1955, pp. 39–40, 76–77) presents them as obliged for a certain period to work on state land. The punishment for flight or desertion was forced labor for life (El-Lahun Papyri, table 6.57): "Order issued by the Great Prison in year 31, third month of the summer season, day 5, that he be condemned with all his family to labor for life on state land, according to the decision of the court."

The Brooklyn Papyrus also provides information about the group of royal servants, or *ḥm.w-nzw* (the feminine equivalent is *ḥm.wt*, "slave women"). Royal servants were Egyptians who shared the status of Asiatics reduced to slavery as a result of military campaigns or trade. Originally prisoners, they were entrusted to individuals as "property," almost always after trying to escape. Fugitives were more frequent in the Middle Kingdom than in previous epochs, despite stricter policing. They are described with particular vividness in the Story of Sinuhe. He emphasizes more than once, albeit indirectly, the frequency with which different categories of citizens were driven to flee from Egypt for a variety of reasons: social, economic, and political:

> One land gave me to another land. I set out for Byblos (near Beirut), and I returned to Kedem. I spent half a year there. It was Amusinenshi who brought me back: he was the chief of Upper Retenu. He said to me: You will be well with me, for you will hear the speech of Egypt. He said this for he knew my reputation. He had heard of my intelligence, for the people of Egypt who were there with him bore witness to me. And he said to me: Why have you come here? Has anything happened at the capital? I said to him: The King of Upper and Lower Egypt, Sehetepibre, has proceeded to the horizon, and no one knows what may happen because of this. I then spoke equivocally. When I returned from an expedition in the land of the Tjemehu, one announced that to me. My mind vacillated. My heart was not in my body, and it brought me to the ways of flight. But no one accused me, no one spat in my face. No reproach was heard, and my name was not heard in the mouth of the town crier. I do not know what brought me to this land. It was like the plan of a God. (Sinuhe B 29–43; Simpson 1973)

Although nominally belonging to the state, that is, to to the king (hence their name "royal servants"), recaptured fugitives, like Asiatic slaves, were assigned to the custody of a master, who could give them away, leave them to his children, or sell them (Brooklyn Papyrus, table 14.26–31; El-Lahun Papyri, table 12.6–11 and see table 13):

> Let my fifteen people (*tp.w*, "heads") and my prisoners of my property (*hnm.w = j*, "associated to me") be given to my wife Senebtisi, in addition to the sixty that I gave her the first time. Now, I make this gift to my wife, to be deposited in the Hall of the Speaker of the City of the South, as a contract that bears my seal and the seal of my wife Senebtisi.
>
> I am making this will for my wife, the woman of the eastern regions Sheftu-daughter-of-Sopdu called Teti, of everything given to me by my brother, the seal-bearer of the director of works, Ankhreni, with all the goods as they should be—of all that he gave me. She herself shall give it to any of her children that she shall bear me. I am giving her the four Asiatics whom my brother, the seal-bearer of the director of works, Ankhreni, gave to me. She herself shall give them to any of her children that she wishes.

Unlike royal servants or Asiatics, a worker (*b3k*) guilty of disservice was sent away from home but not sold. There is proof of this in the correspondence of Heqanakhte, a landowner during the first part of the Middle Kingdom (ca. 2000 B.C.) who, while traveling for work, continued to look after the management of his land by sending written instructions to his family: "Now have the housemaid (*b3k.t*) Senen turned out of my house—take great care!—on the very day when Sihathor reaches you. See! If she spends a single night more in my house, watch out! It is you who let her do evil to my concubine" (Heqanakhte I, 13v–14; James 1962).

The fact that a servant could be so much a part of the family structure that she could disrupt its equilibrium is also demonstrated by a "letter to the dead" inscribed on a vase from the First Intermediate Period in which the sender asks his dead father and his grandmother on his father's side to help his wife Seni bear him a son. Seni had been upset by two housemaids, whose malevolent influence is presented as being responsible for the couple's problems:

> Behold now there is brought to you this vessel in respect of which your mother is to make litigation. It is agreeable that you should support her. Cause now that there be born to me a healthy male

child. You are an excellent spirit. And behold, as for those two, the serving-maids who have caused Seni to be afflicted, namely Nefertjentet and Itjai, confound them and destroy for me every affliction which is directed against my wife; for you know that I need her. Destroy them utterly! (Oriental Institute, University of Chicago, 13945, 3–7)

Although the state of slavery was inherited, as we can see from the fact that Dedisobek, son of the slave woman Ided, was himself a slave (*ḥm;* see Gauthier-Laurent 1931), this did not prevent someone from attaining a higher cultural level: "This communication is to inform my lord, who is occupying himself with your royal servant Uadjhau, teaching him to write without allowing him to flee" (El-Lahun Papyri, table 35.10–13). In contrast to conscripted workers, who were punished with forced labor for life if they attempted to flee, royal servants were executed: "I found the royal servant Sobekemhab, who had run away, and handed him over to the prison for justice. [. . .] He will thus be condemned to death in the Hall of the Speaker" (ibid., table 34.17 ff.).

The varied types of work carried out by slaves recall a point that has already been emphasized when we considered the absence of slaves in Egyptian literary texts. Slavery in Egypt was not so much a "horizontal" phenomenon, or automatically defined state, as a "vertical" one, in which individuals were forced to work within their own trade. We find "royal servants" employed as field-workers, house servants, and cobblers; "slave women" as hairdressers, gardeners, and weavers. It was the same for their Asiatic counterparts, distinguished only by the fact that their names bore an ethnic prefix, despite being, especially in the case of the second generation, Egyptian names: "the Asiatic Aduna and her son Ankhu" (Hayes 1955, p. 87). Both their numbers and the fact that their status as slaves was passed down from parent to child suggest that the position of "royal servant" was comparable to that of Asiatic slave. Of the seventy-nine servants presented in the list on the verso of the Brooklyn Papyrus as belonging to a single owner, at least thirty-three were Egyptians!

The New Kingdom

As we leave the Middle Kingdom, the status of the slave appears to be relatively well established. A document dating to the Second

Intermediate Period—when the Hyksos invasion forced Egypt into the long period of military confrontation with the Asiatic world that characterized the New Kingdom—throws light on some legal aspects of slavery. It examines the granting of citizenship to a slave who had previously been shared between public and private ownership:

> The Overseer of the City, the Vizir, Overseer of the Six Great Courts, Amenemḥēt. An Order to the Reporter of Elephantine Ḥeḳaib to this effect: "An order was issued for the Vizir's Court in Year I, first month of summer, day 27 of the time of Khu-bak— life, prosperity, health. The order concerns the appeal which the (administrator) Itefefsonb son of Ḥeḳaib made, saying, 'Senbet, daughter of Senmut, is a slave-girl (ḥm.t) of the tenants (ḏ.t) of the people of Elephantine, but she is also the slave-girl of Ḥebsy's son Se'ankhu, my lord, and let her be given to me or to the city, according as her owners agree.' So he said. The conclusion is that it shall be done as her owners agree. So run the orders [. . .] A reply to this leather roll of the Vizir's Court has been brought, stating: 'The attorneys of the people about whom you wrote have been questioned. They said: "We agree to the giving of the slave-girl Senbet to the city [as her owners] agree, in accordance with the appeal which our brother, the (administrator) Itefefsonb, has made concerning her.'" Now they are to be made to take the oath upon it, and you shall put the orders before the slave-girl Senbet." (Berlin Papyrus 10470, 1.5–2.9; Smither 1948, p. 32)

This text is novel in two ways. First, it demonstrates the importance acquired by the "town," whose role in the administration of public property has replaced the nominal power of the king, seen in the case of the "royal servants" of the Middle Kingdom. Second, it shows that a slave could become a "citizen," possibly by marriage. Slaves, therefore, now had a similar status to freedmen in Roman times.

Periods of social change in the history of Pharaonic Egypt, however, always possess two sides, one emancipatory and innovative and the other bureaucratic and restrictive. We only have to think of the beginning of the Middle Kingdom, when the rise of a new free middle class was accompanied by increased rigidity in the power structure, causing numerous cases of emigration and flight from the country; or the situation at El-Amarna in the fourteenth century B.C., when Akhenaten's religious reforms were accompanied by the brutal repression of all power centers other than that of the palace. In this case too, as legal opportunities became available to slaves, reflecting their emergence as an essential element in Egyptian society, an autonomous class of "dependents" gradually disappeared. In semantics, an expression that was originally regarded as positive, often tends to acquire a neutral connotation when compared to another, creating the need for a new, more prestigious term. This process was at work in the semantic deterioration of the word "governess," which is no longer the female equivalent of "governor" as it was when used by Elizabeth I to denote her authority, but is now used almost exclusively in the context of looking after young children. The term *mrj* underwent a similar process during the Eighteenth Dynasty (ca. 1540–1293 B.C.). It gradually lost its neutral sense of "dependent" and became used to describe a status not very different from that of royal servants during the Middle Kingdom, as can be seen from the fact that it was possible for the Pharaoh to "donate" personnel to a private individual. The important official Minmose received 150 dependents from the king as a reward for having contributed to the foundation of numerous temples:

> Well, as regards these [temples] that I have just mentioned, I laid their foundations, directing with absolute diligence the work on these great monuments with which my lord has satisfied the gods [. . .] My intelligence was constantly at his service. His Majesty praised me for my great ability and promised me a more rapid promotion than that of other officials: 150 dependents, presents, and clothes were given to me. (*Urkunden* IV, 1444.1–8)

The legal devaluation of local free workers is the most evident sign of an overall restructuring of the Egyptian social fabric in imperial times, as a consequence of foreign policies during the later Eighteenth Dynasty. Military and commercial involvement with the Asiatic world brought many Asiatics to Egypt, either as booty or as slaves bought from slave markets. During the Late Bronze Age in the Near East, Egypt was the main purchaser of slaves in a market that was probably controlled by Asiatic Bedouin. We may remember the biblical tale of Joseph being sold to Ishmaelite traders on their way to Egypt (Gen. 37). The royal servants and conscripts, manifestations of the social structure of the Middle Kingdom, which was founded on internal political (and police) control, now disappeared and were replaced by foreign labor. This was needed to deal with the growing expense of an impressive military apparatus. The auto-biographical text from the tomb at Elkab of General Ahmose, son of Abana (*Urkunden* IV, 1–11), provides the most detailed account of the expulsion of the Hyksos and the rise of the Theban Eighteenth Dynasty under Ahmose I, Amenophis I, and Tuthmosis I (see p. 170). The general provides a typical picture of how foreign slavery emerged during the first part of the New Kingdom, boasting more than once that the king had sometimes allowed him to treat as slaves the Asiatics he had captured as spoils of war. Slaves are constantly associated with a stereotypical depiction of the military world:

> Come, let me describe to you a wretched profession, (that of) chariot-warrior. Because of his mother's father he is assigned to the stable, which has five slaves (*ḥm.w*). He is allotted two men from among them, but they do not obey him [...] People come to collect victuals; he begins to be tormented; he is flung upon the ground and beaten with one hundred blows. (Anastasi Papyrus III, 6.2 ff.; Caminos 1954)

It would appear, however, that this evolution only came to an end when Egypt became an imperial (and imperialistic) power dur-ing the second part of the Eighteenth Dynasty, because at the begin-ning of the New Kingdom, people given away by the king as rewards were still referred to by Middle Kingdom terms, such as "heads" or "people" (see Habachi 1950): "He was praised in the 'House of Recompense' with a reward of twenty men and fifty arourae of land" (1 aroura = 0.677 acres). The Annals of Tuthmosis III continued to define foreign prisoners of war as "men (*rmt.w*) in captivity" (*Urkun-den* IV, 698.6) and used the term "dependent" as it had been used during the Middle Kingdom, to refer to, among others, people handed over to serve in temples. These often included foreign cap-tives (*Urkunden* IV, 172.5, 207.9, 742.14, 1102). From the reign of Amenophis III on, however, forced labor in temples seems to have been reserved for "male and female slaves" (*ḥm.w, ḥm.wt*) and was expressed in a topos that recurs frequently during the Nineteenth Dynasty: "The lake (of the temple) was high because of the great inundation, filled with fish and birds, pure with flowers; his work house was full of male and female slaves, the children of princes in all foreign lands, the spoils of His Majesty" (*Urkunden* IV, 1649.6–8;

see also Kitchen 1968, 2.15, 23.6; Harris Papyrus I, 8.9, 47.10, 58.3, 59.5, 60.3).

By the end of the Eighteenth Dynasty, slaves had become so common in Egyptian society that the term *ḥm* was even applied to *ushabti*. These were statuettes made of wood, terra-cotta, or pottery that formed an integral part of the funerary objects intended for use in the afterlife, where they were called on to work for the dead person. Slaves could be "rented" for a certain period by people whose social conditions were relatively humble, and the motive for hiring out a female slave could be as mundane as the need for new clothes, even though the actual price appears too high:

> Year 27, third month of the summer season, day 20, under His Majesty the King of Upper and Lower Egypt Nebmaatra, son of King Amenophis III, to whom shall be granted eternal life as to his father Re each day. Day in which Nebmehi, a shepherd in the temple of Amenophis, presented himself to the shepherd Mesi saying: "I am without clothes: let me be given the value of two days' work of my slave girl Harit." So the shepherd Mesi gave him a *dꜣjw*-garment worth 3 1/2 *shati* and a *sḏw*-garment worth 1/2 *shati*. Then he came back to me once more and said: "Give me the value of four days' work of the slave girl Henut." So the shepherd Mesi gave him grain [...] worth 4 *shati*, six goats worth 3 *shati*, and silver worth 1 *shati*, for a total value of 12 *shati*. But two of the working days of the slave girl Henut were particularly hot; for this reason he gave me two more days' work of Meriremetjuef and two days' work of the slave Nehsethi in the presence of several witnesses. (Berlin Papyrus 9784, 1–10)

During the Ramesside Period, the relationship between slave and master also became a topos in models for correspondence: "As a slave (*ḥm*) serves his master, so I want to serve my lord" (Lansing Papyrus 11.3). Both the Miscellanies (anthologies of model texts—letters, hymns, prayers—used in schools) and historical and autobiographical texts represent the slave either as booty obtained from war or as someone chosen from among the young nobility of Egyptian-occupied territories:

> I have brought back in great numbers those that my sword has spared, with their hands tied behind their backs before my horses, and their wives and children in tens of thousands, and their live-

stock in hundreds of thousands. I have imprisoned their leaders in fortresses bearing my name, and I have added to them chief archers and tribal chiefs, branded and enslaved, tattooed with my name, and their wives and children have been treated in the same way. (Harris Papyrus I, 77.4–6)

The victory is attained, and the captives and tribespeople destined for Egypt are handed over to His Majesty. The foreign woman has fainted through marching and is placed upon the soldier's neck. (Lansing Papyrus 10.3–5; Caminos 1954)

Apply yourself with extreme zeal, firmness, and efficiency to have things ready before [the arrival of] Pharaoh, your good lord, to wit: bread, beer, meat, sweets, and cakes. Likewise incense, sweet moringa oil, *dft*-oil of Alasia (Cyprus), the finest *kdwr*-oil of Khatti, *inb*-oil of Alasia, *nkftr*-oil of Amor, *gt*-oil of Takhsy, and moringa oil of Nahrin; namely the many oils of the port to anoint his army and his chariotry. And to wit: oxen, fine castrated short-horned cattle of the west, and fat kids of the Southern Province [. . .] Bowls and dishes of silver and gold filled in beneath the window. Slaves of Kerke and striplings from the priestly *phyle* fit to be butlers of His Majesty [. . .], Canaanite slaves of Khor, fine striplings, and fine Nubians of Cush fit to give shelter with the fan. (Anastasi Papyrus IV, 15.1 ff.; Caminos 1954)

During the first part of the New Kingdom, it was still the king (bear in mind the Middle Kingdom term "royal servant" for recaptured fugitives) who maintained legal property rights over foreign prisoners and who decided whether they were to be given to individuals. Observing the oxen and slaves depicted on the walls of his Theban tomb, the treasurer Maia (epoch of Haremhab, 1321–1293 B.C.) remarks:

[This is what was] conceded as a demonstration of the king's favor to he whom the perfect god praises, whom the lord of the Two Lands loves for his character, who bears the fan to the right of the king, the overseer of the Treasury, Maia, the vindicated, among the prisoners taken as spoils by His Majesty among the Asiatics. The king said: "Take them!" (*Urkunden* IV, 2163.7–11)

At its height, the New Kingdom witnessed the development of a legal system that codified the ownership of slaves, who could now be bought and sold by individuals. The Ramesside Cairo Papyrus 65739, for example, describes a long legal dispute between a soldier and a woman concerning the ownership of two Syrian slaves. The legal system was also intended to provide slaves with legal protection. Administrative texts document that slaves could own property. The rigid bureaucratic style of the Wilbour Papyrus, which dates to the time of Ramesses V (Twentieth Dynasty) and is the most important extant Pharaonic administrative register of land assessment and allocation, refers more than once to slaves among the owners of land being assessed. It is probably the most eloquent proof that the law treated free citizens and slaves in the same way.

Slaves also had the right to be treated equally when they broke the law. A female slave found guilty of theft was merely condemned to give back twice the value of what she had stolen (Leiden Papyrus 352; Černý 1937). Emancipation from slavery should be considered in the context of these new legal rights, since it effectively mirrored the presence of slavery as a stable element in Pharaonic society. A number of administrative texts from the New Kingdom present different legal opportunities for slaves to be freed, often linked to a form of *do ut des* between slave and master, as in the case of a slave who agreed to marry an invalid niece:

> Year 27 under His Majesty the King of Upper and Lower Egypt Menkheperre, son of Re Tuthmosis (III), to whom it has been given to live and last as Re in eternity. The barber of the king Sabastet entered into the presence of the young princes of the royal palace, saying: "My slave, a man of my property named Ameniu, whom I had taken prisoner with my own arm when I accompanied the king [. . .] He has never been struck nor imprisoned behind a door of the royal palace. I gave him as wife Ta-Kemnet ("the blind one"), daughter of my sister Nebet-Ta, who had previously lived with my wife and my sister. He now leaves the house, being deprived of nothing [. . .] and if he decides to agree to a legal compromise with my sister, no one will ever do anything against him." (*Urkunden* IV, 1369.4–16)

A slave could also become free by being adopted by his or her owner. In the following Ramesside document, a sterile woman adopts the children her husband has fathered with a female slave, confirming the observation made about the Middle Kingdom that, in the absence of such a procedure, the legal state of slavery must have been hereditary:

> We bought the slave girl Dienihatiri, and she gave birth to three children, a boy and two girls, three in all. And I adopted, fed, and raised them, and to this day they have never treated me badly. On the contrary, they have treated me well, and I have no sons or daughters other than them. And the overseer of the stables, Pendiu, connected to me by family ties, since he is my younger brother, came into my house and took the elder sister, Taimennut, as his wife. And I accepted this on her behalf and he is now with her. Now, I have freed her, and if she gives birth to a son or daughter, they too will be free citizens in the land of the Pharaoh, since they will be with the overseer of the stables, Pendiu, my younger brother. And the other two children will live with their elder sister in the house of this overseer of the stables, Pendiu, my younger brother, whom I today adopt as my son, exactly as they are. (Adoption Papyrus, 16r–1v)

"Freed," in this passage, translates the Egyptian expression "made free (*nmḥj*) in the land of the Pharaoh." From the Middle Kingdom on, this expression was used to describe people who received from the state an allotment of land, often as recompense for military service. The land then became, in practice, their own property. Egypt's military commitment abroad disappeared toward the end of the second millennium. During the first millennium, this social group became one of the rigid "classes" into which Greek authors divided contemporary Egyptian society, as we shall see.

Another way in which a slave might become free was to be "purified" (*swʿb*) by the king, thus entering temple service as a free man or woman. The clearest formulation of this is in the so-called Restoration Stela of Tutankhamun:

> His Majesty built the barques (of the gods) on the Nile in wood of cedar of the best in the Lebanon, of the most prized along the Asiatic coast, inlaid with gold from the finest of foreign lands, so that the Nile was illuminated. His Majesty purified slaves, both men and women, singers and dancing girls who previously had been slave girls assigned to the work of grinding in the royal palace. They were rewarded for the work done for the royal palace and for the treasure of the lord of the Two Lands. I declared them exempt

from slavery and reserved for the service of the father, that is of all
the gods, wishing to satisfy them by doing that which their Ka desires, because they protect Egypt. (*Urkunden* IV, 2030.1–11)

It is useful to consider for a moment the use of the term *sw⁽b*, "to
purify," to indicate emancipation from slavery. We may recall that,
during the Middle Kingdom, the term *w⁽b* described the condition
of the commoner (*nds*) who gained exemption from state service by
becoming a priest. In a sense, the semantic evolution of this term is
the sign of a more general evolution in cultural history. In the aristo-
cratic, "Nile-centered" society of the Middle Kingdom, "purification" was connected to the promotion of a single individual from the
rank of dependent to that of commoner. In the cosmopolitan society
of imperial Egypt, however, it also came to mean promotion from the
status of slave to that of paid temple servant. In the more complex
social structure of the New Kingdom, the semantic range of this
word no longer indicated only the status of an Egyptian who improved his or her social position but also indicated the status of foreign slaves, in a process typical of all phenomena of "democratization": on the one hand, more chance of upward social mobility and,
on the other, a leveling of cultural elites in society. At the beginning
of the New Kingdom, temple service became, along with military
service, one of the two ways in which Egyptian citizens periodically
contributed labor to the state. From this viewpoint, the presence of
slavery should not automatically be regarded as the sign of a politically despotic structure, compared to that of a society (still) without slavery. In New Kingdom Egypt, slavery paradoxically became
one of the signs that the social structure was evolving toward "de-
mocracy."

To modern eyes, however, one of the most disconcerting aspects
of the bureaucratization of slavery is the presence of "houses of female slaves," apparently devoted to the "industrial production" of
children. We have already seen that slavery appears to have been
hereditary (because the son of the Middle Kingdom female slave
mentioned above was himself classified as a slave, and because of
an explicit reference to the emancipation of the children of a New
Kingdom female slave). We possess an image of one of these "houses
of female slaves" in the Eighteenth Dynasty Theban tomb of Rekhmire (Davies 1943, table 23), as well as a reference in the Harris
Papyrus I, another important administrative text from the Ramesside

Period, which lists the property of the most important Egyptian temples. The prayer to Ptah beginning the section devoted to the Memphis temple refers to an "all-women settlement," which seems to have been intended for the production of slave labor:

> I have issued for You great decrees with secret words, recorded in the archives of Egypt, built out of masses of scalpel-worked stone, and I have organized the service at Your noble temple in eternity and the administration of your "all-women settlement." I have gathered their children that had been scattered in the service of others, and I have destined them for You, in the service of the temple of Ptah, as an order established for them in eternity. (Harris Papyrus I, 47.8–9)

The status of slave, however, only seems to have been applied to foreigners. Egyptians who gave up their rights over their own persons, due to economic difficulties or legal constraints, were referred to generically as "servants" (*b3k.w*), even though their human and social conditions must have been very similar to those of foreign slaves:

> Further, I set forth from the broad halls of the Palace in the third month of Shomu, day 9, at the time of evening in the pursuit of these servants. When I reached the keep of Tjeku in the third month of Shomu, day 10, they told me: "They say in the south that they passed in the third month of Shomu, day 10." When I reached the fortress they told me: "Thy groom is come from the desert, reporting they passed the north fortification of the stronghold of Seti-Merneptah, Beloved-like-Seth." When my letter reaches you write to me concerning all that has come to pass with them. Who found their track? Which watch found their track? Who are the men in pursuit of them? Write to me concerning all that has come to pass with them. How many people have you sent in pursuit of them? [Fare you] well. (Anastasi Papyrus V, 19.6 ff.; Caminos 1954)

"Servant" (*b3k*) thus seems to be a generic term, the meaning of which incorporates the foreign slave (*ḥm*). We must not forget that, in biblical tradition, where Egypt is synonymous with "house of slavery," Egyptians could opt to become slaves when forced to do so by famine, selling their possessions and their own persons to the state (Gen. 47:13 ff.). Thus, in a document preserved in the Museum of Turin, a priest of Medinet Habu named Amenkhau discusses the fate of thirteen servants in his second marriage contract, following the death of his first wife. Nine servants are passed on to the children of his first wife, and the other four are given to his second wife, to become her property only if her husband dies or in the event of divorce. The document is interesting because it presents, alongside the local servants, a foreign female slave (*ḥm.t*) and, above all, because the two wives of Amenkhau are described as freedwomen. They bear exactly the same title of "free citizeness" (*ꜥnḫ.t nj.t n'.t*) that we found in the first document discussed in this section, in which the "citizens" of Elephantine accepted a request for emancipation of a female slave who was half owned by the city. In this context, the formula the vizier chooses to express his acceptance of the clauses in the Amenkhau marriage contract is even more revealing. The vizier states:

> Even if it had not been his wife but a Syrian or a Nubian whom he loved and to whom he gave a property of his, [who] should make void what he did? Let the four slaves which [fall to his lot] with the citeness Anoksunozen be given [to her?] together with [all that he may acquire] with her, which he has said he would give her, "my two thirds [in addition to] her one eighth, and no son or daughter of mine (Amenkhau) shall question this arrangement which [I] have made for her this day." (Turin Papyrus 2021, 3.11–4.1; Černý and Peet 1927, pp. 32–33)

Clearly, Egyptian servants could possess property in exactly the same way as foreign slaves could (see the testament of Naunakhte: Černý 1945). In effect, they made up what would now be called a subproletariat, whose status appears from documents to be similar, on the one hand, to that of slaves and, on the other, to that of the waged proletariat of field-workers and craftsmen. This reveals a further aspect of the typically Egyptian phenomenon of camouflaging slavery, which is never explicitly defined in the texts, but whose essential features are simply suggested. At the beginning of the New Kingdom, in the correspondence of a certain Ahmose of Peniati, one of the few administrative archives of the Eighteenth Dynasty to have survived, the mother of a servant (*b3k.t*) complains that the master to whom she has entrusted her daughter has passed her on to someone else. This would suggest that Egyptian servants, unlike foreign slaves, were not normally treated as objects to be traded but were employed for a specific service. The issue then reaches the courtroom, where it becomes somewhat complex:

What Ahmose of Peniati says to his lord, the treasurer, Ty: What is the reason for the carrying off of the servant girl who was with me, now given to another? Am I not your servant, obeying your orders by night as well as by day? Let her value, as far as I am concerned, be taken, for she is indeed young and does not [yet] know work. Let my lord order to have her work carried out like that of any servant girl of the lord's; for her mother sent a message to me, saying: "You have let my child be taken away while she was there with you. But I did not protest to my lord as she was with you as a child." So she said to me in protest. (Louvre Papyrus 3230, 2)

A note to let you know about the business of the servant girl who is in the care of the noble Tetimose. The chief of slaves Abui was sent to him to say: "Come, you should settle the matter with him." He, (that is,) Mini, does not answer what the overseer of field-workers Ramose said. See! As for the servant girl of the noble Mini, the sailor, he does not listen to me over settling the matter with me in the court of magistrates. (British Museum Papyrus 10107, 3–12)

In these administrative texts too, New Kingdom Egyptian society appears to be increasingly divided into professional and craft groups, within which "servants" sometimes represent the lowest segment. The process that we have already witnessed in bud in the Middle Kingdom seems to have continued. In the Satire of the Trades of the classical epoch, stylistic antitheses still indicated a basic contrast between the free world of the aristocracy, represented by the scribe, and dependent Egyptian society in all its complexity, represented by the trades and the professions. These antitheses are found once again, in a more corporativist sense, in the Miscellanies. It is now the professional activity of scribes that is being compared to all other activities, regardless of their social prestige, which—in the case of the prophet or priest in the third text below—must have been much higher than that of the scribe:

Look for yourself with your own eye. The professions are set before you. The washerman spends the whole day going up and down, all his body is weak through whitening the clothes of his neighbors every day and washing their linen. The potter is smeared with earth like a person one of whose folk has died [. . .] The sandal-maker mixes tan; his odor is conspicuous [. . .] The

basket-maker prepares floral offerings and brightens ring-stands;
he spends a night of toil even as one upon whose body the sun
shines. The merchants fare downstream and upstream, and are as
busy as brass, carrying goods from one town to another [...] A
carpenter, the one who is in the ship-yard, carries the timber and
stacks it. If he renders today his produce of yesterday, woe to his
limbs! The shipwright stands behind him to say to him evil things.
His outworker who is in the fields, *that* is tougher than any profession. He spends the whole day laden with his tools, tied down to
his toolbox. (Lansing Papyrus, 4.2 ff.; Caminos 1954, pp. 384–85)

And just now the scribe lands at the riverbank to estimate the
harvest tax with a suite of attendants carrying sticks and Nubians
with rods of palm. They say, "Show us the grain!" But there is
none, and the peasant is mercilessly beaten. He is then tied up and
cast head foremost into a pool, where he gets thoroughly soaked.
His wife is bound in his presence; his children are in shackles.
(Ibid., 7.1 ff.; Caminos 1954, p. 390)

The prophet also serves as a tenant-farmer. The priest performs the service and spends the time—there being three services
daily—soaking himself in the river: he does not distinguish between winter and summer (nor whether) the sky be windy and
rainy. (Anastasi Papyrus II, 7.6–7.7; Caminos 1954, p. 51)

The Late Period

During the first millennium B.C., corporativization became an even
more typical feature of Egyptian society. In the New Kingdom, as
we have just seen, slavery was essentially restricted to imperial prisoners of war and to Asiatics bought in slave markets. It had become
a basic component of Egyptian social structure, even though the autonomous figure of the slave never quite became part of the rich
repertoire of human types found in literary texts. As imperial power
declined and Egypt lost its influence in Asia during the Iron Age,
the number of slaves in the Nile Valley also decreased considerably.
Foreigners in Egypt were now organized autonomously. We only
have to think of the gradual development of the colonies and the
groups of Greek, Semitic, and Carian mercenaries in places such as
Naucratis and Elephantine. Although references to actual slavery can
be found dating back to the beginning of the first millennium, they

are significantly less frequent when compared to the abundance of the Ramesside Period. In the inscription in which the Libyan potentate Sheshonq, "great chief of the Meshwesh" and future founder, as Sheshonq I, of the Twenty-second Dynasty (946–712 B.C.), declares that he wishes to establish a religious foundation in Abydos to maintain the funerary cult of his father, Nemlot, there appears among the personnel of the foundation a field-worker responsible for four slaves (*ḥm.w*): "in total five men for an overall value of four *deben* and one *kite* of silver," according to the typically bureaucratic style of the formula (Cairo stela JE 66285, 13–14). After this period, the term *ḥm* no longer appears in administrative documents.

The situation in the Late Period thus appears to have been very similar to that of earlier times, with no formal codification of slavery, the only mention of it being made in connection with temples and the palace. It comes as no surprise, therefore, that, in the fifth century B.C., Herodotus, the first Western interpreter of Egyptian civilization, did not mention the slave among the "seven classes of Egyptians" (*Aigyptíōn heptà génea*) that he considered representative of society during the Late Period: "The Egyptians are divided into seven classes named after their occupations: priests, warriors, cowherds, swineherds, tradesmen, interpreters, and pilots" (2.164). Nor is it surprising that, a few decades later, Plato's analysis of Egyptian society should resemble that made by Herodotus. In the *Timaeus*, an Egyptian priest talks to the Athenian lawmaker Solon about the laws in his own country:

> In the first place, there is the caste (*génos*) of priests, which is separated from all the others; next, there are the artificers, who ply their several crafts by themselves and do not intermix; and also there is the class of shepherds and of hunters, as well as that of husbandmen; and you will observe, too, that the warriors in Egypt are distinct from all the other classes, and are commanded by the law to devote themselves solely to military pursuits. (24a–b; trans. Jowett)

During the Roman Period, Diodorus Siculus (I.73–74) divided Egyptian society, other than the army, into three classes of free citizens: shepherds, field-workers, and craftsmen.

How should we, in our turn, interpret the Greek interpretation of Egyptian society? Priests, soldiers, and peasants (in the widest sense of "people engaged in agriculture") were the three basic com-

ponents to emerge from the disintegration of imperial society. Priests
occupied a privileged position administering the temple economy,
which had become much greater than that of the palace. Most professional soldiers were mercenaries, employed from time to time by
different dynasties. Field-workers and shepherds were the *nmḥ.w*,
the heirs of those who, in the New Kingdom, were "freed in the land
of the Pharaoh," and whose possession of an allotment of land ensured their economic independence from central power.

In a society whose political (although not necessarily cultural)
horizons had been reduced, and that had once again become centered on the Nile, there was no longer room for slavery. As society
expanded economically, slavery was replaced by forms of "clientship" expressed in two ways: first, in the corporative link between
the individual and his professional group (so tight a link that it appeared to Greek observers to be a sign of closed social groups); and,
second, in the frequent commercial transactions involving servants,
identified once again by the term *bȝk*, meaning "service." Contracts
during the Saite and Persian Periods provide us with numerous examples of the lack of differentiation between Egyptians and foreigners. In these contracts, servile status was regulated by a series of legal
restrictions, from which, however, it was possible to be freed. Servile
status often was the free choice of an individual in search of economic protection and was encouraged by ideological motivations
which clearly suggest that servile status was closer to clientship than
to slavery (Louvre E 706, 3r–7; see Bakir 1952, table 17; Griffith
1909, vol. 3, pp. 52 ff.).

> You have acted so that I am in agreement with you about my price
> to become your servant. I am now your servant, and no one will
> henceforth be able to take me from you, nor shall I be able to as-
> sign myself (become *nmḥ*) to another, but I shall remain in your
> service, along with my children, even in the case of cession of
> money, grain, or any other property of the country.
>
> The servant Tapnebtynis, daughter of Sebekmeni and of her
> mother, Esoeri, said before my lord Sobek, lord of Tebtynis, the
> great god: "I am your servant as are my children and my children's
> children. I shall never be free (*nmḥ*) in your temple, for eternity.
> You will look after me, keep me, safeguard me, keep me healthy,
> protect me from all male and female spirits, from every man in
> trance, from every epileptic, from every drowned man, from every

drunkard, from every nightmare, from every dead man, from every man of the river, from every madman, from every foe, from every red thing, from every misadventure, from every plague." (British Museum Papyrus 10622, 7–14)

The term *nmḥ*, in fact, provides us with the most suitable ending to this brief account of slavery in Egypt. In the Middle Kingdom, it had been used to define people without legal protection (the original meaning of the word was "orphan"). By the end of the New Kingdom it had come to stand for the untaxed small landowner, and it later became used increasingly to refer to emancipation from slavery. Greek papyri in Egypt reveal a rise in Hellenistic forms of slavery, based on capture in war, the purchase of slaves from Syria and Palestine (as described in the papyri of Zeno), the enslavement of debtors, and the inherited status of slaves' children born in their master's house. In the autochthonous texts of the Ptolemaic Period, however, the most common form of servitude (including voluntary servitude) was that of temple service. The "freeborn" person was now contrasted with one "born within the walls of the temple," the last purely Egyptian bastion in an increasingly syncretistic society. It was the temple that protected, reelaborated, and inscribed on its walls the religious texts of the preceding millennium, before collapsing to make room for the new period of Christian Egypt.

Conclusion

Analyzing the figure of the slave in ancient Egypt has a threefold historical function. Above all, it clarifies the significance, and structure, of some important social changes that took place in the Pharaonic world during the three thousand years of its documented history: from the pyramidical society (in all senses) of the Memphite Period to the gradual "meritocracy" (and the humanistic problems related to this) of the Middle Kingdom, and from Ramesside bureaucratic centralism to the emergence of closed professional groups, or "social classes," during the Late Period. Second, it contributes to a critique of a hypothesis, which might be defined as "evolutionary," in the study of human history, according to which the social, economic, and legal developments of classical civilizations represent a step forward from the cultures of the eastern Mediterranean Bronze and Iron Ages. Pharaonic Egypt, in fact, produced different forms of

"slavery" according to its economic needs and changing ideas, ranging from the absence of the state of slavery in the Old Kingdom,
during which the whole of Egyptian society was absolutely dependent on state control, the recognition and presence of "political"
slaves in the Middle Kingdom, the abundance of foreign slaves in
the New Kingdom, and the emergence of different forms of more or
less voluntary servitude during the first millennium B.C. Finally, it
allows us to outline a "social history" of Egyptian culture, revealing
the typical inner workings of the complex social mechanisms that
governed part of the ancient Near Eastern world and, at the same
time, offering the historian glimpses of extraordinary modernity
(such as the distrust of legal codification compared to the system of
precedent; we only have to think of the Anglo-Saxon legal system
compared to Roman law and the Napoleonic Code) and thus encouraging us to reconsider critically the very foundations of Western
culture.

Bibliography

Bakir, Abd el-Mohsen. *Slavery in Pharaonic Egypt*. Supplément aux ASAE
    18. Cairo, 1952.
Berlev, O. D. Review of W. K. Simpson, *Papyrus Reisner I: The Records of a
    Building Project in the Reign of Sesostris I. Bibliotheca Orientalis* 22 (1965):
    263–69.
Blackman, A. M. "The Stela of Shoshenq, Great Chief of the Meshwesh."
    Journal of Egyptian Archaeology 27 (1941): 83–95.
Bresciani, E. "I Semiti nell'Egitto di età saitica e persiana." In *Atti del con-
    vegno "Egitto e Società Antica,"* pp. 93–104. Milan, 1985.
Caminos, R. A. *Late-Egyptian Miscellanies*. Brown Egyptological Studies, 1.
    London, 1954.
Černý, J. "Restitution of, and Penalty Attaching to Stolen Property in
    Ramesside Times." *Journal of Egyptian Archaeology* 23 (1937): 186–89.
———. "Le caractère des oushebtis d'après les idées du Nouvel Empire."
    Bulletin de l'Institut Français d'Archéologie Orientale 41 (1942): 105–33.
———. "The Will of Naunakhte and the Related Documents." *Journal of
    Egyptian Archaeology* 31 (1945): 29–53.
———. "The Stela of Merer in Cracow." *Journal of Egyptian Archaeology* 47
    (1961): 5–9.

Černý, J., and T. E. Peet. "A Marriage Settlement of the Twentieth Dynasty: An Unpublished Document from Turin." *Journal of Egyptian Archaeology* 13 (1927): 30–39.

Clère, J. J., and J. Vandier. *Textes de la Première Période Intermédiaire et de la XIème Dynastie.* Bibliotheca Aegyptiaca, 10, fasc. 1. Brussels 1948.

Cruz-Uribe, E. "Slavery in Egypt during the Saite and Persian Periods." *Revue Internationale des Droits de l'Antiquité* 29 (1982): 47–71.

Daressy, G. "Une stèle de l'Ancien Empire maintenant détruite." *Annales du Service des Antiquités de l'Égypte* 15 (1915): 207–8.

Davies, N. de G. *The Rock Tombs of Sheikh Saïd.* Archaeological Survey of Egypt, 10. London, 1901.

———. *The Rock Tombs of Deir el Gebrâwi I–II.* Archaeological Survey of Egypt, 11–12. London, 1902.

———. *The Tomb of Rekh-mi-rē' at Thebes.* 2 vols. Publications of the Metropolitan Museum of Art, 11. New York, 1943.

Erichsen, W. *Papyrus Harris I.* Bibliotheca Aegyptiaca, 5. Brussels, 1933.

Fischer, H. G. "An Early Occurrence of *ḥm* 'servant' in Regulations Referring to a Mortuary Estate." *Mitteilungen des Deutschen Archäologischen Instituts, Kairo* 16 (1958): 131–37.

Gardiner, A. H. "Four Papyri of the 18th Dynasty from Kabun." *Zeitschrift für Ägyptische Sprache und Altertumskunde* 43 (1906): 27–47.

———. *The Admonitions of an Egyptian Sage.* Leipzig, 1909.

———. "A New Letter to the Dead." *Journal of Egyptian Archaeology* 16 (1930): 19–22.

———. *Chester Beatty Gift.* Hieratic Papyri in the British Museum, 3d ser. London, 1935.

———. "A Lawsuit Arising from the Purchase of Two Slaves." *Journal of Egyptian Archaeology* 21 (1935): 140–46.

———. *Late-Egyptian Miscellanies.* Bibliotheca Aegyptiaca, 7. Brussels, 1937.

———. "Adoption Extraordinary." *Journal of Egyptian Archaeology* 26 (1940): 23–29.

———. *The Wilbour Papyrus.* 4 vols. London, 1941–52.

Gauthier-Laurent, M. "Quelques objets égyptiens du Musée de Langres." *Bulletin de l'Institut Français d'Archéologie Orientale* 30 (1931): 107–25.

Glanville, S. R. K. "The Letters of Aahmose of Peniati." *Journal of Egyptian Archaeology* 14 (1928): 294–312.

Griffith, F. L. *Catalogue of the Demotic Papyri in the John Rylands Library.* Vols. 1–3. Manchester, 1909.

Habachi, L. "An Inscription at Aswan Referring to Six Obelisks." *Journal of Egyptian Archaeology* 36 (1950): 13–18.

Hayes, W. C. *A Papyrus of the Late Middle Kingdom in the Brooklyn Museum.* Wilbour Monographs, 5. New York, 1955.

Helck, W. *Urkunden der 18. Dynastie.* Berlin, 1955–61.

————. "Die soziale Schichtung des ägyptischen Volkes im 3. und 2. Jahrtausend v. Chr." *Journal of the Economic and Social History of the Orient 2* (1959): 1–36.

————. *Wirtschaftsgeschichte des alten Ägypten im 3. und 2. Jahrtausend vor Chr.* Handbuch der Orientalistik, I, 1, 5. 1975.

————. "Kriegsgefangene." In *Lexikon der Ägyptologie*, vol. 3, cols. 786–88.

————. "Sklaven." In *Lexikon der Ägyptologie*, vol. 5, cols. 982–87.

James, T. G. H. *The Heqanakhte Papers and Other Early Middle Kingdom Documents.* Publications of the Metropolitan Museum of Art, 19. New York, 1962.

Kitchen, K. A. *Ramesside Inscriptions.* Vol. 1. Oxford, 1968.

Lepsius, C. R. *Denkmaeler aus Aegypten und Aethiopien.* 12 vols. Berlin, 1849–58.

Lichtheim, M. *Ancient Egyptian Literature.* Vol. 1, *The Old and Middle Kingdoms.* Berkeley and Los Angeles, 1973.

Loprieno, A. *Topos und Mimesis: Zum Ausländer in der ägyptischen Literatur.* Ägyptologische Abhandlungen, 48. Wiesbaden, 1988.

Osing, J. *Der spätägyptische Papyrus BM 10808.* Ägyptologische Abhandlungen, 33. Wiesbaden, 1976.

Peet, T. E. "Two Eighteenth Dynasty Letters: Papyrus Louvre 3230." *Journal of Egyptian Archaeology* 12 (1926): 70–74.

Pernigotti, S. "I più antichi rapporti tra l'Egitto e i Greci (secoli VII–IV a.C.)." In *Atti del convegno "Egitto e Società Antica,"* pp. 75–91. Milan, 1985.

Posener, G. *Littérature et politique dans l'Égypte de la XIIème dynastie.* Paris, 1956.

Posener-Kriéger, P. *Les archives du temple funéraire de Néferirkarê-Kakaï (les papyrus d'Abousir).* 2 vols. Bibliothèque d'Étude, 65. Cairo, 1976.

Roccati, A. "Il quotidiano degli Egizi attraverso i papiri di Torino." In *Atti del convegno "Egitto e Società Antica,"* pp. 41–46. Milan, 1985.

Seidl, E. *Einführung in die ägyptische Rechtsgeschichte bis zum Ende des Neuen Reiches.* Ägyptologische Forschungen, 10. Glückstadt, 1951.

Sethe, K. *Die altägyptischen Pyramidentexte.* 4 vols. Leipzig, 1908–22.

————. *Urkunden des Alten Reiches.* 2d ed. Leipzig, 1933.

————. *Urkunden der 18. Dynastie.* 2d ed. Berlin and Graz, 1961.

Simpson, W. K. *Papyrus Reisner I: The Records of a Building Project in the Reign of Sesostris I.* Boston, 1963.

————, ed. *The Literature of Ancient Egypt: An Anthology of Stories, Instructions, and Poetry.* 2d ed. New Haven, 1973.

Smither, P. C. "The Report Concerning the Slave-Girl Senbet." *Journal of Egyptian Archaeology* 34 (1948): 31–34.

Thompson, H. "Two Demotic Self-Dedications." *Journal of Egyptian Archaeology* 26 (1941): 68–78.

Westermann, W. L. *Upon Slavery in Ptolemaic Egypt.* New York, 1929.

————. "Sklaverei." In *Realenzyklopädie der klassischen Altertumswissenschaft*, Suppl., vol. 6, cols. 894 ff.

8. FOREIGNERS

Edda Bresciani

In 1961, Sergio Donadoni wrote, among other things, about the way in which ancient Egypt dealt with the existence of other, foreign realities beyond its borders: "Universal empires do not suffer from these realities that we see as limits. They see them as a nebulous disorganized chaos, no more than a negative frame to the reality of a politically united and completed cosmos."

This concept was a valuable tool for maintaining royal power throughout the course of Egyptian civilization. It was the task of the Pharaoh, as the gods' representative on earth, to ensure universal order by acting against those who threatened it. Non-Egyptian peoples to the south, east, and west of the country were "conquered" by definition, even before any fighting took place. Scenes and symbols presenting the enemy as a single entity—the "Nine Bows"—are found throughout Egyptian history, even during the Greek and Roman Periods. They acted as an example, and as a warning: the figures of the defeated are shown beneath the soles of the king's sandals, and they are depicted on the floors and under the balustrades of the palace and on the plinths of royal statues.

In the Pyramid Texts, historical and ethnocentric Egypt already regarded itself as the center of the world. As "the eye of Horus," Egypt was destined by the god to be, not "a" nation, but "the" nation, created for Horus-Pharaoh:

> The doors that are on you rise in protection.
> They do not open to the westerners,
> they do not open to the easterners,

they do not open to the southerners,
they do not open to the northerners [...]
They open for Horus! It is he who has made them,
he who has raised them, he who has saved them
against all attacks against them by Seth.

(Pyramid Texts, 1588–1606)

This was the justification, elaborated so early on as myth, of the opposition between Egypt and its neighbors at the four astronomically
oriented corners of the world. It contrasted the kingdom of Horus
with that of Seth. That is, it contrasted Egypt, where everything was
perfectly in order, with the "foreign lands," the kingdom of the "different," and of disorder.

In any case, the kingdom of the Pharaoh was protected, both
officially and ritually, against foreigners who refused to become part
of the most fortunate of all possible states, Egypt. Magical and political maneuvers intended to make hostile foreigners harmless can be
seen in the so-called Execration Texts of the Old Kingdom, written
on vases and clay statues found at Giza and Saqqara. These texts list
the princes and countries of Nubia and Asia to be exorcized "along
with their conquered [subjects]." ("Conquered," in this context,
means those "who will inevitably be conquered.")

> All rebels in this land, all people, all officials, all subjects, all males,
> all eunuchs, all women, all leaders, all Nubians, all soldiers, all
> messengers, all allies, and all confederates of all foreign lands who
> may rebel, who are in the land of Uauat, of Djatiu, Irtjet, Iam,
> Ianekh, Masit, Kaau, who may rebel, who may plot, who may fight,
> who may talk of fighting, or who may talk of rebelling against Up-
> per and Lower Egypt [will be destroyed] for all time.

These very specific rituals date not only from the Old Kingdom
but also from the Middle Kingdom. They reveal a wealth of direct,
concrete knowledge regarding the geography, politics, place-names,
and languages of Africa and Asia, and of the princes over whose lands
the Pharaoh had effective control. Although some of these lands
were actually within Egyptian territory, the possibility of rebellion or
conspiracy was feared. Rarer cases, in which the people being exe-
crated bore Egyptian names, might have been directed at foreigners
who were living in Egypt, or even at Egyptian subjects considered
to be corrupt, or "rebellious."

Defeated, and convinced of their defeat, "foreigners" had no choice but to obey. Whether they remained as oppressed and loyal subjects in their own countries and provided Pharaoh with the riches their lands produced or were taken to Egypt to serve the king or the temples, they had found their role, by this point, in the well-organized world of the Pharaoh's political system. They even bene-fited from their position, in the sense so clearly expressed by the "loyalist" philosophy of Sesostris I in Nubia, in Wadi el-Hudi: "Ev-ery Iunti (nomad) of Nubia who is recognized as a servant acting in accordance with the power of this perfect king will see his descen-dants live eternally."

The difference, or "strangeness," of foreign countries when compared with Egypt was noted, described, and represented with curiosity by ancient Egyptians. It was recognized in the form of a series of anthropological, ethnographic, and even environmental and hydrographical features. Yet even though foreign people were un-doubtedly different, they were also "equal" in the providential cre-ation of the divine demiurge—at least in the highly developed elab-oration familiar to us from the mid–Eighteenth Dynasty. However, this did not exclude an awareness of difference at a day-to-day level: "It is Atum who has created men, / who has defined their nature and has made them live, / who has distinguished one from the other by the color of their skin" (Boulaq Papyrus 17, Hymn to Amun-Re). See also the Hymn to Aten:

Thou didst create the world according to they desire,
[...]
The countries of Syria and Nubia, the land of Egypt,
Thou settest every man in his place,
Thou suppliest their necessities:
Everyone has his food and his time of life is reckoned.
Their tongues are separate in speech,
And their natures as well;
Their skins are distinguished,
As thou distinguishest the foreign peoples.
[...]
All distant foreign countries, thou makest their life (also),
For thou hast set a Nile in heaven,
That it may descend for them and make waves upon the mountains,
Like the great green sea,

To water their fields in their towns.
How effective they are, thy plans, O lord of eternity!
The Nile in heaven, it is for the foreign people
And for the beasts of every desert that go upon (their) feet;
[While the true] Nile comes from the underworld for Egypt.
(Trans. J. A. Wilson, in Pritchard 1969, pp. 370–71)

Foreign countries, with their exotic goods, were created to enrich the temples and storehouses of Egypt, as we can see from the Thousand Songs in honor of Amun:

Foreign countries come to you,
loaded down with marvellous goods,
each district is filled with fear of you:
the inhabitants of Punt come to you,
the Land of God is verdant for you.
The waters bring you [ships] loaded with resin
to celebrate your temple with festive fragrance;
trees of incense ooze balsam for you [. . .]
The cedar grows for you
[from whose wood] your barque is made.
The mountain sends you blocks of stone
to make the doors [of your temple] great;
ships are at sea for you,
vessels are loaded on the shores,
they sail for you. . . .

The universalist, superracial conception of the world found in New Kingdom Egypt is eloquently depicted in the Theban tomb of Sethos I: Asiatics, Nubians, Libyans, and Egyptians, each dressed in national costume, advance under the eye of Horus, each in the same way, toward the same otherworldly destiny ensured by religious belief.

Most foreigners who settled in Egypt to become soldiers or members of the royal bodyguard continued to wear national costume. Their characteristic hairstyles and parades were as common a sight in Egypt as the arrival of exotic merchants and processions bearing foreign tribute.

Soldiers in Nubian (Kushite) divisions, employed from the Old Kingdom on, carried the arms of their country (bows, arrows, and axes), wore wide curved belts decorated with a diamond pattern, and wore ribbons in their hair. Libyan mercenaries continued to tattoo their bodies and wore up to four feathers on their heads. The men in the division of the Shardans (one of the so-called Peoples of the Sea), who served in the bodyguard of Ramesses II, made a striking impression with their sideburns and curled moustaches, their rounded shieldlike helmets, and their doublets covered with metal studs.

The scenes in the New Kingdom tombs of important officials that show the arrival of tribute-bearers from the Aegean world are extremely evocative. The details revealing the identity of the "Cretan" are so precise (long curling hair, knee-high boots of decorated leather, tasseled kilts) that Egyptian artists must have based their work on the actual presence of these exotic models. In any case, painters and sculptors delighted in representing ethnic variety and enjoyed reproducing, and ironically accentuating, certain Negroid and Semitic features.

The difference of color observed between "the eye of an Asiatic" and "the eye of a Nubian" is referred to in a text forecasting birth:

> You must look into the woman's eyes by daylight, and if you find that one of her eyes is like that of an Asiatic and the other like that of a Nubian, [the woman] will not give birth, but if both her eyes are the same color, she will give birth. (Berlin Papyrus 3038, r. 2.1–2)

The letter written by Amenophis II to his viceroy in Nubia, Usersatet (who had it copied onto a stela found at Semna in the Sudan), adopts in part the arrogant tone one might expect from a Pharaoh toward Asiatics and Nubians, immediately recalling the far more lucid and pragmatic diagnosis of the character of "vile Asiatics" offered by Khety II to his son Merikare five hundred years earlier. However, the letter also contains some amusing—and amused—teasing about his official's harem, filled with exotic women, along with advice to be wary of Nubian "witchcraft" (we shall examine this widespread Egyptian prejudice later) and observations on the untrustworthiness of African subjects in positions of responsibility in Egypt, due to their inability to carry out any task beyond that of the storehouse keeper:

Copy of the order which His Majesty wrote himself, with his own
hand, to the viceroy Usersatet. His Majesty was in Thebes in the
kap of the Pharaoh, and he drank and spent the day in merriment:
    Look, this order is brought to you from the king, great in mas-
sacre, strong of arm, victorious with his scimitar, who has bound
the Northerners and prostrated the Southerners in all their cities.
No rebel exists in any country.
    You [live among the Nubians], are a hero who brought booty
from all foreign countries, a charioteer, who takes captures for His
Majesty Amenophis, [who receives tribute from] Naharin, who
makes the land of the Hittites a payer of tribute, you (are) the master of a wife from Babylon and a maidservant from Byblos, a young
girl from Alalakh [in Syria] and an old woman from Arapakha. Now,
these people from Tekhsi (Syria) are worthless—what are they
good for?
    Another message for the viceroy: Do not trust the Nubians but
beware of their people and their witchcraft. Take this servant of a
commoner, for example, whom you have made an official although
he is not an official whom you should have suggested to His Majesty. . . . Do not listen to their words. Do not heed their messages!
(*Urkunden* IV, 1343–44)

Coming from Kush was not, in the eyes of teachers, a guarantee
of high scholastic achievement. Significantly, in one of the texts collected in the Miscellanies (Bologna Papyrus 1094, 3.5–3.10), the unwilling student is compared to a monkey: "Even the monkey is able
to listen to the words, even though it has been brought from Kush."
    The fact that "we are what we eat" is not a discovery of modern
anthropology. For ancient Egyptians, the type, quality, and preparation of food were already, like clothing, characteristics that distinguished one people from another. The Bedouin who welcomed
Sinuhe gave him different food from that of Egypt, since it all was
cooked in milk. "Many sweet things were made for me, and milk in
every kind of cooking." When Sinuhe returned to Egypt, he became
an Egyptian once more, removing, both physically and metaphori-
cally, his Bedouin trappings:

Then his majesty said to the Queen: "Here is Sinuhe, come as a
Bedu (Bedouin), in the guise of the Asiatics." She gave a very great
cry, and the royal children clamored all together. Then they said to
His Majesty: "It is not really he, O Sovereign, my lord!" Then His

Majesty said: "It is really he!" [. . .] Years were made to pass away
from my body. I was plucked and my hair was combed. A load of
dirt was given to the desert, and my clothes to the Sand-Crossers.
I was clad in fine linen and anointed with prime oil. I slept on a
bed. I gave up the sand to them who are in it, and wood oil to him
who is anointed with it.

In a witty and learned article written some years ago, Serge Sauneron showed the low opinion held by Egyptians of their southern
neighbors. Even though the evidence dates from the Late Period, or
even more recently, there is no doubt that such an opinion developed
during the many centuries of contact and coexistence between the
two peoples. In a Demotic tale (Setne, no. 2) in which the main character is the son of Ramesses II, Setne (Setem) Khaemwese, a magician from Kush comes to Egypt, where he challenges the Pharaoh's
magicians to read a letter without unrolling the sealed papyrus scroll.
After having called Kush "the land of resin-eaters," the Pharaoh orders a room and "disgusting things [to eat] according to Ethiopian
tastes" to be prepared for his guest.

Another text, found at Esna and dating from the Trajan age, explains that the providential demiurge Khnum has made the products
of foreign countries (including the kinds of food suitable for the
Nubian constitution) different from those of Egypt:

> Khnum created precious things in their lands,
> That they might bear their products abroad,
> For the lord of the wheel is their father too,
> Tatenen who made all that is on their soil.
> They produce their supplies—thus the people of Ibhat—
> To nourish themselves and their children.
> (Lichtheim 1980, p. 113)

In another Demotic tale (Petubasti; Strasbourg 15, 20–21), Min-
ebemaat, prince of Elephantine, is insultingly called a "black resin-
eater." Even the fact of possessing little food, when compared with
the abundance the Nile provided Egypt, helped to distinguish nomadic foreigners. Asiatic nomads were constantly on the move in
search of new supplies of food. As we can read on the stela of Merenptah at Karnak, the peoples of Libya "wander continuously and have
to fight daily in order to fill their bellies."

The introduction of "foreigners" into the world entrusted to the

Pharaoh was already documented in the Annals, inscribed on the Palermo Stone, and on other monuments. Nubians and Libyans entered the Nile Valley in considerable numbers, labeled as "living prisoners," after having been captured in war or during raids. For the first king of the Fourth Dynasty, Snofru, the Palermo Stone lists seven thousand prisoners "from the land of the Nubians," along with 200,000 beasts, both large and small. For the succeeding dynasty, during the reign of Sahure, the stone lists the importation of large quantities of precious minerals from neighboring countries and Sinai (the "Terraces of Turquoise"), and of exotic materials from Punt (frankincense, electrum, malachite, wood, etc.). Reliefs in Sahure's funerary temple at Abusir provide almost photographic images of the physical features, ways of dressing, and characteristic tattoos of military leaders from different lands in Libya, captured and brought to Egypt with their families and beasts. The following figures refer to the number of animals captured in raids: cattle, 123,400; asses, 223,200; goats, 232,413; and sheep, 243,689. The fact that the capture of prisoners was associated with that of livestock reveals the "economic" motivation behind the Pharaonic domination of foreign lands. These were the riches—minerals, animals, plants, manpower and craftsmanship—to which the Pharaoh needed access and to which he was entitled by divine grace. At Abusir once again, the god Ash, "lord of Libya," says to Sahure: "I will bring you every good thing that is in this land." In other scenes, the god makes statements such as: "I give you all hostile peoples with all the provisions that there are in foreign lands"; and "I give you all the foreign lands to the west and to the east, all the Iunti (Nubian nomads) and the Mentiu (Asiatic nomads) that exist in every land."

The Abusir temple reliefs from the reign of Sahure also show the arrival by sea of Asiatics—not as prisoners but, it would seem, as merchants, probably from Byblos. Men, boys, and women enthusiastically greet the Pharaoh from their boat: "Health to you, O Sahure, god of the living! We see your beauty!" "Health to you, Sahure, loved by Thoth, lord of foreign lands!"

The hieroglyphs that stand for one or more people on board a boat do not seem to have meant "signaler" or "quartermaster signaler," as Boreux (1924) suggests. The proposal of "interpreter," made by A. H. Gardiner and later partly modified by H. Goedicke ("foreigner" acting as a mercenary in the Egyptian army), is more likely. Nevertheless, despite Goedicke's suggestion, the generic translation of "foreigner" does not seem to be possible in the titles of two Old Kingdom palace doctors. In the case of the specialist in internal medicine, Iri, the phrase must be read as "he who recognizes the symptoms of urine in the bladder." In that of the other doctor, Khui, it should be translated as "he who recognizes the symptoms of the hidden tumor (?)." These men, as internal specialists, were able to "interpret" the pathological language of the body.

The need for "interpreters," or, in other words, of "foreigners-who-can-speak-Egyptian," arose because of the intense international trading activity that was so characteristic of the Egyptian world, even in the earliest period. Egyptian speakers can be seen, in texts and punctiliously realistic images, on each boat arriving from Asia in the ports of Sahure. It was their task to translate, and thus render comprehensible, foreigners' exclamations in honor of the Pharaoh.

The existence of a class of bilingual foreigners, or "interpreters," integrated into Egyptian society and employed professionally is quite widely documented in the Old Kingdom, although it is not clear whether they were foreigners by birth or the children of mixed marriages. The Decree of Dahshur (*Urkunden* I, 209.16) refers specifically to a group of interpreters coming from Nubian lands such as Medja, Iam, and Irtjet. These probably formed part of the "pacified Nubians" mentioned in the same decree (211, 3.10). Like others in this group, they were probably at the service of Egypt, where they would have been used as "scouts" or "interpreters" during expeditions to Sinai, Nubia, and the Red Sea, under the command of important officials such as the governors of Elephantine, Herkhuf, Pepinakhte, and Sarenput. Alternatively, they would have been employed in profitable military trading missions to those African lands in which natives and exotic goods could be acquired. The famous dancing dwarf brought back by Herkhuf to the boy-king Pepi II was a Pygmy from the land of Iam, south of the Second Cataract on the Nile.

The fact that interpreters no longer featured among recognized trades, with the exception of very rare cases, in the New Kingdom might be related to the increasingly profound linguistic contact established between Egyptians and foreigners from other countries in the empire and within Egypt itself. There is no further mention of interpreters as a specific class until the seventh century B.C. when, according to Herodotus (2.154), the category was organized by Psamtik I to spread the knowledge of the Greek language in Egypt.

The already massive presence of Nubians in the Egyptian army during the Sixth Dynasty is shown by the inscription of Uni (*Urkunden* I, 98 ff.). Uni was at the head of an army of many thousands of men, not only from Upper and Lower Egypt, but also "coming from Irtjet of Nubia, from Medjai of Nubia, and from the country of Libya." He conducted a series of successful campaigns against the "Sand-dwellers," the nomadic Bedouin of the Carmel region.

From the Old Kingdom on, groups or individuals of African origin (not necessarily prisoners of war) were absorbed into Egypt's indigenous laboring class. This was the case for men and women from Punt, for example, who worked as house servants in the palace of Merur nel Fayyūm and as mercenary troops during the Middle Kingdom. In the case of Nubians and people from Punt, social acceptance and cultural assimilation were encouraged by a basic ethnic affinity. The same process occurred, however, with the African populations from Napata in Kush, who began to arrive in Egypt in large numbers from the middle of the Eighteenth Dynasty on, when the roads that led to Darfur and Kordofan were under the direct control of the Pharaoh. A few figures will give us some idea: the Eighteenth Dynasty Annals of Tuthmosis III (*Urkunden* IV, 708 ff.) state that between the years 37 and 41 of the Pharaoh's reign, over two hundred prisoners were imported from Kush, including four of the Prince of Irem's children. During the Nineteenth Dynasty, Ramesses II lists, at Amara, approximately seven thousand prisoners taken from black African lands.

Captured prisoners were employed in Egypt in a number of ways: within the palace, in temples, and in royal funerary temples. A series of small commemorative stelae found at Qurna in the funerary temple of Tuthmosis IV reveal the existence within the temple estates of African colonies from the "vile land of Kush" and of "Syrians captured by His Majesty in the city of Gezer." These people were employed in specific activities: the Africans worked in the kitchens and bakery, or "house of bread," in the south wing of Tuthmosis IV's funerary temple, and the Palestinians, traditionally experts in the making of wine, worked in the cellars or "house of wine" in the temple's north wing.

Another indication of the servile status imposed on Nubians and Asiatics can be found, during the New Kingdom, in the wooden and ivory cosmetic spoons in which the handle has the form of a servant (a Nubian, an African, or an Asiatic) bent beneath the weight of a large jar, which formed the bowl of the spoon (closed by a hinged lid, this contains the unguent).

During the Eleventh Dynasty, in the First Intermediate Period, a colony of Nubian mercenaries settled at Gebelein in Upper Egypt. They left evidence of themselves in a group of about twenty stelae, Egyptian in their decorative and religious style and use of hieroglyphs, but typical of their own culture in the figures of the people commemorated and of their families. The Nubian soldiers have frizzy hair, often bound by a ribbon and sometimes with a large pin (or bone?) pushed through it; their wide belts often have tassels or animal tails hanging from them. They carry in their hands bows and arrows, the symbols of their trade. On the Nubian stelae of Gebelein, we notice the constant presence of one or two dogs, the friends and companions of soldiers in war (the names of these dogs, however, are not given, unlike the Libyan dogs, with Libyan names, in the famous Cairo Museum relief from the tomb of Antef II at Deir al-Bahri, dating from the same period). Although the wife of the "Nubian Sunu" (Boston Stela MFA, 03.1848) was probably Egyptian, their son, named Nebeska, was also a soldier and wears Nubian national dress on the stela. The "Nubian Tjenenu" (Stela M, Turin, Suppl. 1270) and his four brothers were professional soldiers. They are shown in national costume on the Gebelein stelae.

The ethnic group of mercenaries coming from the Medjay region, at the Second Cataract of the Nile, was particularly important during the Eleventh Dynasty and continued to be appreciated during the Twelfth Dynasty. The name "Medjay" was later used to describe a special police force, often in service at temples.

Not all Africans became part of the Egyptian social fabric by joining the army. Many, either freed or "adopted," became "Egyptians" and advanced within society. The Nubian Ameniu, for example, captured during one of Tuthmosis III's campaigns and ceded by the king to his barber, Sabastet, married the barber's niece and lived happily ever after (see chap. 7, p. 206). The act of emancipation (preserved on a papyrus in the Louvre) was drafted in the twenty-seventh year of the reign of Tuthmosis III "before the 'boys of the *kap* [royal nursery].'" The Nubians who belonged to the Kap (usually educated and of a high social class) clearly had the task of providing "consular" protection for less fortunate Nubians.

The existence of the Kap reveals both a basic absence in ancient Egypt of racial prejudice and a policy of cultural assimilation of the "defeated" by the victors. Already in the Middle Kingdom, the Kap of the royal palaces accepted and trained the sons of the Pharaoh and of Egyptian nobles along with those of Nubian chiefs and nobles. By the New Kingdom, if not sooner, the sons of Asiatics were also accepted. The foreign "boys of the Kap" made their careers in Egypt, within the palace, in administration, and in the army. Alternatively, they returned to their own countries, preserving political and cultural links with the land of the Pharaoh.

Within the palace, the Kap was also a kind of male harem, or all-male club, where the Pharaoh could relax, drink, and enjoy the company of his friends, as we can see from the letter, quoted above, from Amenophis II to his viceroy in Nubia: "His majesty was in Thebes in the Kap of the Pharaoh, and he drank and spent the day in merriment" (*Urkunden* IV, 1343–44). One African "boy of the Kap" was Heqanefer, depicted on the Theban tomb of Hui, viceroy of Kush. Heqanefer, prince of Miam during the time of Tutankhamun, is shown taking part in an exotic procession to render homage to the Pharaoh. He is wearing a mixed Afro-Egyptian costume, although in his own tomb in Nubia, he is depicted in Egyptian dress. The young princes accompanying him, also destined to become "boys of the Kap," are already dressed as Egyptians. The African princess, in white pleated linen, will certainly enter the women's harem. There is doubt about the identity of the black noblewoman on a chariot drawn by oxen. Dressed in an opulent mixture of Egyptian and foreign styles announcing Meroitic splendors, she may have been the bride of the prince of Miam or of Wawat or have been destined for the Pharaoh's harem.

One category of foreigners had a special reputation in Egypt: magicians. They were mainly Nubians and Kushites: even the goddess Isis, as a magician, declared herself to be "Nubian." In magical texts, Nubian names and spells (incomprehensible and thus even more effective) were particularly powerful.

In the chapel of Haremhab at Gebel Silsileh, there is a depiction of the triumphant return of an expedition to Nubia, with its procession of prisoners. Four Nubian magicians can be seen, employed in a magical dance accompanied by singing (in favor, one hopes, of the Pharaoh . . .). Nubian magicians were powerful enough to be dangerous if hostile. We should remember what Amenophis II said to his viceroy in Nubia.

A papyrus containing a magical text (Leiden 343–45, r. VI.8) al-

ludes to powerful Palestinian magicians: "the people of Altaqana
who speak with serpents." The existence in Egypt of a man of Byblos who was an expert in medicine is revealed by the medical Ebers
Papyrus, dating from the Eighteenth Dynasty: "Another remedy
for the eyes that an Asiatic from Byblos has told me about" (63.8–
11). The remedy in question contains the first known mention of
the word "*ibnu*," the Egyptian for "alum," which might indicate that
both the term and the medical adoption of alum were foreign to
Egyptian tradition, having arrived from the Near East.

The fame of Nubian magicians lasted until Greco-Roman times.
As we have seen, the second of the cycle of Demotic tales of Setne
Khaemwese describes how a magician from Kush came to court in
order to challenge Egyptian magicians to read a sealed papyrus scroll
without unrolling it.

The Bedouin shepherds who wandered the edges of the eastern
Delta and the Wadi Tumilat pass were not only familiar to the Egyptians but appear to have been welcomed from the earliest times. In
the Prophecy of Neferti, written in the Twelfth Dynasty, we read:
"They (the Asiatics) will beg for water in their usual way, to give to
their flocks."

From the Middle Kingdom on, Asiatics became increasingly numerous in Egypt. Picturesque caravans moved between the Near
East and Egypt. The famous tomb paintings of Khnumhotep at Beni
Hasan (around 1900 B.C.) depict, in extraordinary detail, the arrival
of an entire tribe of Bedouin: men, women, asses laden with bows,
axes, lances, and wooden harps of a kind not found in Egypt. They
are led by their chief, Abishai, described in a somewhat boastful way
as "Heqa Khasut," "prince of foreign lands."

Among foreign carpenters we find the "Fenekhu," a name that,
from the Old Kingdom on, undoubtedly referred to carpenters from
the wooded land of the Lebanon, although it later began to be used
less precisely to describe various coastal regions in Asia. Later, in the
Ptolemaic Period, the hieroglyph "Fenekhu" was used for the Greek
"Phoinike" (Phoenicia).

Middle Kingdom documents list Syrians who used both their
original names (most of which incorporated the names of gods such
as Reshef, Shamash, Anat, Baal, and Baalat) and Egyptian ones. The
fact that foreigners adopted Egyptian names, however, means that
they were already almost, if not entirely, indistinguishable from
Egyptians.

The Thirteenth Dynasty usurpation of the throne by the Syrian Khendjer ("Wild Boar"), an ex-mercenary from the Pharaoh's divisions, must have encouraged foreigners to come to Egypt. We cannot elaborate here the consequences of the arrival in Egypt of the people from Asia known as the Hyksos and of their gods. They settled in the Delta, where their capital city of Avaris was protected by their official deity, Baal-Sutekh, a god of the tempest. He was later incorporated into the Egyptian deity Seth, already a "suspect" god in Egyptian mythology, where his rule had been "confined" to foreign lands, beyond the border of Egypt.

The Two Lands—the Nile Valley and the Delta—were divided once again under the Hyksos, almost as if they had returned to the chaos preceding historical times. The eastern border had been crossed by Asiatic invaders, who allied, for reasons of mutual interest, with the prince of Kush at the frontier of Upper Egypt. This anomalous situation was perfectly appreciated by Kamose, the prince of Thebes. Addressing his counselors, who wanted to leave things as they were, he said: "I should like to know what my power means when one chief is in Avaris and another is in Kush, and I sit beside an Asiatic and a Nubian, and each has his piece of this Egypt?" (Carnarvon Tablet).

A "war of liberation" followed, during which the Thebans won numerous victories. It came to an end when the enemy's forces were driven back into Palestine, and order was restored in a reunified Egypt. The description of the taking of Avaris, the Hyksos capital, emphasizes the presence of the Hyksos women, delectable spoils awaiting the arrival of the victors:

> I saw on the terraces your women, who looked at the port from between the battlements; they did not move when they heard me, but pushed their noses out through the walls, like owl-chicks from their hole, saying: "All is lost." (Stela of Karnak)

The capture of Avaris and its port, with its ships and wealth, as well as of the inhabitants of the city, who were taken prisoner, is boastfully described by Kamose:

> Your heart is broken, O vile Asiatic! I drink the wine of your cellar, that which has been squeezed for me by Asiatics who are now my prisoners [. . .]
> I have thrown your women into the boats; I have captured the

horses. I have not left a single plank of the three hundred ships of green cedar, full of gold, lapis lazuli, silver, turquoise, innumerable bronze axes, as well as of oil, incense, fat, honey, *ituren*-wood, carob, *sepni*-wood, all prized woods, and all the good products of Syria. (Stela of Karnak)

During the long period, however, in which Thebes and Avaris had coexisted without violent conflicts, the resident invaders had been assimilated by Egyptian culture. The letter to the prince of Kush whose bearer was captured by Kamose was "written by hand by the prince of Avaris," evidently in Egyptian (unlike, for example, the letter carried by the messenger of the prince of Naharin captured by Amenophis II and referred to in the Memphis stela; borne around the messenger's neck, its message was written in cuneiform characters inscribed on clay). It is curious to discover that, in his letter, Apopi accused the king of Thebes of having attacked and betrayed him without warning and of having attacked his territory without provocation. The "barbarian" is accusing the Egyptian of barbarism.

The subsequent centuries of Egyptian domination in Asia led to the arrival in the Nile Valley not only of large numbers of male and female slaves but also of groups of prisoners of war. These became part of Egyptian society, sometimes establishing colonies. An inscription by Ramesses II at Abu Simbel (written to comment on a depiction of the Pharaoh in the act of killing some Libyans) provides important information about the practice of transferring conquered people from one part of the empire to another, or of deporting groups from their original homeland:

> The perfect god, who kills the Nine Bows,
> who crushes the lands of the north
> who is powerful in these lands,
> who bears the land of Nubia into the land of the north,
> and the Asiatics into Nubia.
> He has placed the Shasu Asiatics into the western land,
> he has settled the Libyans in the hills (of Asia),
> filling the fortresses that he has built
> with people captured by his mighty arm.

Produced during the reign of Ramesses V, the Wilbour Papyrus (III, 44 ff.) indicates possible sites of Semitic colonies in Egypt in the region of Oxyrhynchus. Among places listed in connection with plowing, mention is made of Pa-en Shasu (the Shasu established there worshiped "Hathor"), Per-Baalat ("the temple of the goddess Baalat"), Kharu ("Syria"), and Na-Kharu ("the seat of the Syrians"). Other place-names in the same document, such as Pa-en Medjay and Pa-en Nehesu, indicate the existence of settlements of people from Medjay and of Nubians as well.

At the time of Sheshonq III, a community of Shasu Bedouin, originally from central Syria, was to be found at Aphroditopolis. This was almost certainly one of the colonies of soldiers, or of prisoners, established during the Ramesside Period. During the Bubastite Period (Twenty-second to Twenty-third Dynasties), a community of Shardan mercenaries also existed to the north of Aphroditopolis.

The arrival in Egypt of Asiatic prisoners of war was constant and intense. In certain cases, it can be quantified by examining official documents. As booty from a single Asiatic campaign, Amenophis II brought back 838 women, 550 *marianu*-warriors with their 240 women, 328 children of princes, and 2,790 female singers of princes of all foreign lands, with their jewels. After the war fought during the ninth year of his reign, the Pharaoh returned with an even higher number of prisoners: "Princes of Syria (Retenu): 127; brothers of princes: 179; Shasu Bedouin taken prisoner: 15,200; Kharu Syrians: 36,300; people of Nuhasseh (Aleppo) taken prisoner alive: 15,070; their families: 30,652. Total 89,600 people" (Stela of Mit Rahina, CGC 6301). Although the total is, in fact, too high by over ten thousand prisoners, it is nonetheless striking. It is significant in that it indicates the arrival in Egypt of people from a wide range of social classes and ethnic origins.

The number of foreign women to be absorbed into New Kingdom Egypt is also striking. They range from those destined for the harem of the Pharaoh, or of other important figures in Egyptian society, to weavers, maids, singers, and dancers.

Brothels were provided with exotic attractions, and the music performed in them made use of instruments that were new to Egypt. Nubian dancers were accompanied by drums and tambourines. Libyan dancers, identified in the Deir al-Bahri reliefs by three feathers on their heads, performed ritual dances to a rhythm produced by curved sticks, similar to the modern Italian "dance of the batons."

At Luxor, a scene showing the festival of Opet depicts a group of Asiatic singers referred to as "the singers of Khepeshit." In another relief at Thebes, in the scenes of harems carved on blocks from

Karnak dating from the Amarna Period, we find Nubian singers. Syrian singers (recognizable by the layered frills of their clothes) can be seen in harem scenes carved on the walls of the El-Amarna tombs of Ay and Tutu.

By the middle of the Eighteenth Dynasty, Near Eastern influence on Egyptian costume and behavior had even reached the Pharaoh. An extraordinary serpentine statuette (from Thebes, now in the Metropolitan Museum of Art in New York) shows Amenophis III wrapped in a long Asiatic garment with a fringed border. His hands are clasped in front of him in a gesture reminiscent of Elamite or, more precisely, Babylonian statuary of the period. The designs on the tunic of Tutankhamun also reveal the influence of decorative motifs from the Near East. By the time of the Amarna Period at least, Egyptians had adopted a new way of drinking beer, using a squared siphon, as we can see in a stela (Berlin Museum) dedicated by a Syrian soldier named Terera. New Kingdom Egypt also borrowed from its Near Eastern neighbors new types of weapons and vases and skills such as those involved in making glass vessels, as well as new shipbuilding and pottery techniques.

This taste for the exotic also involved botany and the environment. During the Eighteenth Dynasty, the pomegranate was introduced to Egypt. Entire shrubs of incense were uprooted and brought from Punt by Hatshepsut. During his military campaigns in Asia, Tuthmosis III also "conquered" some unusual plants. Each detail of their leaves, flowers, and seeds was observed and drawn, to form the oldest herbarium in the world. Known as the "Botanical Garden of Tuthmosis III," these drawings are reproduced on a wall of the king's temple at Karnak.

Undeniable, albeit infrequent, examples of Asiatic influence on Egyptian literature exist. These include the Tales of Anat and Seth, Astarte and the Sea, the episode (which took place, however, outside Egypt, in the Lebanese Valley of the Cedar) of the girl of Bata desired by the Sea (in the Tale of the Two Brothers), and the allusion (in Anastasi Papyrus I, 23.7) to a story whose leading character, Qagerdi, prince of Iser, is chased by a bear and forced to climb a tree. That literary texts written in cuneiform were read is suggested by the existence of mythological tales among the tablets of El-Amarna (Adapa and the Southern Wind; Nergal and Aresh-kigal). The frequent exchange of correspondence in cuneiform between Egypt and the Near East, revealed by the Amarna archives, required the existence at court of scribes and readers of cuneiform. This has been confirmed by the discovery at El-Amarna of a dictionary of Egyptian words phonetically transcribed into cuneiform.

During the New Kingdom, the Egyptian army contained an ever increasing number of foreign mercenaries. We only have to look at the list of troops on an expedition to Phoenicia (invented by the author of the Satirical Letter, Anastasi Papyrus I, during the reign of Ramesses II, to emphasize his rival's inability to organize): "The troops before you number 1,900: 520 Shardan, 1,600 Qehaq (Libyan), 100 Meshwesh (Libyan), 880 Nubians, 5,000 in all, not counting their officials."

Although the Egyptians had abundant direct knowledge of the Near East by this time, alarming information about foreigners could still circulate. In the Satirical Letter the dangers of a journey in Syria are vividly described: "The narrow path is infested by Shasu (Bedouin) who hide in the scrub; some of them are four or five cubits (2.5 or 3 meters!) tall from head to toe; fierce in face, their hearts are not soft and they do not listen to jokes" (Anastasi Papyrus I, 23.7–8).

Among the enemies brought back to Egypt as prisoners during the Nineteenth Dynasty were the inhabitants of the "land of Kheta." These people—the Hittites—were depicted by Egyptian artists with beardless faces, double chins, and long, ringleted hair. Toward the middle of the thirteenth century, changing historical conditions imposed new, peaceful relations between the two countries. These culminated in a bilateral—and bilingual—peace treaty between Ramesses II and the Hittite king. The long period of negotiation leading up to this treaty meant that many messengers and ambassadors came to Egypt in a spirit of "peace and good brotherhood," as the treaty, in the hieroglyphic version known to us from Thebes, expresses it. The pact between the two long-standing enemies was also witnessed by the gods, a thousand for each country. For the Hittites, these ranged from the sun god, lord of the sky, to the sun goddess of the city of Arinna, the god of storms, and, finally, the Rivers of the Land of Khatti. The Egyptians had Amun, Re, Seth, male and female gods, and those of the rivers and mountains of Egypt.

When, toward the end of the reign of Ramesses II, Khattusili II decided to send his daughter to become the wife of the Pharaoh, the city of Piramesse and the eastern Delta were suddenly filled with Hittites. According to the inscription on the "Wedding Stela" (beside the temple of Abu Simbel), the princess brought with her a splendid dowry ("gold, silver, bronze, slaves, innumerable pairs of horses, livestock, goats, endless thousands of sheep") and was accompanied by Hittite princes. The description in the Wedding Stela of the amicable relations between Egyptians and Hittites is rather disconcerting when one remembers how often Egyptian texts expressed their scorn for "the vile land of Khatti." It is clear that both the new affection and the traditional scorn were, in effect, no more than convention:

> Now, when the daughter of the great prince of Khatti came to Egypt, the infantry, the chariots, and the nobles of His Majesty escorted her and mingled with the infantry, the chariots, and the nobles of Khatti. They ate and drank together, with one heart as brothers, without disturbing one another.

As in all love stories, the Hittite princess—"her face as beautiful as that of a goddess"—enchanted the heart of Ramesses. He gave his royal bride the Egyptian name Maathornofrure ("She who sees the beauty of Re") to replace her Hittite name.

The spread of Egypt's political influence during the Old Kingdom was accompanied by the "exportation" of Egyptian gods (Thoth and Hathor into Sinai and Byblos; Hathor into Punt), increasing constantly from that period on. It is hardly surprising, therefore, that Egypt also "imported," and welcomed as integrated guests, foreign gods from the regions and lands around its borders. In some cases, these gods were allowed to keep their names, appearance, clothes, and myths of origin. In the case of the earliest contacts, they lost their original character and were assimilated (e.g., the Libyan goddess Neith and god Ha; and, from the east, the god Soped, of extremely remote Asiatic origin). A Nubian god like Dedun, "who presides over the land of the Nubians," already mentioned in the Pyramid Texts, remained confined to the lands south of Aswan. There he may be said to have collaborated with the power of the Pharaoh, to whom he gave the exotic produce of Africa. The lion mask and hairstyle of the Pygmy god Bes preserved all the magical fascination of the exotic.

It was only natural that the arrival of Asiatic deities in Egypt should have coincided with that of Asiatic peoples. During the New Kingdom, Syrian and Palestinian deities triumphed in Egypt, alongside other signs of a new cosmopolitanism. Reshef and Baal were warrior gods and wore their exotic national costumes proudly on

Egyptian monuments to them, as did mercenaries serving the Pharaoh. Horon, identified with the Great Sphinx, was worshiped at Giza at least from the time of Amenophis II. The Amorite god of shepherds, Horon was invoked by magical chants preserved (both in Egyptian and in Amorite transcribed in Egyptian signs) in the Harris Papyrus. These chants asked the god to protect herds from wolves and other wild animals.

During the New Kingdom the cult of the "naked goddess," Qadesh, spread throughout the area of Memphis, which contained numerous military and civilian colonies of Syrians and Palestinians. Qadesh was welcomed in the temple of Ptah as his bride (the gods also following the fashion of having foreign women in their harems!). Astarte received particular veneration from Amenophis II as the "rider-goddess" and goddess of war. From his reign on, she was declared the "Lady of Perunefer" ("Good journey"), a river port near Memphis that possessed a shipyard and arsenal. Perunefer was an important center because of the many Asiatic immigrants, merchants, artisans, and mercenaries living there.

The statue of Astarte at Nineveh, believed to have magical healing powers, was originally sent by Tushratta of Mitanni to the sick Amenophis III. Ramesses II declared himself "loved by Anat," who became the titular god of a cult at Piramesse.

The "Asiatic" sickness ("that of the Amorites") also arrived in Egypt from the east. A suggested remedy was to pronounce a magical spell invoking Seth, god of foreign lands, over certain medicinal substances:

> Spell for the Asiatic sickness: "Who is wise as Re, who is wise as Re?" Blacken the body with charcoal to capture the god (the cause of the illness) [and bring him] to the surface. [Say]: "Just as Seth fought against the sea, so Seth will fight against you, O Asiatic, so that you shall not enter in the son of such-and-such." (Hearst Papyrus 170, 11.12–15)

It may have been necessary to address this "Asiatic" illness in its own language. Egyptian doctors were provided with the spell "used in this case by the people of the land of Keftui (Cretans): Saantaka-papiuaia-aiamaantarakukara" (such a gallimaufry of syllables that the spell could hardly have failed to work!).

It has been known for some time that foreigners, particularly

Semites, played an increasingly active role in Egyptian society during the Ramesside Period. Half of the known cupbearers (*udepu*) of the king, for example, are estimated to have been of foreign origin. The position of *udepu* was anything but humble, since the king had to trust the loyalty of his cupbearer (among the members of the palace plot against Ramesses III, however, we find a number of foreign cupbearers).

The highest social level among immigrants was that of the "sons of princes." As a result of a deliberate policy, expressed by Tuthmosis III in a frequently quoted passage describing Egypt's relations with the Near East in the Eighteenth Dynasty, these boys were brought to Egypt as hostages. They were raised in the harem or Kap and were taught to behave as Egyptians so that they would return to their homes as loyal subjects, favorably inclined to the culture of their oppressors. The practice of "diplomatic marriages" had a similar purpose. Princesses and women of the highest birth from every kingdom of the Near East were taken into the harem. The royal fashion for foreign brides was also imitated by others of lesser rank.

It is easy to identify foreigners in documents when they, or their relatives, have non-Egyptian names. Jupa, son of Urkhai, and Lullu, son of Buka, were from Hurru. The grandfather of Paser, vizier of Sethos I, also had a name of Hurrian origin: Papaia. The mother of the vizier Neferronpet was called Qafraiat, a Semitic name that might have meant "She who has blonde hair." The mother of the cupbearer Pentaur was named Aurati, and her sister was Lukasha (Cairo Stela N. Provv. 12/6/24/17). The chief draftsman Bania and the painter Qefaa (Theban Tomb no. 140) were Semitic, as were the goldsmith Pa-tjai-Baal and the naval carpenters Aarusu and Bania (Petersburg Papyrus 1116, B 16). Names such as Ishtar-ummi ("Astarte is my mother": *Urkunden* IV, 11, no. 63), Ynusa, Baal-mahar, and Uarna leave no doubt as to the Semitic origins of their possessors. Names that include a place-name are another clear sign of foreign origin: Pa-Luka ("The Lycian"), Pen-Hazor ("The one from Hazor"), and Pa-assur ("The Assyrian").

From the earliest period, however, immigrants concealed their origins by giving their children Egyptian names. A typical example, from the New Kingdom, is that of Pa-ameru ("The Amorite") and his wife, Karen, who called their two sons Useretmin and Merire. The latter became the squire of Tuthmosis III.

It has been noted that, during the Eighteenth Dynasty, foreigners preferred to adopt names containing the element "heqa" ("to rule," "ruler") (such as Heqanefer), whereas during the Ramesside Period, "loyalist" names, which included the name of the current Pharaoh, were more common. The doorkeeper Akber, for example, changed his name to Ramessenakhte ("Ramesses is powerful"). Ramesse-em-per-re, called Meri-iunu ("Loved by Heliopolis"), an eminent figure at court as "first cupbearer, fanbearer to the right of the king, first herald of His Majesty," was originally named Ben-Azan after Zeri-Basani, a place to the east of the Sea of Galilee.

Tutu followed Akhenaten to El-Amarna and possessed the following titles: "first servant of Akhenaten in the temple of Aten," "first servant of Aten in the barque," "overseer of all the works of the Pharaoh and overseer of all public works," "treasurer," and "chief of all the country." The name "Tutu" derives from the Semitic name "Dudu", and on this basis he has been reasonably identified with the Dudu known to us from letters sent to Akhenaten by Aziru, son of the Amorite king Abdi-ashirta. This hypothesis seems to be confirmed by the fact that Tutu, in an inscription on his tomb, discovered in El-Amarna, describes himself as a man who understands the words of foreign ministers and can report them to the palace:

> As for the messengers from all the foreign lands,
> I reported their words to the palace,
> while I was at the palace daily.
> I was sent as the Pharaoh's delegate with each of
> His Majesty's orders.

Another very interesting case is that of Sarbaina (or Sarbakhana), known as Abi. Abi was a prophet both of Amun and of the Semitic deities Baal and Astarte in the city of Perunefer. He probably lived sometime during the middle of the Eighteenth Dynasty and was buried at Saqqara.

The Semite Aper-ia (or Aper-el) lived at the end of the Eighteenth Dynasty. His rock tomb at Saqqara has recently been discovered and investigated, with extraordinary results, by A. Zivie. Aper-ia actually achieved the rank of vizier, the highest administrative position in the Egyptian state. A parallel with the biblical Joseph's career in Egypt inevitably springs to mind.

The date of the arrival in Egypt of the Hebrew people and of the Exodus still cannot be established with any certainty. Egypt provides the scenario for many of the most important figures in the

Bible, such as Abraham and Sarah, who moved to the verdant Delta (the prototype of the Promised Land), and Joseph, sold as a slave in Egypt by Ishmaelites and bought by Potiphar, one of the Pharaoh's officers and captain of the guard. Joseph later became Potiphar's personal servant and was eventually promoted to the rank of vizier by the Pharaoh. Finally, there is the Egyptianized figure of Moses.

According to the Bible (Gen. 15:13), the Hebrews had lived in Egypt for over four hundred years when Moses led them from the Delta. No trace, however, has been found in Egyptian documents of the Hebrews as a special race. They would have been only one of many groups of Asiatics to have settled in Egypt, where they lived by working as, among other things, brickmakers and masons. Although the term "Apiru" (the designation borne by Semites who seem to have been a kind of mobile workforce, constantly on the move in both Egypt and Asia) might evoke "Hebrew," there is as yet no proof that the two terms refer to the same ethnic group.

As we have already seen, the Libyan race was one of the four peoples of the world according to Pharaonic tradition. In practice, however, up to the Nineteenth Dynasty, Egyptian interests were concentrated on Nubia, Kush, and the internal and coastal regions of Asia. Control over the seminomadic inhabitants of Libya was limited to attempts to halt their constant insidious incursions into the Delta and the oases of the Western Desert by means of deterrent action and raiding parties to capture prisoners and livestock.

During the Nineteenth Dynasty, the pressure of the Tjehenu Libyans and their even more warlike and aggressive allies threatened the border of the Delta, forcing Merenptah to intervene. The Great Inscription of Karnak describes in detail earlier episodes of creeping invasion by the people of Libya, as well as their new and dangerous aggressiveness. It also provides ethnographic comments expressing considerable contempt for the "Peoples of the Sea," "who had no foreskin," that is, who were circumcised. The chief of the invaders was the "vile chief of Libya, Merirei, son of Did"; his allies were "Shardan, Shekelesh, and Equesh from the (foreign) lands of the sea (*n p3 ym*), who have no foreskin. Having no foreskin, these were killed and their hands were cut off." The Lukki and Tursha tribes are also mentioned. It is clear that the Libyans were allied to groups of the Peoples of the Sea. These groups would later, during the reign of Ramesses III, attempt in vain to enter the Delta from the eastern border and the Mediterranean coast.

Merenptah flies into a rage against those Egyptians who had
been failing to keep the foreigners under control for some time:

> Egypt has been abandoned to invasion by every land,
> the Nine Bows have been able to sack its borders.
> Rebels can invade it each day [. . .]
> [so that Libyans] have entered on several occasions
> Egypt's fields from the Great River (Nile),
> passing days and months occupying [the country],
> reaching the hills of the oasis [. . .]
> coming from the district of Farafra:
> this is testified, they say, since the times of the kings
> in documents of other times.
> No one was able to [destroy them] like worms,
> there was no way to overwhelm their bodies,
> because they love life and hate death,
> and their hearts are exalted against those who know (?) [. . .]
> Passing their time wandering around the land,
> fighting each day to fill their bellies;
> they come to Egypt to seek food for their mouths.

In the same inscription, Merenptah boasts about his victory over
the Libyan leader, who fled "leaving behind him, in his haste, his
sandals, bow, and quiver," and from whose camp the victors brought
back his goods, women, and furniture to Egypt. As a result of the
king's victory, the Libyans were no longer feared in the Delta, nor
were foreign languages to be heard there:

> Oh how sweet it is to sit and babble!
> One walks free-striding on the road,
> for there's no fear in people's hearts;
> fortresses are left to themselves,
> wells are open for the messenger's use.
> [. . .]
> There's no calling out at night:
> "Wait, I come," in a stranger's voice.
> (Lichtheim 1976, p. 77)

Up to this point, the Libyans had been elusive enemies due to
their nomadic habits. Now, however, they effectively entered the
universal scheme on which Pharaonic ideology was based. Ramesses
III was able to boast that he had brought the conquered Libyans into

Egypt, where they forgot all notion of nationalism, their native tongue being replaced by Egyptian after a process of cultural brainwashing: "Brought back to Egypt, [the Libyan prisoners] were placed in fortresses. They heard, in the service of the king, the language of the Egyptians; the king made them forget their own speech and overturned their language" (LD III, 218).

The army Ramesses III used against the Libyans was composed of Egyptian troops and groups of mercenaries, including the Shardan, Philistines (the Philistines and Palestinians were part of the Peoples of the Sea), Syrian Shasu, and Nubians. The Shardan had been mercenaries in Egypt since the time of Amenophis III. That they were soldiers of fortune is confirmed by the fact that they appeared among Egypt's enemies during the wars against the Hittites. At the time of Merenptah they were allies of Libya, along with the Philistines (Pereset), who were originally from Crete.

After the Twenty-first Dynasty, the throne of Horus was occupied by dynasties of foreign origin; first Libyans, then Ethiopians of Napata from Kush. This "scandalous" phenomenon was accepted as a result of the cultural assimilation of these "foreigners."

The founder of the Twenty-first Dynasty, Sheshonq I, descended from an old family of military colonists at Herakleopolis known as the "chiefs of Ma" ("Ma" is an abbreviation of "Meshwesh," who were not only in the pay of the Pharaoh but also allied to the enemies of Egypt defeated by the Ramessides). These colonists had established themselves at Bubastis. The founder of the colony was a Libyan with the "barbaric" name of Bui-uaua.

It might be considered one of history's ironies that Egypt acquired new international prestige, not to mention a certain domestic harmony and an economic recovery revealed by large-scale building, precisely during the reigns of these foreigners with the "barbaric" names of Sheshonq and Osorkon. A number of alliances were made in Asia during the same period, and Assyrian aggression was kept under control.

The fear of hostile "foreigners," however, was still alive. It was expressed in the proliferation of "oracular amulets," intended to protect their wearers from all evil: "from the magic of the Syrians (Kharu), from the magic of the Ethiopians, from the magic of the Asiatic Shasu, from the magic of the Puti Libyans, from the magic of the people of Egypt." In this context, the name "Kharu" might indicate the settled Palestinians or the people of the Phoenician coast.

Shasu might refer to the nomadic Semites to the east of the Delta
and in Transjordan: people, that is, such as the Arabs, Kenites, Midi-
anites, Edomites, Amalekites, or even, already, the Jews of Israel.

Tefnakhte of Sais, the founder of the Twenty-fourth Dynasty,
also belonged to a powerful family of the chiefs of the Meshwesh.
At the end of the eighth century B.C. he proclaimed himself "great
chief of the Libyans and great prince of the west" before announcing
that he was king, in opposition to the claim made by the king of
Napata, the Kushite Piankhi (or Peye, according to the proposal to
change the traditional spelling of the name). At this point in Egyptian history, a black African was recognized king of Kush and Egypt,
after a triumphant and victorious march along the entire Nile Valley,
before celebrating the jubilee of the Pharaohs in Memphis.

It is certainly remarkable that the conquest of Egypt by the king
of Kush (the distant country to which triumphant Pharaohs had
taken their culture so many centuries before) was officially presented
by Piankhi (on the Great Stela of Gebel Barkal), in a knowing reference to the glorious model of the great New Kingdom Pharaohs, as
a crusade conducted to crush Egyptians who were rebelling against
the decree of Amun. Amun, god of both Thebes and Napata, had
given the king of Kush sovereign power over all countries:

> Amun of Napata has granted me sovereignty over every land,
> so that he to whom I say, "You are king," [will be king],
> but he to whom I say, "You will not be king," [will not be king].
> Amun of Thebes has granted me sovereignty over Egypt,
> so that he to whom I say, "You are crowned," will be crowned,
> but he to whom I say, "You will not be crowned," will not be crowned.
> Anyone to whom I turn my [benevolent] attention,
> his city will not be destroyed, at least not by my hand.
> It is the gods who create a king—
> even though men can also create a king;
> but me, Amun has made me king.
>
> (Stela 26 of Gebel Barkal)

In seventh-century Egypt, the defence of the eastern borders
against foreign invasion was in the hands of the Africans of Kush.
King Shabataka sent an army to help Hezekiah of Judah (an ineffec-
tive aid, however, compared in the Bible to "a broken reed that
pierces the hand in which it rests"). King Taharqa fought fiercely
before retreating when faced by the attack of the Assyrian king As-

surbanipal, who reached as far as Thebes with his army of Phoeni-
cians, Syrians, and Cypriots, as well as Egyptians from the Delta.
Egyptian princes in the north, in fact, were ready to collaborate with
the Assyrian enemy, in reaction against the intolerable sovereignty
of Napata.

For Assyrian domination in the province of Egypt we have no
direct documentation from monuments. However, we know the procedures the Assyrians used to govern the province, procedures that
resemble those adopted by imperial Egypt in relation to its Nubian
subjects and to those Asiatics brought to Egypt to be educated. Inspired by the same motive, the Assyrians took the young princes of
Egypt's tributary and vassal cities to Nineveh, giving them an Assyrian education and Assyrian names. The name of the prince of Sais,
son of Necho and future founder of the Twenty-sixth Dynasty, was
thus transformed from Psamtik to the Assyrian Nabushizibanni. It is
no accident that Psamtik I, whose experience in Assyria enabled him
to make valuable contacts with the lords of other Assyrian vassal
states, took advantage of the weakness of Napata and of the fact that
Assyria was concentrating its attentions elsewhere to restore Egypt's
liberty and independence. The military supremacy he needed was
provided by recruiting Ionian and Carian mercenaries from Anatolia.

It is well known that pre-Hellenic contacts between the Greek
world and Egypt had been preceded by Egypt's relations, first, with
Minoan civilization and then with the Mycenean world. From the
Eighteenth Dynasty on, Crete's ancient inhabitants appear in tomb
decorations as importers of materials, that is—according to the conventions of Pharaonic iconography—as tribute bearers. With their
customary skill and attention to ethnic details, Egyptian artists distinguished these foreigners by their facial features, hair, clothes,
boots, and the objects they carried. The studies carried out by Jean
Vercoutter, and published some years ago, remain basic texts in this
field. We know that Egyptian texts referred to the Myceneans as the
Keftui (the Kaftor of the Bible). The Keftui (belonging to both the
Aegean world and the countries of the Syrian coast) frequently visited Egypt during the New Kingdom, as merchants and importers of
various "tribute."

Egypt's ports and coasts were not unknown to Homeric Greeks.
We might recall the account in the *Odyssey* of the attempts to disem-
bark in Egypt made by Odysseus—a pirate similar to the "Peoples
of the Sea," but in the eighth century B.C. The recurrence, in Linear

B, of the place-name Aigyptiu, clearly related to the Greek name for Egypt, Aigyptos, is well known. The founding of Naucratis, a Mediterranean hub for Greek commercial activity, which was both intense and highly organized by this time, dates back to the seventh century B.C.

Ionian and Carian mercenaries ("bronze men," in the often-quoted passage from Herodotus, 2.152–53) were engaged by Psamtik, attracted by high wages and promises of land (*stratōpeda*) on which to settle. During the Saite Period, Egypt became the place where Greek mercenaries could make their fortune. An Egyptian statue with a Greek inscription dedicated to an Ionian soldier during the reign of Psamtik I, has recently been discovered at Priene. It is an extraordinary example of the rapidity with which Greco-Egyptian cultural bilingualism developed, as well as of the contacts between Egypt and the Hellenic world of Asia Minor, contacts which had such fertile consequences for archaic Greece. Twenty-sixth Dynasty Egypt still possessed enough cultural prestige to oblige Greek philosophers and intellectuals to visit it.

The ethnically mixed composition of the army of Psamtik II is demonstrated by the famous graffiti in Abu Simbel written in Greek, Carian, and Phoenician. Ionians and Carians continued to live in Memphis during the centuries that followed. Alexander the Great discovered their descendants, the "Hellenomemphites" and the "Cariomemphites," when he arrived in Egypt.

Cambyses' conquests in 525 B.C. transformed the Nile Valley into a satrapy of the Achaemenid Empire. During the fifth and sixth centuries B.C., when Herodotus visited the country, Egypt was even more multiethnic and multilingual than it had been during the glorious period when the empire was "Egyptian." The satrap was Persian and generally a prince in the Great King's family. He resided at Memphis with his court, which included the administrators of the satrapy's wealth and the king's Treasury. Egypt was still home to the mass of scribes, judges, provincial chiefs (*fratarak*), garrisons of soldiers, merchants, and exporters, many of whom were Phoenician. The official language in the provinces of the Achaemenid Empire (and thus in Egypt) was Aramaic, known in Egyptian as "(As)syrian writing." Darius I ordered the body of Egyptian laws "preceding the year 44 of Amasis" to be translated from Demotic into Aramaic (Bibliothèque Nationale, Paris, Papyrus no. 215r).

The area of the border garrisons, stretching from Migdol to

Marea and Elephantine in the south, was home for people of various nationalities and religions. Temples and chapels for foreign gods sprang up throughout Egypt. During the period of Achaemenid domination, chapels existed at Aswan for the cults of Nabo, Melkat Sciamin, and Banit. Even before Cambyses' victory (possibly from the time of the edict of Cyrus permitting the return to Israel of the Babylonian exiles, or, alternatively, from the time of Psamtik II), Judaic military colonists had erected a temple to Yahweh on the island of Elephantine.

In the decades during which independence was wrested back from Persia, Egypt became the ally of, and point of reference for, every enemy of the Great King. The Nile Valley recognized, and welcomed, all kinds of allies and exiles, until the country was conquered by Alexander the Great.

The Libyan Period, the Ethiopian conquest, and, above all, the violent invasions by Assyria and then Persia, followed by the passing of Egypt into the Alexandrian Empire and the periods of Ptolemaic and Roman control, were all seen by the people of Egypt as attacks on the "throne of Horus." They represented the mythological "Return of Seth," who, exiled from Egypt and dismissed to the lands of the Asiatics, "turns back to his deviant ways and returns to plunder" in the guise of an Assyrian conqueror, of Cambyses, or of Xerxes. The last resort of defeated Egypt was ritual exorcism, the magical destruction by fire of the figurine representing Seth, the god of disorder:

> Behind, O rebel vile of character
> whose advance has been blocked by Re! [...]
> You will come near Egypt no longer.
> You will die wandering in foreign lands,
> you will penetrate no more the banks of Horus,
> the kingdom that had been granted to him!
> (ritual against Seth-Apophis, *Urkunden* VI,
> 17.22 ff.)

Similar rituals, intended to protect Egypt from foreign invasion and resembling the Execration Texts from two millennia earlier, can be found at Edfu in the Book to Paralyze [Hostile] Humanity:

> All the princes of all Asiatic lands,
> all their great ones, all their notable ones,

all their soldiers, all their magicians,
all the women magicians who are with them [. . .],
who say that they will be joined together
with the rebels against the Pharoah.

(Edfu, V, 132.5–6)

Foreign invaders were exorcised at Dendera, along with magicians and the wicked, who might profane the crypt:

The place whose secret is hidden,
in case the Asiatics come down to the fortress.
The Phoenicans (Fenekhu) will not come
   near,
the Greeks (Haunebu) will not enter,
the Sand-dwellers will not encircle it,
a magician will not carry out his task there,
its doors will not open for a reprobate.

(Dendera, second crypt)

But by now it was too late to close the doors of Egypt.

During this period the "defeated" Egyptians had nothing but memories of their national pride. All that remained to them was to whisper that Cambyses was the son of the last dynastically legitimate Pharaoh, Apries, or that Alexander was not only the "son of Amun" but also the son of Olympia and Nectanebos II, the magician-king who had sought refuge in Nubia (oh, that Nubian magic!), pursued by the Persian Artaxerxes.

Bibliography

Ampolo, C., and E. Bresciani. "Psammetico re d'Egitto e il mercenario Pedon." *Egitto e Vicino Oriente* 11 (1988): 237–52.

Barns, J. W. *Egyptians and Greeks*. Oxford, 1966.

Bietak, M. *Avaris et Pi Ramesse*. Oxford, 1981.

Boreux, C. *Études de nautique égyptienne*. Mémoires publiés par les membres de l'Institute Français d'Archéologie Orientale du Caire, vol. 50. 1924.

Bresciani, E. "La satrapia d'Egitto." *Studi Classici e Orientali* 7 (1958): 132–88.

———. "La morte di Cambise ovvero dell'empietà punita." *Egitto e Vicino Oriente* 4 (1981): 217–31.

———. "The Persian Occupation of Egypt." In *Cambridge History of Iran*, vol. 2, pp. 502–28. 1985.

———. "Presenze fenicie in Egitto." In *Atti del convegno: Momenti precoloniali nel Mediterraneo antico*. Rome, 1988.

———., ed. *Letteratura e poesia dell'antico Egitto*. Turin, 1970.

Davis, N. de G. *The Rock Tombs of El Amarna*. Vol. 6, *Tombs of Parennefer, Tutu and Aj*. London, 1908.

Desroches Noblecourt, C. "Les enfants du Kep." In *Actes XXI Congrès Orientalistes*, pp. 68–70. Paris, 1947.

———. *La femme au temps des Pharaons*. Paris, 1986.

Donadoni, S. "L'Egitto arcaico come ecumene." *Studi Classici e Orientali* 10 (1961): 97–101.

———. "Gli egiziani e le lingue degli altri." *Vicino Oriente* 3 (1980): 1–14.

———. "Egei e Egiziani." In *Le origini dei greci*, ed. D. Musti, pp. 214–15. 2d ed. Rome-Bari, 1986.

———., ed. *Testi religiosi egizi*. Turin, 1970.

Drioton, E. "Le nationalisme au temps des Pharaons." In *Pages d'Égyptologie*, pp. 375–86. 1957.

Fischer, H. "The Nubian Mercenaries." *Kush* 9 (1961): 44–80.

———. "Milk in Everything Cooked." *Egyptian Studies* 1 (1976): 97–100.

Garbini, G. "Il semitico di Nord-Ovest nell'età del bronzo." *Oriens Antiqui Collectio* 13 (1978): 172–73.

Gardiner, A. H. *Ancient Egyptian Onomastica*. 3 vols. Oxford, 1947.

Giveon, R. *Les Bédouins Shosou des documents ègyptiens*. Leiden, 1971.

Goedicke, H. "The Title *mr a* in the Old Kingdom." *Journal of Egyptian Archaeology* 46 (1960): 60–64; 52 (1966): 172–74.

———. "Papyrus Anastasi VI, 51–61." *Studien zur Altagyptischen Kultur* 14 (1987): 83–98.

Habachi, L. *The Second Stela of Kamose and His Struggle against the Hyksos Ruler and His Capital*. Glückstadt, 1972.

Hayes, W. C. *A Papyrus of the Late Middle Kingdom in the Brooklyn Museum (Pap. Brooklyn 35.1446)*. Brooklyn, 1955.

Helck, W. *Untersuchungen zu den Beamtentiteln des ägyptischen Alten Reiches*. Glückstadt, 1954.

———. *Zur Verwaltung des Mittleren und Neuen Reiches*. Leiden, 1958.

———. *Die Beziehungen Ägyptens zu Vorderasien im 3. und 2. Jahrtausend v. Chr.* Wiesbaden, 1962.

———. "Entwicklung der Verwaltung als Spiegelbild historischer und soziologischer Faktoren." In *Le fonti indirette della storia egiziana*, ed. S. Donadoni, pp. 59–80. Rome, 1963.

———. *Wirtschaftsgeschichte des alten Ägypten im 3. und 2. Jahrtausend vor Chr.* Handbuch der Orientalistik I, 1, 5. 1975.

———. "Nochmals zu Ramses' III Seevölkerbericht." *Studien zur Altägyptischen Kultur* 14 (1987): 129–45.

Holscher, W. *Libyer und Ägypten.* Glückstadt, 1937.

Janssen, J. "Fonctionnaires sémites au service de l'Égypte." *Chronique d'Égypte* 26 (1951): 50–62.

Jonckeere, F. *Les médicins de l'Égypte pharaonique.* Brussels, 1958.

Kakosy, L. "Nubien als mythisches land im Altertum." *Annales Universitatis Budapestiensis,* sect. hist., 8 (1966): 3–10.

———. "Les sciences à l'époque saite et perse." *Annales Universitatis Budapestiensis,* sect. class., 3 (1975): 17–22.

Keeler, D. "Die Asiatenkarawane von Beni Hassan." *Studien zur Altägyptischen Kultur* 14 (1987): 147–65.

Koenig, Y. "La Nubie dans les textes magiques, in L'inquiétante etrangeté. *Revue d'Égyptologie* 38 (1987): 105–10.

Leclant, J. "Astarté à cheval d'après les représentations égyptiennes." *Syria* 37 (1960): 19–67.

———. *Les relations entre l'Égypte et la Phénicie du voyage d'Ounamon à l'expédition d'Alexandre.* Beirut, 1968.

Lichtheim, M. *Ancient Egyptian Literature.* Vol. 2, *The New Kingdom.* Berkeley and Los Angeles, 1976.

———. *Ancient Egyptian Literature.* Vol. 3, *The Late Period.* Berkeley and Los Angeles, 1980.

de Linage, J. "L'acte d'élablissement et le contrat de mariage d'un 'esclave' de Thoutmosis III." *Bulletin de l'Institut Français d'Archéologie Orientale* 37 (1937): 217–34.

Lloyd, A. B. "Nationalist Propaganda in Ptolemaic Egypt." *Historia* 31 (1982): 33–55.

Lorton, D. "The So-Called 'Vile' Enemies of the King of Egypt." *Journal of the American Research Center in Egypt* 10 (1973): 65–70.

Osing, J. "Ächtungstexte aus dem Alten Reich." *Mitteilungen des Deutschen Archäologischen Institut, Kairo,* 32 (1976): 133–85.

Posener, G. *La première domination perse en Égypte.* Cairo, 1936.

———. *Princes et pays d'Asie et de Nubie.* Brussels, 1940.

———. *Cinq figurines d'envoûtement.* Cairo, 1987.

Pritchard, J. B. *Ancient Near Eastern Texts Relating to the Old Testament.* Princeton, 1969.

Roccati, A. *La littérature historique sous l'Ancien Empire égyptien.* Paris, 1982.

Sauneron, S. "L'avis des Égyptiens sur la cuisine soudanaise." *Kush* 7 (1959): 63–70 .

———. "La différentiation des langages d'après la tradition égyptienne." *Bulletin de l'Institut Français d'Archéologie Orientale* 60 (1960): 31–41.

Säve-Söderberg, T. *Ägypten und Nubien: Ein Beitrag zur Geschichte altägyptischer Aussenpolitik.* Lund, 1941.

Stadelmann, R. *Syrisch-palästinensische Gottheiten in Ägypten,* Leiden, 1967.

Uphill, E. "The Nine Bows." *Jaarbericht van het Vooraziatische—Egyptisch Genootschap Ex Oriente Lux* 19 (1965–66): 393–420.

Vandier, J. "Quatre steles de soldats." *Chronique d'Égypte* 35 (1943): 22–29.

Vercoutter, J. *L'Égypte et le monde égéen préhellénique.* Cairo, 1956.

———. "Image du Noir dans l'Égypte ancienne." *Meroitica* 5 (1979): 19–22.

———. "Le pays Irem et la pénétration égyptienne en Afrique." In *Livre du Centenaire de l'IFAO.* Cairo, 1980.

Vergote, J. *Joseph en Egypte.* Louvain, 1959.

Yoyotte, J., and O. Masson. "Une inscription ionienne mentionnant Psammétique Ier." *Epigraphica Anatolica* 11 (1988): 171–79.

von Zeissl, H. *Äthiopen und Assyrer in Ägypten.* Gluckstadt, Hamburg, and New York, 1944.

Zivie, A. *Aper-El et ses voisins, in Memphis et ses nécropoles au Nouvel Empire.* Paris, 1988.

9. THE DEAD

Sergio Donadoni

For those who consider the wealth of material in museums displaying its remains, Egyptian civilization has often acquired, albeit unjustly, funerary connotations. This is due to the way archeological excavations have been carried out in a country whose ancient cities are concealed, not only by the centuries-old presence of people still living on the same sites, but also by the annual deposits of silt left over millennia by the Nile floods. The unavailability of information about how ancient Egyptians lived is in marked contrast to the state of their cemeteries, situated in the desert, far from areas affected by flooding, with climatic conditions that have allowed material, destroyed almost everywhere else, to survive. For too long, this has encouraged practicing archeologists to regard the discovery of objects as their main aim.

The discoveries found in monuments are rendered more explicit and significant (hence their emphasis in research) by ancient Egypt's enthusiasm for writing. Paper and walls were covered with religious texts devoted to the dead. This has allowed us to develop a firsthand, logically organized understanding and convincing interpretations, unequaled in the ancient world, of mythical concepts and rituals.

A society that was fundamentally worldly, rationally pragmatic, and proud of its cheerful vitality has thus been overturned by the accidents of documentation. Any study that attempts to describe ancient Egypt inevitably devotes a considerable part of its description to the funerary aspect of the society.

Nor can we escape, in this essay, from the obligations imposed by the material that has been discovered. However, it is not our task to consider religious anthropology, which describes the religious elements that made up the Egyptian personality and whether these elements survived death. We shall not be considering Egypt's many—contrasting and converging—eschatological concepts, nor shall we attempt to decipher the final meaning of the large anthologies of burial texts, staggered in time and containing collections of spells, or "Guides to the Beyond," representing particular aspects of priestly speculation.

What we are interested in is how individuals managed to remain anchored to the world of the living, determining events and situations even when they no longer played an active part in it. These "dead who seize the living" cannot be ignored. They did not disappear (if only into the pain and regret of memory). They continued to exist by means of a will and capacity to act that had belonged to them when they were alive, in their awareness of being "future dead" (and in some cases, as we shall see, as if they were already dead).

The area of our research is thus more limited than the traditional one. However, its absence from this volume would have detracted from the picture, drawn by different authors, of the Egyptian people and their role in a defined society.

The awareness of a past concretely represented by those immersed in it creates a bond between those who are and those who were. The greater the extent of this awareness, the clearer becomes the debt that the present owes to the past—the idea, that is, of tradition as a valid and vital fulcrum for human activity.

A civilization such as that of Egypt, which held so tenaciously to precedent in all its activities, was particularly likely to place a high value on the continuity of time and on the recurrence—as memory, if nothing else—of that which appears to be concluded. The boundary between this world and the Beyond, which was experienced so profoundly in ancient civilizations, thus was much more fragile.

As an example of this, we only have to consider two cases, typical of innumerable others. The first is the life and adventures of Sinuhe, as narrated by their hero in the most famous work of Egyptian literature. The story is told in the first person, but the final phrase makes it clear that the narrator is already dead: "So I remained in the favor of the king until the day of mooring came." The introduction to the record of the trial following the assassination of Ramesses III relates the selection of the court responsible for judging the case. Here, the nomination is made by the murdered king himself. Although he has gone on to another world and is no longer available to the conspirators, he is still able to act within the society from which he has been divided.

Such an attitude represents one specific aspect of Egypt's rich eschatological imagination. Egyptians never tired of imagining a well-defined and not always reassuring Beyond, with features that could be recognized and described. Guides could be supplied, complete with spells providing answers and ways of addressing the non-human beings that would inevitably be encountered. The Egyptian world, potentially, included death among other natural events, thus finding a way of feeding an optimistic vision of constant return and the recovery of youth, as seen in the daily cycle and the cycles of the sun and moon, plants, and the Nile floods. The oldest existing burial texts, carved inside the royal pyramids of the Fifth Dynasty (second half of the third millennium B.C.), frequently refer to these recurring phenomena. They make us aware not only of their value as an attractive model but also of their profound dialectic significance: "That which they tell you: 'Go, so that you may come back! Sleep, so that you may wake! Die, so that you may live!'" (Pyramid Texts, 1975).

Death was a moment in existence. The period preceding history (during which, however, the king for whom the spell was recited was believed to have been born) was described as an age in which "the sky had not yet come into being, the earth had not yet come into being, men had not yet come into being, the gods had not yet come into being, death had not yet come into being" (Pyramid Texts, 1466b/d). "Being there" meant "dying" and was thus the premise for the concept of "dying in order to live" in the spell quoted above.

This cosmic optimism—if we wish to describe it in this way—naturally does not exclude a very different sense of death. The significance of the fact that the verbs used to indicate "dying" in the Pyramid Texts are only employed in order to be negated has been noted. We should also remember that survival after death could also lead to a total reversal of the earlier state. A magical spell reminded people that honey "is sweet for the living and bitter for the dead." The ancient, and constantly repeated, spells intended to protect the deceased from having to walk on his head, drink his urine, and eat his own excrement should be seen in this light. Reversals of this type were also the result of a strictly consequential dialectic, although they were far less consoling than that which saw the consequence of dying as rebirth.

More simply, we should remember certain texts, ranging from the end of the third millennium B.C. to the Christian era, that describe the immediate experience of rejecting the comfort of mythology. One of these texts is known as the Song of the Harper. According to the papyrus on which it was found, it appeared on the wall of the tomb of a Theban prince, Inyotef, who lived around 2100 B.C.:

> Bodies pass on while others endure [. . .] They built chapels, but their cult stations are no more [. . .] What are their cult places? Their walls are dismantled, and their cult places exist no more, as if they had never been. There is no one who can return from there, to describe their nature, to describe their dissolution, that he may still our desires, until we reach the place where they have gone [. . .] Do not control your passion until that day of mourning comes for you. The Weary-Hearted does not hear their sobbing. Their sobbing cannot save the heart of a man from the tomb. (Simpson 1973, pp. 306–7)

At the other end of the Egyptian tradition, during the Greek period, we find a text that expresses, perhaps more tragically, a terror of the Beyond, encapsulating all the literary texts, from the Song of the Harper on, to have touched on this vital theme:

> The West is the land of torpor, a perpetual darkness and the home of "Those who are There." Sleeping is their occupation; they do not wake up to see their brothers, they do not look at their fathers or mothers; their hearts forget their wives and children.
>
> The water of life, from which all life is nourished, is thirst for me. It comes only to those on earth. I suffer from thirst even though water is nearby [. . .] Death's name is "Come" and each of us is summoned. They come directly to her, even though their hearts tremble in terror before her. Nobody sees her among the gods and among men. The great are as the small in her hands [. . .] She takes the child away from the mother more keenly than the old man who moves beside her [. . .]
>
> O you who come to this cemetery! Make me an offering of burning incense and of water for every festival.

The final, unexpected request for those ritual offerings whose uselessness has just been described appears to add one last touch of bitterness. Nonetheless, in the balanced Egyptian world, it was precisely this painful awareness of annulment that produced its own an-

swer: death was also the reward for those who had been downtrod-
den during their lives. In the same cultural context as that of the
Song of the Harper, although in a different period, two other texts
express a loss of faith in human society and a desire for annulment
and escape. A spectator of a perverted world concludes his conversation with his soul, with whom he has discussed at length the possibility of accepting a wicked society, in the following way:

> Death is before me today,
> like the scent of myrrh,
> like sitting beneath the sail on a windy day.
> Death is before me today,
> like the scent of lotus,
> like sitting on the banks of drunkenness.
> [. . .]
> Death is before me today,
> as when a man wishes to see his own house
> after many years spent in prison.

Thus a wretched man, unable to obtain what clearly belongs to him
before worldly judges, contemplates suicide and says: "As a thirsty
man approaches the well, as a small child holds out his mouth for
milk, thus is death sought."

However, alongside this controversial desire for death, the direct
product of troubled times and equivalent to a political and social accusation, there also existed nonmythological expressions of serene
contemplation of death. A Theban tomb of the Eighteenth Dynasty
contains the most significant text in this context, in explicit contrast
to that of the Song of the Harper (which was also originally written
on the walls of a tomb):

> I have heard those songs that are in the old tombs and what they
> say, extolling existence on earth and denigrating the land of the
> dead. But why do they behave like this toward the land of eter-
> nity, which is just, correct, and without terror? Struggle there is
> an abomination, and there is no one who arms himself against his
> comrade. This land, where all our familiars rest since the First
> Time (the creation), has no enemies. Those that come into being,
> millions and millions of them, will come here, without exception.
> It will never happen that someone will remain in Egypt; there is
> no one who will not join us here. Our timespan on earth is like a

dream; but "Welcome in health and integrity" is said to him who reaches the West.

Instinctive pessimism was constantly counterpoised by a desire for serenity and faith. Death behaved like "a hunter in the desert" (Pyramid Texts, 851b). It seized the living with its lasso as if they were game (Ankhnesneferibre 2.32). At the same time, however, it transformed the individual into a "Luminous Spirit," transporting him to the enchanted world of one of Egypt's Elysiums.

Egyptian survival after death must therefore be seen against a backdrop that is both mythological and human. An emotionally simple fact was transformed into a series of cultural experiences, speculative, ethical, and literary. This was the essential premise behind the various social functions carried out by the figure and personality of the deceased, at different levels and with varying significance, in the Egyptian world. Although no longer part of the earthly scene (no longer "on two feet," as the Egyptians would say), the dead person was still active, directly or indirectly, in the world of the living.

A preliminary distinction must be made at once between what can be said about the death of a king and that of one of his subjects. The enormous implications of a royal death reflected the uniqueness of his nature and role. They assumed a function that was both paradigmatic and inimitable and that is discussed elsewhere in this volume.

The most obvious sign of this distinction is the kind of tomb employed. Kings' tombs were always different from those of their subjects. When the former changed, however, the abandoned model became available to the people. Thus, when royal pyramids were replaced by tombs carved into the rock, necropolises filled up with previously forbidden pyramids. Similar observations might be made about tomb decorations and texts.

Tombs, in all their different forms, provide the clearest and most explicit evidence available of the earliest period. We can also see the relationship between the tomb and the ability of the dead to influence the fate of the living. There were the very poor, who disappear into nothingness at their death, flung into the river like dead animals. There were the poor, "thrown into the desert" after having been "dragged from their houses" as one text says. But the offerings that are found in tombs, even when the owner was relatively poor, testify both to the links with survivors and to the ability to make use in some way of the things that had been offered.

Obviously, these are not the cases that will further our research, which is based on tombs belonging to more important figures in the hierarchy of ancient Egypt. The most ancient Instructions in Egyptian literature, attributed to princes and viziers from the Age of the Pyramids, already talk of the parallel tasks of "founding a house" and preparing one's tomb. Although the Song of the Harper refers specifically to these texts in order to criticize their inanity, the dramatic uncertainty of the First Intermediate Period, which followed the Age of the Pyramids, remains evident. However, no sooner had Egyptian society settled down once more into its pattern than the pessimism of the Harper was confuted (as we have seen in the quotation from an Eighteenth Dynasty text), and the theme of the urgent need to provide for one's future tomb was taken up once again. In the following text Ani, a wise man of the New Kingdom, expresses a serene yet melancholic vision far more complex than those of his ancient, more daring, predecessors. He is also capable of adopting the bitterness of the texts being criticized:

> Make perfect your place that is in the Valley (the necropolis of Thebes), the tomb that must conceal your body. Place yourself before it, among those activities of yours that count in your eyes [. . .] No harm can come to one who does this. And he is happy. Prepare yourself in this way. When your "messenger" arrives to take you, he will find you ready to go to the place of rest. And you will say, "Lo, here comes one who has prepared himself before you."

Even during the Greek period, a Demotic wisdom text advised people not to leave their own land (in the age of Hellenistic cosmopolitanism!) in order not to risk losing the tomb that they might have possessed there: "Whoever dies far from his homeland is buried (only) out of pity" (Insinger Papyrus).

The tomb was the house of the dead and often possessed, in the final analysis, the structure of a house. Part of it was devoted to the social life of its owner. It was here that his heirs gathered to make the appropriate ceremonial offerings, and where the decorations fulfilled a variety of roles as ostentatiously as possible. In Eastern tombs this part was known as the *diwan*, in contrast to the *harim*, or secret part of the tomb in which the body was laid, surrounded by everything he needed for his mysterious survival. This basic scheme varied according to period and changes in custom. It ranged from a perfect imitation of a house (including even a toilet) in the ancient period to a transformation of the significance of the *harim* into myth, as we can see from representations that begin to appear at a certain point and allude to the Beyond and specifically identify it with the burial cell.

The first thing to emerge from this concept of the tomb as a house was the stress placed on the fact that tombs only had meaning if someone lived there. Instead of being annulled, the individual personality acquired strength as it passed from the world to potential eternity. This can be seen in the care given to the body, a care that was immediately expressed in the practice of mummification. Even more important, it is revealed in the identification and definition of memory through words and images. The nature of Egyptian sculpture was primarily determined by the need to provide a physical resting place for the specific "soul" (if we wish to use that term), identifiable in the uniqueness of its name. The statue was not a monument or commemoration. It was a specific form of the person with its own life, as was recognized by the rite carried out in order to "open its mouth" (also carried out on the body after mummification). This fact should be emphasized if we wish to understand the roots that nourished figurative expression in Egypt and the significance of both its standardization and its realism.

Similarly, the name and titles of the deceased evoked a specific individual. This evocation acquired a wealth of narrative detail as the tradition developed. On the one hand, it insisted on generically (and traditionally) praiseworthy aspects. On the other, it emphasized single, characteristic moments in the individual's life or even, in some extreme and illustrious cases, described the entire life, from beginning to end.

The strict parallels that can be established between figurative and verbal representations of the individual reveal that they shared a final value, quite distinct from the artistic values to which they gave rise. When someone passed over to the other world, where his actions could no longer be regarded as unpredictable, his ability to live on lay in the embodiment of a memory. Such a memory, however, did everything in its power to exist autonomously, becoming a personality that did not depend on the emotion and memories of those who were still alive.

Egypt understood "fame." It was possible to say: "I have heard the words of Iyemhotep and of Hardjedef, which are uttered in proverbs and which will never pass away." A literary prophecy came to an end in the following way: "A wise man (in the future) will make me libations, when you will see that what I have said has come to pass" (Neferti). But survival for the buried was not the result of fame. On the contrary, it depended not on the grace of others but on the deceased himself. The statue was a physical presence; biographical accounts, whether long or short, began with "I." They were not, in other words, commemorative texts, but autobiographies. Gravestones or statues representing an eternal pious repose, such as those that decorate the tombs of our own churches, would have been inconceivable in ancient Egypt. Their statues, eyes wide open, lived in their own homes and awaited their guests, with texts on the walls repeating what the master of the house wanted them to say.

To say that this is the source for certain figurative and literary expressions is probably overmechanical (even though all works of art are, in a sense, occasional). In any case, this is not our concern. It is enough to have identified the definite state of *being there* attributable to those who have been removed from the world of day-to-day experience.

"Being there" weighed so heavily on daily life that it became part of it, above all in economic terms. As someone who would later die, the living person set aside part of his belongings to cover his eternal needs in the future. These were represented by offerings of various kinds that would later be brought to his tomb on a vast number of occasions. Before this stage, however, the tomb itself had to be built. This was a complex task, drawing on the work of bricklayers, masons, architects, decorators, and scribes. Autobiographical inscriptions frequently emphasize that these craftsmen were paid, and that nobody was forced to work against his will. On other occasions, the texts record that parts of the tomb (especially those made in valuable materials such as the granite of Aswan or the brilliantly white and compact limestone of Tura) were gifts from the Pharaoh in return for services described, or that palace craftsmen were placed at the disposal of the deceased. Royal offerings to the tomb were soon consecrated by means of a formulaic, generalized expression. What all this means, however, is that it was possible to set aside a certain amount of one's personal belongings from daily requirements for a purpose that was primarily concerned with prestige. This practice was a heavy burden on the economic life of ancient Egypt.

Mummification was the first of a series of operations intended to maintain the personal reality of the dead individual. It demanded technical skill, anatomical and chemical knowledge and experience, and ritual activities. Although the details of the procedure need not concern us here, it should be noted that mummification was considered essential (obviously, since it is the simplest way of preserving the autonomous, concrete personality of the dead person), and that it was a procedure that had its price. Herodotus, the first person to describe the process, already emphasized the basic range of prices involved when embalming a corpse.

We do not have information that allows us to quantify the price of mummification or of the cult activities connected with it. For the Ptolemaic Period, however, certain Theban archives have survived that illustrate the commercial maneuvers of undertakers as they divided up the area among themselves, argued in court about the interpretation of clauses in contracts, reported the theft or movement of mummies, and, in one case, informed the police of a theft worth ten talents, a sum that would have kept five people alive for an entire year. We can glimpse a genuine mummification industry at work during this period, and it is likely that something similar existed in earlier epochs.

We have far more information about the price of coffins in the extensive documentation of daily life left by the workers of the Ramesside village of Deir al-Medina at the Theban necropolis. These texts describe many different types of coffins, along with their prices, as well as those of other objects connected with burial. It is obvious that prices varied according to the type of object produced. The price of a normal wooden coffin ranged from 20 to 30 *deben* (a *deben*, in these calculations, equaled 91 grams of copper) for the actual coffin, and from 8 to 12 *deben* for its decoration (although there are examples that cost as much as 200 *deben*). The average price of other types of coffin (such as those in human form or complete sarcophagi) was slightly different. The information provided here is, in any case, limited in time and space and far from being applicable to all of Egyptian history.

Ensuring the basic survival of the individual by means of mummification and deposition in a coffin was only the first stage. The presence of the mummy as a person who lived in his tomb involved another kind of consumption: that of the funerary furnishings. In the earliest period, these were basically, although not exclusively, consumer goods devoted to the care of the body: vases containing various items, unguents, objects for dressing the hair, and so on. There were also, naturally, personal items that, in some cases, included such precious and splendid jewels as those found in the tombs of the Twelfth Dynasty princesses at Dahshur and El-Lahun, from which the most beautiful Egyptian jewelry probably derives.

But the vitality of the deceased gradually began to require other items, introduced into people's daily needs by the rising standard of living in the Nile Valley. Thus funerary furnishings increased in variety until they included practically everything that might be found in the homes of the living. In order to appreciate what might be found in the tomb of a couple who belonged to a class that, although certainly not low, was not exceptionally elevated, let us look at an inventory of everything found in the tomb of the royal architect Kha and his wife Merit, who lived in Thebes at the height of the Eighteenth Dynasty. Their tomb is, fortunately, intact and perfectly preserved, unlike many others, whose contents were scattered after their discovery.

The tomb, one of the treasures of Turin's Egyptian Museum, was, in fact, one of many. Here is the inventory. The coffins of the couple (three—one inside the other—for the husband, and two for the wife, wrapped in strips of linen fifteen meters long and two meters wide), a wooden statuette of Kha, an illuminated Book of the Dead, and two *ushabti* figurines, workers of the Beyond, are inevitable funerary elements. Everything else, however, is connected to daily life. A trunk contains the personal objects of the husband: a leather bag with five bronze razors, pincers, a whetstone, an alabaster vase with pomade, two bronze needles, a wooden comb, some tubes of antimony, a flask with a cord to hang it up by, a painted terra-cotta funnel, a blue enamel cup, a small cylindrical silver vase, a silver cup, two strainers (one made of silver and the other of copper), two scribe's palettes complete with brushes, four pestles for preparing paint, a plaster-covered panel of wood on which to write, a folding cubit measure, a case for scales, a drill, a carpenter's axe, a bronze scalpel, and three pairs of leather sandals. Among his property there were also a traveling mat, a number of walking sticks, a small chest with toiletry items, and another for his personal linen. This consisted of fifty pairs of underpants, twenty-six loincloths, seventeen summer tunics, and one heavy winter tunic. The chest also contained four pieces of canvas.

The objects buried with his wife included a plaited wig supplied with its own protective case, bronze needles, ridged needles made from bone, a wooden comb, a fringed bathrobe, alabaster vases of perfume, vases made from silver and glass, and so on.

Apart from these personal objects, there were a number of items of furniture and household goods: a chair with a back (on which the statuette of Kha stood), ten stools of various types, two small wooden tables, four small tables made of papyrus trunks and reeds, two beds with head rests, thirteen trunks (five of which imitate inlaid models), not to speak of sheets, towels, carpets, a bronze water jug with bowl, and vases and other objects in bronze. There were also supplies of food and drink: bread, wine, oil, milk, flour, roasted and salted birds, salted meat and dried fish, as well as all kinds of cut vegetables, onions, garlic, cumin and juniper seeds for seasoning, grapes, dates, figs, and *dum*-palm coconuts.

Finally, there were gifts from friends—a chessboard and some precious walking sticks—and a silver hanging vase and a gold cubit measure from the king.

Such an accumulation of goods is depicted in the funeral scenes decorating some Theban tombs. As the coffin is taken to its final resting place, followed by members of the family and mourning women, a procession of people passes bearing a wide variety of objects: furniture, boxes, ornaments. This ostentation was just as valuable as the offerings themselves, since it was believed to help the deceased. Whereas the offerings provided the deceased with everything that might be considered useful, revealing a remarkable faith in the ability of the deceased to make use of worldly goods, the act of presenting the goods was an invitation to consider the importance of the person for whom this quantity of goods was removed from immediate use, since the worth (and identity) of the deceased was precisely defined by such ostentation.

It is obvious that the willingness to face the cost of preserving the body and the willingness to provide the goods that were entombed with the deceased derived from the same emotional and intellectual attitudes. However, it is also clear that death created two quite different economic effects. On the one hand, payment was provided for a service (so to speak); on the other hand, wealth was destroyed since goods were simply taken out of circulation.

But these were not the only ways in which the deceased continued to influence—as a direct result of his death—the economy of the living. Among the oldest and most explicitly significant offerings were those consisting of food, as we have already seen. These offerings reveal that the deceased still belonged to the world. Alongside the original offerings in the tomb's underground storeroom, other offerings were left periodically to make up for the amount consumed by the deceased. The oldest collections of spells in our possession, from the pyramids (probably a particularly ancient nucleus of them), have preserved the words that accompanied this ritual act as uttered by the son as he offered bread and beer to his dead father.

In the tomb of a Second Dynasty woman, an entire meal has been preserved, served on rustic terra-cotta plates: bread made from spelt, barley soup, fish, a pigeon, a quail, two kidneys, beef ribs, roasted figs, berries, honeyed sweets, cheese, and wine. There are many other examples from subsequent centuries. In a typically Egyptian custom, these real offerings were paralleled by a list of the foodstuffs provided, indicating the amounts, placed near the banquet scenes painted on the tomb walls. A typical list recorded a thousand loaves, a thousand jugs of beer, a thousand oxen, a thousand geese, and so on.

Alongside the appeal made by the magic of words, we find that made by the magic of forms (if we wish to express the idea in a rather simplistic way). The walls of tombs were covered with depictions of food offerings made by symbolic figures to the deceased and, in temporal order, the figurative description of how each offering reached its final state (in other words, from the sowing of the grain to the baking of bread and brewing of beer).

In this case too, the need to keep the personality of the tomb's owner alive was the "occasion" for a fundamental artistic experience, that of depicting an entire process. These paintings represented the organic unity of a narrative expressed by means of figures, one of Egyptian art's greatest achievements from the very earliest stages.

Apart from their symbolic, evocative, and even magical role, however, offerings also possessed their own reality. The deceased's need for physical nourishment was provided for by means of a piece of land, whose income was intended to pay for future offerings. This service was entrusted to a figure who might be described as a "funerary priest" (or "servant of the genie," as the Egyptians called him). He was responsible for making sure that the service was carried out, and he may have been the "beloved son" of the deceased. He was obliged to fulfill his role diligently throughout his own life, and because the responsibility did not end with death, he had to leave the land he had been given in payment to one of his own sons (in contrast to the custom in which an inheritance was divided up among the heirs). In this way, something that might be called a funerary endowment was passed on, undivided and at the service of the deceased, from father to son.

The oldest endowments of this type seem to have been made by kings and by members of the court who, by royal grace, obtained not only elements of the structure of their tombs but also the means by which offerings and the future needs of the cult could be provided for. It is therefore no accident that the oldest endowments bear compound names incorporating that of the king. As time passed, however, and private individuals began to amass their own wealth, endowments lost their royal character.

A good example of the conditions to which a funerary priest had to conform in order to enjoy the goods he had been consigned can be found in the inscription of a person whose name has been lost to us. The text on the walls of his tomb refers to agreements made between the deceased and his priest during the Fourth Dynasty:

> I shall permit in perpetuity no funerary priest to be authorized to give away the field, the people, and everything that I have done for him in terms of the funerary offering here (in the tomb) to be sold to any person or to leave it in his will to any person, unless he leaves it to his only son. (*Urkunden* I, 12)

This text is not without parallels. It is judicially significant that a private individual was able to enforce his will by legal means even after his death. However, the mechanism by which these obligations were fulfilled should also be taken into consideration. The offerings taken to the tomb were not consumed by the deceased, unless in some mysterious way that had no effect on their quantity. They could thus be "moved on" to another tomb and then another, satisfying more than one deceased and ending up in the hands of the priest himself. Of course, nothing prevented a single priest from serving more than one tomb and, in particular, a regal tomb, where the revenue was much higher.

We have many extracts from administrative and accounting texts dealing with the funerary priests of a royal temple from the Memphite Period. These papyri reveal complex business activities. In the case of private endowments, however (more interesting to us, since kings did not always represent the standard), we can consider a series of contracts drawn up by the governor of Assiut, a province of Middle Egypt, with his funerary priest. The latter was appointed to make sure that further contracts dealing with the tomb's furnishings were honored by the city temple's priests:

The prince, nomarch, chief of prophets, Hapy-djefa says to his funerary priest: "Here, all these things that I have stipulated with these priests are in your control. Here, in truth, is the funerary priest of a person who maintains his things, who maintains his offering. Here, I have done it so that you may know these things that I have given to the priests in exchange for that which they will give to me. Be careful that nothing of this is taken away. Each word concerning my goods that I have given them, make sure that it is heard by your son and heir, who will inherit the role of funerary priest for me. Here, I have furnished you with fields, people, livestock, gardens, like every official in Assiut so that you can perform the rite for me with a light heart. You will look after all my things that I have placed in your authority. Here, this is before you in writing. These things will be to your only beloved son, who will perform for me the role of funerary priest at the head of your other sons, as a life interest that cannot be reduced and that cannot be divided up among his sons, according to this word that I have given before you." [. . .] Contract made by the nomarch, chief of prophets, Hapy-djefa vindicated, with the temple council. Bread and beer will be given to him on day 19 of the first month of *akhet*, the feast day of *wag*.
    List of that which must be given to him:

LIST OF NAMES	JUGS OF BEER	ROLLS	WHITE-BREAD
Chief of prophets	4	400	10
Herald priest	2	200	5
Provost to the mysteries	2	200	5
Priest of the loincloth	2	200	5
Chief of the warehouse	2	200	5
Overseer of the hypostyle	2	200	5
Chief of palace of the *ka*	2	200	5
Scribe of the temple	2	200	5

| Scribe of the offering table | 2 | 200 | 5 |
| Ritualist | 2 | 200 | 5 |

This is what he gives them for this: 22 temple days of his possessions from the house of his father, certainly not those of the house
of the nomarch. Four days to the chief of prophets, two days to
each of the others.

He told them: "Here, one temple day is 1/360th of the year.
You must thus divide up all the things that enter the temple, such
as bread, beer, and the daily ration of meat—which corresponds to
1/360th of the bread, of the beer, and of everything that enters this
temple—for each of the temple days that I have given you.

Here, these are my possessions from the house of my father;
certainly not from the house of the nomarch, because I am the son
of a *wab*-priest, as each of you are.

Here, these days will pass for all the temple council that will
be (then), given that they are the ones who will provide me with
the beer and the bread that they will give me." And they were
content with this.

The contract containing these complicated accounts, involving a
wide range of responsibilities, was addressed to different ranks and
categories among the staff of the temple.

Considering the document, it is clear that funerary cults created
a series of life interests. These inevitably led to possession and, as
the centuries passed, property. Thus the structure of Egyptian society changed, as new legal and, in some cases, political situations were
created. The personnel of royal endowments were exempted from
taxation and the liturgy, effectively becoming autonomous from the
state. An example of this can be seen in a decree of Pepi II regarding
an endowment at Dahshur for a distant ancestor of his (revealing
how long-lasting such provisions were):

The people working in the endowment of Snefru must not, under
any circumstances, be distracted from their normal duties; it is forbidden to assign them to liturgies or to royal building [. . .] Furthermore, I exempt the said endowment from taxes on canals,
basins, and ditches, on raising and breeding animals, and on trees;
furthermore, from the liturgy that obliges the putting up of royal
messengers passing through the place.

These self-administered endowments, whose constitutions were based on life interests linked to individuals and temples, compromised a previously centralized structure. The crumbling of royal power as a result of this was a decisive factor in the collapse of the Memphite monarchy. Other factors should also be taken into consideration if one wishes to avoid an oversimplified vision of historical processes. Nonetheless, the profound effect that funerary customs had on economic life is another sign of the weight placed on Egyptian society by the personality of the deceased, and by his stubborn vitality beyond natural limits, a vitality granted him by the civilization to which he belonged.

This mechanism, which had such serious consequences, was modified during the New Kingdom, when the "funerary priest" was replaced by libation rituals. But the dead continued to intervene, albeit passively, in the distribution of wealth and in an economy that might be described as "submerged." In a sense, this economy restored the violently disrupted equilibria found in an economy based on ostentation and prestige. Goods that had been so decisively removed from circulation by being deposited in tombs tended to reappear, still possessing their original, less symbolic value. In other words, the existence of rich funerary furnishings inevitably produced grave robbers.

Grave robbing was a standard practice in ancient Egypt from the earliest times. There is archeological evidence, as well as documents, that denounce the opening and looting of tombs. The most famous, and detailed, of the documents deal with robberies from tombs of the late New Kingdom. These acts were sufficiently serious and frequent to lead to the removal of many dead Pharaohs from their own tombs to a single hiding place. This was chosen so well that it was not discovered until the end of the last century (by thieves). However, it lacked the furnishings that had made the repose of the deceased in their official tombs so unpredictable. It is, effectively, no accident that the bodies of so many famous historical figures (offering us the almost unique opportunity to see the features, albeit mummified, of almost legendary rulers) remained hidden until archeological research and, as a result, the market attributed to them a value they had not previously possessed.

Statements made by grave robbers under interrogation have survived, although their confessions were sometimes extorted and clearly cannot always be regarded as true:

We opened their sarcophagi and their coffins in which they lay, and
found the noble mummy of this king equipped with a sword, and
there was a great quantity of amulets and of golden jewels at his
neck. The noble mummy of this king was completely bedecked
with gold and his coffins were adorned with gold and silver inside
and out, and decorated with every precious stone [...] We collected the gold we found on the noble mummy of this god [i.e.,
the king] with his amulets and the jewels that were at his neck and
the coffin in which he lay [...] We also found the queen and we
collected all that we found on her likewise, and we set fire to their
coffins. [...] We took their furniture, articles of gold, silver and
bronze, and divided them among ourselves. This gold that we
found on these two gods and on their noble mummies we divided
into eight shares.

Clearly, entering tombs of this kind involved so many risks and
difficulties that it is impossible not to assume that many people,
some of them undoubtedly highly placed, were involved. Such involvement must have spread until wider and wider groups of people
played a part. During certain epochs, it is quite likely that entire
populations made a living out of the business. A papyrus compiled
in the seventeenth year of the reign of Ramesses IX contains seven
columns of a list of thieves who had stolen metal from royal tombs.
The list includes scribes, merchants, boatmen, temple watchmen,
and the slaves of important figures, all of whom, however, had stolen
only small amounts of bronze. Larger amounts of bronze and more
precious metals had certainly ended up in the hands of more illustrious people than the ones who were rounded up. The unhappy fact
that tombs could be entered, as well as be contaminated by undeco-
rous behavior and rowdiness, was a recurrent fear, expressed in a series of spells found carved in the oldest tombs. The deceased promised success and help to those who, passing his tomb, recited the
spells of the offering. Such spells, however, often turned into specific
threats for those who incited the anger of the deceased. "I shall
wring their necks, like geese," announced one, while another, even
more threateningly, said: "Let the crocodile be against him in the
water, the snake against him on land! If anyone acts aginst this
[tomb], it shall not be I who acts against him, it will be God who
judges him" (*Urkunden* I, 23). Another warns that "he will be judged
by the Great God" (*Urkunden* I, 73). This Great God was originally

the king, in his role as lord and overseer of the necropolis. Gradually, however, he became a cosmic deity, capable of vindicating injustice and defending the rights of those who appealed to him.

The judgment to which the deceased alluded was probably not of this world. But it was likely to have at least some effect on those who might have feared it in the distant future.

In the New Kingdom, the social mechanism of funerary priesthoods fell into disuse. The tone used in requests to survivors also changed in tone, appealing to sentiment rather than to the law. Visitors were asked to recite the offering spell in the following way:

> It is only a reading, there is no expense, there is no blame, no conflict comes from it. There is no fighting with others, no oppression of the wretch in his moment. It is a sweet speech that brings satisfaction, and the heart is never weary of hearing it. It is only a breath of the mouth [. . .] It will be well for you if you do it. *Urkunden* IV, 510)

The relationship between the world of the living and the needs of the deceased has clearly changed. If we wish to understand this change more fully we need to go back in time to consider some other issues.

The dead could influence society, more subtly than through these powerful economic pressures, by presenting themselves as models or, at least, as the origin of concepts that reformulated social ideals.

During the Age of the Pyramids, the regal state possessed a particular significance even after death. The fate of ordinary people was the earth; for kings it was the heavens: "Men hide; the gods fly away" (Pyramid Texts, 459c). Once dead, the king became Osiris, the archetypal dying god and, as such, participated in his resurrection. This luminous destiny was ensured by rites and rituals reserved to the king. His divine survival thus became almost a general guarantee for the entire court, who placed their own tombs (of a different appearance and structure from that of the king) around the pyramid, that point at which the divine nature of the king became eternal. This allowed him to continue to concern himself with the well-being of those who had made up his society and who, more than anyone else, were entitled to remain close to him.

The end of this world was described by Egyptians a number of times. A typical sign of the destruction its end would cause was that tombs would be abandoned and fall into ruin and that those texts ensuring that the king became Osiris would be accessible to everyone. By releasing energies that had previously converged in the unitary structure of the state, centralized authority was weakened. Egypt became a world in which ancient hierarchies were reshuffled, and individuals were given the chance to reach levels they could never have hoped to achieve in a serenely stratified society. The problem of equality arose, as did that of a concept of justice valid in itself rather than merely as adherence to the royal will, however superior it might have been "throughout the heavens."

The potential leveling out of social stratification also gave a more explicit value to individual autonomy. This was revealed most typically by the fact that, as eschatological rituals and concepts linked to royalty became more widespread, everyone could expect to "become Osiris" after death. The name of the god was applied at death, without distinction, to anyone who identified with him.

The utopian equality of the otherworld raised everyone to the same level, but it also affected this world, in an exchange of forces. "Becoming Osiris" effectively meant partaking in the nature of the king. But this did not only involve undergoing the appropriate rituals. It also meant facing in the afterlife the same test of legitimacy that kings had to pass in order to become divine. In other words, individuals had to show that they had adhered to a way of life based on "justice."

Heavenly utopia was transformed into earthly utopia, based on the absolute innocence of individuals and a guarantee of rights and duties (i.e., of the "law," rather than of the specific, passing desire of the king) throughout society. We have seen that the deceased influenced the structure and economy of worldly life in a series of complicated ways. Similarly, the dead god introduced into ideal daily life caused a disintegration of elements deriving from a more archaic vision of the state. He did so by defining what was "good" in itself, in a human world in which respect for one's neighbor represented the measure of what was permitted. (This can be seen from the official list of sins that, one imagines, the deceased had to categorically deny having committed before the tribunal of the afterlife.)

So far, we have examined the dead individual in his role as a member of society in general. We must now consider other aspects of his being, which linked him to living people as individual, and specific, as he was.

Precise occasions existed for this purpose. These were the festivals for the dead, during which families gathered in tombs to make
offerings. Together they held a banquet that was often cheered by
dancing, music, and song, in communion with the person who, although no longer present, continued to ensure the structure of the
family to which he or she had once belonged in life.

In their inscriptions, the dead asked to be provided for on a number of occasions. Although the lists changed, according to place and
period, the dead all asked to be given offerings and to be remembered at each important festival (and also at less important but more
frequent festivals: not only at the New Year but at the beginning
of each month, each fortnight, each ten-day period, and so on). It
is impossible that such continuous celebration actually took place.
Certain occasions, however, such as the Festival of the Valley at
Thebes, from the New Kingdom to the Late Period, really do seem
to have fulfilled this function of linking the two worlds into which
Egyptian humanity was divided.

In the Late Period and, particularly, in Ptolemaic Egypt, there is
evidence that cult associations united people involved in the same
activity. Fraternization of this type imposed rules that had to be observed in daily life. Of particular importance, among the rules that
have survived, were those concerning duties toward members of the
fraternity who died. These rules regarded not only practical matters
but also the provision of material and psychological support to the
family of the deceased:

> The member who dies in the course of the year, we shall weep for
> him and accompany him to the necropolis. Each member will give
> five *deben* as a contribution toward his burial, and ten funerary ra-
> tions will be given to his survivors. We shall take with us the child
> of the dead man, or his father, brother, father-in-law, or mother-in-
> law to drink together, so that his heart may be in peace once more.

Death required compassionate solidarity.

The most explicit manifestation of the deceased's living personality, and his capacity for intervention, can probably be found in the
practice, restricted to Egypt, of writing letters to the dead. Most of
these documents date from the Old and Middle Kingdoms, before
the empire. Some letters are written using normal writing materials—papyrus or canvas. Often, however, the text was written on
terra-cotta plates, and it is likely that these plates were used for offer-

ings. The spirit of the deceased would thus be able to read the requests addressed to him when he approached the plate to eat.

Reading genuinely private letters is always a difficult exercise,
and this is particularly true when they are as distant in time and
space as these "Letters to the Dead." Alluding, in everyday language, to events that took place while their writers were alive, the
details of the letters are often difficult to understand. But it is always
clear that the man—or, more frequently, the woman—who appealed
to the dead needed some kind of supernatural help to solve a problem. The matter was usually dramatically urgent and could not be
solved by everyday means.

In the inscriptions left by the deceased, an attempt was made to
maintain relations—in a sense, legal relations—with the living. He
wished them well or threatened them with a judgment in which he
would be the accuser. The living, on the other hand, asked the dead
to intervene in the life of the family whenever events conformed
neither to the presumed wishes of the deceased nor to the wishes of
the person writing.

Although it is difficult to reconstruct its details without ambiguity, a letter such as the following tells a tale of interests, and thus of
social status:

> A sister who speaks to her brother, a child who speaks to his father.
> Your state is that of one who lives a million times. May Heh, lord
> of the West (the land of the dead), and Anubis, lord of burial, do
> all that you desire. Now I shall remind you of when the envoy of
> Behesti came to your bed, where I sat at your head, calling for Iy,
> son of Irti, to recommend him to the envoy of Behesti, and you
> said: "Protect him!" for fear of the Iy, the ancient one [. . .] But
> now, here is Uabuet, who has come with Isesi to devastate your
> house. She has taken everything that was there to enrich Isesi be
> cause they wanted to impoverish your son to enrich Isesi [. . .]
> How can your heart stay cold in this regard? I would rather you
> took this person who is here in your presence than see your son
> oppressed by the son of Isesi. Wake your father Iy against Behesti,
> get up and run to him. You know who has come for you here for a
> sentence regarding Behesti.

A similar ferment of hatred, along with otherworldly intervention
to establish privileges and rights, can be found in the correspondence
of the funerary priest Heqanakhte, written to his family during the

Middle Kingdom. The letters are so vivid that Agatha Christie made use of them in one of her famous thrillers. The environment is the same, apart from the fact that his authority could no longer be exercised except through this sinister reawakening of the family's dead, called on to carry out sentences that lay beyond the reach of worldly courts of justice.

Another example of this faith in the ability of the dead to influence the affairs of the living comes from a much later epoch, the Ramesside Period. This example, however, reveals the victim's point of view. A papyrus letter has been found, entrusted to the statuette of a woman who was probably regarded as a messenger to the Beyond. It was written by a widower to his dead wife in order to exorcise her spirit and to complain about the wrongs that, in his opinion, he was unjustly suffering. It recalls the affection and devotion with which his wife was treated during their years together in an extremely vivid and immediate way. This time, it was the living man who asked to be judged by the tribunal of the Beyond in order to regain the tranquillity he deserved:

To the excellent spirit Ankhere! What evil thing have I done to you that I should have come into this wretched state in which I am? What have I done to you? What you have done is that you have laid hands on me, although I had done nothing evil to you. Since I lived with you as husband down to this day, what have I done to you that I must hide it? What have I done to you? What you have done is that I must bring this accusation against you. What have I done to you? I will lay a complaint against you in the presence with words of my mouth, in the presence of the Divine Ennead of the West (the gods of the land of the dead), and it shall be decided between you and me by means of this writing, even this which disputes with you what is written about. What have I done to you? I made you a married woman when I was a youth. I was with you when I was performing all manner of offices. I was with you, and did not put you away. I did not cause your heart to grieve. And I did it when I was a youth and when I was performing all manner of important offices for Pharaoh, without putting you away but saying, "She has always been with me"—so said I! And everyone who came to me before you, I did not receive them on your account, saying "I will act according to your desire." And now, behold, you do not suffer my heart to take comfort. I will be judged

with you, and one shall discern wrong from right. Now behold,
when I was training officers for the soldiery and the cavalry of Pharaoh, I caused them to come and lie on their bellies before you,
bringing all manner of good things to lay before you, and I hid
nothing from you in your day of life. I did not cause you to suffer
pain in anything that I did with you, after the fashion of a lord. Nor
did you find me disregarding you after the fashion of a peasant in
entering into a strange house. I caused no man to chide me in anything that I did with you. And when they placed me in the position
in which I am, I became unable to go abroad in my wonted fashion,
and I came to do that which one like me does when he is at home,
concerning your unguent, and likewise your provisions, and likewise your clothes, and they were brought to you, and I did not put
them in a strange place, saying, "The woman is there (?)." So said
I, and did not disregard you. But behold, you do not know that I
have done with you. I am sending to let you know that which you
are doing. And when you did sicken of the sickness that you did
have, I caused to be brought a master-physician, and he treated
you, and he did everything whereof you did say, "Do it." And when
I followed after Pharaoh journeying to the south, and this condition
had come to pass with you, I spent this sum of eight months without eating or drinking like a man. And when I arrived in Memphis,
I asked leave of Pharaoh, and I came to the place where you were
(buried), and I wept exceedingly together with my people in front
of my street-quarter, and I gave linen clothes to wrap you, and I
caused many clothes to be made, and I left no good thing that it
should not be done for you. And now, behold, I have passed three
years dwelling alone without entering into a house, though it be
not right that one like me should be caused to do it. And behold, I
have done it on your account. But behold, you do not know good
from bad. It shall be decided between you and me. And behold,
the sisters in the house, I have not entered into one of them. (Gardiner and Sethe 1928)

The end of the letter suggests that the widower intended to remarry, and that he wanted to clarify his position with his preceding
wife in order to avoid unpleasant rancor. In this case too, the inter-
weaving of this world and the next is expressed with a fluency that
demonstrates how normal such a practice was to Egyptian culture.
   A final example is formulated in an even more complex way. At

the death of Nesikhonsu, wife of a chief priest of Amun who had declared himself king, and daughter of another self-declared king, the bereaved husband of such a clearly dynastic marriage must have felt threatened by the new, barely controllable authority his wife had acquired by leaving the power games of this world behind her. Taking advantage of his priestly position, he obtained from his god Amun an oracle declaring that the princess had been deified and that she enjoyed in the West—the land of the dead—all the offerings made to those who became gods, having been received with due respect by the deities of the region. In return for this treatment, appropriate to her doubly royal nature as daughter and wife of a king, the princess—in compliance with the oracle pronounced by the Theban god—would behave in a benevolent manner toward her surviving husband and toward everything, both people and goods, connected to him. The form of the divine decree, the long text of which has survived on a papyrus and tablet, takes it for granted that the judgment will be favorable to her husband should the same thing occur between him and his dead wife as that which threatened Ankhere's widower.

All these cases show the terrible power that the dead exerted over the living. Although no longer of this world, they could return to revenge themselves in a manner more similar to that of an executioner than of a judge. It is understandable, therefore, that the lists of hostile forces and beings in protective magical texts generally included "each dead man and woman" as beings from whom the spells demanded protection, just as they did from any other "enemy." The apparent serenity of Egyptian necropolises actually concealed primordial fears that could be only partially exorcised. It is precisely because the dead were feared by the living that people presented themselves in their idealized autobiographies not only as having been pious and benign but also as still capable of helping the living. Thus a certain Djedhor, who lived at the beginning of the Ptolemaic Period in Egypt, boasted of having been known as the "Savior." During his lifetime, he had saved more than one person in his city from snakebites. Now dead, with his statue covered in spells, he would help all those who had faith in him.

There are other examples of benign worldly presence in the form of a statue. Nor was it the only way in which someone who no longer existed offered to help the living from the Beyond or, at least, from another level of existence. Certain renowned wise figures became gods. In many cases, we learn about them not only from documents that they themselves left while alive but also from the position they assumed in the eyes of the living, often a considerable length of time later. King Djoser (Early Dynastic Period) and King Amenophis III (Eighteenth Dynasty) both became popular deities, as did several others. These figures owed their divinity to their exemplary lives. Others, however, derived their divine status from having drowned in the Nile: reliving an episode from the myth of Osiris, they were automatically elevated to the rank of gods. Temples could be dedicated and prayers addressed to these people as a result. However, perhaps we are overstepping the intended limits of this chapter by touching on concepts that are more concerned with religion than with society.

Also outside the scope of this survey are a number of explicitly literary documents in which the theme of the narrative concerns relationships with the dead who present themselves to the living, those who are sought in their tombs by the living, or visits, voluntary and otherwise, to the Netherworld. This material, varied, picturesque, and adventurously seductive in more than one case, is extremely interesting for a number of different reasons. Nonetheless, it is somewhat hazardous to adopt it as documentation of that daily concrete reality that, in many other ways, needs to be recognized as belonging to those who have "passed on"—and here the term is not euphemistic but has its own specific value.

"Passing on" expresses precisely the vitality of Egyptian society, so unshakably concerned with the reality of daily events that it could not (or did not want to) believe that a rift might exist between earthly life and no-life. The tombs of ancient Egypt continue to remain the richest, most eloquent, and vital evidence of the life that beat along the shores of the Nile.

Bibliography

Brunner, H. "Der Tote als rechtsfähige Person." *Zeitschrift der Deutschen Morgenländischen Gesellschaft* 105 (n.s. 30) (1955).

Faulkner, R. O. *The Ancient Egyptian Pyramid Texts Translated into English.* Oxford, 1969.

Gardiner, A. H. *The Attitude of the Ancient Egyptians to Death and the Dead.* Cambridge, 1935.

Gardiner, A. H., and K. Sethe. *Egyptian Letters to the Dead.* London, 1928.

Grapow, H. "Der Tod als Räuber." *Zeitschrift für Ägyptische Sprache und Altertumskunde* 72 (1936): 76.

Hornung, E. *Das Totenbuch der Ägypter.* Zurich and Munich, 1979.

Kees, H. *Totenglaube und Jenseitssorstellungen der Alten Ägypten.* Leipzig, 1926.

Sander Hansen, C. E. *Der Begriff des Todes bei den Ägyptern.* Med. Kgl. Vid. Selsk-Medd. 29.2. Copenhagen, 1942.

Scharff, A. *Das Grab als Wohnhaus in der ägyptischen Fruhzeit.* Munich, 1947.

Simpson, W. K., ed. *The Literature of Ancient Egypt: An Anthology of Stories, Instructions, and Poetry.* 2d ed. New Haven, 1973.

Sottas, H. *La préservation de la propriété funéraire dans l'ancienne Égypte avec le recueil des formules d'imprécation.* Paris, 1913.

Spencer, A. J. *Death in Ancient Egypt.* Harmondsworth, 1982.

Zandee, J. *Death as an Enemy according to Ancient Egyptian Conceptions.* Leiden, 1960.

10. THE PHARAOH

Erik Hornung

The social pyramid of humanity, as seen by the Egyptians, culminated in the king. He was closest to the gods and belonged rather in their world, being "indistinguishable" from them. Thus, in one of his aspects the king was a god and received cultic worship.

In his other aspect, however, the king was the protagonist of the cult and hence the representative of humanity vis-à-vis the gods. The walls, pillars, and columns of the Egyptian temples are covered with cultic scenes of the king bringing offerings and praying to the deities of the land. Since he could not be present in all the temples, however, he had to delegate some of his cultic functions to priests, who could legitimize themselves before the gods only by taking the king's place in the celebration of the cult.

No private person, only the king alone, could erect, renovate, or enlarge cultic edifices. Therefore, construction work in Egyptian temples was always carried out in the name of "Pharaoh," even during the Greco-Roman period, when the king was a Ptolemy or a Roman emperor. This is the reason for the continuity of Egyptian kingship, which, beginning with the Hyksos, survived numerous periods of foreign rule. Only the victory of Christianity replaced Pharaoh as the "Son of God" with another Son of God, one who stands above all sovereigns.

Until that time, for three and a half millennia, the institution of Egyptian kingship was never questioned. It was subject to crises, especially following the end of the Old Kingdom and during the Amarna Period, but even detested foreign rulers like the Hyksos and the Persians profited from Pharaoh's religious prestige, which made his person sacrosanct. Criticism of his office was never voiced, and personal criticism of the sovereign was not openly expressed until late sources like the Demotic Chronicle, although some kings, such as Cheops and Pepi II, were portrayed rather negatively even in earlier narratives.

Pharaoh was the focal point not only in ancient Egyptian religion but also in art and history. The time span before Alexander the Great is called the "Pharaonic" period, and our subdivisions of Egyptian history are based on dynasties of rulers. Art and literature were under the auspices of the state and centered on kingship as well. Even where we can catch a glimpse of the world of the "little people," the lower echelons of society, the figure of Pharaoh looms ever present in the background: as the one for whom they worked, from whom they received their livelihood, and in whom they placed their religious hopes. Hence, Egyptian history is still, first and foremost, the history of the Pharaohs.

In earlier times, the person of the king is completely obscured by his ideological role and the ritual encompassing him. Even the individual name he received at birth was often programmatic in character and contained a religiopolitical program. Such is the case, for example, with the names formed with Re (the name of the sun god) since the Fourth Dynasty, or the Amun-names of the Twelfth and Eighteenth Dynasties (Amenemhet = "Amun is at the top"; Amenophis = "Amun is pleased"). No later than the New Kingdom, the birth of the king became obscured by a veil of myth. The god Amun assumed the physical appearance of the father in order to engender the future king with the queen. Wall decorations and texts (especially by Hatshepsut in Deir al-Bahri and by Amenophis III in the temple of Luxor) describe the birth of the semidivine child, his acknowledgment by Amun, and his rearing by divine nurses. The king is frequently described as being called upon to rule even "in the egg."

At his accession to the throne, the name of the king was expanded into a five-part titulature that developed during the Old Kingdom and is headed by the Horus-name, which goes back to prehistoric times. This name identifies the king as the worldly incarnation of the falcon-shaped sky god Horus, as a "Horus in the palace." Along with the lion and the bull, the falcon was the most important animal aspect of Pharaoh, who was sometimes depicted in the New Kingdom as a composite entity with falcon wings or even with a falcon head. When the king died, it was said that "the falcon had flown to the sky."

All kings of the New Kingdom combined the title "Horus" with the element "Strong Bull," an allusion to an ancient embodiment of the king that is documented as early as the Narmer Palette. The god Seth was the other divine power that manifested itself in the king and sometimes appeared in the form of a bull as well. As "Horus and Seth," Pharaoh united the fighting brothers within his person. But Horus was the victor in this struggle, and Seth never found a permanent place in the royal titulature, since he continued to play a negative role as a violent god and the murderer of Osiris. Starting in the Fifth Dynasty, the Horus aspect, on the other hand, gained additional importance through the Osiris myth. Horus was now regarded as the son of Osiris and each king became an "Osiris" when he died; thus the reigning Horus-king was now also the mythical son of his (deified) father.

The second royal title, compounded with the element Nebti, "the two ladies," specifically referred to the two apotropaic goddesses of Upper and Lower Egypt: Nekhbet, in the shape of a vulture, and Uto (Uadjit), in the shape of a cobra. It is by no means unusual that female powers, too, manifested themselves in the male person of Pharaoh. The best known example is the duality of Sakhmet and Bastet: the terrible and the merciful aspect, respectively, of the deity, which the king combines in himself, just as the quarreling brothers Horus and Seth were reconciled within him. The Egyptians liked to think in dualities that formed a whole only in combination; and the king united, above all, the duality of the two halves of the country, Upper and Lower Egypt.

The third title is called the "gold name" (formerly "gold Horus-name"). It, too, hints at the nature of the king as a falcon, but gold is also a symbol for the material of which the gods and their statues are made. The details of the meaning of this title are still disputed.

The throne name proper, which, from Middle Kingdom times onward, always contained the name of the sun god Re, was joined with the fourth title: Nesut-biti, "King of Upper and Lower Egypt," that is, king of the entire country, whose unification marks the beginning of historical times for the Egyptians. The throne name following it was enclosed within a "cartouche," an oval which originally represented a plaited amulet and which surrounded the name of the king protectively on all sides. In hieroglyphic inscriptions, these name cartouches of the king stand out clearly from the rest of the text and were therefore an important aid in the decipherment of the script.

A second cartouche surrounded the king's birth name, which he retained even after his accession to the throne. Beginning with the Fourth Dynasty, it was linked with the title "Son of Re." In his epithets, the king was described as the "son" of many other deities, but only his affiliation with the sun god was reflected in the "official" titulature; even the exceedingly common designation of Pharaoh as the "image" of the sun god was restricted to the epithets. The epithets surrounding the king like a luminescent cloud and changing from inscription to inscription reveal the emphases of each era in its conception of kingship. Epithets like "the one who conquers all countries with his powerful strength" or "the one who creates truth and destroys the lie" or "the Nile of Egypt, who inundates the land with his perfection," shed some light on the expectations and hopes that were placed in Pharaoh, though they say nothing about the individual personality of the ruler.

The royal inscriptions contain a great number of other titles and designations of the sovereign in addition to the "official" parts of his titulature and changing epithets. He was "lord of the Two Lands," "lord of the crowns," and "lord of the cult," but also simply a "good god." His title of "Pharaoh" has been common since the New Kingdom and made its way into the Old Testament and the Coptic texts from Egypt's Christian era. It meant literally "the great (or greatest) house"; that is, it originally referred to the architectural entity of the palace and was later transferred to the institution and the person of the king, in much the same way that the "Sublime Portel" and the "White House" became terms for institutions.

The expression *ḥem.ef*, which we render as "His Majesty," often replaced the title and name of the ruler. Since the word *ḥem* describes not only the king but also slaves, scholars believe it referred to the king's physical presence, his person; Greek inscriptions use the title *basileus* on these occasions. The king was also frequently referred to by impersonal constructions: "one rewarded," "one ordered," "one sent," and so on.

The robes worn by Pharaoh distinguished him clearly from the rest of humanity and shared many features with the garments of the gods. In contrast to Egyptian subjects, who were usually depicted clean-shaven (unlike the bearded Asiatics), gods and kings each wore a long ceremonial beard. On gods it was curled at the tip; on kings it hung straight down and was attached by a ribbon. Since the deceased king became Osiris, however, deceased kings also wore the divine beard in paintings, reliefs, and sculptures; conversely, the god Ptah was almost always depicted with the straight, royal beard.

The only piece of clothing worn by Pharaoh in the older periods was the *shendjut,* "loincloth," a term that survives today in the term *sindone* for the shroud in Turin. It was very short, usually pleated, with a trapezoidal middle piece; a slightly later version had a triangular, protruding middle piece. Both forms were clearly distinct from the loincloths of gods and officials. Although Roman emperors in their role as Pharaoh were still depicted with this archaic *shendjut,* the king often wore a plain long loincloth and covered his upper body with a kind of shirt or vest as early as the New Kingdom. During his anniversary celebration (Sed festival), he was dressed in a short, tight-fitting coat.

The crowns, a good many of which appear in depictions very early on, were the most important component of the royal attire. The White Crown, associated with Upper Egypt, was a high cap of soft material (possibly leather), tapering off toward the top and ending in a round knob. Its counterpart was the Red Crown of Lower Egypt, a flat-topped cap with a "wire" of unknown material that is coiled up in a spiral. Both crowns are combined in the "Double Crown," which designates its wearer as the king of the entire country. Throughout the New Kingdom, the helmetlike Blue Crown was especially popular. It was made of leather, decorated with little metal rings, and worn only by the king, whereas the other crowns could also be worn by gods. In addition, there were a number of feather-crowns that were developed into elaborate composite crowns during the Late Period, embroidered with horns and uraeus-snakes that could be part of basically any crown. Since no original crown has ever been recovered, however, we have to rely exclusively on pictorial representations and do not know which forms were actually worn.

Instead of a crown, Pharaoh very frequently wore a headdress made from a striped rectangular cloth positioned on the head close to the brow and held in place by a headband; the two front corners lay on the chest, and the back corners were twisted into a little braid that fell down the back. Statues, in particular, preferred the headdress to the crowns, and in rare cases both occur in combination. The uraeus-snake formed part of the headdress, too, as a further symbol of kingship, keeping all hostile powers away from the king's person with the "fiery breath" of its poison. Even where the king appeared only with a wig, worn in Egypt by men and women alike, he was clearly distinguishable from all other human beings by the uraeus.

Beginning with the earliest representations the king wore a tied-on bull's tail, a reference to his role as ruler symbolized by the image of the bull. He could also appear wearing a panther's fur, but only when he was carrying out priestly functions. He often wore sandals. Tutankhamun's tomb contained gloves that apparently belonged to the equipment of a charioteer. The two most important tokens of his power that Pharaoh held in his hands were the old rounded shepherd's staff and the so-called flagellum, which might be a fly swatter. Osiris, as the ruler of the dead, took over these two attributes from the king.

The royal attire symbolized a specific role that was more closely defined by Pharaoh's titulature and his epithets. Furthermore, there was undoubtedly an elaborate court ceremonial, although this remains almost completely unknown to us because descriptions of an audience at the royal court, like the one in the Story of Sinuhe, are very rare. But we may believe Diodoros Siculus (1.70), who claims that the entire daily agenda of the king was neatly planned in every detail. In addition, ancient Egyptian sources reveal the taboos that surrounded him. For instance, in an inscription from his Giza tomb, the priest Rawer related a very dangerous incident for him that happened under King Neferirkare (Fifth Dynasty). During a cultic ceremony, he was accidentally touched by the king's mace, whereupon the king had to declare solemnly that he had done this without intention and that the priest was not to be harmed by it. Just like the gods, the king was surrounded by an aura of magical power. When a subject approached the king, he prostrated himself, "kissing the ground" as the Egyptians called it.

The king's individuality receded completely into the background behind the role he had to play. Egyptian art does not represent the king as an individual but as an idealized type. For example, none of the depictions of Ramesses II, who reigned for sixty-six years, show him as an old man; even as an eighty-year-old he still appeared in the youthful vigor that was part of the ideal image of the king. Even the "realistic" royal statues of the Twelfth Dynasty and the Amarna Period are no longer viewed as portraits of these kings but rather as an expression of the changed interpretation of kingship.

Only very few written documents from ancient Egypt allow us immediate access to the personality of a Pharaoh. In contrast to the abundant genre of officials' biographies, which also gave rise to the Story of Sinuhe, no Egyptian king left us his biography. But we do have two Instructions that are attributed to royal authors and in which Pharaoh speaks directly to his son and successor. They are the Instruction for Merikare, a king of the Tenth Dynasty, and the Instruction of Amenemhet I for his son Sesostris I, from the early Twelfth Dynasty. In both texts we find very personal statements and even the admission of having failed in certain situations. Amenemhet even described the attempt on his life, mentioning his own defenselessness and the treason of his confidants; therefore, he urged his son to be suspicious, whereas Merikare was admonished to be lenient. Merikare's father also knew that a king had to live with foreign and domestic enemies, yet he warned him of excessive punishment and praised the "tongue," persuasive speech, as a weapon of the king. Both Instructions can be viewed as governmental declarations of the successor, based on the political experiences of the predecessor and attributed to him.

Among the direct sources on individual kings are also several letters that have been preserved by their "publication" in tombs or on stelae of officials; original drafts of royal letters or their copies preserved in the cuneiform archive at Tell el-Amarna and dating from the time of Amenophis III and Amenophis IV; and others in the archives of the Hittite capital at Bogazköy. Among the "published" letters, two hold special interest. During the second year of his ninety-four-year-reign (in other words, when he was still a child), Pepi II had a letter written to his expedition leader Herkhuf in Nubia:

> The king's decree to the Sole Companion, Lector Priest, Overseer of the Interpreters, Herkhuf:
> Notice has been taken of this letter of yours which you sent to the king at the palace, to let One know that you have come down in safety from Iam (in Nubia) with the army that was with you. You said in this letter of yours that you have brought all kinds of great and beautiful gifts, which Hathor, mistress of Imaau, has given to the ka of the king of Upper and Lower Egypt, Neferkare (Pepi II), may He live forever.
> You wrote in this letter of yours that you have brought a dwarf

of the god's dances from the land of the horizon dwellers, just like the dwarf whom the seal-bearer of the god, Bawerdjed, brought from Punt in the time of King Asosi. You told My Majesty: "Never has someone like him been brought by anyone who traveled to Iam before." You know, indeed, how to do what your lord loves and praises. You spend day and night, indeed, planning to do what your lord loves, praises, and commands. His Majesty will fulfill all of your numerous excellent wishes for the benefit of your son's son, so that everyone will say when they hear what My Majesty will have done for you: "Is there anything comparable to what was done for the Sole Companion Herkhuf, when he returned from Iam, because of the vigilance he displayed in order to do what his lord loves and praises?" So, come downstream to the Residence at once. Leave (everything) and bring this dwarf with you whom you brought alive, well, and living from the land of the horizon dwellers for the god's dances, in order to make the heart of the king of Upper and Lower Egypt, Neferkare, may He live forever, happy and glad.

When he boards the ship with you, place reliable people behind him on both sides of the ship in order to prevent him from falling into the water. When he is asleep at night, have reliable people sleep with him in his tent. Check on him ten times during the night. My Majesty wants to see this dwarf more than the presents from Sinai and Punt. When you arrive at the palace with the dwarf being alive, well, and living, My Majesty will compensate you with more than the seal-bearer of the god, Bawerdjed, received in the time of King Asosi, because of My Majesty's wish to see this dwarf.

Even this stylized version in the courtier's tomb still reflects the childlike joy of the young king that for the first time after more than a hundred years a Pygmy was "imported" to Egypt from inner Africa, not only to fulfill cultic functions as a dancing dwarf, but also to entertain the royal court. Full of expectation, the king urges his official to make haste, but more than that to be careful so as to bring the dwarf safely to the Residence, where Herkhuf will be amply rewarded. Herkhuf was so proud of this personal letter from the king that he included a copy of it in the biographical inscription in his tomb at Aswan.

Usersatet, a viceroy of Kush during the New Kingdom, had a

personal letter from Amenophis II engraved on a stela that was once at the Second Cataract and is now in Boston. The situation here is completely different: the aged king reminded his former brother-in-arms of adventures they had shared in Syria and Palestine, criticizing at the same time the way the latter conducted his office. Thus, the letter bears witness to Amenophis II's very personal style in dealing with the high officials whom he had picked from among the companions of his youth and his wars:

> [Year 23 . . .] Copy of the order which His Majesty wrote himself, with his own hand, to the viceroy Usersatet. His Majesty was in the Residence . . . he spent a holiday sitting and drinking.
>
> Look, this order of the king is brought to you . . . who are in faraway Nubia, a hero who brought booty from all foreign countries, a charioteer . . . you (are) master of a wife from Babylon and a maidservant from Byblos, a young girl from Alalakh and an old woman from Arapkha. Now, these people from Tekhsi (Syria) are worthless—what are they good for?
>
> Another message for the viceroy: Do not trust the Nubians, but beware of their people and their witchcraft. Take this servant of a commoner, for example, whom you made an official although he is not an official whom you should have suggested to His Majesty; or did you want to allude to the proverb: "If you lack a gold battle-axe inlaid with bronze, a heavy club of acacia wood will do"? So, do not listen to their words and do not heed their messages!

The "official" inscriptions sometimes also reveal very personal opinions and actions of the king. Kamose has left us an exceedingly vivid description of his battles against the Hyksos on his victory stela in Karnak. Ramesses II recorded an unusual report about the battle of Kadesh against the Hittites and made himself the spokesperson for his consistent peace policy, which eventually led to a treaty and marriage alliance with the former enemies. A recently discovered stela of King Taharqa (Twenty-fifth Dynasty) recounts a footrace by his troops from their camp near Memphis to the Fayyūm. The king himself raced part of the way, and afterward he rewarded the soldiers with a big feast.

There is something that takes us beyond such biographical details and establishes the closest possible physical contact with individual rulers: mummies. The Egyptian Museum in Cairo houses the mummified bodies of many New Kingdom rulers, and from time to time it puts them irreverently on display. Whereas the bodies of Alexander the Great and Augustus have decayed to dust, these rulers, more than a thousand years older, are still physically palpable, with skin and hair and with the signs of their illnesses.

Although kings were mummified as early as the Old Kingdom, only fragments of their burials have survived, and the early excavators paid hardly any attention to the anthropological material. Had it not been for the priests of the Twenty-first Dynasty who reburied the royal mummies of the New Kingdom in two secret places around 1000 B.C., we would probably have no more than the mummy from the intact tomb of Tutankhamun. One of the two hiding places, a small chamber in the tomb of Amenophis II, was discovered in 1898 by the Egyptian Antiquities Department. The other one, a small tomb south of Deir al-Bahri, had been found in 1871 by modern-day Egyptians, from whom Maspero, as director of the Antiquities Department, wrested the secret about the hiding place ten years later. In 1881 the royal mummies were transferred in a triumphal procession from Luxor to Cairo; they were stored in a mausoleum for a while and eventually moved to a separate room of the Egyptian Museum.

Thus, the mortal remains of important rulers like Tuthmosis III, Sethos I, and Ramesses II are still accessible, and detailed examination has yielded physical features, illnesses, causes of death, and even blood type. We know that Tuthmosis III was 5 feet, 5 inches tall, of petite stature, and died around the age of seventy. Amenophis III suffered from severe toothaches in his old age (whereas Amenophis I, Tuthmosis III, and Ramesses IV had excellent teeth) and from obesity. Siptah showed the effects of poliomyelitis; and Ramesses V, the symptoms of an infection with smallpox, which caused his premature death. Surprisingly, many of these Pharaohs suffered from arthritic conditions.

In contrast to the stylized representations of Egyptian art, the mummies bring us as close as possible to the real appearance of many kings and provide biographical details that no other source mentions. Yet, there are limits to the information provided by this anthropological material, and even the age at the time of death cannot be determined with certainty by today's methods. Most important, the empty shell of a mummy tells us nothing about the thoughts and feelings of the person who once inhabited this body. When it comes to the

life stories and an evaluation of these personalities, we must therefore rely on other sources after all.

The inscriptions of the kings and their officials are disappoint-
ingly silent in this respect, because their focus is often different from
what we would expect. Tuthmosis III "recounts" the decisive battle
at Megiddo, where he defeated an enemy coalition, in only three
verses of his Annals:

> Then His Majesty became powerful at the head of his troops;
> [the enemies] saw that His Majesty was becoming powerful
> and fled in confusion into Megiddo with faces full of fear.

The annalist describes in great detail, however, the consultations of
the king with his army and the deployment of the troops before the
battle. On the other hand, Ramesses II, in describing the battle of
Kadesh against the Hittites two hundred years later, which was anything but an Egyptian victory, provides much more textual as well as
pictorial information. This is part of the style of a new era, which
replaces the ancient symbolic scene of "smiting the enemies" with
detailed representations of Pharaoh's wars against his enemies. But
the lengthy description of the battle of Kadesh, which almost ended
disastrously for the Egyptians, also helped Ramesses II to succeed
with his peace policy. Behind this policy, which doubtless had to
overcome much resistance, was the personality of the king who established a stable peace in his time, a peace that was ended only by
the rise of the Sea Peoples.

The king's very personal imprint on politics becomes visible
also in the sources from the time of Amenophis IV (Akhenaten) and
from the time of his father, Amenophis III. These are rare exceptions, however; the personality of a Pharaoh usually remains hidden
from us.

A random example is Ramesses IV, who lived in a well-documented period. He was born around 1200 B.C., not as a prince, however, because his family had not yet attained rulership. It was not
until after the (possibly violent) death of Queen Tausret that his
grandfather Sethnakht founded the Twentieth Dynasty and was succeeded after a very short reign by Ramesses III, the father of
Ramesses IV. Like the other princes, the future king gained military
experience by participating in the campaigns against the Libyans
and the Sea Peoples. It appears that for a long time Ramesses III

was unable to decide which of his sons to choose as his successor. His decision in favor of Ramesses triggered a conspiracy of the harem with the goal of designating another prince, Pentawer, as heir apparent. Although the old king was assassinated, the conspirators did not succeed with their plan. They were caught and sentenced, and Ramesses IV attained rulership.

Mastering this state crisis and securing his power doubtless required great skill and energy. His legitimacy and recognition by the gods were underscored in unusual documents, such as the Great Harris Papyrus in London. Other documents report the trial of the conspirators, which the king delegated to a special jury of twelve officials. In his royal titulature, Ramesses IV propagated a governmental program that underscored the concept of *maat*, just world order and harmony, and was directed against the corruption that surfaced even in this trial.

Having inherited a stable international situation from his father, he was able to concentrate entirely on peaceful activities. Numerous large expeditions were sent to the quarries of Wadi Hammamat, more than 8,000 men in his third regnal year, for instance. In building his expansive mortuary temple in western Thebes, the king made use of material from older buildings, and in other places he simply "usurped" existing edifices by inserting his cartouches, a common practice throughout Egyptian history. Constrained by the economic situation at the end of the Twentieth Dynasty, Ramesses IV was unable to engage in new large-scale building activities of his own. He managed only to finish his tomb in the Valley of the Kings, though here he developed a new concept that was continued by his successors.

The ground plan and decoration of each royal tomb was individually designed for each new king; often the changes or additions were minor, but in other cases an entirely new design was implemented. It is unclear, however, to what extent the king himself influenced such developments, in other words, whether the new concepts incorporated into the tomb of Ramesses IV were initiated by the king himself or were the work of a group of officials and priests. The king's inscriptions inform us about his religious and intellectual interests; he read old papyri stored in the House of Life and ensured the strict observation of religious rules. It is therefore imaginable that he personally created the new design for his tomb. The overall layout of the tomb was brilliantly simplified, but the dimensions were increased to evoke the impression of a "burial palace," which contained new decorative elements as well. When the king was buried in 1149 B.C., after a six-year reign, the tomb was finished—an astonishing feat considering the corruption mentioned in many documents of the era.

Thus, the personality of a ruler of the well-documented Ramesside Period is visible at least in outline. The same is true for the important Ramesses II—one of the few Pharaohs besides Akhenaten and Hatshepsut about whom a monograph has been published (by K. A. Kitchen). Although Old Kingdom sources are too scarce to justify a monograph on an Old Kingdom Pharaoh, the first rulers of the Fourth Dynasty, Snofru and Cheops, are portrayed in later literary texts as distinct personalities. Poetic compositions of the Middle Kingdom (Westcar Papyrus, Prophecy of Neferti, Instruction of Kagemni) describe Snofru as a kind and charitable Pharaoh who possessed a natural authority and treated his high officials in a friendly, unassuming way. His son Cheops, on the other hand, is portrayed as rather despotic, an image he also has in the antique tradition. Contemporary sources show both kings primarily as pyramid builders. Cheops may have erected the largest one, but Snofru built the most pyramids (three large and several small ones); thus, Cheops's description as "despot" cannot derive only from his building activity.

Although the king of the official inscriptions "never sleeps," watching over the country day and night, the "*roi des contes*," as G. Posener calls him, appears much more human; he is bored and seeks diversion (Westcar Papyrus), he tries to learn the future (Neferti) or to prolong his life (Vandier Papyrus), and in the Story of Neferkare and Sisene he even appears as a homosexual lover who visits one of his generals at night. This is a far cry from the sublime divinity of Pharaoh, and Ramesside picture ostraca even deal with kingship in a satirical way without ever questioning the institution as such; after all, the same period paints a very "human" image also of the gods, as in the quarrel between Horus and Seth and the cunning of Isis.

The status and political influence of queens varied considerably in the different epochs of Egyptian history. As the regent for a king under age, a queen could wield real political power at all times without being Pharaoh. Also, there was always only one "Great Royal Wife," who was ideally the king's sister or half sister. The king had numerous other wives, but descent from the main wife was a decisive factor in succession to the throne and a circumstance that gave legitimacy to a female Pharaoh. Originally a purely male institution, the kingship was flexible enough to admit women to the role of Pharaoh.

As early as the First Dynasty, we encounter an outstanding woman in Queen Meretneith, who probably acted as regent during the minority of King Den. She claimed a number of royal privileges, such as the erection of two tombs as well as statues and stelae; but she had no Horus-name, nor did she count her own regnal years; in other words, she did not appear as the reigning Pharaoh. Only three queens took that step beyond a doubt: Sobeknofru at the end of the Twelfth Dynasty, Hatshepsut in the Eighteenth Dynasty, and Tausret at the end of the Nineteenth Dynasty. The case of Nitocris from the end of the Old Kingdom is uncertain.

Sobeknofru followed her brother Amenemhet IV as ruler because there was apparently no male heir to the throne. The torso of her statue in the Louvre shows the male attire of Pharaoh, headdress and loincloth, on top of her female garments, and in her titulature she appears clearly as a woman in the male role of Pharaoh, calling herself "female Horus." Hatshepsut, clearly following in the footsteps of Sobeknofru, underscored her femininity in the beginning and avoided the common title "Strong Bull." However, during her reign of over twenty years she developed more and more into a male Pharaoh, although she tolerated Tuthmosis III as a male coregent. Tausret assumed many royal prerogatives already as queen, though it was not until the death of her son Siptah that she reigned as a true Pharaoh.

The "Divine Spouses" who exercised the power in Upper Egypt in lieu of the king during the eighth through sixth centuries B.C. form a special case. They were members of the royal family who were officially considered "wives" of the Theban god Amun. Therefore, they remained unmarried and designated their successors by adoption. They had their own abridged royal titulature, counted their own regnal years, and built temples, and their administration was largely a copy of the secular original. Hence, their institution shows great formal similarity to the rule of Pharaoh, though without being a true kingship, unlike the abovementioned female Pharaohs of the Middle and New Kingdoms.

Hatshepsut legitimized her rule as female Pharaoh in three ways. First, she claimed divine origin as a daughter of Amun, born to a human queen but engendered by a divine father. This myth is documented in a detailed sequence of seventeen pictures in her mortuary temple at Deir al-Bahri, which describe Amun's encounter with the queen, the god Khnum forming the child, the birth, her naming, the child in the care of divine nurses, and, finally, her solemn recognition by Amun. A second complete cycle is preserved in the temple of Luxor by Amenophis III. There must have been more parallels, and traces of this Egyptian royal ideology are to be found as late as Alexander the Great, who had himself proclaimed the son of Amun.

Second, Hatshepsut legitimized her rule also through her human father, Tuthmosis I, claiming to have been designated as his heir apparent. As the daughter of his main wife, Ahmes, she had a clear advantage over Tuthmosis III, who was the son of a lesser wife of Tuthmosis II. Third, she legitimized her rule through an oracle ceremony during which the god Amun proclaimed his decision that Hatshepsut was to become king. Scenes show him crowning Hatshepsut, who is kneeling before him, and thereby bestowing the kingship on her. These forms of legitimization were valid for all kings of the New Kingdom.

During the Middle Kingdom, the rulers of the Twelfth Dynasty successfully guaranteed the continuity of their power by a strict system of coregencies. This method was used in the New Kingdom as well (e.g., Hatshepsut and Tuthmosis III), although the Ramessides tried to maintain the ideal fiction of only *one* ruler by calling the heir apparent "generalissimo" and denying him his own titulature and his own regnal year count. The dynasties of foreigners in the Late Period chose quite different, un-Egyptian ways of securing succession to the throne. The Libyans divided the state into many small realms in order to share the rulership with as many relatives as possible, whereas succession among the Nubians was from brother to brother and then down to a nephew. The Ptolemaic Dynasty utilized the coregency again, but preferably with female partners.

The Egyptian ideal throughout all periods of history was that every office, even that of Pharaoh, should be inherited by the son from his father, as it is told in the myth of kingship: Horus wins his father's heritage against all opposition. Seth's violent usurpation of his brother's throne threatens the succession temporarily but ultimately fails. As a rule, a new sovereign represented a new generation, and no generation was skipped. If an heir apparent died before his coronation, it was one of his brothers, not one of his sons, who replaced him. Pharaoh Merenptah, for instance, was the fourteenth son of his predecessor, Ramesses II. The governing principle here was not to choose the oldest son first but to prefer the sons of the main wife, followed by the sons of other wives. Ramesses III apparently hesitated a long time before he picked one of his sons as his successor—one reason for the harem conspiracy that cost him his life.

Even if the Great Royal Wife did not give birth to a son, there were almost always sons of other wives, unless the king died very young. If he had only daughters, like Akhenaten, his sons-in-law gained in importance and were treated like sons. Akhenaten's son-in-law Tutankhamun died too young to establish a new dynasty, but in other cases the king's son-in-law did found a new dynasty. Here we are still following the subdivision of Egyptian history into dynasties which the priest Manetho introduced or copied from older sources under Ptolemy II. Some, though not all, of his thirty dynasties correspond to one family's rule, which was passed on to another family either by the legal designation of a successor or by usurpation.

During the Early Dynastic Period and throughout the Old Kingdom all leading positions in the administration were filled by members of the ruling family; the highest official (vizier) had to be a son of the king, and the highest rank, *repat*, probably was reserved for a member of the ruling clan. Toward the end of the Old Kingdom, the influence of the royal family steadily decreased, and in the Middle and New Kingdoms the princes hardly played a role anymore.

As it was never quite certain which of the princes would be king one day, their education was the same. The heir apparent was taught in the palace school together with all the other princes, with the sons of foreign rulers, and with future officials, whom he would trust on account of their shared upbringing. The position of a teacher at court involved a great deal of responsibility and was given only to seasoned officials. Literacy, the ability to read the "classical" literature, was the foundation of any education. In the Prophecy of Neferti, King Snofru is reported to have taken a papyrus roll and a scribal palette out of its box in order personally to record the words of the sage Neferti. Our sources also mention athletic training in archery and swimming in addition to military training in the "work of (the god of war) Month." Amenophis II, the "athletic king," reports in great detail on his physical prowess, which surpassed that of all his soldiers. Kings of the New Kingdom also had to be skilled in driving a horse-drawn chariot, originally for hunting and warfare and during the Amarna Period as a fast means of transportation in general. In older times, the king was carried in a litter or sailed on a ship. Pharaoh was never pictured on horseback, however, because horses were used only as draft animals.

At any rate, it can be taken for granted that Pharaoh received a thorough intellectual as well as physical education. He also prepared for his religious tasks by studying texts, as we saw earlier in the case of Ramesses IV. The sources do not mention, however, to what extent Pharaoh was prepared for his divine role before his coronation; it has been repeatedly claimed by modern scholars that he was formally "initiated," but this has never really been established. Royal inscriptions and hymns declare that Pharaoh had secret knowledge (for instance, about the arcana of the sun's course) and that he was "wise already in the egg," but these statements refer to the divinity of his office, not to the human individual.

The hopes connected with the beginning of a new reign are best expressed in the New Kingdom hymns on the accession to the throne of Merenptah and of Ramesses IV:

O beautiful day! Heaven and earth are in joy,
you are the good lord of Egypt!

Those who had fled have returned to their towns,
those who had hidden themselves have come out;
those who were hungry are full and happy,
those who were thirsty are drunk;
those who were naked are clad in fine linen,
those who were dirty are resplendent;
those who were in captivity have been released,
those who were in shackles are happy;
those who were quarreling in this country
have become peaceful.

A high Nile has come out of his cavern
in order to refresh the hearts of the people.

The widows, their houses are open, they let wanderers in;
the prostitutes are rejoicing
and singing their songs of joy,

. . . .

Male children are born into a good time,

(because) a progenitor of generations upon generations
is the ruler for all times.

The ships, they are rejoicing on the tide, they need no ropes:
they are landing with sail and rudder.
They are filled with joy, since it was said:
"The king of Upper and Lower Egypt Hekamaatre,
he wears the White Crown again!
The son of Re, Ramesses,
he has received the office of his father!"

The entire double empire says to him:
"Horus is beautiful on the throne of his father Amun-Re,
the god who sends him out, the protector
of this sovereign who conquers every country!"

(Assmann 1970)

Merenptah's counterpart to this hymn to Ramesses IV underscores in addition that the goddess Maat, personifying the just and
ideal order of society and nature, has returned and conquered injustice, so that "one lives in laughter and in wonder." Pharaoh was expected to repeat the actions of the creator god and to restore the
ideal original state of the world. The term "god" is mentioned in his
titulature, the depictions elevate him into the sphere of the gods,
and the Egyptians looked to him for the power of a deity.

In dealing with Egyptian kingship, early Egyptology was too
heavily influenced by classical authors, who either considered Pharaoh just another Eastern despot who had pyramids erected for his
own glory or portrayed him as a Hellenistic conqueror of the world,
as in the legends that coalesced around the figure of Sesostris. It was
only in 1902 that Alexandre Moret clearly pointed out the "religious
character of Egyptian kingship," and this started the discussion
about Pharaoh's "divinity" that has continued to the present day.
This discussion revolves around the "two natures" of the king, since
along with his divine nature there is obviously his human side, which
we mentioned before. It was especially Georges Posener who reem-
phasized this human aspect in his 1960 study, while other authors
focused completely on the divine aspect.

The popular but imprecise term "god-king," coined by Moret
("*le roi dieu*"), lends too much importance to the divine aspect. Pharaoh was human, but his office was divine. In other words, he was a
human being in the role of a god; and at the same time he was a

priest, a servant of the gods representing all humanity vis-à-vis the gods. Furthermore, in Egypt any human being could become a "god." The deceased were generally considered gods, since they inhabited the same sphere as the "real" gods after their death. According to some theories, the Egyptian word for "god" (*netjer*) originally referred only to the dead king; but what makes Pharaoh special is precisely the fact that, unlike all other mortals, he is a god already in his lifetime, a "god on earth" in a manner of speaking!

Thus, it is difficult to define the divine nature of the Egyptian king, and the best point of departure is the textual and pictorial sources of the Pharaonic period. They make several quite different kinds of statements about the relationship between the king and the realm of the gods:

1. Pharaoh is a god.
2. Pharaoh is the son of a god.
3. Pharaoh is the image of a god.
4. Pharaoh is "loved" by or "in the good graces" of the gods.

Only the first two statements are part of the official titulature; the other two are reflected above all in the epithets. The love (*merut*) and grace (*hesut*) which the gods extend to the king characterize the special relationship of trust between them, and it is quite frequently said that a god or a goddess loves the reigning monarch "more than all of his predecessors."

Djedefre of the Fourth Dynasty, the successor of Cheops, was the first king to bear the title "Son of Re," the sun god. Later epithets refer to Pharaoh as the son of Amun, of Ptah, and of many other gods and goddesses; and a wide variety of deities address him as "my son" or "my beloved son" in the inscriptions. The myth of Pharaoh's divine origin shows that he is seen quite physically as the "son" of the sun god and was engendered by him, as attested for the first kings of the Fifth Dynasty in Papyrus Westcar from the Middle Kingdom. But when, during the Ramesside Period, the king is called "son of Seth," a god who has no son in the myths, this addresses rather a similarity in character: Pharaoh shares the belligerent aspect of his nature with the violent god Seth, and the term "son of Seth" means nothing other than "he is like Seth" or "he is a Seth" (when he fights against his enemies). This level of comparison is certainly also aimed at by nonroyal personal names like "Son of (the god/goddess) X" or "Daughter of X," which are not found in the Old Kingdom but enjoyed great popularity during the Middle Kingdom. It is still an open question, however, what religious statement was being made by nonroyal parents who called their child "Daughter of Amun."

The use of the term "image of god" to indicate all humanity (as in Genesis) is found only in the Instruction for Merikare, and the term is afterward restricted to the king. In the Old Kingdom it is absent altogether. During the Thirteenth Dynasty it becomes a new definition of Pharaoh as "the living image of (the sun god) Re on earth" and is henceforward used in numerous variations throughout the New Kingdom and the Late Period. The Egyptians had about twenty different words for "image," expressing fine nuances of meaning. Thus, "image" can also refer to a sign, a statue, or a cult picture. The official titulature covered this aspect of Pharaoh with the designation "Son of Re," and the inscriptions often use "son" and "image" in parallel formulations. Amenophis III, for instance, is called "my beloved son who emanated from my limbs, my image whom I invested on earth" by Amun-Re (*Urkunden* IV, 1676). The earthly son is the reflection of the divine father in every respect: in his shape, in his actions, in his character, but also in his social position, his rank. The designation "representative" of a god, however, as attested in the Ramesside Period, is exceedingly rare, as this was probably considered a demotion in rank.

Gods and goddesses are able to act upon earth not only through their cultic images and sacred animals but also through Pharaoh. The texts even go so far as to identify the king with the gods. For instance, Amenemhet III is called Sia, Re, Hapi, Khnum, Bastet, Month, and Sakhmet in the Loyalistic Instruction of the Middle Kingdom; that is, he is identified with male as well as female deities. We are not dealing with the "incarnation" of deities in the king, however. The context of the entire eulogy on the king makes clear that Pharaoh is a Hapi (inundation of the Nile) for the people in his capacity as nourisher of Egypt, a Khnum (who forms humans on his pottery wheel) as the patriarch of the country, terrible Sakhmet in his wrath, peaceful Bastet in his mercy, and the god of war, Month, on the battlefield. The names of these gods describe briefly the role Pharaoh plays on earth.

The descriptions and depictions of the king as an animal have to be understood at the same level. Attested from the beginning of the historical period, the most important royal animals are the lion, bull, and falcon, with the composite entities of sphinx and griffin later additions (the griffin combines the lion and falcon nature of the king). The bull symbolizes not only fertility to the Egyptians but above all rulership. Hence, Osiris is called "bull of the West"; other gods, "bull of the sky." In scenes of triumph, popular on scarabs and scaraboids from the New Kingdom, the king, in the shape of a bull, strides across an enemy lying on the ground; but the triumphant king can also assume the form of a lion, sphinx, or griffin, and even the horse is included as a new entry in this list of royal animals.

Above all, it is the falcon nature of the king that is most frequently highlighted in inscriptions and depictions. From the beginning of the historic period, Pharaoh is portrayed as Horus in the form of a falcon; his titulature begins with the Horus-name, and he is viewed as the "falcon in the palace," that is, as Horus on earth. Chephren introduced the well-known statue type of the king protected by the Horus-falcon, a type that survives in variations until the end of the Pharaonic period; even Nectanebos II not only is depicted as protected by the great falcon (statue in New York) but is also worshiped as "the falcon." Among the statuary it is the type of the "king in falcon garment" that demonstrates most impressively the penetration of the king with the falcon nature of Horus. The front side of this statue type shows the king in his royal vestments, and the back shows the wings of the falcon. The same aspect of Pharaoh is expressed less boldly by numerous falcon attributes that belong to the king's regalia. Although Ramesses II is often represented in his deified form with a falcon head, this is an allusion to the sun god Re-Harakhte, however, not to Horus.

The Egyptian king is identified with no other deity as frequently and as completely as with the sun god Re. A virtual nonentity during the first three dynasties, Re suddenly gains major importance in the Fourth Dynasty, and in the Fifth Dynasty each king erects a separate sanctuary for him next to his own pyramid. The son and successor of Cheops, Djedefre, defined the relationship between king and sun god by assuming the title "Son of Re," which was borne by all future kings. His successors chose throne names that contained statements about Re, and the epithets of the king describe the close relationship between Pharaoh and Re in various ways. From the Pyramid Texts onward, the sun god is furthermore the dominant deity in the royal Netherworld.

The Middle Kingdom shows an increase in the number of epithets that describe Pharaoh as the "sun king." He is the "sun disk of mankind who dispels the darkness over Egypt," "the sun of the foreign countries," or "the one who illuminates the Two Lands." The development of this "solar" kingship reaches its peak during the New Kingdom, when texts like the "sun litany" strive to achieve a complete identification of the dead king with the sun. This identification is threefold: "I am you, and you are I, your soul (*ba*) is my soul, your course is my course through the Netherworld," Re says to Pharaoh. The identification with the sun, which rises every morning from the Netherworld, rejuvenated and reborn, was the surest guarantee of an afterlife in the Netherworld. For this reason, the nightly voyage of the sun through the Netherworld is the dominant theme in the decoration of the tombs in the Valley of the Kings; representations of the sun god in his barque or in the form of the sun disk appear everywhere.

Even the living king tried to achieve an identification with the sun god, and since Amenophis II the officials called out to him: "You are Re!" Amun, the "king of the gods," says to Amenophis III: "I have invested you as Re of the Two Riverbanks (Egypt)." The same king seems to be the first one to write his name within a sun disk, thus documenting his identification with the sun god also visually.

Apparently it was this solar aspect of the king that gave rise to the veneration of the living king as a god from the time of Amenophis III on. To be sure, Pharaoh had been surrounded by rituals from the very beginning, especially during his investiture and his throne jubilee (Sed festival), but it was only through his death, which made him a god and, specifically, an "Osiris," that he had become the object of a cult. Now, for the first time, the reigning king was represented giving offerings before his own deified picture. The gold and sun land Nubia was the preferred place for this worship, for it was closest to the sunrise as seen from Egypt. There, in Soleb and Sedeinga, Amenophis III erected a double temple for the worship of his wife Tiye and himself; Tutankhamun followed his example in Faras, and Ramesses II built a number of temples in faraway Nubia in addition to his double temple at Abu Simbel in order to have himself worshiped as the sun king. His cultic image, to which he brings offerings himself, is depicted with the head of a falcon and the sun disk (in another he has a human head topped with the sun disk), thus virtually elevating the king to sun god.

This cultic worship of the living king is connected especially with colossal statues that are given their own cultic name and symbolize a separate divine aspect of Pharaoh. Their names appear on scarabs as well, and seals express the deification by depictions of the king in the cultic barque, which was replaced by a litter after the Amarna Period: like a statue of a god during a procession, Pharaoh, dressed with all the attributes of kingship, is borne along on the shoulders of human or divine beings. Like the sun, he influences the course of the world by his mere "appearance." In the cultic barque, his picture can be replaced by his name, and in the scenes of the procession he often remains anonymous.

The Egyptians could understand the sunlike character of Pharaoh in a very real way. Like the sun, he "illuminated" Egypt with the monuments he built everywhere in the country. "You have erected magnificent monuments in my temple, you have illuminated Karnak with works of eternity like the sun when it rises in the morning," says Amun to his "beloved son" Sethos I in the Great Hypostyle Hall at Karnak. Pharaoh's buildings shine throughout the country; Egypt is "flooded" with the splendor that emanates from his temples and is put in a "festive mood" at the same time. The bright colors of the temple reliefs, the gilded tops of the obelisks and other gilded architectural parts, the precious, polished stones of the statues, they all contribute to the splendor of the "sun king." Like the creative light, he shapes the world and lets it shine for his subjects.

And, just as the rays of sunlight dispel the darkness, he scatters the enemies of Egypt wherever he appears. His picture, often engraved on the outer walls of temples, in quarries, or on scarabs and on other small objects, has apotropaic powers and keeps the powers of darkness at bay. In the New Kingdom he is frequently praised and depicted as a good marksman with a bow and arrow; just as the sun "shoots" its rays and disperses all enemies, Pharaoh, speeding along in a chariot, lets fly his arrows and never misses his mark.

The deeper meaning behind this "solar" activity of Pharaoh is clearly addressed in a text of Tuthmosis III: the country will be "as though Re (himself) were its king" (*Urkunden* IV, 1246) or simply "like in the time of Re," when the sun god himself ruled the earth, or "like at the time of creation," when he made the world. Pharaoh's actions as the sun are nothing other than a repetition of the acts of the creator god, a cleansing of all contamination that has happened since the creation, a restoration of the world to its original, perfect state. He enacts the role of the creator god on earth. In an inscription at Tanis, Ramesses II is called "the one who founds the world anew like at the time of the creation." The Restoration Stela, from the end of the Amarna Period, says about the youthful Tutankhamun: "He has scattered chaos . . . , so that order (*maat*) prevails in its place. He makes the lie an abomination, so that the world is like at the time of its creation." These texts reveal the hope that each new successor would remove all evil and make the world perfect again!

This royal ideology draws an ideal picture, but it did influence the reality of Egyptian history. Many of the reported campaigns did not originate in political or economic necessity. They were merely a ritual "smiting of the enemies" by Pharaoh, who had to prove himself as victorious over hostile powers as soon as possible after his inauguration in order to live up to the expectations of his role. Therefore, even peaceful rulers like Hatshepsut and Akhenaten report such military display.

Another way to defeat hostile powers was to go hunting, since the hunted and killed animals were considered enemies of Pharaoh. The depictions, for example, on the painted chest of Tutankhamun treat hunting and warfare scenes as variations on the same theme, varying only the representation of the "enemies" as human or animal while the large figure of the king accompanied by his soldiers and shooting arrows from his chariot remains unchanged. A ring of Amenophis II in the Louvre shows Pharaoh fighting enemies on one side and slaying a lion on the other; and the famous depiction of the wild bull hunt of Ramesses III at the southern end of the pylon at Medinet Habu has a war scene as its counterpart at the northern end. The "tribute scenes" documenting foreign trade relations frequently contain exotic animals like elephants, giraffes, and bears that are presented to the king, demonstrating Pharaoh's rule over even the most remote areas of the ordered world. They were kept in zoological gardens at the royal court to fulfill the same function by their presence.

In analogy to the Egyptian depictions of war and the hunt that place Pharaoh larger than life in the center of the composition, the texts call him "more efficient than millions of soldiers" or "a wall for his army" and recount almost exclusively his actions, whereas the names of generals or other officers are never mentioned. Ramesses II relates the battle of Kadesh as if, his army having failed after an ambush, he had kept the Hittites and their allies at bay and turned the fortunes of war to his favor all by himself, supported only by his god Amun. This stylized version of the events, however, which conforms perfectly to Egyptian royal ideology, symbolizes a very real peace policy that ended the military confrontation between the two great powers and after long negotiations led to a peace treaty, eventually even to a marriage alliance. Doubtless, this did not happen without the strong resistance of a war party, who would not overcome its hostile image of the "miserable Asiatic."

It is also part of the royal ideology that Pharaoh does not wage wars of aggression to conquer but merely reacts to the provocation and the "rebellion" of his enemies. Ramesses II attacks only those who "violated his border," and a typical casus belli is expressed in the statement that says: "One came to report to His Majesty: the miserable country of Kush is rebelling." This aversion to wars of aggression marks a stark contrast to the frequent formula that the king "enlarges the borders of Egypt," which is motivated by another ideological postulate, the "expansion of the existing possessions" (see below). No later than the Middle Kingdom, the king claims to be the ruler of the world, "all lands and all foreign countries" are subject to him, and in the New Kingdom it is accurate to speak of an Egyptian empire that included Palestine, Syria, Lebanon, and vast areas of modern Sudan. Pharaoh's rule over the world is often described in mythical terms; it stretches from the "horn of the earth" in the south to the primeval darkness or the pillars of the sky in the north; in other words, it includes the entire ordered world to the limits of creation. In a nutshell, the king is "lord over everything the sun disk encircles."

The two most important aspects of Pharaoh's historical actions are those of warlord and builder of monuments. His titulature frequently refers to the erection of "monuments" (*menu*): buildings, stelae, obelisks, statues, even a new royal residence (Akhenaten) or small objects of art. Creating such "monuments" was a special task of the king's and pertained to his role as creator god on earth. Every king, in order to fulfill this role, initiated large-scale building programs as early as possible after his accession to the throne, which accounts for the often surprising wealth of monuments that were erected during comparatively short reigns. Ramesses II, who reigned for over sixty-six years, left us three long building inscriptions from his first year and apparently started several gigantic temple projects at once: Abydos, Abu Simbel, the Ramesseum. He also undertook the enlargement of the temple of Luxor, the completion of the Great Hypostyle Hall at Karnak, and the construction of a huge tomb in the Valley of the Kings, with all the stelae and statues that are part and parcel of such edifices—all this on top of his campaigns against the Hittites before his peace policy took effect!

Similar accomplishments are known of King Snofru from the Old Kingdom, who built three large and several smaller pyramids, and in the New Kingdom Amenophis III also figures prominently as a builder of monuments. Amenophis III also commissioned an incredible number of royal and divine statues, more than 700 of the goddess Sakhmet alone. Such an exertion of all the resources of the country, however, was not possible in every reign. Many kings had to be content with a rather symbolic "erection of monuments" by adding inscriptions or merely altering the cartouches of their predecessors on already existing buildings and obelisks in order to ascribe the respective monuments to themselves. These "usurpations" were not considered acts of hostility but were quite legitimate and in accord with the royal ideology.

His role as creator obliged the king to create new things, to exceed the achievements of his predecessors, and to "expand the borders," as he did on his military campaigns. The concept of the Egyptian temple is perfectly adapted to this task, because, unlike Greek temples, it was never finished and could be indefinitely enlarged. The individual elements of the axial temple—hypostyle hall, court, pylon, gates—could be arbitrarily multiplied. Thus, a king could erect new temples, but he could also add new elements to existing temples. The temple of Karnak was constructed over more than two thousand years. This compulsion to add new things is what I call the rule of the "expansion of the existing possessions."

This rule was doubtless in effect as early as the Old Kingdom and determined the development of the pyramid; from the Middle Kingdom, the rule was an integral part of the governmental program of every Egyptian king. The author of the royal Instruction for Merikare wants a successor who surpasses him and "increases what I have achieved," and even young Tutankhamun is said to have "surpassed what had been achieved since the time of the ancestors." In the same inscription, the king orders that the number of the carrying poles for the statue of the god Amun be increased from eleven to thirteen, and from seven to eleven for the statue of Ptah. These measures, too, are an "expansion of the existing possessions," as are an increase in the offerings and the addition of new holidays for the gods.

Systematic, carefully planned expansion is most visible in the buildings, however. Another example in addition to the temples is the development of the royal tombs in the New Kingdom. The oldest, still very modest tombs in the Valley of the Kings consist of only a few small chambers, but with each new reign the size and the richness of their decoration are increased, a development that reached its peak in the "tomb palaces" of the Ramesside Period, which are completely decorated with painted relief and lead more than 300 feet into the limestone. Their ground plans and decoration programs show a steady elaboration: the number of chambers and sometimes also the number of pillars increase, measurements are changed, and new motifs are introduced in the decoration. The sarcophagi of the kings show a development toward larger and more richly decorated forms.

The steady increase led to limits we have nowadays come to know as the "limits of growth." At the beginning of the Twentieth Dynasty, the royal tomb had become so gigantic that a further enhancement no longer seemed possible or desirable. In this situation, Ramesses IV changed the measurements. He removed the pillars, reduced the number of chambers, and made the entire tomb smaller. However, he increased the height and width of the corridors so that the overall impression was very imposing. In this way he stretched the limits again and continued the development.

The dynamics of this process originate in the deep insight of the Egyptians that every living thing needs renewal, regeneration. This is what happened during the great annual festivals in which Pharaoh played an important role. After the permanent move of the Residence to the north (Memphis and the eastern Delta) following the Amarna Period, the Pharaoh still came to Thebes every year to attend the Opet festival, the great procession of the divine barques from Karnak to Luxor and back. During the festival in honor of the god Min, the king's accession to the throne was renewed, and birds were sent in all four directions to announce the renewal of the reign to all the world.

The most important of the royal festivals, however, was the Sed festival, which is inaccurately called a "jubilee." Attested since the beginning of history, it promoted the idea that power and government had to be fundamentally renewed in each generation, and it developed into a general symbol of renewal, even in the Hereafter. Therefore, most Sed festivals that are mentioned in the texts or depicted in reliefs are nothing more than hopes or wishes, with no connection to a real festival. Independently of the real duration of his reign, Pharaoh was supposed to celebrate "millions" or "hundreds of thousands" of Sed festivals, and this count includes his existence in the Netherworld. Apart from a few exceptions, the real celebration took place after thirty regnal years, the equivalent of one generation, and was repeated after that in shorter intervals of three or four years.

Among the documented Sed festivals are the three celebrated by Amenophis III in his palace at Malqata (Molgata, western Thebes), which are attested by countless inscribed deliveries to the palace, special series of statues, and dated depictions (tomb of Kheruef). From the long reign of Ramesses II we know of fourteen Sed festivals that were "announced" by high-ranking officials; concrete evidence like that at Malqata is missing, however, since the palaces of the Egyptian kings are preserved to a much lesser extent than their tombs and temples. For Ramesses III, as well, we have knowledge only of the preparations for the festival and can assume that he was assassinated shortly before the first repetition.

The most complete description of the ritual part of the celebration is found in scenes of Neuserre (Fifth Dynasty) and Osorkon II (Twenty-second Dynasty), as well as in the Dramatic Ramesseum Papyrus, which probably refers to the Sed festival of Sesostris I. The ritual itself revolves around the burial of a royal statue symbolizing the aged king and the repetition of the original accession to the throne and coronation ceremony for the "rejuvenated" king, who demonstrates his physical strength in a cultic run before the gods. In Malqata, even the dais with thirty steps was found on which Amenophis III had sat during his Sed festival.

It is still an unresolved issue whether this festival replaced an original ritual murder of the king. In any case, the human nature of Pharaoh becomes visible once again, since his strength wanes in the course of time and needs a profound renewal to prevent a collapse of order in the state and in nature. The tragedy of an aged, ossified monopoly of power is described in the myth of the Destruction of Mankind from the Amarna Period. Here it is the sun god Re himself who initially rules over humans and gods on earth. "His Majesty having grown old," a crisis develops. His human subjects rebel against him and have to be cruelly punished by the fiery "eye" of the sun god. Sparing a few people (this is the Egyptian version of the deluge motif), he resigns from his rule on earth and is carried to heaven by the heavenly cow. Thus, even Re does not pass his power on to a younger generation until after the painful experiences of a rebellion.

An "abdication" as described in this myth is not attested for any Pharaoh. It became superfluous owing to the idea of the Sed festival, the ritual renewal; in addition, the institution of the coregency guaranteed in many cases the timely transition from one generation to the next. Having grown old, the last Ramesside king, Ramesses XI, inaugurated a "Renaissance Era" at a time when the state was shaken by crises; it did not outlast him, however, nor did it prevent the end of the New Kingdom. In order to document that all of nature regenerates together with the kingship, the Egyptians recorded especially high inundations of the Nile during Sed festival years; the Palermo Stone notes a record high for the Sed festival of Den in the First Dynasty, and Amenophis III makes the same claim (tomb of Khaemhet). A manipulation of history? Just as Egyptian art presents an idealized picture of humanity, the Egyptian Annals draw an ideal picture of history, where it is the necessary that happens, not the accidental.

Harmony between state and nature, which poses such a great problem today, was never questioned in ancient Egypt, despite occasional natural disasters. And the state was identical with Pharaoh. He integrated his buildings into nature and designed them creatively without violating nature; even the gigantic pyramids seem to be a part of nature. Nature and state both share *maat* as their common basis, which is binding for all social levels, including that of the king, and on which justice, truth, and all cosmic and social life are founded. Pharaoh emphasizes that he "lives off *maat*" like the gods; that is, he abides by this principle. Visually the same idea is conveyed by the "offering of Maat": the king hands a small figurine of the squatting goddess with a feather on her head to the gods.

In the social sphere the principle of *maat*, the principle of fair balance, is to prevent injustice being done to the weak. It is the king's responsibility to enforce it against opposing forces and against the natural "right of the stronger." The Instruction for Merikare, for example, explains that rulers were invested in order to "strengthen the back of the weak"; frequently mentioned as socially disadvantaged are widows and orphans, for whom the state is supposed to provide special protection. Although Pharaoh did not appear as a judge in the legal system and there was no formal way of appealing to him, no physical punishments could be carried out without his approval, neither the death sentence nor mutilation of nose and ears.

The ability of kingship to renew itself and to change existing conditions counterbalanced the bureaucracy and prevented Pharaonic Egypt from becoming a purely administrative state. The development of an influential clergy was also averted until relatively late, because, by appointing the highest priests himself, the king prevented the heritability of these offices. The extensive power of Pharaoh, on the other hand, was bound up with the universal principle of *maat* and thus could not very easily turn into despotism and tyranny. Akhenaten used his power to bring about a temporary reorganization of the state in the name of *maat* and to establish a new religion. But he was not able to make his "perestroika" last; it did not survive him, because the traditional religion proved to be stronger.

The obligation of social balance did not keep the Egyptian kingship from distancing itself clearly from the rest of humanity, for which purpose it had recourse to its divine aspect. It developed the tomb type of the pyramid—a royal prerogative that only the queen was allowed to share—along with royal mortuary temples and royal mortuary texts. A first wave of "democratization" made many of these privileges available to everyone after the end of the Old Kingdom. The pyramid, however, remained an exclusively royal tomb form until the beginning of the New Kingdom, when it was abandoned by the king and immediately seized upon by the officials as a now "legal" architectural form. For the new type of royal tomb, the rock-cut tombs in the Valley of the Kings, new mortuary texts were created, the books of the Netherworld, which were a royal prerogative until the end of the New Kingdom. In addition, a complex system of "royal" measurements was developed that was used only in the royal tomb. Among the statue types it is especially the sphinx which was strictly limited to the king, since it refers to the divine aspect of Pharaoh as a lion-shaped guardian and victor.

The king always led the way in creating new forms and ideas, the officials following after a certain time lag. This holds for tomb, coffin, and statue forms but also for religious literature and much else. Even the animal cult, which was later so popular, seems to have originated at the royal court. Thus, time and again Pharaoh was the driving force of historical development.

We are faced here with an institution that is not only one of the oldest but also one of the most durable in the history of humanity. It existed for more than three thousand years without ever being seriously questioned. Even foreign rulers were integrated in an astonishing manner for over one thousand years and transformed into "real" Pharaohs. Even Emperor Trajan still dances before Egyptian deities in the reliefs of the temple of Esna, thus fulfilling the necessary religious role of Pharaoh as the intermediary between the world of humans and the world of the gods. Although the Egyptians turned to other intermediaries in times of weak kings, worshiping sacred animals and deified deceased persons, or turned directly to the gods, this religious function of Pharaoh remained intact until the victory of Christianity.

In Egypt the ever problematic rule of humans over humans found a form that did not lead to oppression, despite the extent of the power of its rulers. The ancient Egyptian state allowed creative, productive powers to unfold, to which we owe the great achievements of this culture. Pharaoh was tied to a clearly defined role that itself called forth creative powers: he was supposed to act as the creator god upon earth and overcome human imperfection with his divine nature.

Bibliography

Assmann, J. *Der König als Sonnenpriester.* Glückstadt, 1970.

———. "Krieg und Frieden im alten Ägypten: Ramses II. und die Schlacht bei Kadesch." *Mannheimer Forum* 83/84 (1983): 175–231.

Barta, W. *Untersuchungen zur Göttlichkeit des regierenden Königs.* Berlin, 1975.

von Beckerath, J. *Handbuch der ägyptischen Königsnamen.* Berlin, 1984.

Blumenthal, E. *Untersuchungen zum ägyptischen Königtum des Mittleren Reiches.* Vol. 1, *Die Phraseologie.* Berlin, 1970.

Bonhême, M.-A., and A. Forgeau, *Pharaon: Les secrets du pouvoir.* Paris, 1988.

Brunner, H. *Die Geburt des Gottkönigs.* 2d ed. Wiesbaden, 1986.

Decker, W. *Die physische Leistung Pharaos: Untersuchungen zur Heldenhaftigkeit, Jagd und Leibesübungen der ägyptischen Könige.* Cologne, 1971.

———. *Sport und Spiel im Alten Ägypten.* Munich, 1987.

Frankfort, H. *Kingship and the Gods.* Chicago, 1948. Reprint, 1978.

Goedicke, H. *Die Stellung des Königs im Alten Reich.* Wiesbaden, 1960.

Grimal, N.-C. *Les termes de la propagande royale égyptienne de la XIXᵉ dynastie à la conquête d'Alexandre.* Paris, 1986.

Habachi, L. *Features of the Deification of Ramesses II.* Glückstadt, 1969.

Hornung, E. "Pharao ludens." *Annales Eranos* 51 (1982): 479–516.

———. *Tal der Könige: Die Ruhestädte der Pharaonen*. 5th ed. Zurich and Munich, 1990.

Hornung, E., and E. Staehelin. *Studien zum Sedfest*. Geneva, 1974.

Jacobsohn, H. *Die dogmatische Stellung des Königs in der Theologie der alten Ägypter*. Glückstadt, 1939.

Keel, O. "Der Pharao als 'Vollkommene Sonne.'" *Scripta Hierosolymitana* 28 (1982): 406–512.

Kitchen, K. A. *Pharaoh Triumphant: The Life and Times of Ramesses II*. Warminster, 1982.

Lexikon der Ägyptologie. Vol. 3, pp. 461–664. Wiesbaden, 1980.

Moftah, R. *Studien zum ägyptischen Königsdogma im Neuen Reich*. Mainz, 1985.

Moret, A. *Du caractère religieux de la royauté pharaonique*. Paris, 1902.

Müller, H. *Die formale Entwicklung der Titulatur der ägyptischen Könige*. Glückstadt, 1938.

Posener, G. *De la divinité du Pharaon*. Paris, 1960.

Radwan, A. "Zur bildlichen Gleichsetzung des ägyptischen Königs mit der Gottheit." *Mitteilungen des Deutschen Archäologischen Instituts, Kairo*, 31 (1975): 99–108.

———. "Einige Aspekte der Vergöttlichung des ägyptischen Königs." *Ägypten—Dauer und Wandel*, pp. 53–69. Mainz, 1985.

Ratié, S. *La Reine—Pharaon*. Paris, 1972.

Sethe, K. *Urkunden der 18. Dynastie, historische-biographische Urkunden*. 4 vols. Leipzig, 1906–9.

Vernus, P., and J. Yoyotte. *Les Pharaons*. Paris, 1988.

Wiese, A. B. *Studien zum Bild des Königs auf Skarabäen und verwandten Siegelamuletten*. Fribourg/Switzerland and Göttingen, 1990.

Wildung, D. *Die Rolle ägyptischer Könige im Bewußtsein ihrer Nachwelt*. Vol. 1. Berlin, 1969.

———. "Göttlichkeitsstufen des Pharaoh." *Orientalistische Literatur-Zeitung* 68 (1973): 549–65.

11. WOMEN

Erika Feucht

Very few sources give us insight into the life of women in Egypt. Most of them are found on monuments or in wisdom texts, myths, and stories written by men, portraying their point of view. Erected by a privileged class, the monuments give us a glimpse of wives, mothers, and daughters in their relationships with kings, officials, and priests. We must be aware, however, that they merely reflect an ideal life according to the principles of *maat* (personified as a goddess of truth, justice, and world order); the reality of everyday life must have been different. As for the daily life and the rights of women of the lower echelons of society, we have virtually no information for the Old Kingdom period. Only the legal documents and letters on papyrus that are preserved in increasing numbers from the Middle Kingdom onward begin to form a mosaic-like picture, however fragmentary.

In the decorations of her husband's tomb, the wife is depicted as an equal, participating in her husband's life on earth as well as in the Hereafter. Not only did she not have to hide her body during any period of Egyptian history, but its charms were even accentuated in wall paintings and reliefs. The male ideal of a woman is expressed in this description of a lover:

Radiant, white of skin with clear, shining eyes,
with lips that speak sweetly; she does not say one word too many;
with a high neck and white breast,
her hair genuine lapis lazuli.
Her arms surpass gold,

315

her fingers resemble lotus blossoms.
Her hips full, her waist supple,
she whose thighs compete for her beauty,
with noble gait when she treads the earth.

(Schott 1950, p. 39)

We encounter this image of women in all periods of Egyptian history, but men were occasionally depicted as well-nourished dignitaries with wrinkled bellies, although youthful representations predominate. From the earliest periods until the beginning of the fourteenth century B.C., reliefs and sculptures in the round showed women clad in tight-fitting dresses that were secured with wide shoulder straps and that revealed their slender figures. When the garment became more voluminous, it was not to veil the body but, rather, to accentuate its charms: the flowing, folded or pleated fabric was so sheer that the shape of the body and even the navel were revealed. In contrast to men, who were depicted either with shaven heads or wearing short or long wigs, the women of all periods had long, thick hair that was supplemented, if necessary, by hairpieces of natural hair, vegetable fiber, or later even wool, or replaced by wigs. The eyes of men and women alike were outlined with makeup. It should be noted that the makeup with its antiseptic components like galena (black) or copper oxide (green) also offered protection from trachoma, still common today.

Although this is an ideal image of women as shaped by men, female members of the lower echelons of society were never depicted in a degrading way either, even if they had bared their chests in the heat of a bakery like their male colleagues.

Though Amenophis III had joyfully added two Mitanni princesses to his harem, he refused to send an Egyptian princess to the sovereign of Mitanni, because "from time immemorial a royal daughter from Egypt has been given to no one" (Knudtzon and Weber 1915, p. 73). This is not only an expression of the feeling of superiority of the Egyptians over the foreigners but at the same time an indication of the solicitude accorded female relatives, who could not be inconvenienced by living among "barbarians."

In his tomb Petosiris, who lived through the conquest of Egypt by Alexander the Great, describes his feelings for his wife in the following way:

His wife, his beloved,
mistress of amiability, sweet in love,
clever in conversation, pleasant in her words,
with excellent counsel in her writings,
everything that passes her lips is like the work of Maat,
a perfect woman, highly regarded in her town,
who lends a hand to everyone and says what is good,
who repeats what people like to hear, who brings joy to everybody,
whose lips no evil word passes, very popular everywhere.

(Lefebvre 1923–24, pp. 85, 101)

The wife of this eminent man, who held a high priestly office in his town, is described as a partner of her husband. Like her husband, she was in contact with the world outside and was able to win the respect of the citizens by her good acts. The occasional statements found in the tombs of men about their wives almost two thousand years earlier, in the latter half of the Sixth Dynasty, are very similar. Besides the usual statements that a wife is "beloved by her husband" or "justified by her husband," there are inscriptions that describe her as "someone who speaks beautifully and loves her husband dearly," as "someone whom people appreciate," or as "someone whom her entire town loves." One man declares: "great was my respect for her. She never uttered a word that was repulsive to my heart, and she was never mean as long as she was youthful in life." These short remarks are surprisingly similar to the later words of Petosiris about his wife. Some of the statements portray a gracious female who makes her husband happy, and some describe her appreciation by her fellow citizens. Twice her actions in the social sphere are characterized in words similar to those of the autobiographical inscriptions of men in which, starting at the end of the Sixth Dynasty, the tomb owner usually emphasizes his concern for the welfare of the poor. The women are called "someone who gives bread to the hungry and clothing to the naked" or "someone who does good things for the heart of the orphan," which is a variation on the common male epithet "he who protects the widow and the orphan."

Diodorus Siculus claimed that Egyptian women had power over their husbands. This impression may have arisen among the Greeks who settled in Egypt during the centuries before and after the birth of Christ and who formed a large part of the population of Lower

Egypt during the Greco-Roman Period. Unlike Egyptian women, Greek women had to spend all their lives in the privacy of their homes tending to domestic duties while their husbands not only went about their business outside but socialized with their colleagues and friends, sought out hetaeras, and satisfied their sexual desires with prostitutes. Greek women were not allowed to go where they pleased and needed a guardian in legal matters. Egyptian women, on the other hand, led much freer lives and were able to decide their own affairs. Women's seeming liberty to go anywhere prompted Herodotus's statement that the Egyptians had reversed the traditions of mankind; women, for instance, went to the market and engaged in commerce while the men stayed at home weaving. Although this was not true for all levels of society, men did, in fact, weave, and women did go to the market and haggled with merchants or sold their own products. Working-class women did not have to be separated from their male colleagues either. In the bakery and the weavers workshop and during the winnowing in the fields, men and women worked side by side.

A papyrus dating from the second century A.D. states that the goddess Isis granted as much power to women as to men. In the following we will investigate to what extent the ancient Egyptian sources confirm this claim.

A married woman of the middle or upper class probably focused on her duties as a wife and mother; her fair skin, as depicted in paintings, indicates that she spent most of her time inside the house, whereas the husband went about his business outside the house. In the Tale of the Two Brothers, the wife awaits her husband's return from the field, pours water over his hands, and lights a lamp. In a lawsuit about the purchase of a female slave, a woman described how she had moved into the house of her husband and began to weave and sew her clothes. In the seventh year of her marriage, she bought a female slave offered to her by a trader. Her husband was not involved either in this transaction or in the later lawsuit; the wife was perfectly free to act on her own behalf and had full legal standing.

The domestic responsibilities could involve the husband's possessions outside the house. The loving obituary that the Twentieth Dynasty scribe Butehamun of the workers' village of Deir al-Medina placed in the tomb of his deceased wife, Akhtay, shows that in the family of an official, whose time was taken up by his professional duties, the responsibility for the personal property outdoors was

shared by the wife, down to physical labor in the field and the care
of the livestock:

> O you beautiful one, without a peer,
> you who brought the cattle home,
> who tended to our fields,
> while all kinds of heavy loads were resting on you,
> although there was no place to put them down . . .
> (Černý 1973, pp. 369–70)

In the Egyptian wisdom texts, the husband is urged to treat his
wife well, since happiness and a harmonious marriage depended
largely upon his behavior toward his wife. The Old Kingdom Instruction of Ptahhotep invokes general human well-being:

> When you prosper and found your house,
> and love your wife with ardor,
> fill her belly, clothe her back,
> ointment soothes her body.
> Gladden her heart as long as you live;
> she is a fertile field for her lord.
> Do not contend with her in court,
> keep her from power, restrain her—
> her eye is her storm when she gazes—
> thus you will make her stay in your house.
> (Lichtheim 1973, p. 69)

During the New Kingdom, Ani advises the husband not to nag
his wife but to appreciate her value and avoid strife in order to live
harmoniously with her (Lichtheim 1976, p. 143). Speaking of "her
house" in this context, he underscores that it is her domain as the
mistress of the house. A thousand years later, Ankhsheshonqi and
the author of the Insinger Papyrus also emphasize the importance of
a woman to her husband. A prudent woman with noble character
who raises her children well is said to replace worldly riches. The
husband should avoid quarrels with his wife and not divorce her,
even if she cannot bear children. Ankhsheshonqi's wish "Oh, were
the hearts of a woman and her husband far from quarreling" reveals
the author's realistic attitude toward marriage. But we also find descriptions of bad women and their effects on the well-being of a man.
There are warning against the seductress, who threatens a man, and
tales reveal the secret desires and fears of a man who meets such a

woman. We hear nothing, however, of the dangers that men can pose to women.

The ideal of marriage as a lifelong companionship is expressed in the New Kingdom in a letter a widower wrote to his deceased wife, by whom he felt threatened. He married her young and remained faithful to her even after his rise in the ranks of the administration. He had not hidden anything from her, nor had he cheated on her like a peasant. He had taken care of her and provided her with everything she needed. Having reached a high position, he had not left as often as he may have wanted. When she fell ill, he summoned the best physician, who treated her according to her wishes. After learning of her death while he was on a journey with the Pharaoh, he had fasted for eight months, and immediately after their return to the Residence in Memphis, he had taken leave in order to mourn her publicly and to bury her with dignity. Even after her death he lived by himself, although that was not right for a man.

The fact that the widower emphasizes his exemplary behavior indicates that not all marriages were so harmonious. The importance of a wife and a family for a man, however, was frequently underscored, and the husband was considered responsible, along with his wife, for a successful marriage. On the other hand, he was supposed to be superior to his wife: Ptahhotep advises him not to give his wife any power, and Ankhsheshonqi recommends that the husband of a young wife (who, by our standards, was still a child when she got married immediately after reaching puberty) form her according to his wishes, keep her financially dependent, and not trust her as he does his mother.

Women were legally protected against physical abuse from their husbands. In a Twentieth Dynasty lawsuit, a man had to swear that he would henceforth refrain from beating his wife, on pain of one hundred blows with a cane and the loss of everything he had acquired together with her.

Men often had to leave their families for months on end: to run administrative errands, attend royal construction works, participate in military campaigns or prospecting expeditions, work on the estates of their lords, or perform compulsory labor. Traveling salesmen fared no better. Men of the lower classes often had to look for work outside their villages and were able to come home only occasionally. Even though the men tried to provide for their wives and children during their absence, the women were largely on their own and were responsible for themselves and their children. They had to take care of everyday problems themselves, although an older son could help them.

The legal documents from the workers' village of Deir al-Medina suggest that family life was not always as harmonious as the wisdom texts counseled. Quarrels between parents and children and between husbands and wives, as well as adultery and rape, were dealt with in court. One woman sent barley to her sister asking her to bake bread for her and to send it back because her husband wanted to divorce her on account of her parents' and her siblings' refusal to provide for her while other women received daily rations of food from their relatives. This demonstrates how much even married women depended on their blood relatives. It also explains the marriage contracts of later periods in which the husband committed himself to provide for his wife or to give her a certain share of grain every year.

Marriage and Family

We have no evidence that premarital relationships between young people were prohibited, and there is no clearly attested Egyptian word for "virgin." Considering the liberty with which women were able to move in society, it is likely that young men and women knew each other before marriage, and, if the Love Songs can be believed, premarital sexual contacts were not precluded, if limited by the early marriage age. It is impossible to determine today whether those Late Period couples who did not sign their marriage contracts until they had children were already married or lived together unmarried.

Ptahhotep's wisdom text from the middle of the third millennium B.C. advises a young man to marry and produce a son after having earned a reputation. About a thousand years later, Ani recommends in his Instruction early marriage and having children while young. The husband should be able to provide for his family, however, which was probably possible after an administrative apprentice had finished his training at the age of about twenty years, an age that Ankhsheshonqi in the first century B.C. quotes to his son as the proper age for marriage as well.

Young girls, on the other hand, usually married after reaching puberty, at the age of twelve to fifteen years. The sage Ptahhotep prohibits men from sleeping with a woman who has not reached sexual maturity; and Padiese sends the admirer of his daughter away with the request that he return after she has reached sexual maturity and after he has been installed as a priest of Amun, which would create a financial basis for a marriage. In addition to the desire to take advantage of a woman's fertile years, preventing premarital relationships may have been another reason why women married young.

Although a papyrus from 163 B.C. mentions that a Greek woman was circumcised in the Egyptian custom upon reaching marriageable age, the only ancient Egyptian text that has been used as evidence for the circumcision of girls is extremely unclear. According to Greek authors, the clitoris was removed when a girl was fourteen years old in order to prevent sexual arousal from the friction of the clothes; circumcision also reduced the desire for sexual intercourse and premarital relationships. Ankhsheshonqi's statement, on the other hand, that a failed marriage was the husband's fault if he neglected his wife sexually speaks against the circumcision of women, since, interestingly enough, the enjoyment of the sexual aspect of marriage is presented here not only as the wife's right but as a main factor in the success of a marriage. Circumcision, which has recently been prohibited in Egypt, deprives Islamic women of this part of marriage. Sexual satisfaction is the prerogative of the husband, whereas the feelings of the wife, who has to be at his disposal at all times, are considered unimportant.

Parents undoubtedly tried to influence their children's choice of a spouse, but they seem to have taken their children's affections into account, since a bond of love between husband and wife was presupposed. This is implied in depictions of married couples when the wife is referred to as "his beloved wife" or "his beloved sister." As early as Old Kingdom times, Ptahhotep had urged the husband to love his wife and treat her well.

Ankhsheshonqi's advice to his son not to marry a godless woman, on the one hand, and his instruction to find a sensible husband for his daughter, on the other hand, indicate that in those days the groom had more liberty in searching for a spouse than the much younger girl did.

We know little about weddings in Pharaonic times. They were not performed by a secular or a religious official but were apparently strictly private affairs. The future husband had to ask the father of the bride for his daughter's hand and make a marriage contract with him, which remained in the possession of the latter. If the father had already died, he was represented by a male relative or by the mother of the girl. The purpose of this custom, still widely practiced today, is to prevent the husband, who is several years his wife's senior, from taking advantage of the usually very young woman, or to prevent her from marrying a man with a bad reputation or someone from the lower classes. Starting in the late sixth century B.C., both parties signed the marriage contract themselves; each kept a copy, or the contract was deposited with a state official or in a temple. The wife was thus an equal contract partner with her husband.

Since marriage contracts regulated the possessions of the wife and the children, they could only be drawn up for couples with a certain amount of property. Consisting in many cases of no more than a bed, a copper kettle, grain, a donkey, and the like, it may seem very little to us, but the majority of the population probably possessed even less, so that most of them did not bother to sign a contract. The early contracts vary considerably. One such contract from the Nineteenth Dynasty awarded the wife one-third, and the children two-thirds, of the husband's property upon his death, a division that seems to have become the basis for later contracts as well.

The numerous marriage contracts dating from the sixth century B.C. until the Roman Period clearly show that monogamy was the norm, as both partners were unable to remarry until after a divorce. Around 20 percent of these contracts were drawn up for couples who already had children. The wife's legal situation prior to the contract remains unknown to us.

The contracts concerned the possessions of the husband to which the wife was entitled after a divorce. We know of real or fictitious dowries—often of modest value—which the husband pledged to double in the event of a divorce, and of a bridal gift that was used to buy household utensils which remained in the wife's possession after a divorce. The husband could also transfer his possessions as well as future acquisitions to his wife and children while retaining only the usufruct rights. In case of a sale he consequently needed the consent of his wife and his children. A woman could also pay the husband to become his wife, thereby obligating him to support her. In case of a divorce, he had to repay the entire sum, or he had to continue providing for her should he be unable to make the lump-sum payment.

Among the poorer part of the population, a divorce settlement secured for the wife in this way was just as insufficient to support her and her children as an inheritance from a dead husband. However, they formed the basis for a new marriage or provided support during an interim period if necessary.

Marriage contracts could include divorce clauses that imposed special obligations on the husband if he separated from his wife through no fault of her own. These could consist of payment of twice the amount of the dowry fixed in the marriage contract, one-third of his possessions (up to two-thirds if he took a new wife), one-third or all of the gains made during the marriage, or even a hundred blows with a cane. If the wife left her husband without the fault being his, however, she lost part or all of her rights; if she had committed adultery, she received nothing.

A divorce, possibly aggravated by divorce stipulations, left a simple man with very little, so that he could contribute hardly anything to a new marriage and he and his new wife had to depend entirely on his income. Only if he had been promoted and hence earned a higher income was he better off than during his first marriage. Rich men, on the other hand, retained enough for a new marriage.

Patrilocal marriage was the customary form of marriage; that is, the wife moved out of her father's house into the house of her husband. If he still lived with his parents and was unable to afford a house of his own, the young couple moved into the house of the groom's parents. Thus removed from her own family, the usually very young bride became dependent on her husband and his family. Matrilocal marriages, where the groom moved into the house of the bride or merely visited her occasionally, were the exception. After a divorce, the wife returned to the house of her parents or moved into the house of a male relative.

Both bride and groom usually belonged to the same social stratum, although marriages between partners from different echelons of society were possible. Marriage between siblings was rare among Egyptian subjects before the Late Period, and even then it is attested only between half siblings. Among the royalty, marriages between brothers and sisters from different mothers but the same father occurred occasionally in Pharaonic times; marriages between brothers and sisters from the same mother and father, however, were rare as well. It was not until the Ptolemaic Period that this form of marriage became customary. Only Roman citizens were not permitted to marry a brother or sister, and when all Egyptians became

Roman citizens by virtue of the Constitutio Antoniniana in A.D. 212, this prohibition applied to them as well. Late Period family archives show, on the other hand, that marriages between uncle and niece or between cousins were quite customary.

Herodotus's claim that only priests were monogamous, while all other Egyptians were polygamous, is only partly true. Monogamous marriages were the norm, not only due to the financial limitations of the husband but also due to the esteem in which a wife was held.

Starting with the Old Kingdom, the wife was called "his woman" on the monuments (tombs, stelae, statues) of men, thus emphasizing her bond with him. From the New Kingdom onward, the term "his sister" indicated that she was considered a member of the family, a blood relative. Starting in the Middle Kingdom, at the latest, the main wife, who was the head of the household, bore the designation "mistress of the house," a title that could occur next to "his wife" and that she probably kept even after the death of her husband. The other wives were considered to be "supported" by him. Whereas relationships with dependents seem to have been permitted to a husband, we know nothing about the rights of these women and their children.

Polygamous marriages were, at least at times, possible mainly for the wealthier class. We know of a few cases from the First Intermediate Period and the Middle Kingdom, especially among nomarchs. The several wives that are mentioned in the tombs of some New Kingdom officials and priests, however, seem to have been successive wives. The main wife of the king appeared as the queen, whereas the other wives had no official function. Among the commoners, the first wife and her children had more rights than the subsequent, or lesser, wives and their children. This probably gave rise to the Middle Kingdom practice of indicating descent through the mother, thereby specifying one's position and rights within the family. Maybe this is also the origin of a convention attested for the first time in a Nineteenth Dynasty marriage contract and then during the Late Period and in Ptolemaic times. According to this convention, the first wife inherited one-third of the husband's property and her children inherited the other two-thirds, while the second wife was entitled to the possessions that were acquired during the marriage. If the husband was not bound by a marriage contract, he could dispose of his belongings differently by means of a will. His wife and children seemed to have had certain privileges, however. We should not see matriarchal or matrilinear features in the filiations, especially since narrative texts from the same period indicate descent from the father, and in the Old Kingdom the mother is mentioned only in a few cases.

The wife was free to dispose of her own possessions, whether she had inherited them from her parents or acquired them herself. Her husband was permitted to manage them but not to sell them; and in the case of a divorce he had to return them in full. She also had full executive power over the property to which she was entitled in the event of a divorce or over the inheritance of her deceased husband. She was able to bequeathe different shares to her children and, in the case of a sizable fortune, determine that it had to be handed down in direct lineage. If a woman neglected to write a will, her children inherited her entire property, and her husband was not entitled to any part of it.

The listed conventional punishments show, however, how much the wife depended economically on her husband. Although an un-married, divorced, or widowed woman was not discriminated against and was able to (re)marry, she could live autonomously only if she was independently wealthy or had her own source of income; other-wise, she was soon at the mercy of her relatives' goodwill and finan-cial status. If she could move into the house of her parents or a male relative, she had a roof over her head, but she and her children were dependent on those who had taken them in. Thus, life was certainly difficult for such women of the lower classes. Household lists from the Middle Kingdom show that not only a man's mother could live in his house but also his grandmother, aunts, and sisters, some of them with their own children. This usually stretched the budget of a man and his own family considerably. Earning a living would have been very difficult for a divorced woman or widow with small chil-dren, especially if she had no education. As demonstrated below, few women had a profession that would have enabled them to live a life-style comparable to their husband's. Considering the early marriage age, a divorcée or widow could still have been very young and inex-perienced, which probably made her an easy victim for fraud and abuse. If no one was willing to take care of her, her fate must indeed have been deplorable. There are occasional depictions of women gleaning in the fields, an activity that Amenemope must have had in mind when he advises in his Instruction not to drive a widow from a field. And that is also why it was a virtue of the rich to take care of widows and orphans.

Adultery with a married woman entailed drastic punishment for the man as well as the woman, such as death, banishment, mutilation of nose and ears, a thousand lashes, or large fines. A wife was considered her husband's legal possession, for whom she was supposed to bear legitimate heirs. Although literary narratives mention executions, punishment in real life was generally less rigorous, as a legal document from the workers' village of Deir al-Medina suggests. Here a man was forbidden to continue his adulterous relationship with a married woman on pain of banishment to Nubia and mutilation of his nose and ears. When he repeated the offense, he was warned again, this time on pain of working in a quarry in Elephantine. We are not told, however, whether the mutilation threatened on the first occasion was carried out, or whether the woman was punished. In another case, however, a majordomo barely succeeded in keeping an infuriated crowd from forcing their way into the house of a woman who had had an eight-month relationship with a married man and beating her. He suggested to the husband, on the other hand, that he divorce his wife and return to the house of his mistress. This apparently unmarried woman was held responsible for seducing the man into committing adultery. Even if we do not know whether the wrath of the villagers had other causes, the advice to the husband shows how easily a man could ask for a divorce and how important the rejection stipulations in the marriage contracts were.

The purpose of marriage was procreation. A son was supposed to succeed his father in office, take care of his sick or old parents and his siblings, bury them after they had died, and secure their mortuary cults in order to "keep their names alive."

Ancient Egyptians knew that the reasons for infertility could lie with the husband as well as the wife. They tried to cure it with prayers and pledges to the gods or with magic spells. Although infertility was not considered a reason for divorce, in reality it could, and probably often did, lead to a divorce. Egyptian women tried to prevent too quick a succession of children by using contraceptives, which were not altogether unsuccessful, as we know by now. For instance, a rinsing with sour milk or with a mixture of acacia tips, colocynth, dates, and honey seems to have had an effect similar to that of the gels based on lactic acid that are used today. Camel dung soaked with vinegar and inserted into the vagina probably worked like the little sponges that are used today. Ancient Egyptians presumably noticed that nursing delays a new conception, although the effectiveness decreases drastically after the first five months. They were aware of the connection between intercourse, cessation of menstruation, and pregnancy. They observed changes in the breast and the face, the change of the linea alba to the linea fuchsia, and nausea; interior and exterior palpating could reveal the size and development of the uterus. Barley and wheat were moistened with the urine of a pregnant woman to see if the grain would sprout, a custom still practiced today even in Europe. In modern experiments, 40 percent of the grain treated this way sprouted, whereas grain that was moistened with the urine of men and nonpregnant women did not sprout. However, determining the gender of the child, as is described in an Egyptian text, is not possible with this method.

A pregnancy was calculated to last nine months by the Egyptian solar calendar, ten months according to the Greek lunar calendar. The womb was considered a vessel in which the male sperm developed through the milk of the mother, the child thus receiving a share of each parent. According to an old tradition, the heart—seat of emotions, character, and mind—came from the mother. A much later one claimed that the bones were formed out of the father's sperm, and the skin and flesh were formed out of the mother's milk inside the womb, an idea that was taken over by Greek authors and has also survived in some African tribes. The embryo was considered a living being inside the womb and was commended to the gods for protection. Premature babies who died were buried.

The mother gave birth in a birthing hut erected on the roof of the house or next to it. She knelt on bricks while supported by midwives. In later periods, birthing chairs were also used. She spent the ensuing two weeks of her cleansing period here, protected by amulets and magic spells that were supposed to ward off illness and death from mother and child; many women died in childbed, and children frequently did not survive infancy. These spells illustrate the desperate fight of mothers for sick children, and the woeful mourning over children who died early is an eloquent testimony of the love of mothers for their children.

If a mother and her baby died at the same time, they could be buried together. Older children could be buried along with their mother or father as well. If the baby survived, it was given a name that was chosen by both parents. In addition, there was a name that was apparently picked by the mother alone.

Mothers nursed their children for up to three years. The ancient Egyptians probably realized that children who were nursed for a longer period had a better chance of survival. Wet nurses could take over the nursing, and through their milk they became related to the child. Thus, divine nurses were believed to transfer their divine powers to the king through their milk. Human nurses were held in high esteem and even accepted into the family. The king's wet nurse came from a prominent family and was so highly respected that Tuthmosis III, for instance, married the daughter of his nurse. They had probably been raised together, just as the daughter of a royal nurse and mother of the vizier Rekhmire had been raised with the royal children. Being chosen as a wet nurse certainly benefited the careers of their own children and their husbands, who had their wives or mothers depicted in their tombs holding the princes on their laps. Wet nurses of private persons appear occasionally on tomb walls or stelae. They probably also participated in the upbringing of the child, since male tutors and wet nurses bore the same title, which was indicated in writing with a female breast.

During the Roman Period, nursing contracts for a period of eighteen months to two years were drawn up. Thereafter the children could be left in the care of the nurses for up to three years. The nurses took the children into their homes, as was later customary in Europe, but were not allowed to nurse any other child or to have intercourse with a man during this time. Interestingly enough, in the Roman Period people did not hire nurses for their own children but for children that had been adopted. These were probably children of a deceased relative, foundlings, or even the children of the house slaves or children bought as slaves, whereas mothers raised their own children and hired nurses who came to the house only on rare occasions.

The mother also saw to her children's education. The Instruction of Ani, dating from the fourteenth century B.C., says the mother sends her child to school and takes care of him at home. A thousand years later, Ankhsheshonqi warns his son: "Do not marry a godless woman lest she rear your children badly." In the Tale of Setne Khaemwese the mother asks the teacher whether her son is stupid.

In return, children owed their mothers love and honesty, and sons were supposed to support their aged mothers and maintain their mortuary cults.

The mother of an illegitimate child was despised like a prostitute.

A happy family life was the ideal of the ancient Egyptians, and they emphasized in texts and paintings the value of the family and being united with one's family in life and death. Love between spouses and between parents and children was taken as a given. The nuclear family was regarded as a social unit. The bonds between its members were considered so strong that in the time of Ramesses III, women and children joined their husbands and fathers in strikes to support their demands, and if a man committed a crime, his family could be held accountable.

These family ties are reflected in the tombs and monuments that were erected by members of the higher classes during their lifetime. Children had to bury their parents adequately and to carry out their mortuary cult with means provided by the parents. Few women could afford their own tombs. Usually a woman was buried with her husband and represented side by side with him on his monuments, which sufficed to secure her existence in the Hereafter. Men who depicted only their children in their tombs but not their wives, especially in the Old Kingdom, were probably divorced. If the separation had brought about hard feelings, the husband could even go so far as to have the depiction of his wife removed from reliefs or statues that showed them as a couple, thus carrying the separation from her husband and children over into the next world.

Although the wife appears side by side with her husband in the tombs of men, almost as a part of him, it is striking that the husband is depicted neither in the few tombs that women had built for themselves nor in the section of a man's tomb that was reserved for his wife. A typical case in point is the tomb of Mereruka, who is shown with his wife and children in his part of the tomb, whereas his wife— a princess—does not even mention his name in her section; only her son is depicted with her. The son, in turn, shows neither of his parents in his area of the tomb.

Accompanying her husband with her children on inspection tours of his estates and workshops, an upper-class lady was always informed about his business and thus able in his absence to act and make decisions on his behalf, as we can see from New Kingdom documents. The children, sons as well as daughters, were introduced to their later responsibilities early on.

The entire family could accompany the husband when he went hunting and fishing for sport, gliding with him through the papyrus marshes in his boat as he swung the throw-stick and cast the spear.

Depictions of festivities show husband and wife at times separated according to gender, while at other times they celebrated together, as suggested by the harpist's songs of the New Kingdom: "Celebrate a holiday, . . . with the woman of your heart sitting next to you." During funeral feasts she sat by his side or across from him. The couple received presents either alone or with their children. In Ramesside times, when tomb scenes focused more and more on life in the Hereafter, man and wife approached the gods or the court of the Hereafter as a couple, or they worked together in the fields of the Hereafter.

At funerals, women, separated from their husbands, represented the world of emotion: they tore their hair and garments as they accompanied the funeral procession while the men strode in quiet dignity. It is only after the Amarna Period that we occasionally see men showing emotion.

Education, Rights, and Professions of Women

Ancient Egyptians wanted children of either gender, as we learn from expressions of gratitude for the birth of a healthy son or daughter that are incorporated into personal names. Magical spells or requests to the gods asking for male or female offspring have been preserved as well. Although a son was required to take over the office of the father, daughters were welcome too, and the son's obligation to bury the parents could be transferred to a daughter or even to an outsider.

Exposing or killing a child was condemned and occurred only during the most troubled times. Although both practices were customary among the Greeks who lived in Egypt later on, the victims being especially girls, such acts were clearly at variance with Egyptian ethics, and Herodotus's report that the Egyptians fed all children is probably based on fact.

Until their tenth year, children were considered ignorant and hence innocent. The little ones went naked in the heat. In scenes of daily life, girls—often depicted with a hint of breasts and, in the

New Kingdom, also with dark pubic regions—are usually shown close to their mothers rather than their fathers. Sons, on the other hand, are shown next to their fathers; but both daughters and sons participated in their parents' life in the same way. In the Old Kingdom they accompanied their parents on their inspections of the estates, and in the New Kingdom during the performance of the cult.

Adolescents were probably separated according to gender, since girls practiced dancing, ball games, or acrobatics while the boys developed dexterity and speed in their own games. Daughters were now probably increasingly involved in the work of their mothers, whereas sons received instruction in their future professions from their fathers, at local schools, or at palace schools. The professional training of the administrative apprentices was handled by teachers who assumed the role of the father. We know nothing about the education of girls, as all the preserved instruction texts are addressed to boys only. Therefore, it is generally believed that girls did not go to school. They were not denied access to knowledge, however; otherwise we could not explain the letters to and from women from Deir al-Medina. D. Sweeney (1993) has shown that they account for 14 percent of the 470 letters preserved. In contrast to the correspondence of the men, which deals predominantly with business matters, they contain private matters one would not very willingly have dictated to a scribe. It is therefore safe to assume that they were written by the women themselves; when and how they acquired this skill, however, is unknown to us. According to modern estimates, only 0.3–1 percent of the ancient Egyptian population was literate. Given the complexity of the Egyptian writing system, it is unlikely that women acquired the ability to read and write simply by watching their brothers. They must have had competent training.

If we can thus assume that a fraction of middle-class women had some schooling, the number must have been greater still among upper-class women. Women who held a secular or priestly office had to have the same qualifications as their male colleagues. The "chantresses of Amun" and the "great entertainer of Amun," who are depicted holding scribal palettes in their husbands' tombs, probably had not only basic reading and writing skills but an above average command of the Egyptian writing system, which consequently would have played a major role in their lives. The accomplishments of the wife of Petosiris, whose "excellent counsel in her writings" was praised by her husband, have already been mentioned.

Princesses were probably introduced to the principles of government and the general knowledge necessary for a future queen or wife of a prince or high official by a high-ranking civil servant who was responsible for their education as a male "nurse." Their education certainly included reading and writing. Female "nurses" probably not only breast-fed the princesses but also taught them female behavioral patterns as they grew up.

Possible proof of female literacy is the controversial motif of a scribal palette next to the twenty-fourth-century B.C. representation of Princess Idut. Two fourteenth-century B.C. scribal palettes belonging to two daughters of Akhenaten and Nefertiti have been preserved, and Princess Ahure of the Setne Khaemwese tale picks up the book of Thoth that was stolen from her brother and reads in it.

The mere fact that the goddess of the art of writing was a woman and that Isis is said to have been taught to read and write by her father seems to indicate that school knowledge was not considered a purely male domain from which women were excluded. Although following in the father's professional footsteps was not the goal of the education of the daughters of officials and priests, as it was for their brothers, it was not impossible for a woman to get a predominantly male job, if she had the education. This remained the exception, however. Though the title "scribe" was being commonly used for officials, it is not until the Eleventh and Twelfth Dynasties that we know of women bearing this title, and not until the Twenty-sixth Dynasty, almost 1,500 years later, that it is attested again for a woman, who was in the service of the Divine Spouse Nitocris.

"Citizeness" or "townswoman" was a common term for a married or a widowed woman from the Middle Kingdom on. Unlike Greek women, she could conduct business independently of her husband. Beginning in the middle of the third millennium B.C., legal documents attest the right of unmarried and married women to dispose of their own property. A woman's property was not transferred to her husband's control upon marriage, unlike the case in Europe for a long time. In England, for instance, women acquired this right only in 1888 with the Married Women's Property Act. Before the introduction of equal rights in Germany in 1953, the husband, who was the head of the family, became the administrator and usufructuary of the wife's property and wages in many regions, unless separate property had been set aside for the wife; and without her husband's permission, a wife was not allowed to sell property or to mortgage it.

Only after his death did she assume the administration of the common property.

As early as the Old Kingdom, Egyptian women could inherit and bequeathe, buy property without spousal consent, take a job, hold a secular or religious office, and have income. Ptahhotep's recommendation to the aspiring official that he "not contend with her in court" and "keep her from power" indicates that women had rights even vis-à-vis their own husbands, which is also attested in documents. We know of lawsuits concerning assault, testimonies on behalf of a daughter against her husband, as well as a charge of embezzlement against a father. A father sued his daughter, and one daughter promised to pay twice the amount embezzled by her father. In addition, testimonies in court and the signing of legal documents by female citizens are well attested in the documents of the New Kingdom; and in the twelfth century B.C., two women appear as members of the local jury of Deir al-Medina, a right that German women have enjoyed for less than a century. An Egyptian woman was able to represent her children or underage siblings in court and be appointed as their trustee.

As shown above, a woman could know enough about the job of her husband that she was able to conduct business in his absence and take care of his affairs. Even if the women are presumed to have acted on their husbands' orders in those cases, they had to be sufficiently familiar with the tasks in order to be able to perform them. When it came to their own affairs, women acted with full legal rights. One woman was even able to influence her husband's decision: he revoked the cancellation of his lease when his wife objected.

By the same token, women were fully punishable. In one case, for example, a woman received the same punishment of a hundred blows with a cane as the three men who were sentenced along with her.

A female officeholder had the same power of command as a man. In the New Kingdom during a time of weak rulers when wages were not paid and the necropolis workers in Thebes went on strike, the "foremost of the musicians and dancers of Amun-Re" assumed responsibility for the provisions of the necropolis workers and was able to order a troop commander to find grain and issue it to them. The chantress of Amun Nesimut probably had her majordomo distribute grain rations to people who lived within the enclosure walls of the temple of Medinet Habu, and another holder of the same title,

Nedjmet, along with two other officials, even received secret orders from a royal general to execute two policemen after an interrogation and to throw their bodies into the Nile at night. Nobody was to know anything about this. These women, often the wives, sisters, or daughters of high-ranking officials, had more power than they are usually credited with.

A landownership list in the Wilbour Papyrus from 1143 B.C. tells us that 11 percent of the listed property belonged to women, and later documents in which women lend money (even to their own husbands) or purchase, sell, or lease landed property or slaves demonstrate how free and independent they were in economic affairs.

In Ptolemaic times, impoverished women sold themselves and their children into slavery. Others sold their children for adoption or hired them out for work. This might be attested as early as the New Kingdom in a letter. Ahmose wrote to his superior that after a female servant who was still a child unfamiliar with work had been taken away from him, the girl's mother complained to him because she had entrusted her daughter to him as "a child." He promised to give a maidservant in exchange for the girl.

The fate of female farmhands and workers was probably no different from that of their husbands (see chaps. 1 and 7). They helped their parents from their childhood on. Decrees dealing with exemptions from corvée labor are indirect evidence that women as well as men could be pressed into it.

If a man was able to support his family, the wife's main task was to manage the household and take care of the children. If his income was insufficient, she had to take on a job either at home or somewhere else on top of her responsibility for her household and her children in order to generate additional income. In tomb paintings of the kitchens of Ti and of Niankhkhnum and Khnumhotep, for example, we see small children holding on to their mother as she grinds grain and a woman nursing her child while she fans the fire underneath the baker's oven.

Both men and women could wait on their lords and ladies. Old Kingdom depictions show women attending only ladies. By the time of the New Kingdom, they served beverages to male guests as well and adorned them with blossom wreaths during festivities.

Scenes in tombs show us workers and craftsmen in the workshops of the rich, the king, or the temples. There were only a few tasks in which women participated, mainly those she was familiar with as a housewife and that were performed indoors. It was rare that women performed outdoor tasks. In workshops almost all women's jobs could be handled by men, whereas women did not take on the responsibilities of men.

In the Third Dynasty, there was a "house of the (female) millers," a "house of the (female) weavers," and a "house of the (female) washers" within the royal palace, and later on the grain-grinding maid was a popular motif for reliefs and sculpture in the round, although occasionally men were depicted in this activity, too. Both worked side by side brewing beer and baking in the large-scale kitchen operations; meat and fish, however, were cooked and dried only by men. The function of overseer of the weavers was exercised by women as well as men as early as the Old Kingdom. In the Middle Kingdom the horizontal weaver's loom was worked almost exclusively by women, while men spun yarn next to them. But when the vertical loom, which is harder to handle, was introduced in the New Kingdom, men took over in this profession. The Satire of the Trades says the fate of the weaver is harder than that of a woman, shedding light on the hard work women had to perform. When the harem (the private quarters of the queen mother, the royal wives, the princesses of several generations, and their numerous entourage) was moved from El-Lahun to Abu Gurob in the New Kingdom, a busy textile manufacturing operation and processing workshops for the produced fabrics were established at Abu Gurob. Both the production and the processing of the fabrics were also done at home or by captured Asiatic women in workshops under the supervision and training of high-ranking ladies, although here the overseers were usually men.

From the late Old Kingdom on, men washed laundry on the banks of the Nile, where crocodiles posed a threat. Outdoor jobs like tilling the fields, fishing and fowling with nets, and hunting and breeding animals were the responsibility of men; women were called in for winnowing or tearing out flax. Agricultural produce and the finished products of manufacturing workshops were brought to the lord by men and women in farmers' or workers' processions. The tomb scenes, however, reflect only the state of affairs on the domains of the rich. If a commoner possessed a piece of land or animals, the women often had to help out, as indicated by the letter of Butehamun quoted above and texts of later periods.

Women in high positions were rare. Although the mother of Cheops, as "overseer of the butchers of the acacia house," was responsible for the meat offerings for the cult of her deceased husband, she probably never went anywhere near a slaughterhouse but delegated the work, checking on its proper performance and enjoying the income connected with the title.

Women in responsible positions in the Old Kingdom were usually employed by a female relative of the king's. A (female) "steward" managing the domains of the queen with all their personnel must have had just as much organizational talent as a (female) "overseer of the mortuary priests of the queen mother," who was responsible for the personnel, the fields, and the manufacturing workshops that were necessary for the adequate support of the lady in the Hereafter. Like these women, a (female) "overseer of the physicians" had the confidence of a queen mother.

In addition to administrative positions in the households of princesses or high-ranking officials, women could be put in charge of midlevel offices in the royal palace or mortuary temple, which brought with them important privileges. The most profitable leading positions, however, were held by men. Even the overseers of the female dancers, female acrobats, and female singers in the palace and of the royal harem were men more often than not.

The incomes of these women must have corresponded to those of their male colleagues, since Neferreses, the "first royal dancer," paid for a tomb to be built for her mortuary cult from her daily income in the palace.

If only a few of the higher positions were held by women in the Old Kingdom, the situation deteriorated dramatically for women in the Middle Kingdom, when the Egyptian state slowly began to consolidate again after a prolonged period of political and economic decline. Now, women could assume only low-level positions in the administration and were rarely in charge of domains or personnel any more.

The priestly titles suggest the same state of affairs. In these professions as well, women were represented in very small numbers. An Old Kingdom list of a hundred names and their priestly titles shows only three women, and among the numerous personnel of the mortuary temple of King Neferirkare (Fifth Dynasty) we know of only three women, who worked as singers. A study of seventeen deities of the Old Kingdom shows that women of the royal family or wives of high-ranking officials or priests served only three of them. A rule is not recognizable. While for the goddess Neith only priestesses are attested, the goddesses Bastet, Seshat, and Maat had a strictly male personnel. Thoth, on the other hand, appears to have had only queens performing his cult. Hathor had predominantly female personnel from the middle and upper classes, though the overseer positions were filled exclusively by men. Until the Eleventh Dynasty, and again later in the New Kingdom, even princesses and queens were no more than plain Hathor priestesses, and only a few men shared their rank. Queens often served several goddesses in the Old Kingdom without ever holding the office of an overseer of the priests, which was a male prerogative. Also, the office of a simple priestess was not heritable, in contrast to the office of an overseer, which was handed down from father to son.

The nature of the tasks of a priestess is not attested anywhere, but priestesses bear the epithet "musician of Hathor" and are depicted rattling sistrums or *menit*s in honor of the deity. Although this function has been held in low esteem, it should not be considered negligible or unimportant. It is the essential cultic function that soothes and delights a deity and maintains the course of the world. In the Pyramid Texts and later, the king himself appears singing, rattling the sistrum, and dancing in front of Hathor.

The upper-class ladies who served a local or major deity as "dancers" or "musicians" from the New Kingdom onward, and who had to perform their monthly duty in phyles without holding the title of priestess, seem to have been cultic singers as well. Many wives of Theban officials were "singers of (the state god) Amun" and performed in his honor under the leadership of the "greatest" among them, who was a member of the royal family or the wife of a high priest of Amun.

In the Old Kingdom, the wives of Pepi II are depicted making offerings. In the New Kingdom, women of the royal family and wives of high officials are so depicted. This was usually a prerogative of the king or his representative, and it indicates the high esteem in which these women were held.

Princesses participated not only in the cults of deities but also, as mortuary priestesses, in the funerary cults of their deceased fathers or grandfathers. Among commoners, the wives, daughters, and sons carried out the mortuary cults of husbands and fathers. They provided for the deceased in the afterlife and for themselves as well by means of the income from the mortuary estates.

The title of "priestess of Hathor" is attested again in Ptolemaic times for wives of high priests. Women now also served the nome deities, and the funerary priestesses as well as priestesses of animal cults, otherwise attested only in the Old Kingdom, gained importance. Their numbers matched those of the men, and they obtained the same salary for their offices as their male colleagues. Like their male counterparts, the women in higher offices no doubt delegated the actual work to their employees and kept the considerable income.

As early as the Middle Kingdom we know of Divine Spouses of various gods. In the New Kingdom, the office of the Divine Spouse of Amun that Ahmose-Nefertari endowed with a staff of priestesses at the beginning of the Eighteenth Dynasty was usually held by a wife or a daughter of the reigning king. The Divine Spouse fulfilled the same functions as the high priest and helped maintain world order. She had a whole staff of personnel at her disposal, who administered the estates and manufacturing workshops connected with the office under the supervision of a majordomo.

During the Twenty-first Dynasty (eleventh century B.C.), the Theban theocracy developed into a state within a state. The king, ruling far away in the north, sent one of his daughters to Thebes, first as the wife of the high priest, later as a Divine Spouse in her own right, in order to strengthen his own position by forging an alliance with the priests. Under the rule of the Kushite and Saite kings, the reigning Divine Spouse adopted a daughter of the king as her successor. The Divine Spouse, identified with Mut, the wife of the god Amun, had similar power at her disposal within the Theban theocracy as the king, though she remained subordinate to him. Two of them shared the highest priestly office, just as the king shared the high priesthood of Amun. Among the officials who administered the possessions of the Divine Spouse were several women whose large tombs have been preserved. They prove that these women held high offices like their male colleagues and received the corresponding income.

Queens

As in other ancient Middle Eastern cultures, an Egyptian queen enjoyed an elevated status based on her relationship with her husband or son. She did not have to be of royal descent. The main wife (Great Royal Wife) of a king had her own household with estates and separate administration. An adequate tomb was erected for her, and the personnel necessary for the maintenance of her funerary estates and the dignified performance of her mortuary cult were provided for her afterlife. Whether or not the main wife of the king had authority over the minor wives cannot be established with certainty.

The mother of a king was held in high esteem by her son, whether she was the main wife or a minor wife of the deceased king, or not married to a king at all, as in the case of the mother of the founder of a new dynasty. As early as the Annals of the Early Dynastic Period her name was listed next to the name of the reigning king, her son, and until the Eighteenth Dynasty, she ranked above the queen, the wife of her son. During the Ramesside Period she lost her importance.

Several strong queens figure prominently in the three thousand years of Egyptian history. Their number is smaller than that of women in other leading positions, however. Manetho's claim that the Second Dynasty king Ninetjer-Binothris decided that women could assume the office of kingship is probably based on an old tradition. Manetho himself, in his list of five hundred rulers, names no more than four ruling queens who are also otherwise known to us as independent sovereigns. After Manetho's death, Cleopatra joined the list. In addition, queens acted as regents for a successor who was still under age, and we know of Great Royal Wives who are mentioned by the king's side.

During the First Dynasty, two queens, Neithhotep and Meretneith, ruled as regents while the heir apparent was still a minor. During the Sixth Dynasty, two wives of Pepi I, who were daughters of the nomarch Khui and sisters of the vizier Djau, governed on behalf of their minor sons: the first one until the death of Merenre, the second one from the time her son Pepi II was six years old until he came of age. Since Pepi II is depicted on his mother's lap, in full royal array, he was considered the reigning monarch. In the absence of a male heir apparent, the wives of the last kings of the Old and Middle Kingdoms, respectively, Nitocris and Sobeknofru, led the government until they were replaced by male pretenders.

During the Second Intermediate Period, following the death of her husband, Tao II, and after heavy fighting during which her son Kamose was killed, Ahhotep I apparently succeeded in expelling the Hyksos from Upper Egypt and in restoring order. Her second son, Ahmose, was crowned king at age eleven. Ahmose called her

the one who knows the issues, who takes care of Egypt.
She gathered its (i.e., Egypt's) officials and protected it.
She returned its refugees and united its emigrants.
She pacified Upper Egypt and expelled its rebels.

(*Urkunden* IV, 21)

Ahmose's wife, Ahmose-Nefertari, also led the government after his premature death until her son Amenophis I came of age. Her rule must have been especially prosperous for her land, because she and Amenophis I were both honored as gods until the late Ramesside Period. Ahhotep and Ahmose-Nefertari were Great Royal Wives and mothers of the successor to the throne.

Hatshepsut, daughter of Tuthmosis I and Great Royal Wife of Tuthmosis II, gave birth only to a daughter. A strong woman, she became the regent for young Tuthmosis III, the son of a minor wife of her husband's who had either died early or fallen from grace because of Hatshepsut. She arranged a marriage between Tuthmosis III and her own daughter, Neferneferure. On account of her close connection to both preceding kings, she probably had a strong following which enabled her to have herself crowned Pharaoh. Tuthmosis III, whom she allowed to reign as coregent, was overshadowed by her until her death, after which he became one of Egypt's most expansionist rulers.

Tuthmosis IV's minor wife Mutemwia led the government for her twelve-year-old son, Amenophis III, even though she was not of royal descent. Sethos II's wife Tausret, after being regent on behalf of her son Siptah, had herself crowned Pharaoh after Siptah's death. It is unknown whether Siptah died of natural causes or whether she ordered his assassination.

Three other queens who were highly valued by their husbands should also be mentioned. Two of them were not of royal blood. Queen Tiye must have been fully involved in the administration of Amenophis III, for after the latter's death Mitanni's ruler Tushratta wrote to her son Amenophis IV (Akhenaten) and asked him to consult his mother because she knew the treaties between the two countries. Tushratta also sent her a letter to the same effect.

During Akhenaten's early regnal years, a temple was erected in Karnak for his wife Nefertiti in honor of the new state god Aten, who was regarded as her father. She and Akhenaten were identified with Shu and Tefnut, the first divine couple of creation. She appeared together with the king and her daughters in all official ceremonies and supported the cult of Aten, whom her husband had elevated above all other gods. Like her mother-in-law, Tiye, she was identified with Maat, and, like Tiye, she was depicted in the posture of the king smiting his enemies.

Ramesses II must have appreciated his wife Nefertari very much. Although in his statues she was depicted *en miniature* by his side, he honored her by erecting a temple next to his own in Abu Simbel, and her tomb is among the most beautifully decorated in the Valley of the Queens in Thebes.

The last woman on the throne of Egypt was a descendant of the Macedonians who were installed by Alexander the Great and who ruled over Egypt for more than three hundred years as Ptolemy I–XIV. The last two Ptolemies were husband and coregent, respectively, of their older half sister Cleopatra, who, as Egypt's last ruler, tried in vain to protect the country from Rome by her relationships with Julius Caesar and Mark Antony.

It was by virtue of their husbands' position that these women reached their prominence. Supported by his loyal followers after his death, some of them became the regent for the underage heir apparent or, if there was no heir, exercised power in their own names. Hatshepsut and Tausret were the only regents who succeeded in expanding their power so much that they were able to push aside the heir apparent and exercise de facto rule. Hatshepsut alone was able to tolerate the rightful heir to the throne by her side so that he could attain power after her death. Interestingly enough, she is the only queen who, after a transition period, is represented as a man in her depictions and inscriptions.

In Pharaonic times, succession to the throne was not always determined by the status of the mother, as is still claimed, following Bachofen, in publications on matriarchy. We know of several king's mothers who were not of royal ancestry. Furthermore, the theory that a prince whose mother was not a member of the royal family had to marry a princess in order to secure his succession is false as well. Thus, it is incorrect to speak of matrilinearity.

The Gods

In keeping with the dualistic approach of the ancient Egyptians to the world, their pantheon consisted of male and female deities.

There were primeval gods and goddesses; the creator god, albeit masculine, was androgynous and created the first divine couple, who were the mother and father of the Egyptians. Similarly, the Nile and fertility gods were represented as men with female breasts. The Egyptians did not have the concept of a mother earth. The sky and the earth were embodied by the goddess Nut and the god Geb in the third generation of the Egyptian creation myth, and Osiris symbolized the fertile soil out of which the new crops grew.

The absence of a dominant god in the Egyptian pantheon reflected the everyday world. Gods and goddesses enjoyed cults of greater or lesser importance. They could stand alone or be joined as couples. Occasionally the couples had a child; the primeval gods of the cosmologies even had several children. The partners in these divine couples could be of equal importance and play individual roles outside the family, like Osiris, Isis, Horus, Ptah, Sakhmet, and Nefertem. In addition, there were gods who had unimportant partners, Amun and Amaunet being the most prominent case. While Amun developed from a local god into the state god, his wife, Amaunet, who had been created as his partner at the very beginning, as her name indicates, never attained any standing of her own.

Osiris, the ruler of Egypt who was murdered by his brother, became the most important figure in the Egyptian mortuary beliefs as lord of the Hereafter. His sister-wife Isis, who remained loyal to him after his death, raised their posthumously conceived son Horus by herself and promoted his rights as his father's heir. As the ideal wife and mother, Isis gained more and more importance during the Late Period, not only as a mother goddess. Feminists like to use her as proof of an Egyptian matriarchy. In her role as mother, however, she limited women to Lévi-Strauss's "natural sphere" of the house, like the Christian mother of god, which kept her away from the "cultural" public sphere of society outside.

The conflation of Ptah, Sakhmet, and Nefertem was a secondary development in the New Kingdom after all three deities had had their own traditions. The development of the lion goddess Sakhmet is interesting. From a gentle, catlike mother goddess nursing the king, she became a furious lioness who slayed the king's enemies. She was also known for her attempt, following the wish of her aged father, Re, to destroy humanity, who had turned against him. Re appeased her before she could finish the task. In both cases she served a man, helping the king and Re to conquer their enemies and becoming a furious murderer in the process. She was soothed by her father but retained her destructive qualities as the goddess of sickness and disease.

Despite the existence of important goddesses who had their own cults, the greatest deities were male. No goddess attained the status of state goddess, even though the deities of Upper and Lower Egypt (the crown goddesses of the king), the vulture and the uraeus, were both female. Among the great goddesses were the war goddess Neith; Hathor, the goddess of love and joy who receives the deceased as a necropolis deity and gives birth to them again as the sky goddess; Isis, the faithful wife and caring mother; the scribal goddess Seshat; and the goddess Mut. They enjoyed their own cults and were held in high esteem.

Conclusion

Summing up the described sources, we can say that although women in ancient Egypt were respected and their legal status was favorable, they certainly did not have the same rights as men. Even though Egypt had a large number of female deities, it is not possible to infer from this, as Sanday has, that women held a high social position.

Women of all levels of society were largely dependent on the men in their families, although they had their own rights vis-à-vis them. But how many women actually knew their rights or dared to take legal action against one of these men? They lived in the households of their male relatives: their fathers, husbands, sons, or brothers. Only through means given to them by their parents, their husbands, or their children, in rare cases earned by their own efforts, were they able to attain independence. Their opportunities to enter secular and priestly professions were limited, and here, too, they were usually subaltern to men. Even female members of the royal family hardly ever reached top positions. And although women of the ruling class had a high social and religious status compared to the lower echelons of society, with very few exceptions they did not exercise power either. Those few women who held positions of power, however, did so owing to their social context as wife, mother, or daughter of a high-ranking man, and in many cases they wielded this power on behalf of the man (as regent or Divine Spouse). There were exceptions, of course, as there are in any male-dominated society.

In comparing the rights of ancient Egyptian women with those of modern Islamic women, we find a number of parallels, but also differences. As in ancient Egypt, modern Egyptian women are entitled to inherit from their parents. Their share, however, is only half as much as the share of their brothers. In ancient times this share could vary. Since today's marriages are based on a separation of property, women are able to dispose of their possessions independently, as in Pharaonic times. The dowry given by the bride's parents also remains in her possession, even if she is the one filing for divorce. Already known in ancient times, the groom's gift to the bride is a common tradition in modern Egypt. The smaller part is payable to the parents of the bride prior to the wedding in order to cover the cost of the bride's dress and other items; the larger part is due after a divorce. In ancient Egypt the bride received the whole gift herself.

An Islamic woman is entitled to inherit only one-eighth of her husband's property; his children get the rest. The ancient Egyptian marriage contracts show a ratio of 1:2. A Muslim bride can incorporate the right to a divorce in her marriage contract, which is usually done by women who are wealthier than their husbands. If this right is not included in the contract, she can still file for divorce, but she loses all claims on her husband. In ancient Egypt this was the case only if she had committed adultery. However, we do not know the rights of women who failed to draw up marriage contracts.

As in ancient times, the modern Egyptian husband can contractually relinquish his claims to his own possessions for the benefit of his wife and children. Today, as in Pharaonic Egypt, the wife can sue her father or husband on behalf of herself or her children. In contrast to ancient Egyptian women, modern female Egyptian citizens cannot become judges. According to Islamic law, a father can conclude a marriage contract for his son as well as for his daughter. If he is deceased, a male relative, friend, or even stranger has to sign the contract. In ancient Egypt the mother possessed this right as well. In Pharaonic times, the groom negotiated with the father of the bride; women acquired this right in the sixth century. Although nowadays the imam can legalize the marriage only with the consent of both partners, many young people, especially in rural areas, do not know this; and even if they do, tradition prohibits a child from opposing his or her father. A child refusing to get married or a woman suing her father or husband is ostracized by society. It is no longer possible to determine today to what extent women in ancient Egypt were

subject to similar societal pressures. But some offenses for which
women sued their fathers or husbands in the workers' village of Deir
al-Medina seem too trivial to risk discrimination by their families or
the villagers. The social pressures that subject Muslim women to
their husbands even against their rights do not seem to have existed
for women in ancient Egypt. Their position was thus stronger than
that of their modern sisters.

Bibliography

Černý, J. *A Community of Workmen at Thebes in the Ramesside Period*. *Bulletin d'Égyptologie* 50. Cairo, 1973.
Knudtzon, J. A., and O. Weber. *Die El-Amarna Tafeln*. 3 vols. Leipzig, 1915.
Lefèbvre, G. *Le tombeau de Petosiris*. 3 vols. Cairo, 1923–24.
Lichtheim, M. *Ancient Egyptian Literature*. Vol. 1, *The Old and Middle Kingdoms*. Berkeley and Los Angeles, 1973.
———. *Ancient Egyptian Literature*. Vol. 2, *The New Kingdom*. Berkeley and Los Angeles, 1976.
Schott, S. *Ägyptische Liebeslieder*. Zurich, 1950.
Sethe, K. *Urkunden der 18. Dynastie, historische-biographische Urkunden*. 4 vols. Leipzig, 1906–9.
Sweeney, D. "Women's Correspondence from Deir El-Medineh." In *Sesto Congresso Internationale di Egittologia: Atti*, ed. Silvio Curto et al., vol. 2, pp. 523–30. 1993.

INDEX

Accounting: lists of craftsmen and laborers, 35–36; writing required for, 66

Achaemenid Empire, 248–49

Administration: of craftsmen activities, 46; hieratic writing of, 67; military, 77–78, 172–74; of temple economy, 214. *See also* Bureaucracy; Overseers; Scribes

Adultery, 327

Africans: as mercenaries in Egypt, 231; populations in Egypt, 230; as workers/laborers, 230. *See also* Libyans; Nubians

Age of the Pyramids: Instructions from, 261; significance of king after death, 273

Agriculture: effect of Nile River flooding, 4–6; implements used in, 6–11; irrigation system, 4, 6, 8–9; peasant abandonment of, 22–23; peasant's work in, 1–6; viniculture, 13. *See also* Flooding, Nile River;

Implements; Irrigation; Peasants; Viniculture

Amenemope, onomasticon of, 41–42, 91–94, 108–9

Amenophis (scribe), 75–76, 97

Amun (Theban god), 246, 296

Anastasi Papyrus, 109, 238

Architecture: of royal tombs, 294–95; study of, 75; of temple, 135–37; of tomb, 261–62

Army, Egyptian: composition and function of standing, 156; development of professional element, 158; effect of existence of regular army, 172; foreign mercenaries in, 238; hierarchy of, 169; Nubians in, 230; organization of, 172–74. *See also* Mercenaries; Soldiers

Artists, 33–34

Asia: Egyptian domination in, 235; influence on Egyptian design, 237

Asiatics: gods of, 239–40; influx of, 164, 202; as prisoners of war,

348

vival after death, 273–74; education and preparation for role as, 298–99; as a god, 132, 283; implications of death of, 260; inheritance of title, 297–98; as innovator, 312; as king of Upper and Lower Egypt, 132; limited individuality of, 288–89; as military leader, 166–74, 178; mummies of, 291–92; perception after revolution of year 19, 103–4; personality of, 289–95; as priest, 133; as protector of Egypt, 152, 222; as representative of humanity, 283; role in protection of land and water, 159; role in real and divine worlds, 132–33; titulature of, 284–86. *See also* Pharaoh

Kushites: conquer Egypt, 246; as magicians, 232–33; as prisoners in Egypt, 230

Lamentations of Ipuwer, 156, 188
Land: allotment as symbol of freedom, 207; owned by bureaucrats, 115–16; system of land tenure, 3; used by soldiers, 171, 181–82. *See also* Cleruchy, the
Lapidaries, 51
Lector priests: difference from scribe, 64; as leader, 65–66; as magician, 65, 140; as scribes, 65–68
Legal system, x–xi; access of slaves to, 201–2, 205–6; enforcement of wills, 268–70; examples of actions taken under, 147–48; issue of slave ownership, 211;

laws related to adultery, 327; laws related to women's ownership of property, 333–35; New Kingdom laws related to, 205–6; restrictions related to servile status, 214–15; treaties, 80–81, 238. *See also* Contracts; Property
Letters to the Dead, 275–79
Libraries: in temples, 145
Libyans: as dancers, 236; as invaders, 243–44; Libyan Period, 180–81; as mercenaries, 155, 225
Literacy: female, 333; of king, 298
Literature: Asiatic influence on, 237–38; interest in bureaucratic, 102; military spirit revealed in, 163–64; promotion of, 69; Satire of the Trades, 188; for transmission of ideology, 189–90. *See also* Entertainment literature
Living, the: ability of the dead to influence, 260–67; linking of the dead to, 274–80
Living conditions: of peasants, 23–28; workers, craftsmen and foremen, 40, 42–45, 52–54
Locusts, 9
Lower Egypt: goddess of, 285; unification with Upper Egypt, 132
Loyalistic Instruction, 71–72, 118

Maat (goddess), 300
Maat principle, 132–33, 189–90, 29, 311–12, 315
Macedonian occupation of Egypt, 82
Magicians: Egyptians as, 233;

Magicians (*continued*)
foreigners as, 232–33; lector
priest as, 65
Marriage contracts, 322–24
Marriages: between close relatives,
325; monogamous and polygamous, 323–25; patrilocal, 324;
between ruling families, 165,
238–39; between siblings, 324
Masters of works, 48
Medicine: medical care of peasant,
25–26; study of, 75
Medjay region, 231
Megiddo, battle of: development
of, 169–70; events preceding,
167–68, 293; king's comments
on, 293
Melkat (cult), 249
Memory: autonomous existence of,
262; identified and defined in
tombs, 262
Memphite Theology, 81
Mercenaries: foreign, 238; Greek,
Semitic, and Carian, 181–82,
212, 247–48; Ionians as, 247–48;
Libyan, 180; from the Medjay
region, 231; Nubian, 231;
Shardans as, 245
Merchants, 228, 247
Meretneith (queen), 296
Merseankh III (queen), 37
Middle class, 171–72, 176, 201
Military sector: depictions as evidence of activity in, 153; description of rising class, 158–
59; descriptions of battles,
156–57; as hereditary caste,
171; propaganda, 178–79;
scribes in administration of,

77–78; structure in Libyan Pe-
riod, 180. *See also* Conscription;
Forts; Garrisons; Mercenaries;
Soldiers
Military service: as corvée labor,
152, 158; exemptions from,
192–93
Minoa, 247
Miracle-workers, 95–97
Money, 181. *See also* Coins
Monogamy, 323–24
Mummification, 262, 264, 291–92
Mycenea, 247
Myths: of ancient sages, 82; of Hat-
shepsut's divine origin, 296–97;
Osiris, 285; Pharaoh's divine
origin, 301

Naucratis (Greek city), 181–82, 248
Nekhbet (goddess), 285
Nile River: annual flooding of, 4–6,
88; Nile Valley, 234–36
Nomads: Asiatic, 227; attacks from,
152; Bedouin Sand-dwellers,
230; as hunters in service of
Egypt, 161, 180; Libyans as,
244; as "others," 151–52
Nomarchs, 37, 90, 112–13
Nomes, 90
Noria, or waterwheel (*saqqiah*), 9
Nubia: expedition to, 161–62; as
gold and sun land, 304; Old
Kingdom fortresses in, 155
Nubians: in Egypt, 81, 230–31; in
Egyptian army, 154–56, 158,
160, 224–25, 230; as interpret-
ers, 229; kidnapped, 193; as
magicians, 232–33; as mercenaries, 231; national dress of